AN OUTLINE OF ENGLISH PHONETICS

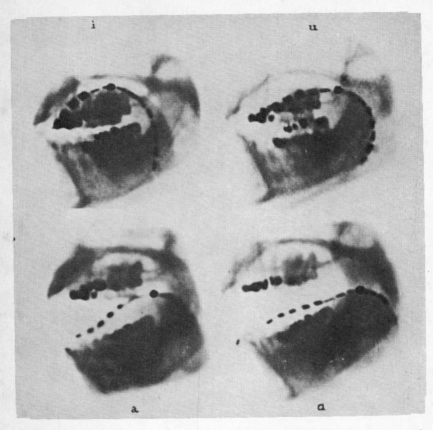

X-ray photographs of the tongue positions of the cardinal vowels **i**, **a**, **ɑ** and **u** pronounced by the author (reduced to $\frac{2}{5}$ of the original size).

A chain of small lead plates strung together was placed on the tongue to show its outline. The large dot added on each photograph marks the highest point of the tongue. The cross is a point of reference (near the end of the hard palate). By measuring from the point of intersection of the cross it is found that the dots have the relative positions shown in Fig. 23.

The photographs were taken by Dr. H. Trevelyan George in St. Bartholomew's Hospital, London, in January, 1917.

AN OUTLINE OF ENGLISH PHONETICS

by

Daniel Jones

M.A. (Cambridge), Dr. phil. h.c. (Zürich), Hon. LL.D. (Edin.)
Professor Emeritus of Phonetics in the University of London
Corresponding Member of the German Academy of Sciences, Berlin
Honorary Member of the Royal Irish Academy

NINTH EDITION

WITH 116 ILLUSTRATIONS
And with Appendices on
Types of Phonetic Transcription
and
American Pronunciation

CAMBRIDGE
UNIVERSITY PRESS

Published by the Press Syndicate of the University of Cambridge
The Pitt Building, Trumpington Street, Cambridge CB2 1RP
40 West 20th Street, New York, NY 10011–4211, USA
10 Stamford Road, Oakleigh, Melbourne 3166, Australia

Library of Congress catalogue card number: 75-26274

ISBN 0 521 29041 4 paperback

First published 1918
Second edition (reprint, with new preface) 1922
Third edition (rewritten) 1932
Fourth edition (reprint, with minor alterations) 1934
Firth edition (ditto) 1936
Sixth edition (ditto) 1939
Seventh edition (reprint, with an Appendix on American pronounciation) 1949
Eighth edition (reset, with numerous additions and improvements and with
a new Appendix on 'Types of Phonetic Transcription') 1956
Reprinted with frontispiece and minor alterations 1957
Ninth edition (reprint, with minor alterations 1960)
Reprinted with further alterations 1962, 1964
Reprinted 1969
Reprinted with minor alterations 1972
First paperback edition 1976
Eleventh printing 1993

This book was formerly published by W. Heffer and Sons Ltd, Cambridge.
It was published for the first time by Cambridge University Press in 1975.

Printed in Great Britain by W. Heffer & Sons Ltd, Cambridge
Reprinted in Great Britain at the
University Press, Cambridge

Preface to the Ninth Edition

It is now forty-two years since this book first appeared. It was re-written (as a third edition) in 1932, and the fourth to the seventh editions were in the main reprints of the third, except that an Appendix on American Pronunciation was added in the seventh edition (1949).[1] In 1956 the time arrived for issuing the book in a completely revised form incorporating all the improvements that had occurred to me, or had been suggested to me by colleagues, in the course of the previous twenty years.

Some of the alterations in the eighth edition were rendered necessary by the fact that the pronunciation of English has undergone changes.[2] Others were attributable to the discovery of new phonetic facts and by advances in our knowledge of phonetic theory. Others again were merely improvements in the mode of presenting facts which have long been known.

The following is a list of the major additions and alterations which were carried out in the eighth edition. An important footnote concerning 'Received Pronunciation' and transcription was appended to § 64. As the use of a vowel **a** intermediate between **æ** and **ɑ** in such words as *ask, plant* is now obsolete, the old §§ 294, 295 relating to that sound were replaced by new ones dealing with the distribution of **æ** and **ɑ:**

---

[1] That edition was, like all previous editions, printed and published by the B. G. Teubner Verlag in Leipzig. It was reproduced in England, by arrangement, by W. Heffer and Sons of Cambridge, who, with the consent of the B. G. Teubner Verlag, printed and published the eighth edition.

[2] The following are a few instances. A relatively new variant of the diphthong here written with **ei** has become very common (§ 388). Words like *lost, cross, cloth* are now pronounced with **ɔ** much more commonly than with **ɔ:**, so that alterations had to be made in §§ 300 and 308. Many Southern English people now hardly use 'linking **r**' at all (§ 758). Changes of stress have been taking place in many words: some words, such as *greatcoat* (§§ 947 (i), 954), which used to have double stress are now often said with single stress on the first syllable; and several words like *hospitable, justifiable, controversy*, which I have been accustomed to stress on the first syllable (**'hɔspitəbl, 'dʒʌstifaiəbl, 'kɔntrəvə:si**) are now often said with stress on another syllable (**hɔs'pitəbl, dʒʌsti'faiəbl, kən'trɔvəsi**).

in various words. Parts of the book relating to diphthongs were
considerably   developed: the   former   § 378   was   expanded
into   three   paragraphs;   a   necessary   distinction   was   drawn
between two classes of words containing the diphthong uə, and
this   necessitated   re-writing   §§ 460–463;   the   subject   of   the
'rising' diphthongs ĭə and ŭə, as in *glorious, influence,* was
dealt with at some length in twenty-one new paragraphs (§§ 466a–
466u), and some information concerning a few other less common
diphthongs was supplied in three further new paragraphs (§§ 466v–
466x). Several paragraphs in the chapters on assimilation and
elision were re-cast, and Fig. 116, illustrating the assimilation
tj > tʃ, was re-drawn in a more accurate form; the term
'coalescent   assimilation'   was   introduced   for   the   first   time
(§ 837). The definition of stress was improved (§ 909), and
§§ 914–916, 919 and 920 in the chapters on stress were considerably   elaborated.   A   few   additions   were   made   in   the
chapter on intonation. A chapter of some importance was
added on syllable separation (Chap. XXXII). A new Appendix of
twenty pages on *Types of Phonetic Transcription* replaced the
previous single page of rules for converting a 'broad' transcription
of English into a 'narrower' one. And finally the Appendix on
American Pronunciation was revised and enlarged.

The old numbering of paragraphs and footnotes was adhered
to as far as possible, so that references to earlier editions remain
in the main correct. Added paragraphs were distinguished by
putting *a, b,* etc., after the number of the preceding paragraph.

The present (ninth) edition is a reprint of the eighth incorporating a few necessary corrections.

As in previous editions, Figs. 3, 4, 15–22, 88, 89 and 90 are
photographs of my mouth. The other photographs (Figs. 36,
38, etc.) are of the mouth of my late brother Arnold Jones, whose
pronunciation of English was almost identical with mine.

The phonetic alphabet used is that of the International Phonetic
Association (I.P.A.) in its most up-to-date form, as set out in the
Principles of the International Phonetic Association, 1949.[3]

---

[3] This booklet, which illustrates the use of the phonetic alphabet by
transcripts of 51 languages, is obtainable from the Secretary of the Association, Department of Phonetics, University College, London, W.C.1.

I am indebted to several friends, and particularly to Professor David Abercrombie, Head of the Department of Phonetics in the University of Edinburgh, to Mr. J. L. M. Trim, Lecturer in Phonetics in the University of Cambridge, and to Miss B. Honikman, for helpful suggestions for this edition. Professor Abercrombie has made a special study for some years of problems connected with the elaboration of different types of phonetic transcription. He very kindly put all his findings at my disposal when I was drafting the new Appendix A, and they proved invaluable to me. Mr. Trim too has been interesting himself in the same problems, and made me a number of excellent recommendations. In particular, the wording of the definition of 'broad transcription' in § 5 of Appendix A is his; I find it to be a considerable improvement on other definitions that have been proposed. Mr. Trim has also aided me by pointing out several instances where stressings different from those to which I am accustomed are now in use, and by calling my attention to some examples in the seventh edition which for some other reason were not entirely appropriate. His notes enabled me to make a number of improvements in Chapter XXIX. Lastly I would express special thanks to my colleague, Miss A. D. Parkinson, for much assistance in connexion with the preparation of the manuscript.

DANIEL JONES.

March, 1960.

In this 1962 reprint the expression 'syllable division' has been changed to 'syllable separation' wherever it occurred in previous editions. The § 555 and footnote 15 of the last reprint have been deleted, and a new paragraph (numbered 560) replaces that footnote.

D. J.

March, 1962.

Contents

Contents

List of Illustrations

List of English Speech-sounds with Key Words

In order to ascertain the values of the phonetic symbols from the key words, these words must be said by a person who has the pronunciation described in § 61.

Each symbol has the sound represented by the italic letter or sequence of letters in the word placed next to it.

Phonetic Symbol	Ordinary Spelling of Key Word	Phonetic Transcription of Key Word	Phonetic Symbol	Ordinary Spelling of Key Word	Phonetic Transcripton of Key Word
ɑ	*fa*ther	ˈfɑːðə	m	*m*ake	meik
a	*fly*	flai	n	*n*o	nou
æ	*ha*t	hæt	ŋ	lo*ng*	lɔŋ
ʌ	*cu*p	kʌp	o	No*v*ember	noˈvembə
b	*b*oat	bout			(see § 403)
d	*d*ay	dei	ou	*go*	gou
ð	*th*en	ðen	ɔː	*saw*	sɔː
e	*ge*t	get	ɔ	*ho*t	hɔt
ei	*day*	dei	p	*p*ay	pei
ɛ	*fai*r	fɛə	r	*r*ed	red (see
əː	*bi*rd	bəːd			§§ 747 ff.)
ə	*a*bove, chin*a*	əˈbʌv, ˈtʃainə	s	*s*un	sʌn
f	*f*oot	fut	ʃ	*sh*ow	ʃou
g	*g*o	gou	t	*t*ea	tiː
h	*h*ard	hɑːd	θ	*th*in	θin
iː	*see*	siː	uː	f*oo*d	fuːd
i	*i*t	it	u	g*oo*d	gud
j	*y*es	jes	v	*v*ain	vein
k	*c*old	kould	w	*w*ine	wain
l	*l*eaf, fee*l*	liːf, fiːl (see	z	*z*eal	ziːl
		Chap. XX)	ʒ	mea*s*ure	ˈmeʒə

ː means that the sound represented by the preceding symbol is long.

ˈ means that the following syllable has strong stress.

ˌ means that the following syllable has secondary stress.

ˌ placed under a consonant-symbol (as in n̩, l̩) means that the sound is syllabic.

ᵕ indicates that a sound is extremely short, or that it constitutes the less prominent part of a diphthong.

- is occasionally used to indicate syllable-division.

Table of English Sounds

CONSONANTS

	Labial — Bi-labial	Labial — Labio-dental	Dental	Alveolar	Post-alveolar	Palato-alveolar	Palatal	Velar	Glottal
Plosive	p b			t d				k g	
Affricate					tr dr	tʃ dʒ			
Nasal	m			n				ŋ	
Lateral				l				(l)	
Fricative		f v	θ ð	s z	r	ʃ ʒ			h
Semi-vowel	w						j	(w)	

VOWELS

	Bi-labial	Front	Central	Back
Close	(uː) (u)	iː, i		uː, u
Half-close	(o)	e	əː, ə	o
Half-open	(ɔː)	ɛ	ʌ	ɔː
Open	(ɔ)	æ	a	ɑ

xvii

List of other Phonetic Symbols used in this Book

References are to paragraphs, where not otherwise indicated.
Numbers in bold type indicate paragraphs in which the sounds
are described.

App. = Appendix.

Consonants

ḅ   **174**, 505, 567, 573, 576.

ṭ   App. D *5, 10, 11, 17–19*.

t   note 1 to 169, **517**, 828, 829.

ṯ, d   App. A note 15 to § *23*.

ḍ   **174**, 518, 567, 573, 576, 611, 615, 789.

ḍ   531, **827**, 828, 829.

c   171, **181**, 538, 599, 847 (ii) (p. 223).

ɟ   **548**, 599.

g̊   **539**, 549, 567, 573, 576.

q   note 1 to 169, App. A *14, 15, 21*.

ʔ   note 8 to 217, 495, 552, **553**, 554–557, 594, App. B III,
     App. D *12*.

m̥   **176**, 845 (i)*a*, App. B III.

ɱ   **641**.

ɳ   **827**, 828, 829.

ɲ   App. A *19*.

ɲ   note 4 to § 6, **655**, 656, App. B III.

l̥   **176**, 193, 835, 836, App. A *9*, App. B III.

ɫ   note 2 to 176.

ɬ   661, 662, **668**, 676, App. A *9*.

l¹, lᵉ, etc.   **665**, 666, note 9 to 670, 671, 672, 676.

ɭ   **827**, 828, 829.

ɾ   746, **753**, Fig. 107, App. A *11, 12, 18*.

ɽ   746, **828**, 830.

ʀ   309, 347, 746, **762**, 764, 765.

ɸ   194, 596, **685**, 692, 806, App. B III.

β   347, 509, 595, 596, 685 **692**, 806, App. A *18*, App. B III.

ʋ   **693**.

ʋ   **690**.

ᶻ	note 9 to 709, **722**, 724, 789.
ʒ	**611**, 615.
ç	171, **180**, 194, 198, 784, **820**, 821, App. B III.
ɾ	568, 596, 600, 624, **775**
ɹ	57, 746, **747**, Fig. 106, 796, App. A *9, 11, 12, 17, 18, 20.* App, B III, App. D.
ʂ	**827**, 828, 829.
ʐ	**827**, 828.
x	171, 194, **782**, App. B III.
ɣ	**550**, App. B III.
ʁ	note 5 to 132, 297, 746, **763**, 764, 765, 798.
ɦ	**779**, 845 (i)*b*
ʍ	**810**, 811, 812, App. A *19, 23*, App. D *15*.
ɥ	**808**.
ɟ̆	note 5 to 251 (p. 66).

Vowels

i̠, a̠, etc.	**777**, note 43 to 778, 783.
i̧, į	251 and note 3.
ī	823, App. B III.
ɩ	**201** (4), 251, 259, note 10 to 879, App. A *28, 33, 36*, App. D.
ɩ̹	App. D *8*.
ɪ	App. A note 23 to *36*.
ɨ	**146**, App. A *13, 17*.
ï	**146**, 847 (v) (p. 224).
ē	App. D *8*.
ɛ̄	165, **822**, 823, App. B III, App. D *8*.
æ̃	823.
a̧	**430**, 431–433, 435.
ã	823, App. D *8*.
ã	164, **822**, App. B III.
ɑ	**832**.
ɒ	**145** (2), note 10 to 879, App. A *28*.
ɔ̃	**822**, App. D *8*.
ɒ̧	**832**.
o:	**309**, 397, 401, 847 (v) (p. 224).
ö	398, 847 (v) (p. 224).
õ	**822**, 823.

ᴏ   **201** (4), **330**, note 10 to **879**, App. A *28, 33, 36*, App. D.

u̯, ʉ̯   **330** and note.

ᴜ   App. A note 23 to *36*.

ü̃   App. B III.

ü   **146**, **845** (v), **847** (v) (p. 224), App. D *5*.

ʉ   **146**.

ʙ   **365, 366, 367**.

ə̃   App. D *8, 11*.

 əₗ (ɚ)   **832**, App. D note 1 to *3*.

y   **145** (1), **201** (2), note to **438**, **847** (iv) (p. 224), App. B III.

ø   **145** (1), **201** (2), **347**, note 77 to **347**, **398**, App. B III.

œ   **145** (2), **201** (2), **338**, **347**, note 77 to **347**, App. B III.

œ̃   **822**.

ɤ   **145** (3), Fig. 33.

ɯ   **145** (3), Fig. 33, **351**, App. B III.

Chapter I

INTRODUCTORY

The Nature of Speech

1. Spoken language consists of successions of sounds[1] emitted by the organs of speech, together with certain 'attributes'.[2]

2. These successions of sounds are composed of (1) speech-sounds proper, and (2) glides.

3. *Speech-sounds* are certain acoustic effects voluntarily produced by the organs of speech; they are the result of definite actions performed by these organs. A *glide* is the incidental transitory sound produced when the organs of speech are passing from the position for one speech-sound to that of another by the most direct route.

4. Speech-sounds are made voluntarily; they require that the speech-organs shall be placed in certain definite positions or moved in certain definite ways. The speaker has to go out of his way in order to make a speech-sound.

5. On the other hand the speaker does not have to go out of his way in order to make a glide; glides occur as the natural and inevitable result of pronouncing two speech-sounds one after the other.[3]

6. Most glides are inaudible or hardly audible even to the most practised ear; most of the glides occurring in English require no special consideration in the practical teaching of the language.[4]

---

[1] Also called 'phones' or 'linear' or 'segmental' features of speech.

[2] Also called 'prosodies' or 'suprasegmental' features of speech.

[3] In the technical term 'independent vowel-glide' the word 'glide' is used in a different sense. It there denotes a particular kind of speech-sound (see §§ 219, 800).

[4] But some glides occurring in foreign languages are distinctly audible and require special mention in descriptions of pronunciation. For instance, the glide between the French ɲ (§ 655) and a following vowel is always clearly audible.

1

Difficulties of Pronunciation

7. The student of spoken English or any other spoken language is faced at the outset with difficulties of five kinds in the matter of pronunciation. They are as follows:

8. Difficulty No. 1. He must learn to *recognize* readily and with certainty the various speech-sounds occurring in the language, when he hears them pronounced; he must moreover learn to *remember* the acoustic qualities of those sounds.

9. Difficulty No. 2. He must learn to *make* the foreign sounds with his own organs of speech.

10. Difficulty No. 3. He must learn to *use* those sounds in their proper places in connected speech.

11. Difficulty No. 4. He must learn the proper usage in the matter of the 'sound-attributes' or 'prosodies' as they are often called (especially length, stress and voice-pitch).

12. Difficulty No. 5. He must learn to catenate sounds, i.e. to join each sound of a sequence on to the next, and to pronounce the complete sequence rapidly and without stumbling.

13. The ultimate object of the language learner is to be able to pronounce properly without having to pay any particular attention to the way in which he does it. To attain this end he must in the initial stages of his study focus his attention continually on the above-mentioned details of the mechanism of speech. After long practice he will gradually acquire the power of pronouncing correctly without thinking of these details.

14. The student who wishes to become proficient in the written as well as the spoken language, has an additional difficulty, which we may call **Difficulty No. 6.** He has to learn the shapes of the conventional letters and the relations between the conventional orthography and the pronunciation.

15. Ability to *speak* a language or *understand it when spoken* does not involve the ability to read or write it in the conventional way. One may learn to speak English perfectly without ever seeing ordinary English orthography. And conversely it is possible to learn to read and write the language without being able to pronounce it.

16. As, however, those who wish to learn to speak and understand English almost always wish to be able to read and write it as well, a good deal is said in this book about 'orthoepy' or the relation between pronunciation and conventional spelling. Every word given as an example is accordingly shown both in phonetic transcription and in ordinary spelling.

How to surmount the Difficulties of Pronunciation

17. We will now explain more fully the nature of the five difficulties of pronunciation, and indicate shortly the appropriate methods for enabling the student to surmount them.

18. Difficulty No. 1 is a matter of 'ear-training' or more accurately 'cultivation of the auditory memory.' No one can hope to be a successful linguist unless he has a *good ear*. If his ear is unsensitive by nature, it may be made more sensitive by training; and if his ear is good by nature, it can be made still better by training.

19. The possession of a good ear is necessary to the linguist for two reasons. (1) If he has a good ear, he will be able to tell whether he pronounces the foreign sounds correctly or not. (2) A good ear helps him to understand the language readily when spoken by natives; he recognizes words instantly, and does not mistake one word for another.

20. The possession of a good ear involves (1) ability to *discriminate* between sounds, (2) ability to *remember* the acoustic qualities of foreign sounds, and (3) ability to *recognize* foreign sounds with ease and certainty. In other words, the student must be able (1) to hear the differences between the various sounds of the foreign language, and between foreign sounds and sounds of his mother tongue, (2) to bring into his consciousness, without the aid of any external stimulus, memories of foreign sounds previously heard, and (3) to compare sounds subconsciously with the memory-images of sounds previously heard.

21. To cultivate a good linguistic ear requires systematic practice in *listening for sounds*. There is only one effective exercise for this purpose, namely, dictation of isolated sounds and meaningless words by a teacher who can pronounce the foreign sounds accurately. The pupil should write down these sounds and words phonetically. If he makes a mistake in his transcription, it shows that he has confused one sound with another. The teacher will in this case repeat the two sounds a number of times (both isolated and in syllables) in order to impress on the pupil's mind the difference of acoustic quality.[5]

22. If the pupil is a beginner, the teacher may use for ear-training exercises real words which the pupil has not yet learnt.

23. Examples of invented words suitable for training the ear to recognize the English sounds are given in § 237 and in Appendix B.

24. A few invented words for ear-training practice should be given at the beginning of every pronunciation lesson, until the pupil can be fairly certain of doing the exercises without mistakes.[6]

25. **Difficulty No. 2** is a matter of *gymnastics of the vocal organs*. In order to learn to form the speech-sounds of a foreign language, the student has to learn to put his tongue, lips, and other parts of the organs of speech into certain definite positions, or to perform with them certain actions. He will learn to make such sounds with the greatest accuracy and in the shortest time if (1) he is told precisely what to do with his organs of speech, and (2) he is given, as far as may be necessary, exercises which help him to carry out the instructions.

26. In other words, the language learner should (1) study *phonetic theory*, and (2) do, when necessary, *exercises* based on that theory.

27. **Difficulty No. 3** requires very different treatment. The student has to learn what is the appropriate *order* in which to

---

[5] See also my book, *The Pronunciation of English*, 1950 and subsequent editions, § 490 (Cambridge University Press). When a teacher is not available, ear-training may be done with a gramophone, provided the records are good and there is a key giving a phonetic transcription of the words of the record.

[6] The 'ear-training exercise' was, I believe, first invented by Jean Passy, the brother of Paul Passy. See his article *La dictée phonétique* in *Le Maître Phonétique*, Feb., 1894 (particularly pp. 36, 37).

A dictation of meaningless words for testing the sharpness of candidates' ears forms part of various examinations in Phonetics in the University of London, and in the examinations held by the Association Phonétique Internationale.

place the sounds so as to make intelligible words and sentences. This is a matter of *memorizing*.

28. The student of spoken English has, for instance, to know that if he wishes to communicate the idea expressed in French by 'armoire' and in German by 'Schrank,' he must form the English sounds **k ʌ b ə d**[7] one after the other in this order. No

---

[7] Letters in thick type are phonetic symbols. The various sounds denoted by them are fully described further on (Chap. XIV, etc.), and lists with key-words are given on pp. xvi–xx.

Every teacher should adopt a definite method of naming the symbols and sounds. As to the *symbols* some teachers simply call them by the sounds they represent, e.g. if they want to mention the phonetic letters **p, l, ʃ, ɔ**, they call them by the isolated sounds **p, l, ʃ, ɔ**. There are some objections to this system. One is that some sounds (e.g. plosive consonants) cannot be said without another sound to accompany them (§ 563). Another is that isolated sounds are often indistinct, especially when uttered in a large room, and a third is that learners not yet fully familiar with foreign sounds do not always recognize which sound is meant. On the whole I am inclined to recommend giving names to the consonant letters—the ordinary names for the letters of the ordinary alphabet and the following special names for new letters:

letter	name
ŋ	iŋ
θ	iθ
ð	ðiː or ðɑː
ʃ	iʃ
ʒ	ʒiː or ʒɑː

The naming of vowel-symbols presents some difficulty. Probably the best plan is to say the sound with a defining adjective, and speak of 'the close **e** letter,' 'the open **ɛ** letter,' 'the back **ɑ** letter,' 'the neutral **ə** letter,' etc. Some teachers, however, use non-technical language and speak of 'Greek *e*' (for **ɛ**), 'broken *o*' (for **ɔ**), 'round *a*' (for **ɑ**), 'inverted *e*' (for **ə**). Another plan is to use key-words and speak of 'the *cup*-symbol' (for **ʌ**), 'the *lock*-symbol' (for **ɔ**), etc.

Sounds may often be named by simply uttering them. But here again confusion may arise in practical teaching through the indistinctness of isolated sounds (especially in a large room) or failure on the part of the pupil to recognize which sound is meant. Greater clearness is ensured by speaking of 'the **kei**-sound' (for **k**), 'the **el**-sound' (for **l**), 'the **iθ**-sound' (for **θ**), etc. In the case of vowels the mention of a key word is often helpful: 'the *cup*-sound' (for **ʌ**), 'the *bird*-sound' (for **əː**), etc. Another plan which gives excellent results in practice is to number the vowels, and designate them when necessary by their numbers; thus **ʌ** may be called 'English No. 10,' **a** may be called 'Cardinal No. 4,' etc. (see §§ 235, 236).

other English sounds will do, nor may these sounds be placed in any other order. However well the student may pronounce the sounds, he will not convey the meaning, unless he uses this particular sequence of them. He must therefore take care to remember that this is the required sequence.

29. The task of learning to remember what is the appropriate sequence of sounds to use in any given word or sentence is greatly facilitated by the use of *Phonetic Transcription*.

30. Phonetic transcription may be defined as an unambiguous system of representing pronunciation by means of writing, the basic principle being to assign one and only one letter to each phoneme of the language. (See Chap. X and Appendix A.)

31. Phonetic transcription, then, is a convenient method of showing sound-order graphically. This graphic representation of sound-order appeals to the visual memory and thus assists the auditory memory.

32. Conventional English spelling is far from being phonetic; it does not give the accurate information as to sound-order required by the student of spoken English. In the first place English assigns to many of the letters of the alphabet values quite different from those which people in foreign countries are accustomed to associate with them: e.g. the *a* in *gate*, the *i* in *find*, the *u* in *tune*.[8] Doubtless these values may be learnt without difficulty; but as soon as the foreign student has learnt them, he finds innumerable words in which these letters have quite different values: compare the *a*'s in *father, fall, any, fat, watch*,[9] the *i*'s in *wind* (noun), *machine, bird*,[10] the *u*'s in *rule, put, hut*[11]; compare also the *o*'s in *stove, move, love*,[12] the *ea*'s in *meat, head, great, bear*,[13] etc.

33. He also finds that many English sounds may be spelt in a large number of different ways. Thus the words *meet, meat, niece, pique, key, quay, seize* all have the same vowel-sound[14]; so also

---

[8] These words are phonetically **geit, faind, tju:n.**

[9] Phonetically **'fɑ:ðə, fɔ:l, 'eni, fæt, wɔtʃ.**

[10] Phonetically **wind, mə'ʃi:n, bə:d.**

[11] Phonetically **ru:l, put, hʌt.**

[12] Phonetically **stouv, mu:v, lʌv.**

[13] Phonetically **mi:t, hed, greit, bɛə.**

[14] Phonetically **mi:t, mi:t, ni:s, pi:k, ki:, ki:, si:z.**

have the words *sauce, lawn, stalk, stork, board, warn, thought, broad, floor* (in Southern English).[15]

34. Discrepancies between pronunciation and ordinary spelling are not confined to the English language. In French -*lle* has different values in *ville* and *fille*,[16] *o* has different values in *grosse* and *gosse*,[17] *portions* is pronounced in two different ways according as it is a noun or a verb[18]; on the other hand, the sound **o** is spelt differently in the words *mot, tôt, beau, chevaux*.[19] In German *ch* has different values in *rauchen* and *Frauchen*,[20] and *u* has different values in *Fuss* and *Nuss*.[21]

35. The result of such inconsistencies is that the foreign learner who depends solely on ordinary orthography is in innumerable cases at a loss to know what sounds should be used, and is continually mispronouncing words. Such mispronunciations may, however, be avoided by the use of Phonetic Transcription.

36. The phonetic alphabet used here is that of the *Association Phonétique Internationale*.[22] A list of the symbols used for transcribing English in this book is given on p. xvi. Further information regarding phonetic transcription is given in Chap. X and in Appendix A.

37. It must be borne in mind that phonetic transcriptions are valueless to students who have not learnt to form the sounds which the phonetic letters represent, i.e. who have not surmounted with tolerable success Difficulty No. 2. When, however, the student can make the individual sounds with fair accuracy, he will be in a position to begin learning sequences of sounds; phonetic transcriptions will tell him *what are the proper sequences to learn* in order to express the ideas he wishes to communicate.

---

[15] Phonetically **sɔːs, lɔːn, stɔːk, stɔːk, bɔːd** (also **bɔəd), wɔːn, θɔːt, brɔːd, flɔː** (also **flɔə**).

[16] Phonetically **vil, fiːj**.

[17] Phonetically **groːs, gɔs**.

[18] Phonetically **pɔrˈsjõ, pɔrˈtjõ**.

[19] Phonetically **mo, to, bo, ʃəˈvo**.

[20] Phonetically **ˈrauxən, ˈfrauçən**.

[21] Phonetically **fuːs, nus**.

[22] Particulars of the *Association Phonétique Internationale* (in English *International Phonetic Association*, often abbreviated to I.P.A.; in German *Weltlautschriftverein*) are obtainable from the Secretary of the Association, Department of Phonetics, University College, London, W.C.1.

38. Unless the student can pronounce every one of the sounds k ʌ b ə d with tolerable accuracy, he will not be able to say the English word for 'armoire' ('Schrank') in an intelligible manner, even if he is furnished with a phonetic transcription. If on the other hand he has learnt to make those sounds, he will be able to say the English word *provided he knows in what order the sounds are to be placed.* He will remember this order if he sees the word written 'kʌbəd better than he would if he simply heard the word pronounced and never saw it written.

39. Difficulty No. 4 concerns certain characteristics which sounds and syllables have relative to other sounds and syllables in the sentence.[23] In particular the student will generally be able to pronounce correctly in the matter of length, stress, and pitch, if accurate information as to the foreign usage in regard to these matters is supplied to him. Sometimes such information may be supplied by means of rules, and sometimes (as in the case of English stress) it is better conveyed by marks in the phonetic transcriptions. There is as a rule nothing particularly difficult in carrying out such instructions. The main difficulty in connexion with them is to bear them in mind—again a question of memory.

40. Difficulty No. 5 must be carefully distinguished from all the preceding. It sometimes happens that a student can pronounce isolated sounds correctly, knows what sequence of sounds to use in a given word or sentence, and knows the necessary details in regard to length, stress, and pitch, but he stumbles over the sound-sequence. He has not acquired facility in passing from one sound to another, and he cannot always say sequences of sounds rapidly and without stumbling. In other words, he does not 'catenate' properly.

41. Moreover he may have acquired the bad habit of stopping between words; he has not realized the important principle that the only places where pauses are normally made are at the ends of certain *grammatical groups* called *sense-groups* (Chap. XXX).

42. Ability to catenate sounds, i.e. to pronounce sequences of sounds with rapidity and without stumbling, can be cultivated by continued repetition of such sound-sequences as present difficulty. The required sequences must be pronounced at first slowly and then with gradually increasing speed. Some suggestions for such

---

[23] I.e. 'prosodies' or 'suprasegmental' elements of speech.

repetition exercises will be found in Appendix C. Exercises of this type may with advantage be followed by systematic fluency exercises on the lines of 'substitution tables.'[24]

43. It must be borne in mind continually that in ordinary conversation people say their sentences at an average rate of some 300 syllables to the minute or five syllables per second. This then is the ideal rate at which the student should aim, when practising any given sentence. When practising catenation exercises the student should frequently time himself, to see how near he can get to this ideal rate.

44. It is worse than useless to try to say words fast or to attempt catenation exercises until the individual sounds have been thoroughly mastered. Above all, the student must beware of being led astray by an idea that he can learn to make a difficult foreign sound by merely repeating words containing that sound. That idea is an absurd one. Repeating words with badly pronounced sounds has the precisely opposite effect of fixing the student's bad pronunciation. Speech-sounds are learnt by the methods referred to in § 25.

Need for Oral Instruction

45. Some features of pronunciation can only be learnt with the aid of a teacher; others can be learnt from books.

46. The services of a teacher are required mainly in connexion with Difficulties Nos. 1 and 2.

47. The functions of the teacher in regard to these difficulties are: (1) to act as a model of pronunciation, (2) to give the pupil ear-training exercises as described above (§ 21), (3) to tell him whether his attempts at the pronunciation of the foreign sounds and sound-sequences are successful or not, and (4) where the instructions in books are inadequate, to devise means which will help the pupil to improve his pronunciation of the difficult sounds and sound-sequences.

48. Good gramophone records can to some extent relieve the teacher of the first of these duties.

49. In regard to the teacher's fourth duty, it should be remarked that all students do not have the same difficulties, and a book

---

[24] See *100 English Substitution Tables*, by H. E. Palmer (published by Heffer, Cambridge).

on pronunciation cannot provide for the needs of every individual student. The most that a book can do is to deal with the difficulties of pronunciation most frequently met with. The rest must be left to the phonetically trained teacher.

50. Sound-order can be learnt from books of phonetic texts. Usage in regard to length, stress, and pitch can likewise be ascertained from books. To attain ability to catenate properly requires neither book nor teacher; it is a matter of private practice on the part of the student.

Utility of Books on Pronunciation

51. It will be seen from what has been said, that though the acquisition of a spoken language is essentially an oral process, yet a book on pronunciation may be of service in several ways.

52. The directions in which such a book may assist the language learner are illustrated by the present 'Outline' which contains:

(1) descriptions of the English speech-sounds together with information as to their usage (Chaps. XIV–XXVII),

(2) information as to English usage in the matter of length, stress, and pitch (Chaps. XXVIII–XXXI),

(3) descriptions of mistakes of pronunciation that foreign learners frequently make (Chap. XIV, etc.),

(4) indications of methods which will help them to avoid such mistakes (Chap. XIV, etc.),

(5) specimen catenation exercises and lists of words illustrating the use of the various sounds (Chaps. XIV–XXVII and Appendix C),

(6) specimen exercises to be dictated for ear-training (Chap. XIII and Appendix B).

53. To perfect his pronunciation the learner should do a considerable amount of reading aloud from phonetic texts. He should also have much practice in transcribing phonetically passages of the language he is learning. His transcripts should, as a rule, be corrected by his teacher. He may, however, derive much benefit from transcribing passages from a book of phonetic texts containing a key in ordinary spelling (by transcribing from the key and correcting his transcripts by reference to the phonetic version).

Chapter II

TYPES OF PRONUNCIATION

54. The first question that confronts a person wishing to acquire an acceptable pronunciation of a foreign language is: Which of the various forms of pronunciation ought he to learn?

55. No two persons of the same nationality pronounce their own language exactly alike. The differences may arise from a variety of causes, such as locality, social surroundings or early influences, and there are often individual peculiarities for which it is difficult or impossible to account.

56. Thus, the pronunciation current among people brought up in Manchester differs from that of those from Exeter, and both differ from the pronunciation of those brought up in Edinburgh or in London. The French of Paris is different from that of Marseilles or Lausanne; the pronunciation of educated Germans from Berlin differs considerably from that used by those coming from Dresden, Cologne or Hamburg.

57. An example of differences of English pronunciation according to locality may be found in the treatment of the letter *r* in such words as *part*. In Scotland the *r* in this word is generally pronounced as a slightly rolled or flapped **r**, but in London English the pronunciation is **pɑːt**. In many parts of the North and the West of England on the other hand, the effect of the *r* appears as a modification known as 'retroflexion' or 'inversion' of the preceding vowel, thus **paɹt** or **pɑ̢ːt** (see §§ 831–833). In the South of England the vowels in *boot* and *book* are different (phonetically **buːt, buk**), but in Scotland a short close **u** is generally used in both words.

58. The following are examples of differences between 'educated' and 'uneducated' speech. People of limited education in many parts of England omit the sound **h** altogether; they say **elp** for **help**. In London Dialect (Cockney) words like *name* are pronounced with a diphthong **ai** or **æi** instead of with **ei**; and words like *house*, *about* are pronounced with **æu**, or sometimes **æə**, instead of **au** (**æus, əˈbæut** or **əˈbæət**). In uneducated Yorkshire speech the vowels of *put* (**put**) and *cut* (**kʌt**) are levelled to a vowel intermediate between these two.

11

59. Differences between the pronunciation of old and young people, and between that of women and men of the same locality and similar position, may sometimes be observed. Thus in English the word *soft* is pronounced **sɔːft** in the South by many educated elderly men, but younger people, and particularly the women, pronounce for the most part **sɔft**[1]; and the use of **hw** in place of the more usual **w** in such words as *which, when,* would seem to be more prevalent among women than among men (in the South of England).

60. Individual peculiarities may be the result of habit, e.g. childish mispronunciations which have never been corrected, or they may arise from some physical defect.

61. The existence of all these differences makes it difficult for the foreign learner to know which type of English pronunciation to acquire. I do not consider it possible at the present time to regard any special type as 'Standard' or as intrinsically 'better' than other types. Nevertheless, the type described in this book is certainly a useful one. It is based on my own (Southern) speech, and is, as far as I can ascertain, that generally used by those who have been educated at 'preparatory' boarding schools and the 'Public Schools.'[2] This pronunciation is fairly uniform in these schools and is independent of their locality. It has the advantage that it is easily understood in all parts of the English-speaking countries; it is perhaps more widely understood than any other type. For further information about it, see the Introduction to my *English Pronouncing Dictionary*, 11th ed., re-set, 1956[3]; also Wyld's *History of Modern Colloquial English*,[4] Chap. I.

62. The term 'Received Pronunciation' (abbreviation RP) is often used to designate this type of pronunciation. This term is adopted here for want of a better. I wish it, however, to be understood that other types of pronunciation exist which may be considered equally 'good.'

63. It should be noticed here that all speakers use more than one style of pronunciation. A person may pronounce the same word or sequence of words quite differently under different circumstances. Thus in ordinary conversation the word *and* is frequently

---

[1] The use of short ɔ in words like *soft, cross, lost* is much on the increase. It would not surprise me if the pronunciation **sɔːft** (which I use) were to disappear within the next fifty years.

[2] 'Public School' in the English sense, not in the American sense.

[3] Published by Dent (London).

[4] Published by Blackwell (Oxford).

pronounced n when unstressed (e.g. in *bread and butter* 'bred n 'bʌtə), but in serious recitation the word, even when unstressed, might often be pronounced ænd rhyming with *hand* hænd.

64. Several different styles of pronunciation may be distinguished. Notable among them are the rapid familiar style, the slower colloquial style, the natural style used in addressing a fair-sized audience, the acquired style of the stage and the acquired styles used in singing. Of these the slower colloquial style is probably the most suitable for the use of foreign learners, and is the style indicated throughout this book, except where the contrary is stated.[5]

---

[5] Although those who use RP have much in common in their speech, it must not be thought that RP is absolutely uniform. Quite a number of variations are to be found in it. For instance, the qualities of sounds used in some words vary from speaker to speaker (see, for example, §§ 271, 330, 388). And in the case of some words two distinct pronunciations must both be considered as belonging to RP; examples of such words are *been* (§ 471), *off*, *cost*, *loss*, etc. (§ 300), the words ending in *-aph* (§ 294), *threepence* (§ 257), *association* (footnote 28 to § 732).

The following are some variations within RP which require special mention, since their occurrence has determined certain features of the system of phonetic transcription used in this book: (1) many of those who speak with RP lengthen the traditionally short sound of *a* (æ) in various words (§874), (2) the sequences eiə, ouə, are often reduced to diphthongs eə, oə, distinct from εə, ɔə (§§ 392a, 403), (3) a diphthong of the aə-type or a pure vowel of the aː-type distinct from ɑː is often used in place of aiə and auə (§§ 414, 430), (4) a monophthongal o-sound often takes the place of ou in unstressed positions (§ 403).

Although the form of transcription here adopted allows for these four variations, it must be understood that none of these variants are essential to acceptable pronunciation. Consequently, if greater simplicity is desired, a simpler form of transcription may easily be devised by taking as a basis for study a type of English pronunciation in which the above-mentioned alternatives do not occur. Such a simplified transcription is described in Appendix A, *44–49*; it is perfectly adequate for enabling foreign students to learn to pronounce English like English people. In a 'broad' transcription (§ 200) of this particular kind of speech the special letters æ, ε, ɑ, and ɔ are not needed; they may be replaced without ambiguity by the common letters a, e, a, and o respectively, in accordance with the principle of substituting familiar for unfamiliar letters formulated in §20 of the *Principles of the International Phonetic Association*, 1949. Transcription simplified on these lines, in which the number of special letters is reduced to a minimum, is very convenient for use by the numerous foreign learners whose sole object is to learn to speak English well, but who have no need either to become specialized phoneticians or to concern themselves with more than one variety of English pronunciation.

For further information concerning different types of phonetic transcription see Appendix A.

Chapter III

THE ORGANS OF SPEECH

65. It is necessary that the student of phonetics should have a fairly clear idea of the structure and functions of the organs of speech. Those who have not already done so should make a thorough examination of the inside of the mouth by means of a hand looking-glass. The best way of doing this is to stand with the back to the light and to hold the looking-glass in such a position that it reflects the light into the mouth and at the same time enables the observer to see in the glass the interior thus illuminated. It is not difficult to find the right position for the glass.

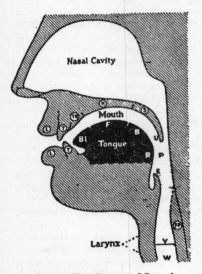

Fig. 1. The Organs of Speech.

B Back of Tongue. *Bl* Blade of Tongue. *E* Epiglottis. *F* Front of Tongue. *FP* Food-passage. *H* Hard Palate. *LL* Lips. *P* Pharyngal Cavity (Pharynx). *R* Root of the Tongue. *S* Soft Palate. *TR* Teeth-ridge. *TT* Teeth. *U* Uvula. *V* Position of Vocal Cords. *W* Windpipe.

66. Models of the organs of speech will be found useful. Suitable models of sections of the head, mouth, nose, larynx, etc., may be obtained from dealers in medical instruments.

67. Figs. 1 and 2 show all that is essential for the present book.

68. A detailed description of the various parts of the organs of speech is not necessary; the following points should, however, be noted.

69. The roof of the mouth is divided, for the purposes of phonetics, into three parts called the teeth-ridge, the hard palate, and the soft palate. The *teeth-ridge* is defined as the part of the

14

roof of the mouth just behind the teeth which is convex to the tongue, the division between the teeth-ridge and the palate being defined as the place where the roof of the mouth ceases to be convex to the tongue and begins to be concave (see Fig. 1). The remainder of the roof of the mouth comprises the other two parts, the front part constituting the *hard palate*, and the back part the *soft palate*. These two parts should be examined carefully in the looking-glass; they may be felt with the tongue or with the finger. The soft palate can be moved upwards from the position shown in Fig. 1, and when raised to its fullest extent it touches the back wall of the pharynx as shown in Fig. 10, etc. (see also § 165).

70. The *pharynx* is the cavity situated in the throat immediately behind the mouth. Below it is the *larynx* which forms the upper part of the *windpipe* (the passage leading to the lungs). The *epiglottis* is a sort of tongue situated just above the larynx. It is probably contracted in such a way as to protect the larynx during the action of swallowing, but it does not appear to enter into the formation of any speech-sounds.

Fig. 2. The Mouth.

AA Pharyngal Arch. *PP* Pharyngal Cavity (Pharynx). *S* Soft Palate. *T* Tongue. *U* Uvula.

71. For the purposes of phonetics it is convenient to imagine the surface of the *tongue* divided into three parts (see Fig. 1). The part which normally lies opposite the soft palate is called the *back*; the part which normally lies opposite the hard palate is called the *front*; and the part which normally lies opposite the teeth-ridge is called the *blade*. The extremity of the tongue is called the *tip* or *point*, and is included in the blade. The definitions of 'back' and 'front' are particularly important. It is sometimes convenient to use the term *middle* of the tongue to denote a part of the surface of the tongue including the fore part of the 'back' and the hinder part of the 'front.'

72. The tongue is extremely mobile. Thus the tip can be made to touch any part of the roof of the mouth from the teeth to the

beginning of the soft palate. The other parts of the tongue may likewise be made to articulate against different parts of the roof of the mouth.

Fig. 3. Lateral Spreading of the Tongue.

Fig. 4. Lateral Contraction of the Tongue.

73. Moreover it is possible to spread out the fore part of the tongue laterally (after the manner shown in Fig. 3), or to contract it laterally (after the manner shown in Fig. 4). The presence or absence of such lateral contraction is probably immaterial for most sounds, but there are a few in which lateral contraction appears to play an essential part (see particularly §§ 747, 831).

74. The *vocal cords* are situated in the larynx; they resemble two lips (see Fig. 6). They run in a horizontal direction from back to front. The space between them is called the *glottis*. The cords may be kept apart or they may be brought together so as to touch and thus close the air passage completely. When they are brought near together and air is forced between them, they vibrate, producing a musical sound (see Chap. V).

75. In the larynx just above the vocal cords is situated another pair of lips somewhat resembling the vocal cords and running parallel to them. These are known as the *false vocal cords* (see § 82).

Chapter IV

EXPERIMENTAL METHODS

76. The analysis of speech-sounds in general and the differences in articulation between English sounds and foreign sounds which resemble them may, if desired, be investigated and demonstrated by means of specially designed apparatus. Such demonstrations belong to the branch of phonetic science known as 'experimental' or 'instrumental' phonetics.

77. It is not suggested that experimental phonetics is a necessary study for all those who wish to pronounce a foreign language correctly, but demonstrations by means of special apparatus are sometimes found helpful by students as fixing in the memory facts which they have previously learnt by the ordinary methods of practical phonetics.

78. The apparatus used in elementary experimental phonetics includes the artificial palate, the phonetic kymograph, the laryngoscope, X-ray photography, sensitive flames, tape recorders and other recording and reproducing machines. In more advanced work use is made of apparatus for enlarging the curves on records, cathode ray oscillographs, harmonic analysers, spectrographs and much other apparatus. It is not necessary for the purposes of this book to say much about experimental methods, beyond giving palatograms of various sounds.[1]

79. A palatogram is a drawing showing the parts of the roof of the mouth with which the tongue makes contact in pronouncing sounds. Palatograms may be made by means of a special kind of artificial palate. Suitable palates in metal or vulcanite can be made by any dentist. They should be of the form shown in Fig. 5, the material must be very thin, and the palate must fit the observer's mouth exactly. It must be so made that it will keep in position by itself, and it should be provided with little projecting

---

[1] A number of kymographic tracings were reproduced in the first and second editions of this book (1918 and 1922).

pieces in the front (*AA* Fig. 5) so as to admit of its being removed from the mouth easily. If the material is not black the under side should be blackened with varnish.

80. The artificial palate is used as follows. The under side of the palate is first covered with a little finely powdered chalk and inserted into the mouth. A sound is then pronounced and the palate is withdrawn. The parts of the palate from which the chalk has been removed show the points at which the tongue touched it. These marks on the artificial palate may then be examined at leisure. They

(I)

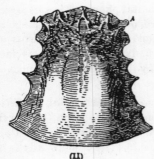 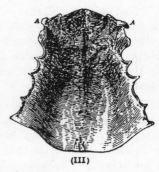

(II)   (III)

Fig. 5. The Artificial Palate.

(I) Side View.   (II) Seen from above.   (III) Seen from below.

may also be photographed if desired, or the marks may be copied in projection on outline diagrams of the palate. D. Abercrombie, of the University of Edinburgh, has recently devised a means of photographing the palate directly, thus dispensing with the use of an artificial palate. See his article *Direct Palatography* in the *Zeitschrift für Phonetik* (Berlin), 1955.

81. The palatograms in this book have been drawn from observations made with vulcanite palates. These palates extend so as to cover the whole of the front teeth. The limits of the gums adjoining the front teeth are marked on the present diagrams by the dotted line (Figs. **37, 39,** etc.).

Chapter V

BREATH AND VOICE

82. The vocal cords are capable of acting in much the same way as the lips of the mouth. Thus they may be held wide apart, they may be closed completely, or they may be held loosely together so that they vibrate when air passes between them. When they are held wide apart (i.e. when the glottis is open) and air passes between them, the sound produced is called *breath*. When they are drawn near together and air is forced between them so that they vibrate, the sound produced is called *voice*. If the false vocal cords (§ 75) are drawn towards each other leaving only a narrow space for the air to pass between them, the resulting sound is one variety of *whisper*. It is believed that certain positions of the glottis intermediate between those for breath and voice give rise to other varieties of whisper.

83. The vocal cords may be made to touch tightly along their whole length so that no air can escape at all. This is the position known as *closed glottis*. The explosive sound heard when this position is released is known as the 'glottal stop' (see §§ 552, ff.).

84. Breath is heard most clearly in the sounds represented by **h**. Voice occurs as part of the articulation of numerous speech-sounds, and particularly of the vowels.

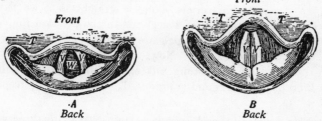

Fig. 6. The Larynx as seen through the Laryngoscope. *A* Position for Breath. *B* Position for Voice. *TT* Tongue. *VV* Vocal Cords. *W* Windpipe.

85. The positions of the vocal cords in the production of breath and voice are shown in Fig. 6. These diagrams show the larynx as seen from above through a laryngoscope.

19

86. The *Laryngoscope* in its simplest form is a small circular mirror, about ¾ of an inch in diameter, which is fixed to a long handle at an angle of 120°. When the instrument is held in the

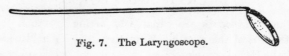

Fig. 7. The Laryngoscope.

position shown in Fig. 7 and inserted into the mouth so that the mirror is pressed against the soft palate as far back as possible, and is adjusted so that a strong light is reflected down the throat, the interior of the larynx is visible in the mirror.

87. Breath and voice may be illustrated artificially by the following experiment. Take a short tube of wood or glass T, say 4 cm. long and 1 cm. in diameter, and tie on to one end of it a piece of thin rubber tubing R, of a somewhat larger diameter, say 3 cm., as shown in Fig. 8. The tube is taken to represent the windpipe, and the rubber part the larynx. The space enclosed by the edge of the rubber E, E, represents the glottis. If we leave the rubber part in its natural position and blow through the tube, air passes out, making a slight hissing sound. This corresponds to breath. If we take hold of two opposite points of the edge of the rubber tube, E, E, and draw them apart so that two edges of the rubber come into contact along a straight line, we have a representation of the glottis in the position for voice, the two edges which are in contact representing the two vocal cords. Now, if we blow through the tube, the air in passing out causes the edges to vibrate and a kind of musical sound is produced. This sound corresponds to voice.

Fig. 8. Instrument to illustrate Breath and Voice.

88. Most ordinary speech-sounds contain either breath or voice. Those which contain breath are called *breathed* or *voiceless*[1] sounds,

---

[1] It is convenient to use the term 'breathed' in speaking of continuant sounds and 'voiceless' in speaking of plosive consonants. It can hardly be said that during the 'stop' of a plosive consonant there is a current of air passing between the vocal cords.

and those which contain voice are called *voiced* sounds. Examples of breathed sounds are **f**, **s**; examples of voiced sounds are **v**, **z**, **b**, and the vowels.

89. When people speak in a whisper, *whispered* sounds are substituted for all the voiced sounds, the breathed sounds remaining unaltered.

90. It is possible to pronounce various sounds with simultaneous closure of the glottis (§§ 83, 569–571). Sounds so pronounced are neither breathed nor voiced. Sounds of this type do not occur in English.

91. It does not require much practice for a person with a fairly good ear to be able to recognize by ear the difference between breathed and voiced sounds. Any students who have difficulty in this should practise prolonging such sounds as **s**, **z**, **f**, **v**, **ʃ**, **ʒ**, **θ**, **ð**.[2] They may also try the following well-known tests. (1) Stop the ears with the fingers, and pronounce the following sounds **p**, **a**,[3] **f**, **v**; a loud buzzing sound will be heard during the utterance of **a** and **v**, but not when **p** and **f** are sounded. (2) Pronounce the same sounds while touching the outside of the larynx with the fingers; the vibrations will be felt in the case of the voiced sounds. (3) Notice that voiced sounds such as **a**, **v**, can be sung, while breathed sounds cannot.

92. When an assimilation (Chap. XXVI) takes place by which a voiceless sound is substituted for a voiced sound, the voiced sound is commonly said to become *unvoiced* or to be *devocalized* or better *devoiced*.

93. The presence or absence of voice may be demonstrated experimentally in various ways. One method is to use a metal

Fig. 9. Zünd-Burguet's Voice Indicator.

ring placed loosely in a tin match-box. A flat side of the box is placed firmly against one side of the larynx; when voiced sounds

---

[2] ʃ is the English sound of *sh*; ʒ is the sound of *s* in *measure*; θ and ð are the sounds of *th* in *thin* and *then*.

[3] As in *half*, *father*.

are produced the ring rattles, though when breathed sounds are produced it remains silent.

94. Zünd-Burguet's Voice Indicator (Fig. 9) is a convenient instrument for demonstrating the presence of voice in a similar way.[4]

95. The presence or absence of voice may also be shown by means of a phonetic kymograph, and voice vibrations appear very clearly on magnifications of sound-tracks.

---

[4] These voice indicators respond excellently to voiced consonants and close vowels, but do not always respond well to the opener vowels, especially the opener front vowels such as ɛ, a.

Chapter VI

VOWELS AND CONSONANTS

96. Every speech-sound belongs to one or other of the two main classes known as Vowels and Consonants.

97. A *vowel* (in normal speech[1]) is defined as a voiced sound in forming which the air issues in a continuous stream through the pharynx and mouth, there being no obstruction and no narrowing such as would cause audible friction.

98. All other sounds (in normal speech[1]) are called *consonants*.

99. Consonants therefore include (i) all sounds which are not voiced (e.g. **p**, **s**, **ʃ**), (ii) all sounds in the production of which the air has an impeded passage through the mouth (e.g. **b**, **l**, rolled **r**), (iii) all sounds in the production of which the air does not pass through the mouth (e.g. **m**), (iv) all sounds in which there is audible friction (e.g. **f**, **v**, **s**, **z**, **h**).

100. The distinction between vowels and consonants is not an arbitrary physiological distinction. It is in reality a distinction based on acoustic considerations, namely on the *relative sonority* or *carrying power* of the various sounds. Some sounds are more sonorous than others, that is to say they carry better or can be heard at a greater distance, when pronounced with the same length, stress, and voice-pitch. Thus the sound **ɑ** pronounced in the normal manner can be heard at a much greater distance than

---

[1] Whispered speech is not considered as normal. In whispered speech 'voice' is replaced throughout by 'whisper' and every sound consists of audible friction and nothing else (except the 'stops' of voiceless plosives, which have no sound at all). The term 'whispered vowels' is commonly used to designate sounds produced with the organs in the same positions as for the sounds defined as 'vowels' in § 97, but with 'whisper' substituted for 'voice.' There is no objection to this terminology, but it should be noted that if a whispered vowel were to occur in speech next to a voiced one, the whispered vowel would have to be regarded as a consonant. This may be seen by pronouncing a whispered **ɑ** immediately followed by a voiced **ɑ**. The result resembles **hɑ** with a strong kind of **h**.

the sound **p** or the sound **f** pronounced in the normal manner. It so happens that the sounds defined as vowels in § 97 are on the whole more sonorous than any other speech-sounds (when pronounced in the normal manner)[2]; and that is the reason why these sounds are considered to form one of the two fundamental classes.[3]

101. The relative sonority or carrying power of sounds depends on their inherent quality (tamber) and must be distinguished from the relative 'prominence' of sounds in a sequence; *prominence* depends on combinations of quality with length, stress and (in the case of voiced sounds) intonation.   When length and stress (degree of push from the chest wall) are constant and the intonation is level, the sounds defined as vowels are more prominent than the sounds defined as consonants; 'open' vowels (§ 153) are mostly more prominent than 'close' vowels (§ 153); voiced consonants are more prominent than voiceless consonants; l-sounds and voiced nasal consonants are more prominent than other voiced consonants.   The voiceless consonants have very little prominence in comparison with the voiced sounds, and the differences in prominence between the various voiceless consonants may as a rule be considered as negligible for practical linguistic purposes.   It must always be remembered, however, that *more sonorous* sounds may become *less prominent*, and therefore more consonant-like, by diminishing length or stress, and that sounds of relatively *small sonority* may be made *prominent* by increasing length or stress.

102. It is as a consequence of this principle of relative prominence that certain short vowel-glides must be regarded as

---

[2] With the exception apparently of 'cardinal' **i** (see the article on *The Perceptibility of Sounds*, by Stephen Jones, in *Le Maître Phonétiqúe*, January, 1926).

[3] The line of demarcation between vowels and consonants might have been drawn elsewhere.   Thus since speech-sounds which consist wholly or in part of 'noise' (as distinguished from 'musical sound') are less sonorous than those which contain no perceptible 'noise,' a logical classification into vowels and consonants might be based on the presence or absence of perceptible 'noise.' If this classification were adopted, the voiced sounds **m**, **n**, etc., and the voiced l-sounds would have to be classed as vowels, because in normal pronunciation they are not accompanied by any perceptible 'noise' or 'audible friction.'   This method of classification would, however, be less convenient in practice than that given in § 97.

consonants. Such are the English **j** (as in *yard* **jɑːd**) and **w** (as in *wait* **weit**). In making these sounds the speech-organs start in the position of **i** and **u** respectively and without remaining there any appreciable time proceed very quickly to the position of another vowel (**ɑ** in the case of *yard* and **e** in the case of *wait*). Such vowel-glides are often called *semi-vowels*. It must be remembered that such sounds have to be regarded as consonants on account of (1) their gliding nature, (2) their shortness and (3) their lack of stress as compared with the succeeding vowel. (See § 800.)

103. In the case of the word *you* **juː** the sound **uː** is actually less sonorous than the **i** with which the **j** begins. Nevertheless, the shortness and lack of stress of the vowel-glide suffice to render the sound consonantal. (For further information regarding prominence, see Chap. XII.)

Chapter VII

VOWELS

How to learn Vowels

104. Practical experience in teaching pronunciation shows that *consonants* are as a rule best acquired by directing attention to tactile and muscular sensations, whereas in learning *vowels* it is necessary to direct attention more particularly to the acoustic qualities of the sounds.

105. This does not mean that the learner is expected to acquire vowels by 'simple imitation.' On the contrary, he will find a knowledge of the organic formation of vowels of considerable use to him. But this knowledge is not in itself sufficient. The finer adjustments of the tongue have to be done by means of sensory control from the ear.

106. In order to be able to use this sensory control properly, the student must learn to estimate by ear the extent and nature of the acoustic differences between one vowel and another. Fortunately it is not difficult to devise a means by which he can learn to do this, and hence to know what to do in order to make any given foreign vowel.

How to describe Vowels

107. The method consists in explaining to the student the relations between the foreign vowels and certain vowels already known to him.

108. A bare description, however accurate, of the tongue-position of a foreign vowel cannot convey much to the learner. A most accurate diagram of the tongue-position obtained by X-ray photography will not of itself enable the student to pronounce the sound correctly.

109. If, however, the descriptions or diagrams are such as to show the exact relations of the foreign vowel to certain known vowels, they immediately become intelligible.

110. Thus, if a certain foreign vowel is known to be formed with a tongue position half-way between two sounds familiar to the student,[1] that student will with practice be able to adjust his tongue until he hears an acoustic quality which seems to have an equal amount of resemblance to each of the two known sounds.

111. Those whose ears are naturally very keen will be able to acquire the foreign vowels in this way with little or no trouble. With those whose ears are duller by nature the process will take longer; with many, a course of 'ear-training' of some length may be necessary before they can learn to pronounce foreign vowels with success.

112. An apt student whose ear has been well trained can estimate pretty accurately not merely whether a sound is half-way between two known sounds, but whether it is one-third or one-quarter or even a smaller fraction of the distance between two known vowels.

113. The process of acquiring vowels by means of estimates of the acoustic distances between them and known vowels may be carried out with tolerable success by a student working without a teacher. But the results will be more successful and will be attained in a shorter time if he has a teacher. Not only will the teacher tell the student when he has hit upon the required intermediate shade of sound, but if the student's attempt is unsuccessful, the teacher will tell him in which direction to modify his sound in order to improve it.

114. The lesson may be conducted in the following way: *Teacher*: 'I want you to try and make a vowel-sound about one-third of the way from so-and-so (which we may call X) to so-and-so (Y). Will you please say these two sounds (X, Y)? Now try to make the intermediate one. No, that won't do; that's hardly different from X; make it sound more like Y. It's still too near X; make it still more like Y. Now you've gone too far in the other direction; it mustn't be quite so much like Y as that. Etc., etc.' By proceeding in this way the student learns to produce the exact shade of sound required, generally in a very short time.

---

[1] We assume in this simple case that the lip-positions required for forming the two known sounds and the foreign sound are identical.

115. In some cases the directions will take the following form. *Teacher*: 'Now put your lips into this position, and while keeping them there, try as hard as you can to say the vowel so-and-so.'

116. Now how are the principles above described to be applied to the teaching of English vowels to foreign learners? With reference to what vowels should the English vowels be described?

117. One answer is that the English vowels may be described with reference to the vowels of the learner's mother tongue. A phonetically trained teacher can easily ascertain the nature of his pupil's vowels and use them as a basis for getting him to make English vowels.

118. The author of a book cannot, however, base his descriptions of foreign vowels on the vowels occurring in his readers' pronunciation of their mother tongue, because all the readers of a particular nationality do not have the same pronunciation. Thus there exist several different ways of pronouncing the French word *bonne*; the shade of vowel used depends on the locality from which the speaker comes. So also the pronunciation of the first vowel in the German *Vater* varies considerably according to locality. It is therefore meaningless to speak of 'the French vowel-sound in *bonne*' or 'the German vowel-sound in *Vater*.' Any description of an English vowel which compared it to 'the French vowel in *bonne*,' without further explanation, would be ambiguous; it would be interpreted in different ways by different French readers.

119. There is only one way of making written descriptions of vowels intelligible to a large circle of readers of different nationalities, and that is to describe the sounds with reference to a scale of 'Cardinal Vowels,' i.e. a set of fixed vowel-sounds having known acoustic qualities and known tongue and lip positions.

120. It has been found by experience that a scale of eight cardinal vowels forms a convenient basis for describing the vowels of any language. They are represented in the International Phonetic Alphabet by the letters i e ɛ a ɑ ɔ o u. (See *The Principles of the International Phonetic Association*, 1949, pp. 4–6.)

Chapter VIII

THE CLASSIFICATION OF VOWELS

The Nature of Vowels

121. It follows from the definition of a vowel given in Chap. VI that the characteristic qualities of vowels depend on the shape of the open passage above the larynx. The passage forms a resonance-chamber which modifies the quality (tamber) of the sound produced by the vibration of the vocal cords. Different shapes of the passage modify the tamber in different ways and consequently give rise to distinct vowel-sounds.

122. Now the shape of this passage can be varied very greatly, even when the organs are limited to vowel positions. Fig. 10 illustrates the approximate limit of vowel-positions; if the breath-force is normal, the tongue must be in a position below the dotted line in order to produce a vowel. It will be seen from this figure that the number of

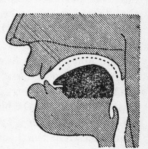

Fig. 10. Limit of Tongue-positions for Vowels.

possible vowels is very large. A good ear can distinguish well over fifty distinct vowels (exclusive of nasalized vowels, vowels pronounced with retroflex modification [§ 831], etc.). In any one language, however, the number of distinct vowels is comparatively small. In English it is not essential for ordinary purposes to distinguish more than twelve pure vowel-sounds and nine diphthongs.

123. The effect of a resonance-chamber in modifying tamber may be illustrated experimentally by means of an instrument

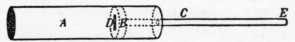

Fig. 11. Instrument to show the effect of a resonance-chamber in modifying quality of tone.

such as that illustrated in Fig. 11; it is made by Messrs. Spindler and Hoyer of Göttingen. It consists of a cylindrical resonator A, open at one end, fitted with a piston B, the rod of which C passes out at the other end. The piston-rod is hollow and the piston contains a reed D, so that by blowing down the piston through the opening E at the end of the rod, a musical sound of definite pitch is produced by the reed. The tamber of this sound depends on the length of the part of the cylinder projecting beyond the piston; by varying the position of the piston a large number of distinct tambers are obtainable, some of the sounds having resemblance to well-known vowels.

124. The chief organs concerned in modifying the shape of the passage are the tongue and the lips. Vowels are classified for linguistic purposes according to the position of the *tongue*. (Note that the position of the tip of the tongue has no great effect on vowel quality, except when the tip is very much retracted or very close to the roof of the mouth; see footnote to § 831.)

125. Some vowels have a clear and well-defined quality; others have a more obscure sound. The latter are chiefly those which are formed with the tongue in an intermediate vowel-position, not raised markedly at the back or in the front, and not too low down in the mouth. The most typical intermediate position gives rise to the sound known as the 'neutral vowel' or 'schwa' (phonetic symbol ə).[1]

126. The vowels of well-defined quality are chiefly those in which the tongue is remote from such intermediate position, that is to say, they are those in which the tongue is markedly raised in the front or at the back or is quite low down in the mouth. It is from among these vowels which are as remote as possible from 'neutral' position that it has been found convenient to select the eight 'Cardinal Vowels' referred to at the end of the last chapter.

127. The positions of the tongue in the formation of the different vowel-sounds may, to a large extent, be felt, and in many cases they may be seen by means of a looking-glass. They may also be determined experimentally in various ways.

128. Palatograms are useful in this connexion (see Figs. 37, 39, etc.). It is desirable in making palatograms of vowels to

---

[1] The English sound of *a* in *about* ə'baut is a characteristic variety of neutral vowel.

take care that the teeth are always kept at the same distance apart, because the diagram obtained depends not only on the height of the tongue, but also on the degree of separation between the jaws. The distance between the jaws may be kept constant by holding the end of a pencil firmly between the teeth. The pencil should not be more than 1 cm. in diameter.[2] When the teeth are kept at a constant distance apart, the palatograms show the correct relative positions of the tongue independently of the jaw.

129. The late Dr. E. A. Meyer of Stockholm obtained excellent diagrams of the tongue-positions of vowels by means of a row of fine leaden threads attached to an artificial palate along its centre line. An account of this work was given in his *Untersuchungen über Lautbildung* in *Festschrift Wilhelm Viëtor*.[3]

130. Valuable results have also been arrived at by means of X-ray photography by E. A. Meyer (who invented the system of laying a light metal chain on the tongue), Trevelyan George, O. Russell, H. Gutzmann, and others.

Description of the Cardinal Vowels

131. Cardinal vowel No. 1 (i) is the sound in which the raising of the tongue is as far forward as possible and as high as possible consistently with its being a vowel[4] (see Figs. 10, 12), the lips being spread.

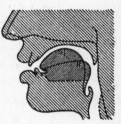

132. Cardinal vowel No. 5 (ɑ) is a sound in which the back of the tongue is lowered as far as possible and retracted as far as possible consistently with the sound being a vowel[5] (see Fig. 12), and in which the lips are not rounded.

Fig. 12. Approximate Tongue-positions of the Cardinal Vowels i and ɑ

---

[2] If the distance between the teeth is much greater than 1 cm., some vowels (e.g. English iː and əː) cannot be pronounced quite correctly. And if the distance is much less than 1 cm., other vowels (e.g. English ʌ and ɔː) cannot be pronounced quite correctly.

[3] Published by Elwert, Marburg a. L., Germany, 1910.

[4] If the tongue were raised higher, the breath-pressure remaining constant, the result would be a fricative j (§ 818).

[5] If the tongue were retracted further, the breath-pressure remaining constant, the result would be a variety of ʁ (§ 763).

133. Cardinal vowels 2, 3, and 4 (**e, ε, a**) are vowels of the 'front' series chosen so as to form an acoustic sequence between the vowels 1 and 5 such that the degrees of acoustic separation between each vowel and the next are equal, or, rather, as nearly equal as it is possible for a person with a well trained ear to make them. Cardinal vowels 6, 7, and 8 (**ɔ, o, u**) are vowels of the 'back' series chosen so as to continue this series of acoustically equidistant vowels.

134. The approximate tongue-positions of these vowels are shown in Figs. 13 and 14. The drawings of the tongue-positions of Cardinal

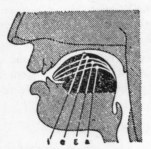 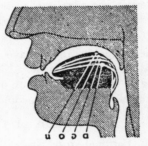

Fig. 13. Approximate
Tongue-positions of the Front
Cardinal Vowels, **i, e, ε, a**.

Fig. 14. Approximate
Tongue-positions of the Back
Cardinal Vowels, **ɑ, ɔ, o, u**.

vowels 1, 4, 5, and 8 are adapted from X-ray photographs.[6] The drawings of the remaining vowel-positions are approximate.

135. The lip-positions of the Cardinal vowels are shown in Figs. 15–22.

136. It will be observed that in passing from vowel No. 1 to vowel No. 2 and then to No. 3 and then to No. 4, the tongue is lowered through approximately equal intervals. Also that in passing from No. 5 to No. 6 and then to No. 7 and then to No. 8, the tongue is raised through approximately equal though smaller intervals.

---

[6] These photographs were of my mouth. They were taken by Dr. H. Trevelyan George of St. Bartholomew's Hospital by Dr. E. A. Meyer's method of placing a very thin metal chain on the tongue. They were first published in the *Proceedings of the Royal Institution*, Vol. XXII, Part 1, Oct., 1919. The originals may be seen in the Department of Phonetics, University College, London, W.C.1. Reproductions of them on a small scale are given in the frontispiece of this book.

Fig. 15.
Lip-position of Cardinal i.

Fig. 16.
Lip-position of Cardinal e.

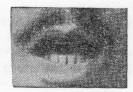

Fig. 17.
Lip-position of Cardinal ɛ.

Fig. 18.
Lip-position of Cardinal a.

Fig. 19.
Lip-position of Cardinal ɑ.

Fig. 20.
Lip-position of Cardinal ɔ.

Fig. 21.
Lip-position of Cardinal o.

Fig. 22.
Lip-position of Cardinal u.

137. The differences in tamber between Nos. 1, 2, 3, 4, and 5 are produced mainly by means of differences of tongue-position; such differences of lip-position as there are (see Figs. 15, 16, 17, 18, 19) have but little effect on the sounds.

138. But the differences in tamber between Nos. 5, 6, 7, and 8 are produced by differences of tongue-position combined with important differences of lip-position (see Figs. 19, 20, 21, 22).

139. It is for this reason that the distances between the tongue-positions of Nos. 5, 6, 7, and 8 are less than the distances between the tongue-positions of Nos. 1, 2, 3, and 4 (Figs. 13, 14).

140. The values of cardinal vowels cannot be learnt from written descriptions; they should be learnt by oral instruction from a teacher who knows them. The teacher will impart them to the student by the means described in §§ 107–115, basing his instruction on the sounds which he finds the learner to possess in his mother tongue.

141. The cardinal vowels here referred to have been recorded on gramophone discs.[7] The student who has not access to a teacher familiar with the cardinal vowels may learn them with fair accuracy by listening over and over again to the sounds as reproduced by the gramophone, and adjusting his speech-organs till he makes a sound indistinguishable (to his ear) from that produced by the machine. His success will depend mainly on the sharpness of his ear. A study of the tongue and lip positions will help him in some measure, especially if he has been able to cultivate some control over the movements of his tongue.

---

[7] E.g. on double-sided record No. ENG 252–3, published by the Linguaphone Institute, 207 Regent Street, London, W.1. There exists also a record of these vowels made in 1917 by the H.M.V. Gramophone Co., 363 Oxford Street, London, W.1, and numbered B 804. Although this record was made before the invention of electric recording, the reproduction is very good. It is no longer on sale through the ordinary channels, but the H.M.V. Gramophone Co. have preserved the matrix, and are willing to print off copies specially for anyone who orders a sufficient number.

Tape recordings of these cardinal vowels said on various pitches by twelve reliable phoneticians have recently been made by Mr. P. Ladefoged, Lecturer in Phonetics in the University of Edinburgh, as part of a research programme. Copies of these recordings can be made available for linguistic research institutions. (Particulars on application to the Secretary, Department of Phonetics, Minto House, Chambers Street, Edinburgh.)

142. Those who have access neither to a qualified teacher nor to a gramophone cannot expect to learn the values of these or any other cardinal vowels with accuracy. For the benefit of such students we append some very rough indications of the values of our cardinal vowels by means of key-words. It must be remembered, however, that to attempt to describe cardinal vowels by means of key-words is to put the cart before the horse. It is the vowels of the 'key-words' that should be described with reference to the cardinal vowels. Moreover, most 'key-words' are pronounced in different ways by different people; accordingly descriptions of sounds by reference to key-words convey different meanings to different readers.

143. In the following table Eng. refers to what I believe to be the average speech of educated Southern English people; Fr. means French as spoken (as far as I am able to judge) by the average educated Parisian; Ger. means German as spoken (as far as I am able to judge) by the average educated inhabitant of Berlin.

144. Number of cardinal vowel	Phonetic sign	Nearest equivalent in Eng., Fr. or Ger.
1	i	Fr. sound of *i* in *si*; Ger. sound of *ie* in *Biene*
2	e	Fr. sound of *é* in *thé*; Scottish pronunciation of *ay* in *day*
3	ɛ	Fr. sound of *ê* in *même*
4	a	Fr. sound of *a* in *la*
5	ɑ	Nearly what is obtained by taking away the lip-rounding from Eng. sound of *o* in *hot*; Fr. vowel in *pas*
6	ɔ	Ger. sound of *o* in *Sonne*
7	o	Fr. sound of *o* in *rose*; Scottish pronunciation of *o* in *rose*
8	u	Ger. sound of *u* in *gut*

Secondary Cardinal Vowels

145. A set of secondary cardinal vowels may be derived from the eight primary cardinal vowels by changes of lip-position. The most important of these are:

(1) the sounds obtained by adding close lip-rounding to Cardinal Vowels Nos. 1 and 2 (phonetic signs **y, ø**);

(2) the sounds obtained by adding open lip-rounding to Cardinal Vowels Nos. 3 and 5 (phonetic signs œ and ɒ[8]);

(3) the sounds obtained by combining the tongue-positions of Cardinal Vowels Nos. 6, 7, and 8 with lip-spreading (phonetic signs ʌ, ɤ, ɯ).

146. Further secondary cardinal vowels may also be selected in 'central' (§ 155) positions. Thus vowels having tongue-positions half-way between those of **i** and **u** may be considered as cardinal vowels. The unrounded and rounded vowels with this tongue-position are represented by the letters ɨ, ʉ. When they occur as subsidiary members of **i** or **u** phonemes, they may according to the usage of the I.P.A. be represented by ï, ü.

147. It is possible, though perhaps hardly necessary, to fix other cardinal vowels in lower central positions, namely, sounds having tongue-positions half-way between those of **e** and **o** and between those of ɛ and ɔ. The rounded central vowel half-way between **o** and ø is represented in International Phonetic notation by ə.

Details of Vowel Classification
Tongue Positions

148. The tongue-positions of the eight primary cardinal vowels (see Figs. 13, 14) may be represented diagrammatically as in Fig. 23 where the relative positions of the highest points of the tongue are shown by dots.

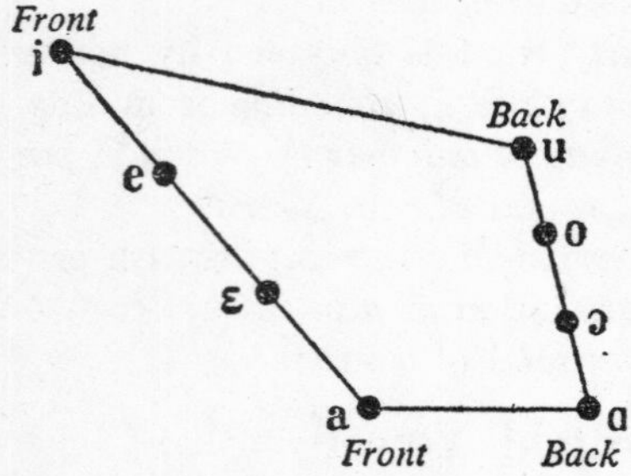

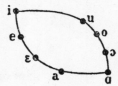

Fig. 23.   Diagram illustrating the Tongue-positions of the eight primary Cardinal Vowels.

Fig. 24.   A more accurate Form of Vowel Diagram.

---

[8] In broad transcriptions of particular languages it is generally convenient to use the symbol ɔ in place of ɒ.

149. The shape of this diagram is a compromise between scientific accuracy and the requirements of the practical language teacher. Scientific accuracy would require a diagram with curved sides somewhat as shown in Fig. 24. This shape, however, is inconvenient for use in practical teaching. Practical teaching requires a definiteness which can only be attained by means of a figure bounded by straight lines. Fig. 23 indicates with very considerable accuracy the relative tongue-positions of the vowels, the relative positions of **i**, **a**, **ɑ**, and **u** having been obtained from X-ray photographs.[9]

150. The cardinal vowels have by definition (§ 126) tongue-positions as remote as possible from 'neutral' position. Accordingly if other vowels are represented by dots on the above geometrical figure, they will be situated either on the circumference of that figure or within it. Thus a dot placed on the circumference of Fig. 23 half-way between the second and third points would indicate a sound which (if unrounded) would have an acoustic quality half-way between the cardinal sounds **e** and **ɛ**.

151. The tongue-positions of vowels can thus be classified by means of a system similar to the latitude and longitude principle used in geography. They are classified (1) according to the height

---

[9] Though this figure combines accuracy with definiteness, some teachers find that its unsymmetrical shape renders it difficult for ordinary pupils to draw. When such a difficulty is experienced, it is well to adopt the modified shape shown in Fig. 23a. In this simplified form the lines **a**—**ɑ**, **ɛ**—**ɔ**, **e**—**o**, **i**—**u** are parallel, the angles at **ɑ** and **u** are right angles, and the lines **a**—**ɑ**, **ɑ**—**u**, **i**—**u** are in the proportion 2 : 3 : 4.

The symmetrical form shown in Fig. 23b has been widely used. It appears to be preferable, however, to adopt a form which shows that the distance **i**—**a** is longer than the distance **ɑ**—**u** and which does not suggest that **u** has a more retracted tongue-position than **ɑ**.

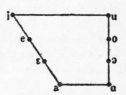

Fig. 23a. Simplified Form of Fig. 23.

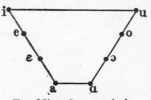

Fig. 23b. Symmetrical Arrangement of Vowels.

to which the tongue is raised, and (2) according to the part of
the tongue which is raised highest.

152. When we classify according to the height of the tongue,
we distinguish four classes. Vowels which have their tongue-
positions on the line i—u (Fig. 23) are called *close vowels*; those
which have their tongue-positions on the lines e—o, ɛ—ɔ, a—ɑ,
are called *half-close vowels*, *half-open vowels* and *open vowels*
respectively.

153. The terms *close, half-close, half-open* and *open* may be
defined more precisely as follows:

Close vowels are those in which the tongue is raised as high as
  possible consistently with the sounds remaining vowels
  (see §§ 97, 122);

Open vowels are those in which the tongue is as low as possible;

Half-close vowels are those in which the tongue occupies a position
  about one-third of the distance from 'close' to 'open';

Half-open vowels are those in which the tongue occupies a position
  about two-thirds of the distance from 'close' to 'open.'

154. When we classify vowels according to the part of the tongue
raised, we distinguish three classes. The vowels which have their
tongue-positions on or near the line i—a (Fig. 23) are called *front
vowels*; in other words, *front vowels* are those in the formation of
which the 'front' of the tongue is raised in the direction of the
hard palate. Vowels which have their tongue-positions on or
near the line ɑ—u are called *back vowels*: in other words, *back
vowels* are those in the formation of which the 'back' of the tongue
is raised in the direction of the soft palate.

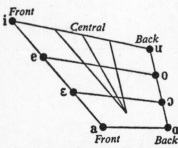

Fig. 25. The Central Vowel area.

155. Vowels in which the
highest point of the tongue is in
the centre part of the vowel
figure are called *central vowels*.
They lie in an area which is
triangular in shape, when refer
red to a diagram bounded by
straight lines such as Fig. 23.
The limits of this triangle are
necessarily arbitrary. Convenient
limits in the longitudinal direction

are two lines parallel to the lines i—a, ɑ—u and placed so that they meet on the central line at a point intermediate between the lines ɛ—ɔ and a—ɑ, as shown in Fig. 25.

Lip Positions

156. Vowel quality, though chiefly dependent on the position of the tongue, is also affected to a considerable extent by the positions of the lips. The lips may be *spread*, *rounded* or *neutral*. Vowels with spread lips or neutral lips are generally grouped together under the term *unrounded*.

157. Two degrees of lip-rounding may be distinguished, if desired, viz. *close lip-rounding* and *open lip-rounding*.

158. Cardinal i is characteristic of a vowel formed with spread lips (Fig. 15); cardinal ɑ (Fig. 19) may be considered as having neutral lips; cardinal ɔ and u have open lip-rounding and close lip-rounding respectively (Figs. 20, 22).

Tenseness and Laxness

159. Another element which is considered by some to be of importance in determining vowel quality is the state of the tongue and lips as regards muscular tension. Those who consider that vowels may be differentiated by degrees of muscular tension distinguish two classes, *tense* vowels and *lax* vowels. Tense vowels are those which are supposed to require considerable muscular tension on the part of the tongue; lax vowels are those in which the tongue is supposed to be held loosely. The difference in quality between the English vowels in *seat* siːt, and *sit* sit is ascribed by some writers to a difference of tension (the vowel in *seat* being considered tense and the vowel in *sit* lax).

160. It is not by any means certain that this mode of describing the sounds really corresponds to the facts. A description of the English short i as a vowel in which the tongue is lowered and re-tracted from the 'close' position (see Fig. 34) is generally sufficiently accurate for ordinary practical work. The term 'lax' may also be used to describe the organic position of the English short u (in *put* put) as compared with the long 'tense' uː (in *boot* buːt). Here the organic characteristics of short **u** as compared with long **u:** might be more accurately described as a lowering and advancement of the tongue and a wider opening of the lips.

161. Although the terms 'tenseness' and 'laxness' probably do not describe accurately the action of the tongue in differentiating certain vowels, nevertheless some teachers can actually get good results by telling pupils to make their tongues tense or to keep them lax. If a teacher can impart correct sounds by such instructions, he should certainly do so.

162. It is generally advisable to apply the terms *tense* and *lax* only to the case of close vowels. It is extremely difficult to determine in the case of the opener vowels whether the sensation of 'tenseness' is present or not, and there is in regard to some vowels considerable difference of opinion on the subject.[10]

163. The 'tenseness' or 'laxness' of a vowel may be observed mechanically in the case of some vowels by placing the finger on the outside of the throat mid-way between the larynx and the chin. When pronouncing for instance the English i (as in *sit*), this part of the throat feels loose, but when pronouncing the corresponding tense vowel (the i: in *seat*), the throat feels considerably tenser and is somewhat pushed forward.

Nasalized Vowels

164. The position of the soft palate may affect vowel quality. In the articulation of normal vowels the soft palate is raised so that it touches the back of the pharynx as shown in Figs. 12, 13, 14. The result is that no air can pass through the nose. It is, however, possible to lower the soft palate so that it takes up the position shown in Fig. 1; the air can then pass out through the nose as well as through the mouth. When vowels are pronounced with the soft palate lowered in this way, they are said to be nasalized. Nasalization may be expressed in phonetic writing by the symbol ˜ placed over the symbol of the sound which is nasalized. An example of a nasalized vowel is the French ã, as in *cent* sã.

---

[10] See, for instance, the remarks on æ, p. 72, footnote 15.

165. The movements of the soft palate may be observed by means of a pencil about 15 cm. long inserted into the mouth. If this is held between the finger and the upper teeth so that the end inside the mouth rests lightly against the middle of the soft palate, and groups of sounds such as ɑŋɑŋ . . ., ɛ̃ɛɛ̃ɛ̃ . . . are pronounced, the outer end of the pencil is seen to rise for the sounds ŋ, ɛ̃ and to fall for the sounds ɑ, ɛ. Again, if we breathe in through the nose and out through the mouth the end of the pencil rises and falls in a similar manner.

Chapter IX

CONSONANTS

Cardinal Consonants

166. The principle of cardinal sounds, which is so fundamental for the proper study of vowels, is not applicable to consonants as a whole. It is only applicable in cases where it is possible to pass from one sound to another through a series of sounds each of which is hardly distinguishable from the preceding, and where it is therefore necessary to fix arbitrarily some points to which any given sound in the series may be referred.

167. There are only a few limited families of consonants within which these conditions prevail. As a rule it is not possible to pass by almost imperceptible degrees from one consonant to another. For instance, there is no continuous series of sounds between **t** and **m**, nor is there between **p** and **r**.

168. The fact is that most consonants fall naturally into well-defined classes, classes which are clearly separated from the neighbouring classes by essential differences in the place or manner of articulation.

169. The chief cases where the principle of cardinal sounds can be applied to consonants are those in which the sounds under consideration all belong to one class as regards *manner* of articulation, and are all articulated by the *tongue* against the roof of the mouth.[1] Descriptions of such sounds may in some cases be made more intelligible to the reader by referring their tongue-positions to certain cardinal tongue-positions.

170. It has been shown (§§ 140–142) that the nature of cardinal sounds cannot be explained by means of key-words. It should be noticed, however, that key-words are as a rule less open to

---

[1] E.g., the series of so-called 't-sounds' ranging from dental **t** through alveolar **t** to the retroflex **ţ** (Chap. XXV), or the series of plosive consonants ranging from **c** (Fig. 29) through **k** (Figs. 30, 31) to the uvular plosive **q**, or the series of fricatives comprising sounds of the types **θ**, **s**, **ʃ**, **ç**.

objection in describing consonants than in describing vowels, because in many cases consonants are not subject to notable variations in the speech of different individuals. Thus the tongue-position of the sound **k** in the English word *back* does not vary to any marked extent with different English speakers. Consequently a definition of cardinal **k** as 'the final consonant of the English word *back*' will give to most English readers a fairly accurate idea of what cardinal **k** is.

171. Some cardinal consonants can be deduced from sounds of particular languages with fair accuracy; thus a French speaker may deduce cardinal **ç** (Fig. 113) from **i**, and cardinal **x** (Fig. 110) from the **k** in *cas* **kɑ**; a German can deduce cardinal **c** (Fig. 29) from **i** or **j**. But to make quite certain of these cardinal sounds oral instruction is required as in the case of cardinal vowels.

172. Fortunately most consonants either cannot be or do not need to be referred to cardinal consonants. Consonants can as a rule be learnt from plain descriptions of the actions which have to be performed by the organs of speech.

Breathed and Voiced Consonants

173. Some consonants are *breathed*, others are *voiced* (see Chap. V). To every breathed sound corresponds a voiced sound, i.e. one articulated in the same place and manner, but with voice substituted for breath, and vice versa; thus **v** corresponds to **f**, **z** to **s**, **b** to **p**. It should be noted that voiced consonants are usually pronounced with less force of exhalation than breathed consonants.

174. Breathed consonants pronounced with weak force occur in some languages. Such sounds are common in South German and occur as occasional variants of **b**, **d**, **z**, etc., in English (see §§ 567, 789). These sounds are sometimes called 'mediae.' They may be represented thus **b̥**, **d̥**, **z̥**, etc. People accustomed to strong breathed consonants are apt to mistake them for voiced sounds. People accustomed to hear very fully voiced consonants in initial and final positions, e.g. the French, are liable to mistake 'mediae' for strong breathed consonants in these positions.

175. The distinction between breathed and voiced consonants is a very important one. Some foreign people have difficulty in recognizing the difference between them, and in bringing out the distinction clearly in their speech.

176. It is a good phonetic exercise to deduce unfamiliar breathed consonants from familiar voiced ones, e.g. to deduce from **m**, which is a voiced consonant, the corresponding breathed consonant (phonetic symbol **m̥**), and to deduce from **l** the corresponding breathed consonant **l̥**.[2] This is done by practising sequences such as **vˆivˆi . . ., zszs . . .**, until the method of passing from voice to breath is clearly felt, and then applying the same method to **m**, **l**, etc., thus obtaining **mm̥mm̥ . . ., ll̥ll̥ . . .**, etc. (In practising these exercises, the sounds should follow one another continuously without break.)

177. The distinction between the breathed and voiced 'plosives' (**p**, **t**, **k**, and **b**, **d**, **g**) offers special difficulty to some foreign people (particularly to Germans, Scandinavians and some Chinese). The difficulty generally lies in the voiced sounds, for which 'unaspirated' breathed sounds ('mediae')[3] are commonly substituted. When the attention of foreign learners is called to the nature of the fully voiced sounds, they sometimes imitate them by prefixing a nasal consonant, saying for instance **mpɑ**, **ntɑ**, instead of **bɑ**, **dɑ**. A true voiced **b** may be acquired by practising the exercise **pmpmpm . . .** pronounced *without opening the lips*, followed by the exercise **bmbmbm . . .** also pronounced *without opening the lips*, and taking care that voice is distinctly heard during the pronunciation of the **b**. The student should also practise repeating the 'stop' (§ 562) of **b**, i.e. pronouncing **bbbb . . .** *without separating the lips*. (Take care that this exercise does not degenerate into **mmmm. . . .**) Voiced **d**, **g** may similarly be acquired by practising **tntntn . . ., dndndn . . ., dddd . . ., kŋkŋkŋkŋ . . ., gŋgŋgŋ . . ., gggg . . .**, *without moving the tongue*. These exercises present considerable difficulty to some learners, and they should be practised until thoroughly

---

[2] This sound exists in French in such words as *peuple* when final (**pœpl̥**); a variety of it is the sound of Welsh *ll*, as in *Llangollen* (**l̥anˈgoɬen**. When the sound occurs in a language as a separate phoneme, it is better to represent it by the special letter **ɬ** as in S. Jones' *Welsh Phonetic Reader* (University of London Press) and C. M. Doke's *The Phonetics of Zulu* (University of the Witwatersrand Press, Johannesburg).

[3] §§ 508, 528, 549, 566, 567.

mastered. Besides being useful in teaching voiced sounds, they are of value for obtaining control over the movement of the soft palate.

Further Classification of Consonants

178. Descriptions of the manner of forming consonants should take into account the following particulars: (i) the place (or places) of articulation, (ii) the state of the air-passage at the place (or places) of articulation, (iii) the position of the soft palate if not already mentioned under (i) or (ii), (iv) the state of the larynx if not already mentioned under (i) or (ii).

179. The chief classes which have to be distinguished under heading (i) for the purposes of English may be termed *bilabial*, *labio-dental*, *dental*, *alveolar*, *post-alveolar*, *palato-alveolar*, *palatal*, *velar* and *glottal*. Of these the classes *dental*, *palatal* and *velar* may be considered as cardinal classes of tongue consonants.[4] It has been suggested also that *alveolar* (with tongue-tip articulation) should be considered as a cardinal class of tongue consonants.

180. The above terms are defined as follows:

Bilabial: articulated by the two lips. Examples **p**, **m**, **w**.

Labio-dental: articulated by the lower lip against the upper teeth. Example **f**.

Dental: articulated by the tip of the tongue against the upper teeth. Examples **θ**, **ð**, Spanish **t**.

Alveolar: articulated by the tip or blade of the tongue against the teeth-ridge. Example English **t**.

Post-alveolar: articulated by the tip of the tongue against the back part of the teeth-ridge. Example English **r**.

Palato-alveolar: articulated by the blade of the tongue against the teeth-ridge with raising of the main body of the tongue towards the palate. Examples **ʃ**, **ʒ** (Fig. 99).

Palatal: articulated by the 'front' of the tongue against the hard palate. Example **ç** (one variety of German *ich*-sound).

---

[4] In general phonetics at least two other classes of tongue consonants have to be distinguished. They are *retroflex* consonants (articulated by the tip of the tongue against the hard palate) and *uvular* consonants (articulated by the 'back' of the tongue against the extremity of the soft palate).

Velar: articulated by the 'back' of the tongue against the central and forward part of the soft palate.   Example the **k** in *pack*.

Glottal or *laryngal*: articulated in the glottis.   Example the 'glottal stop' (§ 553).

181. Typical tongue-positions of the chief classes of tongue-consonants are shown in Figs. 26–31.   They illustrate the following sounds: cardinal dental **t** (Fig. 26), cardinal alveolar **t** (Fig. 27), a retracted variety of **t** (Fig. 28), the cardinal palatal sound represented in international phonetic notation by the letter **c** (Fig. 29), an advanced variety of **k** (Fig. 30), and cardinal **k** (Fig. 31).

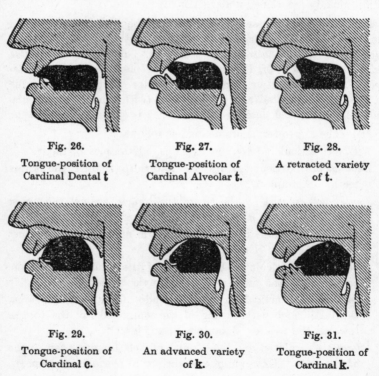

Fig. 26.

Tongue-position of
Cardinal Dental **t**

Fig. 27.

Tongue-position of
Cardinal Alveolar **t**.

Fig. 28.

A retracted variety
of **t**.

Fig. 29.

Tongue-position of
Cardinal **c**.

Fig. 30.

An advanced variety
of **k**.

Fig. 31.

Tongue-position of
Cardinal **k**.

182. The chief classes of consonants which can be distinguished under heading (ii) (§ 178) are called *plosive, affricate, nasal, lateral, rolled, flapped, fricative, frictionless continuant* and *semi-vowel.*

183. These terms are defined as follows:

Plosive: formed by complete closure of the air-passage during an appreciable time; the air is compressed (generally by action of the lungs) and on release of the closure issues suddenly, making an explosive sound or 'plosion.' Examples **p, d**.

Affricate: formed as plosive consonants, but with slower separation of the articulating organs, so that the corresponding fricative is audible as the separation takes place. Examples **tʃ** (as in *choose* **tʃuːz**), German **ts** (as in *zehn* **tseːn**).

Nasal: formed by a complete closure in the mouth, the soft palate being, however, lowered so that the air is free to pass out through the nose. Examples **m, n**.

Lateral: formed by placing an obstacle in the centre of the air-channel, but leaving a free passage for the air on one or both sides of the obstacle. Example **l**.

Rolled: formed by a rapid succession of taps of some elastic organ. Example rolled **r** (§ 752).

Flapped: formed by a single tap of some elastic organ; the position of contact is not maintained for any appreciable time. Example flapped **r** (§ 753).

Fricative: formed by narrowing the air-passage to such an extent that the air in escaping produces audible friction (i.e. some kind of hissing sound). Examples **f, z**.

Frictionless Continuant: made with the organic position of a fricative consonant, but pronounced with weak breath-force so that no friction is heard.[5] Example the principal English **r**.

Semi-Vowel: a voiced gliding sound in which the speech organs start by producing a weakly articulated vowel of comparatively small inherent sonority and immediately change to another sound of equal or greater prominence (§§ 101, 102). Examples: English **j** (as in *yard*), **w**.

---

[5] The palatal and velar frictionless continuants have the organic positions of close vowels. They are, however, uttered with very little breath-force as compared with the normally pronounced vowels which adjoin them in connected speech. These frictionless continuants are to be considered as consonants on account of their consequent lack of prominence as compared with the adjoining vowels.

184. Two classes of consonants are distinguishable under heading (iii) (§ 178), according as the soft palate is raised, as shown in Figs. 26, 27, etc., or lowered, as shown in Figs. 74, 75.   Different names are given to these classes according as the mouth-passage is completely closed or not.

185. The combination of complete closure in the mouth with raised soft palate gives rise to *plosive* consonants, as already mentioned (§ 183). The combination of complete closure in the mouth with lowered soft palate gives rise to *nasal* consonants, as already mentioned (§ 183).

186. When there is not complete closure in the mouth, sounds are distinguished as *oral* (or *buccal*) and *nasalized* according as the soft palate is raised or lowered.   (See § 164 and Chap. XXIV.)

187. There are several classes of consonants distinguishable under heading (iv) (§ 178). The four principal classes have been described in §§ 82, 83.   Only two of them, the *breathed* and *voiced* classes, occur in normal English; the 'glottal stop' occurs, however, as an occasional sound.

188. Consonants which can be held on continuously without change of quality are sometimes classed together as *continuatives* or *continuants*; they include nasal, lateral, rolled and fricative consonants and the frictionless sounds described in § 183. Nasal, lateral and rolled consonants are sometimes classed together under the not very satisfactory name *liquids*. (Some writers do not include nasal consonants among 'liquids.')

Chapter X

PHONEMES, PRINCIPLES OF TRANSCRIPTION

Phonemes

189. In describing the sound-system of any language it is necessary to distinguish between speech-sounds and what are called *phonemes*.

190. A *speech-sound* is a sound of definite organic formation and definite acoustic quality which is incapable of variation.

191. A *phoneme* may be described roughly as a family of sounds consisting of an important sound of the language (generally the most frequently used member of that family) together with other related sounds which 'take its place' in particular sound-sequences or under particular conditions of length or stress or intonation.

192. For detailed information regarding the theory of phonemes readers are referred to my book, *The Phoneme, its Nature and Use*.[1] A few examples must suffice here to give an idea of what is meant by the term 'phoneme.'

193. The **k**'s in the English words *keep, cool, call*, are three distinct sounds articulated at different parts of the palate; but they are regarded as belonging to the same phoneme, since the use of these different varieties of **k** is dependent solely upon the nature of the adjoining vowel. The **j**'s in the French *yeux* **jø** and *pied* **pje** are distinct sounds, the **j** in *yeux* being fully voiced and the **j** in *pied* being breathed (or with some speakers partially voiced); the sounds must, however, be regarded as members of a single phoneme in French, since the breathed (or partially voiced) **j** occurs only after **p** or **t** or **k**, while the fully voiced **j** never occurs in this position. The l-sound in the French *loup* and *boucle* (in final position) are different; the words may be transcribed allophonically (§ 200) as **lu, bukl̦**, **l̦** representing a voiceless **l**. They are members of the same phoneme, because **l̦** never occurs initially in French, while voiced **l** does not occur finally when **k** precedes. It does not occur to ordinary French people that the sounds are different.

---

[1] Published by Heffer, Cambridge.

194. The German x's in *Buch* and *ach* are different sounds, but as their use is dependent upon the nature of the adjoining vowel, they must be considered as members of the same phoneme.[2] The initial consonants in the Japanese words *hito* (man), *hata* (flag), *huzi* (*fuji*) (wistaria) are very different to the ears of a European, the first resembling a German *ich*-sound (ç), the second being an ordinary **h**, and the third being a 'bi-labial *f*' (φ); but in the Japanese language the three sounds are merely members of a single phoneme, their use being determined by the vowel following.   In the Japanese '*Kunreisiki*' *Rōmazi* spelling introduced in 1937 they are represented by a single letter (*h*).

195. On the other hand, sounds of the **n** and **ŋ** types belong to separate phonemes in English, because the use of the two sounds is not dependent upon neighbouring sounds in words.   **n** can occur in positions which **ŋ** can also occupy, e.g. in the terminations **-in**, **-iŋ**.   The **h**-sounds and **ç** (the *ich*-sound) belong to separate phonemes in German, since **ç** and the appropriate varieties of **h** may occur in identical phonetic contexts.

196. But though **ŋ** occurs occasionally in French, it does not constitute a separate phoneme in that language.   It is only found as a member of the **g**-phoneme, as when *langue maternelle* is pronounced **lɑ̃ŋ matɛrnɛl**.   Most French people are unaware of the existence of **ŋ** in their language, and they have difficulty in making the sound properly in English words (see §§ 655, 656).   In Italian and Spanish **ŋ** also exists, but only before velar consonants (e.g. Italian *banca* **'baŋka**, *lungo* **'luŋgo**, Spanish *cinco* **'θiŋko**, *venga* **'βeŋga**).   As **n** never occurs in such positions in Italian or Spanish, **ŋ** is to be regarded as a member of the **n**-phoneme in these languages.

197. The most frequent sound of a phoneme may be called its *principal member* or *norm*.   It is usually the sound which would be given if a person with unstudied pronunciation were asked 'to say the sound by itself.'   The other sounds belonging to the phoneme are called *subsidiary members*.   The term *allophone* is used to denote a particular member (principal or subsidiary) of a phoneme.

---

[2] According to one theory, first propounded by J. L. M. Trim in *Le Maître Phonétique*, July, 1951, p. 41, the German x-sounds should be held to belong to the **h**-phoneme, **ç** constituting a separate phoneme. (Formerly it was thought that the German **ç** and x-sounds were assignable to a single phoneme.) I believe Trim's view to be the correct one for most German speakers.

198. Phonemes are capable of distinguishing one word of a language from other words of the same language. There is an English word **sin** and another English word **siŋ**. There is a German word **'çɔrdə**[3] (*Chorde*) and another German word **'hɔrdə** (*Horde*). The existence of such words is a proof that the **n** and **ŋ** sounds belong to separate phonemes in English, and that the **ç** and **h** sounds belong to separate phonemes in German.

199. The *distinctive* elements of language, i.e. the elements which serve to distinguish one word from another are the phonemes (not the sounds). The distinction between two phonemes is *significant*, i.e. capable of distinguishing one word from another; the distinction between two sounds is not necessarily significant. Different sounds which belong to one phoneme do not distinguish one word of a language from another; failure on the part of the foreigner to distinguish such sounds may cause him to speak with a foreign accent, but it will probably not make his words unintelligible.

Principles of Transcription

200. As a general rule it is only necessary in practical phonetic writing to have symbols for the phonemes. The use of allophones (special members of the phonemes) is, in most languages, determined by simple principles which can be stated once for all, and which can be taken for granted in reading phonetic texts. A transcription based on the principle 'one symbol per phoneme' is called a *'phonemic'* or *'linguistically broad' transcription*. A transcription which provides special signs for allophones (special members of phonemes) is called an *'allophonic'* or *'linguistically narrow' transcription.*

200a. There are also *'comparative'* or *'typographically narrow'* forms of transcription, in which special symbols are introduced in order to show that certain sounds of the language transcribed differ from sounds of another language. For a full discussion of the subject of types of transcription, see Appendix A.[4]

---

[3] More usually pronounced **'kɔrdə**.

[4] The form of transcription of English adopted in this book is a very nearly 'broad' one allowing for the speech of those who use the variant pronunciations mentioned in footnote 5 on p. 13. It is 'allophonic' in one particular only, namely in that it provides a letter to denote the monophthongal o-sound that sometimes takes the place of the diphthong ou in weak positions. It is 'comparative' in some respects. See Appendix A.

The Phonetic Representation of Vowels

201. In transcribing particular languages the following mode of representing vowels is recommended[5]:

(1) When the principal member of a vowel-phoneme is identical with a Cardinal Vowel, the appropriate cardinal vowel symbol should as a rule be used to represent it.

(2) In cases where the principal members of vowel-phonemes are not cardinal vowels, the cardinal vowel letters **i e ɛ a ɑ ɔ o u y ø œ**, etc., should, as far as possible, be used to represent vowels lying within certain *areas* in the vowel figure, as shown in Figs. 32 and 33.

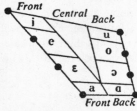

Fig. 32. Areas served by the eight primary Cardinal Vowel letters.

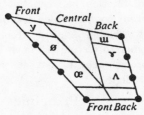

Fig. 33. Areas served by the secondary Cardinal Vowel letters **y, ø, œ, ʌ, ɤ, ɯ.**

(3) **ə** is the letter normally used to represent an unrounded vowel lying within the inner central triangle.

(4) When a vowel lies near the boundary of a vowel area, and is in consequence acoustically remote from any cardinal vowel, it is sometimes necessary to represent it by a special (non-cardinal) symbol. Thus in some types of transcription of English the symbols **æ, ɪ, ɵ** are introduced to represent the vowels in *hat, bit, put.* (In broad transcription[6] these sounds may be written with **a, i, u.**)

The Phonetic Representation of Consonants

202. Principles similar to the above must be adopted in transcribing those consonants which have to be described in relation to cardinal consonants. Other consonants are represented by arbitrarily chosen symbols.

---

[5] See *The Principles of the International Phonetic Association*, 1949, §§ 17–22.

[6] Of the kind of English in which these vowels are not lengthened (§§ 874–878 and Appendix A).

Chapter XI

DIAPHONES

203. It often happens that a certain sound used by one speaker of a language is consistently replaced by another sound by another speaker of the same language. Thus different speakers of Southern English pronounce the word *get* with vowels of different degrees of openness (§ 271). The diphthongal sound **ou** in such a word as *home* is not pronounced by all English people exactly in the manner described in § 394; with some the initial element is more retracted, with others it is opener, with others it is more advanced; the degree of lip-rounding is not the same with all speakers, and with some (most Scotsmen and many in the North of England) the sound in *home* is not diphthongal but is a pure long **oː**.

204. The term *diaphone* is suggested to denote a sound used by one group of speakers together with other sounds which replace it consistently in the pronunciation of other speakers. Thus the various kinds of **ou** mentioned in § 203 and the Scottish and Northern English **oː** may be said to be members of the same diaphone.

205. It has been mentioned in § 63 that everyone has different styles of pronunciation. Such different styles are merely different ways of pronouncing the language. When a person consistently uses one sound in one style of speech but substitutes another for it in another style, it is as if two different people were speaking, and the two sounds must be regarded as two members of the same diaphone.

206. Examples are when an actor pronounces such a word as *possible* with a 'dark' **l**[1] in ordinary conversation, but uses a 'clear' **l**[1] when reciting on the stage,[2] or when a 'forward' **a** is substituted for **æ** in singing, or where a variety of **a** is substituted for **ai** in very rapid pronunciation of such an expression as *I'm going* (normally **aim ˈgouiŋ**, very rapidly **am ˈgoiŋ**).

---

[1] See Chap. XX.

[2] This is often done in accordance with a tradition, the origin of which is obscure.

207. Care must be taken to distinguish diaphones from phonemes. The different members of one phoneme are sounds used by *one single person* speaking in one particular style; their use is conditioned by the nature of the surrounding sounds in the sequence and on the degree of stress, sometimes also on length and intonation. The different members of one diaphone are found in *comparing the speech of one person with that of another*, or in comparing two styles of speech of the same person.

207a. The theory of diaphones is discussed at greater length in my book *The Phoneme*, Chap. XXVII.

Chapter XII

PROMINENCE, SYLLABLES, DIPHTHONGS

208. In every spoken word or phrase there is at least one sound which is heard to stand out more distinctly than sounds next to it. Thus in the English word *letter* 'letə the sounds e and ə are heard more distinctly than the l or the t. If the speaker is at a certain distance, or if the word is spoken on the telephone or on a gramophone, the e and ə may be heard clearly, while l and t are often indistinct. The e and ə are in fact the sounds of the word *letter* which are 'prominent' in the sense explained in §§ 100, 101.

209. The prominence of sounds may be due to inherent sonority (carrying power, § 101), to length or to stress or to special intonation, or to combinations of these.

210. Thus in every sentence there is a kind of undulation of prominence which is easily perceived by the hearer. This undulation may be visualized as a wavy line with 'peaks' (denoting maxima of prominence) and 'troughs' (denoting minima of prominence). It is generally quite easy to count the number of peaks of prominence in a word or phrase.

211. Each sound which constitutes a peak of prominence is said to be *syllabic*, and the word or phrase is said to contain as many *syllables* as there are peaks of prominence. In the word 'letə the e and ə constitute peaks of prominence (by reason of their inherent sonority) and are therefore called 'syllabic,' and the word is said to contain two syllables. In *button-hook* 'bʌtnhuk there are three peaks of prominence and therefore three syllables, the syllabic sounds being ʌ, n and u.

212. In theory a syllable consists of a sequence of sounds containing one peak of prominence. In practice it is often impossible to define the limits of a syllable because there is no means of fixing any exact points of *minimum* prominence. In many cases the bottoms of the 'troughs' must be considered as flat, that is to say there is no one point which can be regarded as the point of syllable separation.[1]   Fortunately the exact determination of points of syllable separation is a matter of no practical importance to the language learner.   When it is desirable to divide words into syllables for the purpose of practising pronunciation or for finding a convenient place to put a stress-mark in phonetic transcription, the separation often has to be made in some conventional way.   For instance, it is customary to divide the spoken word *extremity* thus **iks-'tre-mi-ti**, though the **m** (or part of it) may well be considered to belong to the same syllable as the **e**.   Many teachers would divide *astray* thus **ə-'strei** on account of the *derivation* of the word, although from the point of view of prominence **əs-'trei** is a better division.   The actual minimum of prominence continues through the whole of the 'stop' of the **t**.[2]

213. The syllabic sound of a syllable is generally a vowel, but consonants may also be syllabic.   The more sonorous consonants such as **n, l** often are so, as in the English words *people* **'piːpl**, *little* **'litl**, *button* **'bʌtn**.[3]

214. When it is necessary to show in phonetic transcription that a consonant is syllabic, the symbol **ı** is placed under the letter.

215. When a consonant is immediately followed by a vowel, it is usually not syllabic, since the vowel has the greater inherent sonority.   However, a consonant in this position is sometimes given extra prominence by increasing its length, and it may thus become syllabic.   Examples are found in such English words as *gluttony* **'glʌtni**,[4] *muttony*[5] **'mʌtni**, *lightening* **'laitniŋ**, *bubbling* **'bʌbliŋ**, *flannelly*[6] **'flænli**.   The **n** and **l** in these words are quite distinct from those in *Putney* **'pʌtni**, *lightning* **'laitniŋ**, *publish* **'pʌbliʃ**, *manly* **'mænli**.   In the latter cases the **n** and **l** are very short; in the

---

[1] Thus as the 'stop' of **t** has no sonority at all, it is impossible to say at which part of the **t** the syllable separation of the word **'letə** takes place.

[2] The word *tray* **trei** consists of a single syllable.   The word *stray* **strei** is conventionally considered also to form a single syllable in spite of the fact that **s** has some sonority while the stop of the **t** has none.   The **s** is rather short, and its prominence is ignored in conventional syllable separation.

[3] Many foreign people mispronounce these words by inserting a vowel-sound, generally **ə** or **e**, thus **'piːpəl**, **'litel**, etc.   See § 590.

[4] Alternative pronunciation of **'glʌtəni**.

[5] As in *This meat has a muttony taste.*

[6] As in *This material has a flannelly feeling.*

former they are lengthened so that their prominence is sufficient to make them syllabic in spite of the greater sonority of the adjacent vowel. (Further information concerning the use of syllabic consonants in English is given in my article *The Use of Syllabic and Non-syllabic* l *and* n *in Derivatives of English Words ending in Syllabic* l *and* n in *Zeitschrift für Phonetik und allgemeine Sprachwissenschaft* Berlin, Vol. 12, No. 1–4, 1959 (Calzia-Festgabe).

216. In the comparatively rare cases when two consecutive vowels form two syllables, the necessary diminution of prominence between them is generally supplied by the glide (§ 3) which connects them. This glide is a transitory sound of very short duration and consequently of little prominence. Thus the word *create* kri'eit consists of two syllables because the first i is clearly pronounced, and in passing from it to the e a very short j-glide is present. (The -eit counts as one syllable because the ei is a diphthong, see §§ 219–221.) Other examples of two consecutive vowels forming two syllables are *react* ri:'ækt, *he ought* hi: 'ɔ:t, *screwing* 'skru:iŋ, *freer* 'fri:ə. (When the first syllable has the stronger stress, there is a tendency in some sequences to reduce the two vowels to a single diphthong; thus *screwing, freer* are sometimes pronounced skruiŋ, friə. See further my article *Falling and Rising Diphthongs in Southern English* in *Miscellanea Phonetica* II, 1954, published by the I.P.A.)

217. In cases like *chaos* 'keiɔs,[7] *co-operate* kou'ɔpəreit, *high up* 'hai 'ʌp, *coward* 'kauəd, *buoyant* 'bɔiənt, the syllable separation is marked by the ends of the diphthongs ei, ou, ai, au, ɔi.[8]

218. When a vowel is immediately followed by the same vowel, as in *bee-eater* 'bi:ˌi:tə, *we saw all of it* 'wi: 'sɔ: 'ɔ:l əv it, the syllables are generally separated by a slight diminution of loudness of the vowel due to a diminution in the force of exhalation.[9]

---

[7] Also pronounced 'keɔs, in which case the syllable separation is marked by the glide from e to ɔ.

[8] Many foreign people, and especially Germans, mark the syllable separation in such words as kri'eit, kou'ɔpəreit by inserting the sound ʔ (§ 553), thus kri'ʔeit, kou'ʔɔpəreit (see §§ 557–559).

[9] Very often the effect of syllable separation in such cases is produced by a sudden change of *pitch* (intonation). It must always be remembered that where there is a sudden change of pitch, it is extremely difficult to ascertain, even with the aid of apparatus, whether there is any simultaneous variation in *force*.

219. A *diphthong* is defined as an independent vowel-glide not containing within itself either a 'peak' or a 'trough' of prominence. By a vowel-glide we mean that the speech-organs start in the position of one vowel and move in the direction of another vowel. By 'independent' we mean that the glide is expressly made, and is not merely an unavoidable concomitant of sounds preceding and following.

220. During a diphthong the prominence may fall continuously or it may rise continuously,[10] but by definition it may not contain a fall of prominence followed by a rise nor a rise of prominence followed by a fall.

221. A diphthong must necessarily consist of one syllable. In order that a vowel-glide should constitute two syllables, it would be necessary that it should contain a 'trough of prominence,' i.e. a fall of prominence followed by a rise.

222. Diphthongs may be long or short, according as the glide is performed slowly or quickly. They may also be 'wide' or 'narrow' according as there is a large or a small movement from the initial position.

223. One end of a diphthong is generally more prominent than the other. The greater prominence may be due either to greater inherent sonority (§ 100) or to stronger stress or to a combination of the two. When the beginning of a diphthong is more prominent than the end, the diphthong is said to be *falling*. When the beginning is less prominent than the end, the diphthong is said to be *rising*. Most of the English diphthongs (Chap. XV) are falling diphthongs, but there are two important rising diphthongs, ĭə and ŭə (§ 378) and four unimportant ones, ŏi, ŭi, ĕə and ŏə (§§ 466v, 466x).

224. When a diphthong is 'falling' as the result of a gradual diminution of inherent sonority, the correct effect will generally be given if the speech-organs perform the greater part of the movement towards the second vowel; it is not necessary that the limit of the movement should be actually reached. Thus the English diphthong **ai** is one which begins at **a** and moves in the

---

[10] It is also theoretically possible to make diphthongs in which the prominence remains constant.

direction of **i**. To give the right effect it is not necessary that **i** should be quite reached; the diphthong may and generally does end at an opener vowel than this, such as a fairly open variety of **e**. **i** merely represents the furthest limit of movement; if the movement were to extend beyond this point, the diphthong would not sound correct.

225. When the vowels beginning and ending a diphthong are of approximately equal inherent sonority, one end of the diphthong is generally rendered less prominent than the other by reducing the force of exhalation. Thus the sounds ε and ʌ when isolated and pronounced with equal stress (push from the chest wall) have approximately equal sonority, but in the English diphthong εʌ (a variant of εə, § 449) the beginning of the glide is pronounced with greater stress than the end and therefore has greater prominence. The diphthong is in consequence a falling diphthong. Again, the English sound **i** is normally less sonorous than ə; nevertheless in the English iə (§ 440) the first part of the diphthong is pronounced with so much more stress than the latter part that its prominence is greater, and the diphthong is a falling one (ĭə).[11]

226. Rising diphthongs are sometimes difficult to distinguish from sequences consisting of a semi-vowel followed by a vowel. Some authorities consider the English juː, as in *music* ˈmjuːzik, and ju, as in *monument* ˈmɔnjumənt, to be rising diphthongs (ĭuː and ĭu rather than juː, ju).

227. Another kind of diphthong, called an *imperfect* diphthong, is produced (1) when the initial vowel of a falling diphthong is appreciably lengthened before the glide begins, or (2) when the final vowel of a diphthong (falling or rising) is lengthened after the glide ends. Thus if the initial element of the English diphthong **ai** is prolonged, as is done in singing, the result is the first type of imperfect diphthong. The second type of imperfect diphthong is heard if the final element of the English diphthong **ou** is prolonged, as is sometimes done when saying the interjection *Oh*.

228. An imperfect diphthong forms only a single syllable.

---

[11] It is, however, not uncommon to meet with Southern English speakers who in many words do not give sufficient force to the **i** to make it predominate over the latter part of the diphthong. The diphthong is then a rising one of the type ĭə. Some people use the sequence jəː in these words (see § 442a).

229. It is convenient to represent diphthongs in phonetic transcription by digraphs (sequences of two letters), the first letter representing the commencement of the glide and the second representing its termination or its direction of movement. In the case of many falling diphthongs the point of termination is somewhat variable (§ 224); when this is so, the second letter is selected so as to show the termination most remote from the initial element of the diphthong. Thus the transcription **ai** is used to represent the English diphthong in *fly* **flai**; the glide begins at **a** and proceeds in the direction of **i**, but it seldom reaches **i** (see § 224).

230. When it is desired to show in phonetic transcription which part of a diphthong is the least prominent, the mark ˇ is placed over the letter indicating the less prominent part. Thus the English falling diphthongs **ou, ai, au, ɛə**, etc., may, if desired, be written **oŭ, aĭ, aŭ, ɛə̆**, etc., and the rising diphthongs are denoted in this book by **ĭə, ŭə, ŭi**, etc. (see §§ 466a–466x).

231. The term *consonantal vowel* is sometimes used to denote the less prominent part of a diphthong. Thus it is sometimes said that the English diphthong **ai** consists of 'an **a** followed by a consonantal **i**.' This manner of regarding a diphthong, though not quite accurate, is sometimes convenient in practical teaching.

232. When a vowel glide contains a peak of prominence (i.e. a rise followed by a fall), it is called a *triphthong*. **ŏaĕ**, a careless way of pronouncing *why* (normally **wai**) is a triphthong.

233. The English sequences commonly written **aiə, auə** in phonetic texts are not triphthongs; they are disyllables, since the **i** and **u** are less prominent than the **a** and **ə**. These **i** and **u** are often lowered towards **ɛ** and **ɔ** (§§ 414, 430); the groups then approach nearer to triphthongs, but even then they are not actually true triphthongs. In their extreme forms these sequences are reduced to diphthongs of the type **aə** or to a single long vowel of the type **aː** (§§ 414, 430). It is, however, sometimes convenient to call **aiə** and **auə** 'triphthongs' for want of a better name and in view of the fact that they are often treated in poetry as forming single syllables.

Chapter XIII

EAR-TRAINING FOR THE ENGLISH VOWELS AND DIPHTHONGS

234. Those learning to speak a foreign language should begin their study by ear-training, which will enable them to recognize the sounds of the language. We therefore give in this chapter some exercises for learning to recognize by ear the English vowels and diphthongs, before proceeding to explain how the sounds are formed.

235. The general principles of ear-training have been indicated in §§ 18–24. It must be added here that, at any rate as far as vowels and diphthongs are concerned, it is convenient to assign numbers to the sounds. The teacher should begin by dictating isolated sounds, or single syllables containing easy consonants combined with the various vowels and diphthongs. In the earlier lessons the teacher should ask the pupil to name the numbers of the vowels and diphthongs dictated. Later he should ask the pupil to write with phonetic symbols the sounds or words he dictates.

236. The following system of numbering the English vowels and falling diphthongs is a convenient one. The first line contains the 'pure' vowels, the second line contains the diphthongs ending in **i** and **u**, and the third line contains the diphthongs ending in ə. The pupil should have a copy of this table always ready at hand for reference.

iː	i	e	æ	ɑː	ɔ	ɔː	u	uː	ʌ	əː	ə
1	2	3	4	5	6	7	8	9	10	11	12

		ei	ou	ai	au	ɔi
		13	14	15	16	17

		iə	ɛə	ɔə	uə
		18	19	20	21

The rising diphthongs ĭə and ŭə (Nos. 22 and 23), important though they are, need not be introduced until a later stage. Nor need the unimportant rising diphthong ŭi, or the non-essential diphthongs oi, ui, oə, ŏi, ŏə (§§ 466v–466x).

237. The following are some examples to illustrate the most elementary type of exercise to be dictated. The teacher should vary the lengths of the isolated sounds; pronouncing some of them fully long and some quite short and others of medium length. This is in order to familiarize the student with the differences in tamber apart from the differences of length. (It is, however, unnecessary to dictate ə (No. 12) in isolation, this sound being always very short in English; if lengthened, it is difficult to distinguish from əː (No. 11).) In the syllables it is better to say the vowels with the lengths they would usually have in English words. Their lengths depend (1) on their nature (iː, ɑː, ɔː, uː, əː being longer than the other pure vowels in similar positions), (2) to a large extent on the nature of the following consonant (§§ 863 ff.).

(1) Isolated vowels and diphthongs and single syllables:

uː, æ, ɔ, i, u, e, ɑː, i, ɔː, əː, ʌ, e, iː, æ, uː, əː, iː, ʌ, ɑː, ɔː, u, ɔ; ei, əə, ɔi, au, ou, ai, ɛə, ou, iə, ei, ɛə, uə, əə, ou, ɔː, ɑː, ɔ, əə, ʌ, ai, iə, e, ɔ, ɛə, ou, uə, ɔː, i, əː, ʌ, iə, e, i, æ, ei, əə, u, ɔ, ɛə, ɔː, əː, ou, e, ɔ, æ; pəːt, pʌt, pet, pæt, pɔt, pæt, puːt, put, pɔːt, pɛət, pait, piːt, pit, pɔit, den, dɔːn, dɔn, doun, dɔən, dən, dəːn, dʌn, duən, diən, dɑːn, diːn, dɛən, doun, etc.

(2) Sequences of more than one syllable:

tinɑːlɔd, sumiːdef, bækɑːzug, pesiːvɔː, gʌmuːbik, fægɔʒis, brigetæ, nɑːkɔːndu, lesæʃkʌl, θɔːŋez. nəːf, kʌrmædiguː, trəː-simɑːfgæk, ðuːgʌʒtelezæ, plerkjɑːfkɔː, muːləːvɛəs.

238. When the teacher finds that the pupil has difficulty in distinguishing certain vowels, he should repeat them a number of times in various orders and with various surrounding consonants. Thus if the pupil has difficulty in distinguishing æ from e and ʌ, the teacher should dictate e, e, æ, æ, ʌ, ʌ, æ, ʌ, æ, e, e, ʌ, ʌ, æ, e, ʌ, e, ʌ, ʌ, æ, etc., tæm, tem, tæm, tem, tʌm, tem, net, nʌt, næt, nʌt, net, lʌp, læp, etc., etc.

239. A complete course of ear-training includes much more difficult combinations of sounds than those given above; it includes also sounds other than those of the language studied. Teachers should, when possible, pay some attention to the sounds of the pupils' mother tongue, and give some ear-training exercises containing those sounds which resemble but are not identical with sounds of the language studied. Some graduated exercises are given in Appendix B.

Chapter XIV

THE ENGLISH VOWELS

240. The term 'pure' vowel is used in this book to designate a vowel (during which the organs of speech remain approximately stationary) in contradistinction to a 'diphthong' (during which the organs of speech perform a clearly perceptible movement).

241. There exist many shades of pure vowel-sound in Southern English. Of these twelve are of special importance for the foreign learner of English. They are represented in this book by the notation iː, i, e, æ, ɑː, ɔ, ɔː, u, uː, ʌ, əː, ə. It is convenient to number them 1 to 12 as shown in the first line of the table on p. 61.

242. Four pairs of these vowels may be considered as belonging to single phonemes in one type of Southern English, viz. long iː and short i, long ɔː and short ɔ, long uː and short u, and long əː and short ə. The tamber of the English short i differs considerably from that of the English long iː, but in this kind of English the difference in tamber always coincides with a difference of length; that is to say iː is always longer than i when surrounded by the same sounds and pronounced with the same degree of stress. Similarly with the pairs ɔː, ɔ, and uː, u. There is not much difference in tamber between the long əː and the most frequently used short ə (ə₁, § 356). There are thus eight pure vowel phonemes in Southern English (represented in this book by the letters i, e, æ, ɑ, ɔ, u, ʌ, ə). For further particulars concerning the phonemic classification of the Southern English vowels, see my book on *The Phoneme* (Heffer, Cambridge), especially §§ 510 ff.

243. Of the above-mentioned important vowel-sounds eight (iː, i, e, æ, ɑː, ʌ, əː, ə) have spread or neutral lips, while four (ɔ, ɔː, u, uː) have various degrees of lip-rounding.

244. The approximate tongue-positions of these vowel-sounds are shown in Fig. 34 (p. 64). In this diagram the vowels are placed in relation to the Cardinal Vowels (for which see Chap. VIII). The tongue-positions of the Cardinal Vowels are represented by the small dots in Fig. 34, while the tongue-positions of the English vowels are shown by the large dots. The nature of the tongue-positions will be realized by comparing these diagrams with Figs. 13 and 14.

245. Fig. 35 is a simplified chart of the chief English vowels. It is less accurate than Fig. 34, but is a convenient form for use in practical teaching.

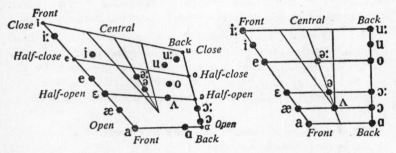

Fig. 34. Diagram showing the relations of the chief English Vowels to the Cardinal Vowels. (*Small dots* represent Cardinal Vowels. *Large dots* represent English Vowels.)

Fig. 35. Simplified Chart of English Vowels for use in practical teaching of the language.

The English Vowels in Detail

English Vowel No. 1: iː

246. iː is the member of the English i-phoneme used when the vowel is relatively long.

247. Its tongue-position is shown by the position of the dot in Fig. 34. The following is a formal description of the manner of forming the vowel:

Fig. 36. Lip-position of English long iː.

(i) *height of tongue*: nearly 'close' (§ 152);

(ii) *part of tongue which is highest*: centre of 'front';

(iii) *position of lips*: spread or neutral (see Fig. 36);

(iv) *opening between the jaws*: narrow to medium.[1]

The sound is considered by many to be pronounced with considerable muscular tension of the tongue (see §§ 159–163). In normal speech the tip of the tongue touches the lower teeth, but small variations in the position of the tongue-tip do not materially affect the acoustic effect of the sound.

248. A palatogram of the vowel as pronounced by me is shown in Fig. 37.

249. iː is the so-called 'long' sound of the letter *e*; examples: *tree* triː, *see* siː, *even* 'iːvn, *complete* kəm'pliːt, *immediate* i'miːdjət. iː is also the sound of *ea, ie, ei* and *i* in many words, examples: *sea* siː, *east* iːst, *field* fiːld, *seize* siːz, *machine* mə'ʃiːn. Note the exceptionally spelt words *key* kiː, *quay* kiː, *people* 'piːpl.

Fig. 37. Palatogram of English long iː.

250. The English iː is similar in tamber (quality) to the French sound of *i*, as in *ici* isi, and to the German 'long' iː as in *mir* miːr, *sie* ziː. It is, however, less close than these sounds. The average continental close i does not, however, sound wrong (in quality)[2] when used in English words such as *sea, even*. But those foreign people (mainly French and German) who use a particularly close i should endeavour to hold their tongue a little more loosely in pronouncing the English iː.

251. Many English people use a diphthong in place of a pure iː. The diphthong begins with an open variety of i and moves to a closer position; it may be represented by i̯i[3] or ui[4] or

---

[1] To make the description complete it is necessary to add (v) *position of the soft palate*: raised: (vi) *action of vocal cords*: vibrating, producing voice. This addition is to be understood in the case of all the subsequent descriptions of vowels.

[2] The vowel as pronounced by foreign people is often wrong in *quantity* (length); see §§ 901 ff.

[3] i̯ denotes a very open i, similar to the English short i. i denotes a very close variety of i.

[4] ʊ is a symbol used in narrow transcription for the English short i.

ij.[5] It is not necessary for foreign learners to attempt this diphthongal pronunciation. An exaggerated diphthongal pronunciation sounds dialectal, an extreme form of the diphthong being used in the local dialect of London (Cockney), where *see* is pronounced səi.

252. Words for practice: *peak* piːk, *beak* biːk, *team* tiːm, *dean* diːn, *keen* kiːn, *geese* giːs, *chief* tʃiːf, *Jean* dʒiːn, *meat, meet* miːt, *need* niːd, *leaf* liːf, *wreath* riːθ, *feel* fiːl, *veal* viːl, *these* ðiːz, *siege* siːdʒ, *zeal* ziːl, *shield* ʃiːld, *heap* hiːp, *yield* jiːld, *queen* kwiːn.

English Vowel No. 2: i

253. The letter i without the length-mark stands for the members of the English i-phoneme used when the sound is relatively short (§ 863). The distribution of these members in words is determined by the nature of the surrounding sounds in the sequence and on the degree of stress (see §§ 260–263). For the purposes of practical teaching it is sufficiently accurate to use the commonest of them in all cases.

254. In pronouncing this common sound, the general position of the tongue and lips resembles that of the long iː (§ 247), but the tongue is lower and retracted. Its nature is shown by the position of the dot in Fig. 34. Some writers express the difference by saying that for the short i the speech organs are 'lax' or held loosely, while for the long iː they are more 'tense.'

255. The following is a formal description of the manner of forming this English short i:

(i) *height of tongue*: nearly 'half-close' (Fig. 34);

(ii) *part of tongue which is highest*: the hinder part of the 'front' (Fig. 34);

(iii) *position of lips*: spread or neutral (Fig. 38);

(iv) *opening between the jaws*: narrow to medium.

---

[5] The symbol j is used here in a sense somewhat different from that assigned to it in § 813. The two values are, however, closely related. The similarity between them lies in the fact that the tongue-position reached at the end of the diphthong written ij, is about the same as the tongue-position assumed at the beginning of the sequence ji. Those who would prefer not to use the same symbol j in these two different senses, are recommended to use ǰ in the diphthong, thus iǰ, the mark ˘ indicating that the sound is to be regarded as a consonantal vowel (§ 231) and not as a semi-vowel (§ 183).

In normal speech the tip of the tongue touches the lower teeth, but small variations in its position do not materially affect the tamber. As with all normal vowels, the soft palate is in its raised position and the vocal cords are in vibration.

Fig. 38. Lip-position of
English short i.

Fig. 39. Palatogram
of English short i.

256. A palatogram of the vowel as pronounced by me is shown in Fig. 39. It will be observed that the air-passage is considerably wider than in the case of the long i: (Fig. 37).

257. i is the 'short' sound of the vowel letters *i* and *y*; examples: *fit* fit, *rich* ritʃ, *king* kiŋ, *symbol* 'simbl. It is also the sound of *e* and *a* in various prefixes and suffixes when unstressed; examples: *become* bi'kʌm, *descend* di'send, *remain* ri'mein, *engage* in'geidʒ, *except* ik'sept, *examine* ig'zæmin,[6] *horses* 'hɔːsiz, *useless* 'juːslis, *goodness* 'gudnis, *village* 'vilidʒ, *private* 'praivit[7]; it is also the sound of unstressed *-ies, -ied*, as in *varieties* və'raiətiz, *carried* 'kærid[8]. Note also the miscellaneous words *minute* 'minit, *three-pence* 'θripəns or 'θrepəns, *women* 'wimin, *Sunday* 'sʌndi, *Monday*

---

[6] Note the difference between *explain* iks'plein and *explanation* eksplə'neiʃn, *exhibit* ig'zibit and *exhibition* eksi'biʃn, etc. The prefix is quite unstressed in *explain, exhibit*, but it has secondary stress in *explanation, exhibition*.

[7] Unstressed *-ate* is pronounced -it in most nouns and adjectives. In verbs on the other hand the termination is pronounced -eit. Thus the nouns *estimate, associate* and the adjectives *appropriate, intimate, separate* are pronounced 'estimit, ə'souʃiit, ə'proupriit, 'intimit, 'seprit, while the similarly spelt verbs are pronounced 'estimeit, ə'souʃieit, ə'prouprieit, 'intimeit, 'sepəreit. *Intermediate* and *immediate* are exceptional words in which the vowel of the termination is usually ə (intə'miːdjət, i'miːdjət). The -it is often changed to -ət in derived adverbs; thus though the adjective *deliberate* is normally di'libərit, yet the adverb *deliberately* is pronounced di'librətli by many.

[8] Foreign people often use the long iː in the terminations *-ies, -ied*.

ˈmʌndi, etc.,⁹ *pretty* ˈpriti, *England* ˈiŋglənd, *English* ˈiŋgliʃ, *busy* ˈbizi, *business* ˈbiznis, *lettuce* ˈletis.⁹ᵃ

258. Many foreign people, and especially speakers of Romance languages, use a sound which is too 'tense'; in fact they do not make the necessary difference of tamber between the English short i and long iː. They pronounce *rich* too much like *reach* riːtʃ and *sit* too much like *seat* siːt, etc. The correct vowel may be acquired by trying to pronounce the sound in a slack sort of way, or by making it more like e. French learners should notice that the English short i resembles the French sound of *é*.

259. The English short i is slightly opener than the corresponding German vowel as in *bitte* ˈbitə, *Sinn* zin, etc., but it is less open than the Dutch sound of *i*, as in *ik* ʊk (I), *dit* dʊt (this).

260. A notable subsidiary short i is a 'lower' variety, i.e. a vowel having a tongue-position lower than that of the i just described. It resembles in quality a not very close e. It may be written with the letter e when it is desired in transcription to distinguish the two members of the phoneme; this transcription, however, involves writing vowel No. 3 with ɛ in place of e.

261. This subsidiary i is used in final positions, for instance in such words as *heavy* ˈhevi, *city* ˈsiti (second i), *many* ˈmeni, when a pause follows.¹⁰ If another word follows in the same sense-group, the ordinary short i is used; thus the ordinary short i is used in both syllables of *city* in the expression *the City of London* ðə ˈsiti əv ˈlʌndən.¹¹

262. A minute analysis of the pronunciation of words containing short i reveals the existence of a number of shades of

---

⁹ Also pronounced ˈsʌndei, ˈmʌndei, etc., especially by younger people.

⁹ᵃ There is a modern tendency in England to substitute ə for i in some of the prefixes and suffixes, e.g. to pronounce bəˈkʌm, rəˈmein, ˈgudnəs. This is not as a rule done with -*es* and -*ed*, presumably because it is felt to be desirable to maintain the distinction between -iz and -əz, e.g. in *offices* ˈɔfisiz and *officers* ˈɔfisəz, *charted* ˈtʃɑːtid and *chartered* ˈtʃɑːtəd. See the special section on *Variant Pronunciations of* -*less*, -*ness*, etc., in the 11th (1956) edition of my *English Pronouncing Dictionary* (Explanations XXII).

¹⁰ These words may also be transcribed ˈhɛve, ˈsite, ˈmɛne, when they stand in final position.

¹¹ In many forms of dialectal English the final vowel of *heavy*, *city*, etc., is *closer* than the common short i; often too it is lengthened or replaced by the dialectal diphthong əi (§ 251).

i-sound ranging mainly between the common i and the subsidiary i described in § 260. The use of these intermediate shades of sound varies with different speakers, and the shade used depends on the nature of the surrounding sounds in the sequence, and on the degree of stress. For instance, it is not uncommon to hear the termination -*ity* (as in *ability* ə'biliti or ə'bilete) pronounced with the penultimate i lower than the ultimate; some use ə in this position, pronouncing ə'biləti. It is instructive to observe the different pronunciations of *visibility* used by radio news readers announcing the weather reports.

263. There is a tendency with some English speakers to use lowered varieties of i in unstressed positions generally, as well as when final. Their pronunciation might be represented thus (using e to represent the lowered i, and ɛ to represent vowel No. 3): *waited* 'weited, *ladies* 'leidez, *goodness* 'gudnes, *become* be'kʌm, *except* ek'sɛpt, *village* 'viledʒ, *limit* 'limet, *Cambridge* 'keimbredʒ, *profit* 'prɔfet (= *prophet*), *indeed* en'diːd, *bringing* 'briŋeŋ, *solid* 'sɔled. These speakers also have distinct weak forms for words like *it*, *this*, *in*, *if*, when unstressed, thus: *I'll get it in the morning* ai l 'gɛt et en ðə 'mɔːneŋ, *I wonder if it is* ai 'wʌndər ef e 'tiz.

264. Although it is desirable that the foreign learner should be aware of the existence of a number of shades of i, yet it is in my view not necessary that he should make any special effort to use them in his speech. If he ignores the differences altogether, it does not matter; with many English speakers the differences are so small as to be negligible.

265. Words for practice: *pin* pin, *bill* bil, *tip* tip, *dish* diʃ, *kitten* 'kitn, *give* giv, *chin* tʃin, *Jim* dʒim, *milk* milk, *knit* nit, *lip* lip, *risk* risk, *fit* fit, *village* 'vilidʒ, *thin* θin, *this* ðis, *sing* siŋ, *zip* zip, *ship* ʃip, *hill* hil, *winter* 'wintə.

266. A sound of approximately the quality of short i also occurs in English at the beginning of the diphthongs iə (§ 440) and ĭə (§ 466a) and at the end of the diphthongs ei (§ 386), ai (§ 406), ɔi (§ 437), oi (§§ 403, 466x, 869), ui (§§ 327a, 869), ŭi (§ 466v). Foreign learners should be careful not to use a close i in these diphthongs.

English Vowel No. 3: e

267. The English phoneme e, in my speech, has several allophones, i.e. it comprises several shades of sound, the use of which is determined by the nature of the surrounding sounds in the sequence (see § 274). The differences are, however, slight and of no importance for the foreign learner. If the foreign learner always uses the principal member of the phoneme, his pronunciation will always sound correct.

268. The tongue-position for the principal English e is shown by the position of the dot in Fig. 34. The following is a formal description of the manner of forming the sound:

Fig. 40.   Lip-position of
English e.

(i) *height of tongue*: intermediate between half-close and half-open;

(ii) *part of tongue raised*: the 'front';

(iii) *position of lips*: spread or neutral (Fig. 40);

(iv) *opening between the jaws*: medium.

In normal speech the tip of the tongue touches the lower teeth, but small variations in its position do not materially affect the tamber. As with all normal vowels, the soft palate is in its raised position and the vocal cords are in vibration.

269. A palatogram of the sound as pronounced by me is shown in Fig. 41. It will be observed that the air-passage is wider than in the case of short i (Fig. 39).

270. e is the so-called 'short' sound of the letter *e*[12]; examples: *pen* **pen**, *red* **red**, *seven* **'sevn**.   e is also the sound of *ea* in many words; examples: *head* **hed**, *breath* **breθ**. Note the exceptional words *any* **'eni**, *many* **'meni**, *Thames* **temz**, *ate* **et**, *Pall Mall* **'pel'mel**.[13]

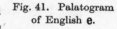

Fig. 41.   Palatogram
of English e.

271. The vowel in these words varies a good deal with different English speakers. Some Londoners use a closer sound than that described above; other speakers use an opener sound nearer to cardinal ε. The symbol e may in fact be taken to represent a diaphone (Chap. XI) with several members. The intermediate or 'average' sound described

---

[12] With some speakers the sound is sometimes long (see § 876).

[13] These are the only words in which the sound e is represented in spelling by the letter *a*. Note that *The Mall* is pronounced **ðə 'mæl**. Some English people pronounce *Pall Mall* as **'pæl'mæl**.

in § 268 is recommended for foreign students of English. Slight divergences from this will, however, not cause the student's pronunciation to sound un-English.

272. Many foreign people, and especially the French, replace the English **e** by a very open **ɛ**. This is especially the case when **r** follows, as in *very* **'veri**. This mispronunciation may be rectified by remembering that the sound to aim at for English is not identical with the French sound in *même* **mɛːm**, *père* **pɛːr**, *belle* **bɛl**, etc., but is intermediate in quality between this and the sound of French *é*.

273. Words for practice: *pen* **pen**, *bed* **bed**, *text* **tekst**, *deaf* **def**, *kept* **kept**, *get* **get**, *check* **tʃek**, *gem* **dʒem**, *men* **men**, *neck* **nek**, *lend* **lend**, *red* **red**, *fed* **fed**, *very* **'veri**, *then* **ðen**, *seven* **'sevn**, *zest* **zest**, *shed* **ʃed**, *head* **hed**, *yes* **jes**, *well* **wel**.

274. The only subsidiary member of the English e-phoneme worthy of note is an opener and retracted variety, which is used when 'dark' l follows, as in *tell* **tel**,[14] *shell* **ʃel**,[14] *felt* **felt**, *else* **els**, *elder* **'eldə**. It is not necessary for the foreign learner to make any special effort to use an opener **e** in these cases. The use of the same **e** as in other words does not sound un-English.

275. An opener variety of **e** (**ɛ**) occurs in English as the first element of the diphthong **ɛə** (see § 446).

English Vowel No. 4: æ

276. The English phoneme represented in this book by the symbol **æ** may, from the point of view of the foreign learner, be regarded as comprising only one sound. There is one member of the phoneme which differs from this sound, namely a rather opener variety used before 'dark' l (as in *alphabet* **'ælfəbit**); this is a variety which may, however, be ignored by the foreign learner.

277. It will be seen from Fig. 34 that in forming **æ** the tongue is low in the mouth, and occupies a position which is roughly

---

[14] When words ending in **-el** are immediately followed by a word beginning with a vowel, they are said with 'clear' l (§ 668) and the vowel is then the principal **e** and not the opener variety. This would be the case, for instance, in *tell it* **'tel it**.

intermediate between the positions for cardinal ε and cardinal a.[15]
The following is a formal description of the manner of forming æ;

Fig. 42. Lip-position of
English æ.

(i) *height of tongue*: between half-open and open;

(ii) *part of tongue which is highest*: the 'front';

(iii) *position of lips*: spread or neutral (Fig. 42);

(iv) *opening between the jaws*: medium to wide.

In normal speech the tongue-tip touches the lower teeth, but small variations in its position do not materially affect the tamber. As with all normal vowels, the soft palate is in its raised position and the vocal cords are in vibration.

278. A palatogram of the sound as pronounced by me is shown in Fig. 43.

279. æ is the so-called 'short' sound of the letter a[16]; examples: *glad* glæd or glæːd, *bag* bæg or bæːg, *pad* pæd, *cat* kæt, *lamp* læmp. The sound is regularly represented by the letter

Fig. 43. Palatogram of English æ.

a, the only exceptions being *plait* plæt, *plaid* plæd, *Plaistow* ˈplæstou. Note that *have* is hæv (strong form),[17] and that *bade* is often pronounced bæd but has an alternative form beid.

---

[15] This seems for practical purposes the most satisfactory way of regarding the tongue-position of this vowel. It must be admitted, however, that the exact analysis of the manner of forming this sound presents some difficulties. Some authorities regard ε as a tense vowel and æ as the corresponding lax vowel. In passing from ε to æ there is (at any rate in my pronunciation) a distinct raising of the *sides* of the tongue; this can be felt, or it can be seen in a looking-glass; it is also indicated by the fact that æ gives a palatogram while cardinal ε does not, though the middle of the tongue seems to be lower for æ than for ε. I am also conscious of a contraction in the pharyngal region in the production of æ. Other observers have also remarked this. This pharyngal contraction is too vague to define precisely, though it appears to be an inherent characteristic of the sound. I have often been able to improve foreign students' pronunciation of æ by telling them to tighten the throat. (The existence of the contraction in the throat is no doubt the reason why the sound æ cannot be pronounced with good voice-production. Singers commonly use a modified æ, or substitute a for it.)

[16] The vowel is in reality often lengthened; see § 874.

[17] The weak forms of this word are həv, əv, and v.

280. Many foreign people, and especially the French, replace the vowel æ by an opener sound of the **a**-type (§ 409), which is the sound in the French *patte* **pat**, *cave* **kaːv**, and the initial element in the variety of English diphthong **ai** described in this book. Germans, on the other hand, commonly replace æ by some variety of ɛ, thus making no difference between *man* **mæn** and *men* **men**, *pat* **pæt** and *pet* **pet**.

281. The correct sound of æ can generally be obtained by remembering that æ must have a sound intermediate in quality between an ɛ and an **a**. It is useful in practising the sound to keep the mouth very wide open.

282. The sound may also be obtained by trying to imitate the baaing of a sheep, which resembles **'bæːˈbæː**. Those who are unable to obtain the exact quality by practising such exercises should note that it is better to err on the side of **a** rather than on the side of ɛ. **a** is actually used for æ in many parts of the North of England.

283. Words for practice: *pat* **pæt**, *bad* **bæd** or **bæːd**, *tax* **tæks**, *damp* **dæmp**, *cat* **kæt**, *gas* **gæs**, *chat* **tʃæt**, *jam* **dʒæm** or **dʒæːm**, *man* **mæn** or **mæːn**, *nap* **næp**, *lamb* **læm** or **læːm**, *rash* **ræʃ**, *fat* **fæt**, *van* **væn**, *thank* **θæŋk**, *that* (demonstrative pronoun) **ðæt**,[18] *sand* **sænd** or **sæːnd**, *exact* **igˈzækt**, *shall* **ʃæl**,[19] *hang* **hæŋ**, *wag* **wæg**.

English Vowel No. 5: ɑː

284. The English phoneme represented in this book by the symbol **ɑ** may be regarded as comprising only one sound[20]; there

---

[18] This word has no weak form. The conjunction *that* has a weak form **ðət**; the relative pronoun *that* (meaning 'which' or 'whom') is always pronounced **ðət** in conversational speech.

[19] This word also has weak forms **ʃəl**, **ʃl**.

[20] In simplified transcription (see Appendix A) the symbol **aː** is used to represent this sound. The use of **aː** for this vowel and **a** in the diphthongs **ai, au** does not cause one word to be confused with another in phonetic transcriptions. The letter **ɑ** is used in this book for 'comparative' reasons, namely, to demonstrate in writing that the initial elements of **ai, au** are different from Vowel No. 5, and to allow for the reduced forms of **aiə** and **auə** (§§ 414, 430). There is, however, much to be said in favour of representing Vowel No. 5 by **aː** in practical textbooks, and explaining once for all the special values to be attached to the symbol **a** in **ai, au**.

are no members of the phoneme which differ to any marked extent
from this sound. It is always relatively long and is therefore
generally written with a length-mark.

285. It will be seen from the position of the dot in Fig. 34
that in forming the English ɑː the tongue is held very low down
in the mouth, and that the vowel is nearer to cardinal ɑ than to
cardinal **a**. The following is a formal description of the manner
of forming the sound:

Fig. 44. Lip-position of
English ɑː.

    (i) *height of tongue*: fully open;

    (ii) *part of tongue which is highest*: a
point somewhat in advance of the
centre of the 'back';

    (iii) *position of lips*: neutral (Fig. 44);

    (iv) *opening between the jaws*: medium
to wide.

The tip of the tongue is generally, though not necessarily,
somewhat retracted from the lower teeth. As with all normal
vowels, the soft palate is in its raised position and the vocal cords
are in vibration.

286. The sound ɑː gives no palatogram.

287. ɑː is the usual Southern English sound of the sequence of
letters *ar* when at the end of a word or when followed by a
consonant; examples: *far* fɑː, *part* pɑːt, *garden* 'gɑːdn. *A* has
the sound ɑː in *half* hɑːf, *calm* kɑːm, and several other words in
which the *l* is silent (see § 662); also in numerous words when
followed by *ff*, *ss*, or by *f*, *s*, or *n* followed by another consonant,
e.g. *staff* stɑːf, *class* klɑːs, *pass* pɑːs, *after* 'ɑːftə, *fast* fɑːst, *castle*
'kɑːsl, *ask* ɑːsk, *command* kə'mɑːnd, *grant* grɑːnt, *can't* kɑːnt, also
in most words ending in *ath*, e.g. *bath* bɑːθ; also in some words
of recent foreign origin, e.g. *moustache* məs'tɑːʃ, *drama* 'drɑːmə,
tomato tə'mɑːtou, *vase* vɑːz. Note also the words *ah* ɑː, *are* ɑː,[21]
aunt ɑːnt, *draught* drɑːft, *laugh* lɑːf, *clerk* klɑːk, *Berkeley* 'bɑːkli,[22]
Berkshire 'bɑːkʃiə or 'bɑːkʃə, *Derby* 'dɑːbi, *Hertford* 'hɑːfəd, *sergeant*
'sɑːdʒənt, *example* ig'zɑːmpl, *heart* hɑːt, *hearth* hɑːθ, *father* 'fɑːðə,

---

[21] *Are* has also a weak form ə.

[22] The American name is 'bəːkli.

rather ˈrɑːðə, and words borrowed from modern French, such as *memoir* ˈmemwɑː, *reservoir* ˈrezəvwɑː,[23] *barrage* ˈbæɾɑːʒ. (See further §§ 294, 295.)

288. The English vowel ɑː is about the same as the vowel used by many Parisians in *pâte* pɑːt.

289. Most Germans[24] and people from many other foreign countries (e.g. Scandinavians, Hungarians, Portuguese) have a tendency to use a forward ɑ approaching Cardinal Vowel No. 4 (§§ 133, 144) in place of the English ɑː. By practising a fully back variety of ɑ with the tongue held as low down and as far back as possible, they will realize better the nature of the English ɑ. It should also be noticed that the English ɑː is somewhat similar in quality (though not in quantity) to the English short ɔ. thus *card* kɑːd is rather like *cod* kɔd with the vowel lengthened. It is helpful to practise the sound with the tip of the tongue touching the lower teeth.

290. When ɑː is followed by a nasal consonant, the Portuguese often replace it by a vowel resembling ə: (§ 343), pronouncing for instance *answer* (Southern English ˈɑːnsə) almost ˈəːnsər (or ˈə̃ːsər with a nasalized ə:).

291. Foreign learners wishing to acquire the pronunciation described in this book must be careful not to add a r-sound of any sort after the sound ɑː unless a vowel follows. Thus the English word *marsh* mɑːʃ is practically identical with the French *mâche*; many Germans (from Saxony, Hamburg, etc.) pronounce *Bahn* exactly like the English *barn* bɑːn; *far* is pronounced fɑː, though *far away* is ˈfɑːr əˈwei (§ 756).

292. Some English speakers diphthongize slightly the sound ɑː especially when final, saying for instance fɑə for fɑː. This pronunciation is not, however, the most usual in educated Southern English.

293. Words for practice: *palm* pɑːm, *bath* bɑːθ, *task* tɑːsk, *dark* dɑːk, *carve*, *calve* kɑːv, *guard* gɑːd, *charm* tʃɑːm, *jar* dʒɑː, *marsh*

---

[23] Also pronounced ˈmemwɔː, ˈrezəvwɔː.

[24] Except Saxons, Bavarians and some from the extreme North (Hamburg, Lübeck, etc.), who often use an ɑ similar to the English one.

maːʃ, *nasty* ˈnaːsti, *clerk* klaːk, *rather* ˈraːðə, *far* faː, *vase* vaːz, *psalm* saːm, *sharp* ʃaːp, *hard* haːd, *yard* jaːd.

294. A number of words written with *a* are pronounced with æ by some Southern English people but with aː by others. Such are the words ending in *-aph*, like *photograph* ˈfoutəgræf or ˈfoutəgraːf, *telegraph, cenotaph,* various words where the vowel is followed by s, z, θ, ð, ns, nt, such as *ass* æs or aːs,[25] *mass* (catholic service) mæs or maːs, *masque, masquerade, contrast* (noun) ˈkɔntræst or ˈkɔntraːst, *contrast* (verb) kənˈtræst or kənˈtraːst, *blasphemy, askance* əsˈkæns or əsˈkaːns, *ant, lather, catholic,* and all the words beginning with *trans-,* such as *translate* trænsˈleit or traːnsˈleit, *transfusion, transparent, transatlantic* ˈtrænzətˈlæntik or ˈtraːnzətˈlæntik, *transact* trænˈzækt or traːnˈzækt (also trænˈsækt, traːnˈsækt), *transmit* trænsˈmit or traːnsˈmit (also trænzˈmit, traːnzˈmit).[26]

295. Many similarly spelt words are not subject to this variation of sound. Some are pronounced with æ and others with aː. There are no rules governing the use of one vowel or the other, so that the foreign student is obliged to learn the words individually. Examples of words pronounced with æ are: *photographic* foutəˈgræfik, *and* (strong form) ænd, *band, hand, land, sand, romance, finance* fiˈnæns or faiˈnæns, *manse, substantial* səbsˈtænʃl, *bass* (fish),[27] *Bass* (name), *crass, lass, mass* (quantity), *morass* məˈræs, *molasses, Passe* (surname), *Passfield, crevasse, gas, Ascot, aster, bast, cant, Levant, rant, scanty.* Examples of words pronounced with aː are: *after* ˈaːftə, *calf, half, giraffe, laugh* laːf, *craft, draft, draught, raft, shaft, waft,*[28] *demand, remand, command, reprimand, advance, chance, dance, glance, lance, trance, advantage* ədˈvaːntidʒ, *chant, grant, plant, slant,*[29] *an't,*[30] *can't* (cannot), *ask* aːsk, *bask, basket, cask, flask, mask, task, brass, class, glass, grass,*

---

[25] Usually æs for the animal, but aːs (less frequently æs) when applied to a person as a term of contempt.

[26] These variations do not exist in Northern English. In the North all the words written with aː in §§ 294, 295 are pronounced with æ or with the Northern variant of this (a).

[27] The musical term *bass* is beis.

[28] Also wɔft.

[29] *Want* is wɔnt.

[30] Colloquial abbreviation of *am not,* used in the expression *an't I?* ˈaːnt ai.

*pass, blast, fast, aghast, last, mast, past, repast, vast, castle, caster,
Castor* 'kɑːstə, *master, plaster, bath* bɑːθ, *lath, path,*[31] *father, rather.*

English Vowel No. 6: ɔ

296. The English vowel represented in this book by the symbol
ɔ without length-mark is the member of the English ɔ-phoneme
used when the vowel is relatively short.

297. It will be seen from the position of the dot in Fig. 34
that in forming short ɔ the tongue is held in the lowest and most
backward position possible. Any further retraction of the tongue
would give rise to a fricative consonant of the ʁ-type (§ 763).
The vowel has the tongue-position of Cardinal Vowel No. 5 (ɑ)
combined with open lip-rounding.

298. The following is a formal description of the manner of
forming the sound:

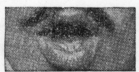

Fig. 45. Lip-position of
English short ɔ.

  (i) *height of tongue*: fully open;

  (ii) *part of the tongue which is highest*:
the back;

  (iii) *position of lips*: open lip-rounding
(see Fig. 45);

  (iv) *opening between the jaws*: medium
to wide.

The tip of the tongue is generally, though not necessarily, somewhat retracted from the lower teeth. As in the case of all normal
vowels, the soft palate is in its raised position and the vocal cords
are in vibration.

299. English short ɔ gives no palatogram.

300. ɔ is the short sound of the letter *o*; examples: *not* nɔt,
pond pɔnd, *dog* dɔg, *sorry* 'sɔri, *solid* 'sɔlid. *O* is also pronounced ɔ
with a variant ɔː in many words where f, s or θ follows; examples:
off ɔf (or ɔːf), *often* 'ɔfn (or 'ɔːfn), *loss* lɔs (or lɔːs), *cost* kɔst (or kɔːst),
cloth klɔθ (or klɔːθ). *Ou* is similarly pronounced in *cough* kɔf (or
kɔːf) and *trough* trɔf (or trɔːf). *A* often has the sound ɔ when the
vowel is preceded by w and not followed by k, g or ŋ; examples:

---

[31] But *wrath* is rɔːθ. The place-name *Wrath* is generally pronounced rɔːθ
by English people, but in Scotland it is raθ (which is sometimes imitated by
English people as rɑːθ or ræθ).

want wɔnt, *what* wɔt, *squash* skwɔʃ, *quality* ˈkwɔliti[32] (but *wax* wæks, *wag* wæg, *twang* twæŋ). Many Southern English people use ɔ instead of the older ɔː before l or s followed by a consonant, e.g. *false* fɔːls or fɔls, *fault* fɔːlt or fɔlt, *halt* hɔːlt or hɔlt. *Austria* and *Australia* are now generally pronounced ˈɔstrïə, ɔsˈtreiljə (less commonly ˈɔːstrïə, ɔːsˈtreiljə). Note the exceptional words *gone* gɔn (rarely gɔːn), *shone* ʃɔn, *because* biˈkɔz, *cauliflower* ˈkɔliflauə, *laurel* ˈlɔrəl, (*ac*)*knowledge* (ək)ˈnɔlidʒ, *Gloucester* ˈglɔstə, *yacht* jɔt.

301. Foreign people generally do not make the English sound ɔ open enough. The French use their vowel in *note* nɔt, *bonne* bɔn; Germans use their vowel in *Gott* gɔt; and so on. The usual German vowel in *Gott* is about Cardinal Vowel No. 6. This word is very distinct from the English word *got* gɔt; the tongue-position of the German ɔ is notably higher than that of the English ɔ. The French (Parisian) vowel in *note* nɔt is not merely higher than the English ɔ but also more advanced. The relations between the English short ɔ and these French and German vowels are shown in Fig. 46.

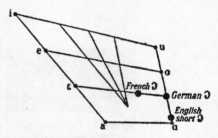

Fig. 46. Relation between English short ɔ and French and German ɔ-sounds. (The small dots represent Cardinal Vowels.)

302. Foreign learners must remember that in pronouncing the English short ɔ the tongue must be held as low down and as far back as possible. Usually the best way of acquiring the vowel is for them to aim at a sound intermediate between ɑ and their variety of ɔ.

303. Cases in which the sound ɔ occurs in unstressed syllables often seem particularly difficult to foreign learners and require special practice. Examples: *cannot* ˈkænɔt,[32a] *a day on the river* ə ˈdei ɔn ðə ˈrivə, *What are you thinking of?* ˈwɔt ə juː ˈθiŋkiŋ ɔv?

---

[32] Foreign learners often make the mistake of pronouncing this word with ɔː instead of ɔ.

[32a] Pronounced ˈkænət by some English people.

304. Words for practice: *spot* spɒt, *bother* 'bɒðə, *top* tɒp, *cotton* 'kɒtn, *got* gɒt, *chop* tʃɒp, *John* dʒɒn, *moss* mɒs, *not* nɒt, *long* lɒŋ, *rock* rɒk, *foreign* 'fɒrin, *involve* in'vɒlv,[33] *methodical* mi'θɒdikl, *sorry* 'sɒri, *shop* ʃɒp, *hop* hɒp, *yacht* jɒt, *squash* skwɒʃ, *watch* wɒtʃ.[34]

English Vowel No. 7: ɔː

305. ɔː is the member of the English ɔ-phoneme which is used when the vowel is relatively long. Its tongue-position is low, though not quite so low as for the short ɔ. The lips are rounded so as to leave an opening which is much smaller than in the case of the short ɔ (see Fig. 47). The vowel differs from Cardinal ɔ in two respects: (i) it is formed with the tongue a little lower than for Cardinal ɔ, (ii) the lips are more closely rounded than for Cardinal ɔ (see Fig. 20).

306. The following is a formal description of the manner of forming the English long ɔː:

(i) *height of tongue*: between half-open and open;

(ii) *part of tongue which is highest*: the back;

(iii) *position of lips*: between open and close lip-rounding (Fig. 47);

(iv) *opening between the jaws*: medium to fairly wide.

Fig. 47. Lip-position of English long ɔː.

The tip of the tongue is generally, though not necessarily, slightly retracted from the lower teeth. As with all normal vowels, the soft palate is in its raised position and the vocal cords are in vibration.

307. The sound ɔː gives no palatogram.

308. ɔː is the regular sound of *aw* and *au*; examples: *saw* sɔː, *lawn* lɔːn, *author* 'ɔːθə.[35] It is also the regular sound of *or* when final or followed by a consonant; examples: *nor* nɔː (like *gnaw*),

---

[33] Often pronounced in'vɔːlv by foreign people.

[34] Often pronounced wɔːtʃ by foreign people.

[35] In the sequences *aus* + consonant and *aul* + consonant many speakers substitute the short ɔ, see § 300.

short ʃɔːt, *form* fɔːm.   The groups *ore, oar* are commonly pronounced ɔː, though a diphthong ɔə is also frequently used in such cases (see § 458); examples: *more* mɔː or mɔə, *roar* rɔː or rɔə, *board* bɔːd or bɔəd.   ɔː with the variant ɔə is also heard in some words spelt with *our*; examples: *pour* pɔː or pɔə, *course* kɔːs or kɔəs.[36]   *A* frequently has the value ɔː when followed by l final or followed by a consonant; examples: *appal* ə'pɔːl, *all* ɔːl, *halt* hɔːlt.[37]   *Ar* frequently has the value ɔː when the vowel is preceded by **w** and followed by a consonant, examples: *swarm* swɔːm, *quart* kwɔːt.   *O* is pronounced ɔː by some in words like *off, loss, cost, cloth, cough,* as mentioned in § 300.[38]   *Ough* has the value ɔː when followed by **t**, as in *bought* bɔːt, *thought* θɔːt.[39]   Note the exceptional words, *broad* brɔːd, *door* dɔː or dɔə, *floor* flɔː or flɔə, *water* 'wɔːtə, *wrath* rɔːθ.

309. The sound ɔː is best acquired by imitation, while observing carefully the position of the lips.   A very near approach to the correct quality is obtained by trying to produce the tamber of the English short ɔ with lips in the position for the continental close o (as in the French *côte* koːt, German *wohl* voːl).   Many foreign people do not use sufficient lip-rounding in pronouncing the English ɔː, especially when there is no *r* in the spelling (as in *all, saw, thought*).   When there is an *r* in the spelling (as in *sore, soar, four, nor*), Germans generally replace the vowel by the close oː and say soːʀ, foːʀ, etc.

---

[36] Many people from the North and West of England use a close o or a diphthong oə in words spelt with *ore, oar, our* and in many of the words spelt with *or* + consonant.   Thus *more, board, course, port* are pronounced by them moə (or moər or moːr), boəd (or boərd or bord), koəs (or koərs or kors), poət (or poərt or port), while the Received Pronunciation of these words is mɔː (or mɔə), bɔːd (or bɔəd), kɔːs (or kɔəs), pɔːt.   The chief words written with *or* + consonant which have such alternative pronunciations with close o are: *afford, ford, horde, sword, fort, port* (and the compounds *export, important,* etc.), *sport, proportion, forth, divorce, force, borne, sworn, torn, worn, forge, pork.*   The chief words having no alternative pronunciation with close o are: *cord* (and compounds *record,* etc.), *chord, lord, order, form* (and *reform,* etc.), *storm, adorn, born, corn, horn, morn, scorn, shorn, cork, fork, stork, York, sort* (and compounds *resort,* etc.), *short, snort, north, George, gorge, horse, gorse, remorse, corpse.*

[37] The sequence represented by *al* + consonant has short ɔ in the speech of some English people, e.g. hɔlt for the more usual hɔːlt.

[38] This is my natural pronunciation; it is now becoming old-fashioned.

[39] Except *drought* draut.

310. Foreign learners wishing to acquire the pronunciation described in this book must be particularly careful not to add a r-sound of any sort after the vowel ɔ:, unless a vowel follows. *Nor* said by itself is pronounced exactly like *gnaw* nɔ:, *stork* is identical with *stalk* stɔ:k. Note, however, cases like *more easily* mɔ:r 'i:zili where a 'linking' r is inserted on account of the following vowel.

311. Some foreign people (and especially the French and Italians) have difficulty in distinguishing the sound ɔ: from the diphthong ou. Those who have this difficulty should study carefully the differences between the two sounds (§§ 305, 394).

312. Words for practising the sound ɔ:; *paw, pour, pore* pɔ:,[40] *bought* bɔ:t, *talk* tɔ:k, *door* dɔ:,[40] *caught* kɔ:t, *Gordon* 'gɔ:dn, *chalk* tʃɔ:k, *George* dʒɔ:dʒ, *more* mɔ:,[40] *gnaw, nor* nɔ:, *law* lɔ:, *raw, roar* rɔ:,[40] *drawer* (sliding box in a table or cupboard) drɔ:,[41] *for, four, fore* fɔ:,[42] *Vaughan* vɔ:n, *thought* θɔ:t, *sauce, source* sɔ:s,[43] *short* ʃɔ:t, *horn* hɔ:n, *your* jɔ:,[44] *warn, worn* wɔ:n.

313. A sound near in quality to ɔ: occurs as the first element of the diphthong ɔə (see § 455) and a very similar sound occurs as the first element of the diphthong ɔi (see § 437).

English Vowel No. 8: u

314. The sound represented in this book by u without length-mark is the member of the English u-phoneme used when the vowel is relatively short.

315. It will be seen from the position of the dot in Fig. 34 that the English short u has a tongue-position considerably higher than that of the English long ɔ:, and somewhat advanced. The tongue is not so high as for long u:. The lips are rounded fairly

---

[40] *Pour* and *pore* have the variant pronunciation pɔə. *Roar* has the variant pronunciation rɔə. *Door, more* have the variant pronunciations dɔə, mɔə.

[41] In the less common sense of a 'person who draws,' the word is always pronounced 'drɔ:ə. *Drawers*, the article of clothing, is drɔ:z (identical in pronunciation with *draws*).

[42] *For* has also a weak form fə. *Four* and *fore* have the variant pronunciation fɔə.

[43] *Source* has the variant pronunciation sɔəs.

[44] Less commonly juə. There are also variants jɔə, jɔə.

closely, but not so closely as for the long **u:** (see Figs. 48, 49). The distance between the jaws is less than for **ɔ** and **ɔ:**. Some writers call this sound a 'lax' vowel (see §§ 159–163).

316. The following is a formal description of the manner of forming the English short **u**:

Fig. 48. Lip-position of English short **u**.

(i) *height of tongue*: just above half-close;

(ii) *part of tongue which is highest*: the fore part of the back;

(iii) *position of lips*: fairly close lip-rounding (Fig. 48);

(iv) *opening between the jaws*: medium.

The tip of the tongue is generally, though not necessarily, somewhat retracted from the lower teeth. As in the case of all normal vowels, the soft palate is in its raised position and the vocal cords are in vibration.

317. The English short **u** gives no palatogram.

318. **u** is one of the two so-called 'short' sounds of the letter *u*; examples: *put* **put**, *full* **ful**, *bush* **buʃ**, *cushion* **'kuʃin**.[45] *Oo* has the sound **u** when followed by *k*, as in *book* **buk**, *look* **luk**,[46] and in the following miscellaneous words: *foot* **fut**, *good* **gud**, *hood* (and the suffix *-hood*) **hud**, *stood* **stud**, *wood* **wud**, *wool* **wul**. In *broom* (for sweeping),[47] *groom*, *room*, and *soot* both **u:** and **u** are heard, the u-forms **brum**, **grum**, **rum**, **sut** being perhaps the more usual in Received English.[48] *Soon* is generally **su:n**, but some English people pronounce **sun**. Note the miscellaneous words *bosom* **'buzəm**, *bouquet* **'bukei**, *could* **kud**,[49] *courier* **'kurïə**, *should* **ʃud**,[49] *wolf* **wulf**, *Wolverhampton* **'wulvəhæmptən** (and a few other similar names), *woman* **'wumən**, *Worcester* **'wustə**, *worsted* (woollen material) **'wustid**,[50] *would* **wud**.[51]

---

[45] Or **'kuʃn**.

[46] The only exception is the rare word *spook* **spu:k**.

[47] In *broom* (plant), however, **bru:m** seems more frequent than **brum**.

[48] I pronounce these words with short **u**. But the use of **u:** in *broom*, *groom*, and *room* is quite common in London.

[49] Weak forms **kəd**, **ʃəd**.

[50] *Worsted* from the verb *to worst* is **'wə:stid**.

[51] Weak forms **wəd**, **əd**, and **d**.

319. Many foreign people, and especially speakers of Romance languages, use a sound which is too 'tense'; in fact they do not make the necessary difference of tamber between the English short **u** and long **u:**. Thus they will pronounce *pull* too much like *pool* **pu:l**, and *full* too much like *fool* **fu:l**. The correct sound of the short **u** may be generally acquired by trying to pronounce the vowel in a slack sort of way, using only the amount of lip-rounding shown in the photograph, Fig. 48.

320. Words for practising short **u**; *push* **puʃ**, *butcher* **'butʃə**, *took* **tuk**, *could* **kud**, *good* **gud**, *nook* **nuk**, *look* **luk**, *room* **rum**, *full* **ful**, *soot* **sut**, *hook* **huk**.

321. A sound of approximately the quality of short **u** also occurs in English at the beginning of the diphthongs **uə** (§ 460), **ŭə** (§ 466*m*), **ui** (§ 327*a*) and **ŭi** (§ 466*v*), and at the end of the diphthongs **ou** (§ 394) and **au** (§ 420).

English Vowel No. 9: **u:**

322. The notation **u:** is employed to denote those members of the English **u**-phoneme which are used when the vowel is relatively long. Two of these members require notice here, the common long **u:** and an 'advanced' variety (see § 326).

323. The tongue-position of the common long **u:** is shown by the position of the dot in Fig. 34. It will be seen that the sound is noticeably different from Cardinal Vowel No. 8, its tongue-position being rather lower and more forward than the cardinal sound. The lips are fairly closely rounded as shown in Fig. 49; the lip-rounding is normally a little less close than that of cardinal **u**, but when pronounced with exaggerated distinct-ness the close lip-rounding of cardinal **u** may be used. The distance between the jaws is less than for the short **u**.

Fig. 49. Lip-position of English long **u:**.

Some writers call the English long **u:** a 'tense' vowel.

324. The following is a formal description of the manner of forming this English long **u:**:

   (i) *height of tongue*: nearly close;

   (ii) *part of tongue which is highest*: the back;

(iii) *position of lips*: close lip-rounding (Fig. 49);

(iv) *opening between the jaws*: narrow to medium.

The tip of the tongue is generally, though not necessarily, some-what retracted from the lower teeth. As in the case of all normal vowels, the soft palate is in its raised position and the vocal cords are in vibration.

325. This **uː** gives no palatogram.

326. The most important subsidiary long **uː** is an 'advanced' variety. It is used when **j** precedes, as in *music* **ˈmjuːzik**, *tube* **tjuːb**, *deluge* **ˈdeljuːdʒ**. By calling it 'advanced' we mean that the part of the tongue which is highest is the central part—a part more forward than the 'back'. The use of this advanced variety is not essential for foreign learners.[52]

327. **uː** is the so-called 'long' sound of the letter *u* (the sound **j** being inserted before it in many cases, see rules in § 817); examples: *rule* **ruːl**, *June* **dʒuːn**, *blue* **bluː**, *music* **ˈmjuːzik**, *future* **ˈfjuːtʃə**, *tube* **tjuːb**. *Oo* has the sound **uː** in most words in which the *oo* is not followed by *r* or *k*; examples: *too* **tuː**, *food* **fuːd**, *spoon* **spuːn** (for exceptions see § 318). *O* has the sound **uː** in *ado* **əˈduː**, *do* **duː**,[53] *to* **tuː**,[54] *who* **huː**, *whom* **huːm**, *lose* **luːz**, *move* **muːv**, *prove* **pruːv**, *tomb* **tuːm**. *Ou* has the sound **uː** in some words, the principal being *routine* **ruːˈtiːn**, *soup* **suːp**, *croup* **kruːp**, *douche* **duːʃ**, *group* **gruːp**, *rouge* **ruːʒ**, *route* **ruːt**,[55] *through* **θruː**, *uncouth* **ʌnˈkuːθ**, *wound* (injury, injure) **wuːnd**,[56] *you* **juː**, *youth* **juːθ**.[57] **uː** (with or without a preceding **j**, see rules in § 817) is also the usual sound of *eu*, *ew* and *ui*; examples: *feud* **fjuːd**, *new* **njuː**, *crew* **kruː**, *suit* **sjuːt**,[58] *fruit* **fruːt**. Note the exceptional words *beauty* **ˈbjuːti** (and its derivatives) and *shoe* **ʃuː**, *canoe* **kəˈnuː**, *manoeuvre* **məˈnuːvə**.

---

[52] It is not as a rule necessary to represent this advanced **uː** by a special phonetic symbol; **üː** is, however, available for those who find a need for one.

[53] This word has weak forms **də** and **d**. Before vowels the word *do* (whether stressed or not) is generally pronounced **du**.

[54] This word has weak forms **tu** and **tə**. Before vowels the word *to* (whether stressed or not) is generally pronounced **tu**.

[55] Also **raut** in *route-march* (**ˈrautmaːtʃ** or **ˈruːtmaːtʃ**).

[56] *Wound* from the verb *wind* is **waund**.

[57] The name *Brougham* used to be pronounced **bruːm**, but is now pronounced **bruəm** or **ˈbruːəm**. The noun *brougham* is also pronounced **bruəm** or **ˈbruːəm**.

[58] Also pronounced **suːt**.

327a. When stressed **uː** is followed by **i**, the sequence is sometimes reduced to a falling diphthong **ui**. Thus *ruin, bluish* are pronounced **'ruːin** or **ruin, 'bluːiʃ** or **bluiʃ**, and *doing* **'duːiŋ** is often reduced to **duiŋ**. When **uː** is followed by **ə** there is generally an alternative pronunciation with the diphthong **uə** (No. 21). For instance, *fewer, doer* are pronounced either **'fjuːə, 'duːə** or **fjuə, duə**. See § 461.

328. The common English long **uː** has nearly the same quality as the normal French vowel in *rouge* **ruːʒ**. It differs slightly from the usual North German vowel in *gut* **guːt**, which is cardinal **uː**. The result is that the **uː** of Germans speaking English generally sounds somewhat too 'deep' in quality. This deep quality of **uː** is often very noticeable when Germans pronounce the phrase *How do you do?* The correct pronunciation is **'hau dju 'duː** with the English variety of **uː**; Germans often say **hɑu 'duː juː 'duː** with the deeper German variety of **uː**.

329. This 'deep' variety of **uː** sounds particularly unnatural to English ears in the words requiring the advanced **uː** (§ 326), e.g. in *new* **njuː**, *music* **'mjuːzik**, *tube* **tjuːb**, *produce* (verb) **prə'djuːs**, *few* **fjuː**. The use of a 'deep' **uː** is less objectionable in other words, such as *food* **fuːd**, *lose* **luːz**, *soup* **suːp**.

330. Many English people diphthongize slightly the sound **uː**, especially when final. This diphthongization takes the form of a gradual increase of the lip-rounding; it may be symbolized phonetically by **ųu**[59] or **ɷu**[60] or **uw**[61]: thus, *shoe, few* are pronounced **ʃuː, fjuː**, or **ʃuw, fjuw**.

331. It is better for foreign learners not to attempt to diphthongize the English **uː**, because an exaggeration of the diphthong sounds incorrect.

332. Words for practising the sound **uː**; *pool* **puːl**, *boot* **buːt**, *tomb* **tuːm**, *doom* **duːm**, *cool* **kuːl**, *goose* **guːs**, *chew* **tʃuː**, *June* **dʒuːn**,

---

[59] **ų** denotes a very open **u**, similar to the English short **u**. **ụ** denotes a very close **u**.

[60] **ɷ** is a symbol used in narrow transcription for the English short **u**.

[61] The symbol **w** is used here in a sense different from that assigned to it in § 802. The two values are related in the same way as the two values of **j**; see footnote 5 on p. 66.

move **muːv**, *noon* **nuːn**, *loose* **luːs**, *lose* **luːz**, *blue* **bluː**, *rule* **ruːl**, *root* **ruːt**, *food* **fuːd**, *soup* **suːp**, *Zoo* **zuː**, *shoe* **ʃuː**, *who* **huː**, *you, yew* **juː**, *woo* **wuː**, *pew* **pjuː**, *beauty* **ˈbjuːti**, *tune* **tjuːn**, *dew* **djuː**, *cue, Kew* **kjuː**, *music* **ˈmjuːzik**, *new* **njuː**, *lute* **luːt** (or **ljuːt**), *few* **fjuː**, *view* **vjuː**, *sue* **sjuː**, *presume* **priˈzjuːm**,[62] *hew, hue, Hugh* **hjuː**.

English Vowel No. 10: ʌ

333. The English phoneme represented by ʌ may be regarded as comprising only one sound; there are no members of the phoneme differing to any marked extent from this sound. It is heard in such words as *cup* **kʌp**, *lump* **lʌmp**.

334. It will be seen from the position of the dot in Fig. 34 that the tongue-position of my variety of ʌ is that of an advanced ɔ. The vowel is, however, pronounced with lip-spreading (see Fig. 50). The distance between the jaws is wide; the sound cannot be pronounced properly with a narrow opening between the jaws.

335. The following is a formal description of the manner of forming my English ʌ:

Fig. 50. Lip-position of my English ʌ.

(i) *height of tongue*: half-open;

(ii) *part of tongue which is highest*: the fore part of the back;

(iii) *position of lips*: spread (Fig. 50);

(iv) *opening between the jaws*: wide.

The tip of the tongue generally touches the base of the lower teeth, but its precise position does not appreciably affect the tamber. As in the case of all normal vowels, the soft palate is in its raised position and the vocal cords are in vibration.

335a. The vowel in the above words varies to some extent with different Southern English speakers. In particular there are many who use a more 'advanced' and less ə-like vowel than mine. Their sound tends towards Cardinal a. In the North of England a raised and retracted variety resembling ə is very commonly heard. So the letter ʌ may be taken to denote a diaphone comprising several members.

336. My ʌ gives no palatogram; nor do the other varieties.

---

[62] Pronounced by some **priˈzuːm**.

337. ʌ is one of the two 'short' sounds of the letter *u*; examples: *cut* kʌt, *mutton* ˈmʌtn, *hurry* ˈhʌri. *O* has the sound ʌ in a good many words; the principal are: *among* əˈmʌŋ, *come* kʌm, *comfort* ˈkʌmfət, *company* ˈkʌmpəni, *compass* ˈkʌmpəs, *conjure* (to do things as if by magic) ˈkʌndʒə,[63] *constable* ˈkʌnstəbl, *done* dʌn, *front* frʌnt, *frontier* ˈfrʌntjə,[64] *honey* ˈhʌni, *London* ˈlʌndən, *Monday* ˈmʌndi, *money* ˈmʌni, *-monger* -mʌŋgə, *mongrel* ˈmʌŋgrəl, *monk* mʌŋk, *monkey* ˈmʌŋki, *month* mʌnθ, *none* nʌn, *one* wʌn (same pronunciation as *won*), *once* wʌns, *onion* ˈʌnjən, *pommel* ˈpʌml, *some* sʌm,[65] *Somerset* ˈsʌməsit, *son* sʌn (same pronunciation as *sun*), *sponge* spʌndʒ, *stomach* ˈstʌmək, *ton* tʌn, *Tonbridge* ˈtʌnbridʒ, *tongue* tʌŋ, *won* wʌn, *wonder* ˈwʌndə, *above* əˈbʌv, *cover* ˈkʌvə, *covet* ˈkʌvit, *covey* ˈkʌvi, *dove* dʌv, *glove* glʌv, *govern* ˈgʌvən, *love* lʌv, *oven* ˈʌvn, *shove* ʃʌv, *shovel* ˈʃʌvl, *slovenly* ˈslʌvnli, *borough* ˈbʌrə, *thorough* ˈθʌrə, *worry* ˈwʌri, *other* ˈʌðə, *brother* ˈbrʌðə, *mother* ˈmʌðə, *smother* ˈsmʌðə, *nothing* ˈnʌθiŋ, *dozen* ˈdʌzn, *colour* ˈkʌlə, *twopence* ˈtʌpəns.[66] *Ou* has the value ʌ in a few words; the principal are: *courage* ˈkʌridʒ, *country* ˈkʌntri, *cousin* ˈkʌzn, *couple* ˈkʌpl, *double* ˈdʌbl, *enough* iˈnʌf, *flourish* ˈflʌriʃ, *hiccough* ˈhikʌp, *nourish* ˈnʌriʃ, *rough* rʌf, *southern* ˈsʌðən, *southerly* ˈsʌðəli, *Southwark* (London borough) ˈsʌðək,[67] *tough* tʌf, *trouble* ˈtrʌbl, *young* jʌŋ. Note also the exceptional words *does* dʌz,[68] *blood* blʌd, *flood* flʌd.

338. Foreign people generally replace this vowel by some variety of a (§§ 133, 409) or ɑ (§ 285), or by some variety of *front rounded* vowel, for instance the half-open front vowel (phonetic symbol œ) heard in the French *œuf* œf, German *zwölf* tsvœlf.[69] Thus they commonly pronounce *up* as ap or ɑp or œp.

339. ʌ as I pronounce it can often be acquired without much difficulty by imitation, provided that care is taken not to add any

[63] But *conjure* (to appeal solemnly to) is kənˈdʒuə.
[64] Also ˈfrontjə.
[65] This word also has weak forms səm, sm.
[66] *Brompton* used to be ˈbrʌmptən, but is now more usually pronounced ˈbromptən. I pronounce *accomplish* with ɔ (əˈkɔmpliʃ), but a great many English people pronounce əˈkʌmpliʃ.
[67] *Southwark Bridge Road* appears to be, however, more usually ˈsauθwək ˈbridʒ ˈroud, *Southwark Bridge* is ˈsʌðək ˈbridʒ or (less usually) ˈsauθwək ˈbridʒ.
[68] This word has also a weak form dəz.
[69] œ is obtained by adding lip-rounding to ɛ (§ 145 (2)).

trace of lip-rounding. Some foreign people are able to obtain the sound by unrounding continental varieties of ɔ, such as those heard in the French *bonne* bɔn, German *Kopf* kɔpf, etc.; it is also sometimes useful to start by unrounding the German close o: in *wohl* vo:l, and then to lower the tongue. There is, however, no objection to using a more a-like sound, as long as the 'fronting' is not overdone; but it is essential to keep the vowel well separated from æ. *Much* mʌtʃ and *struggle* 'strʌgl must be distinguished clearly from *match* mætʃ and *straggle* 'strægl.

340. It is a good plan to learn Vowel No. 11, ə: (§§ 343 ff.), before learning ʌ. It will be seen from Fig. 34 that ʌ, as I pronounce it, is intermediate between ə: and ɑ:, and in practice it is found that ʌ may often be taught by directing the learner to make a sound about half-way between ə: and ɑ:.

341. Words for practising ʌ: *sponge* spʌndʒ, *butter* 'bʌtə, *tug* tʌg, *dull* dʌl, *come* kʌm, *gun* gʌn, *chuckle* 'tʃʌkl, *judge* dʒʌdʒ, *money* 'mʌni, *nothing* 'nʌθiŋ, *luck* lʌk, *trouble* 'trʌbl, *fuss* fʌs, *vulture* 'vʌltʃə, *thumb* θʌm, *thus* ðʌs, *such* sʌtʃ, *result* ri'zʌlt, *shut* ʃʌt, *hurry* 'hʌri, *young* jʌŋ, *won, one* wʌn.

English Vowel No. 11: ə:

342. The English sound represented in this book by ə: is the member of the ə-phoneme used when the vowel is relatively long. (Reasons for regarding ə: and ə as belonging to the same phoneme are given in my book, *The Phoneme*, §§ 197 ff.) The sound ə: varies to some extent with different speakers of Southern English; the vowel described in the next paragraph is the one used by myself, and I believe it to be the most frequent variety.[70]

343. It will be seen from the position of the dot in Fig. 34 that ə: is a central vowel; in other words the central part of the

---

[70] We have here again a case of a *diaphone* with several members. Some people use a sound which has a lower tongue-position and is therefore more ʌ-like in quality than that described in § 343. (Henry Sweet was one of these; I remember well his variety of ə:, which was a distinctly opener vowel than mine.) Other Southern people have a closer ə: than mine, i.e. a sound resembling ə₁ (§ 356) but lengthened. An exaggeration of this combined with tongue retraction, producing almost an ɯ (§ 351), may be observed in the 'clerical' accent.

tongue is raised in order to make it. The tongue is raised to about mid-way between the 'half-close' and 'half-open' positions, or perhaps a shade higher than this. The lips are spread almost as for iː (compare Figs. 51 and 36). The opening between the jaws is narrow; it is impossible to make the sound properly with a wide open mouth; the sound is in this respect very different from ʌ (see § 334).

344. The following is a formal description of the manner of forming my variety of English əː:

(i) *height of tongue*: about half-way between 'open' and 'close';

(ii) *part of tongue which is highest*: the central part, culminating at the junction between 'front' and 'back';

(iii) *position of lips*: spread (Fig. 51);

(iv) *opening between the jaws*: narrow.

Fig. 51. Lip-position of English long əː.

The tip of the tongue generally touches the base of the lower teeth, but as long as it is near the lower teeth, its precise position does not appreciably affect the quality of the sound. As in the case of all normal vowels, the soft palate is in its raised position, and the vocal cords are in vibration.

345. The vowel əː, as I pronounce it, gives no palatogram.

346. əː is the usual sound of stressed *er, ir, ur,* and *yr* when final or followed by a consonant; examples: *her* həː,[71] *fern* fəːn, *fir* fəː, *bird* bəːd, *fur* fəː, *turn* təːn, *myrtle* 'məːtl. *Ear* followed by a consonant is generally pronounced əː; examples: *earn* əːn, *earth* əːθ, *heard* həːd.[72] *Or* is generally pronounced əː when preceded by w; examples: *work* wəːk, *world* wəːld; it is also pronounced so in *attorney* ə'təːni. *Our* is pronounced əː in *adjourn* ə'dʒəːn, *courteous* 'kəːtjəs,[73] *courtesy* 'kəːtisi,[74] *journal* 'dʒəːnl, *journey* 'dʒəːni, *scourge* skəːdʒ. Note the exceptional words *colonel* 'kəːnl, *amateur* 'æmətəː,[75]

---

[71] When unstressed this word is often pronounced əː or hə or ə.

[72] Exceptions are *beard* biəd, *heart* hɑːt and *hearth* hɑːθ.

[73] Also pronounced 'kɔːtjəs.

[74] Also pronounced 'kɔːtisi.

[75] Also pronounced 'æmətə, æmə'təː and (rarely) 'æmətjuə.

connoisseur **kɔni'səː**, *chauffeur* **ʃou'fəː**[76] and a number of other words ending in *-eur*. *Year* is pronounced **jəː** or **jiə**. (I pronounce **jəː**.) The word *were* has two pronunciations, **wəː** and **wɛə** (besides a weak form **wə**). The word *girl* is usually pronounced **gəːl**; **gɛəl** and **giəl** are also not infrequent. Foreign learners are recommended to use the forms **wəː**, **gəːl**.

347. The English **əː** is a very difficult sound for most foreign people. They often replace it by some variety of *front rounded* vowel such as **œ** or **ø**,[77] and in addition to this, they usually add some kind of **r**-sound at the end. The word *word* **wəːd** will generally betray a foreigner. Germans usually pronounce it as **vœrd** or **βœrt**.

348. The most important point to be borne in mind is that there is no lip-rounding in pronouncing a normal **əː**; the lips are spread as for **iː** (Figs. 51, 36). Foreign learners who wish to pronounce in the manner described in this book must take care that the quality of the sound remains absolutely unchanged while it is being pronounced, and that no trace of a **r**-sound is added after the vowel (unless another vowel follows, as in *stirring* **'stəːriŋ**, § 756).

349. Many foreign people have a tendency to curl back or 'invert' the tip of the tongue (§ 831) when trying to pronounce the English sound **əː**. This is especially the case with Norwegians and Swedes. Such a pronunciation is common in American and various forms of dialectal English, but it is not used by Londoners. The usual sound of **əː** may be acquired by keeping the tip of the tongue firmly pressed against the lower teeth, holding it there if necessary with the finger, or with the end of a pencil. It is useful to practise the exercises **kəːkəːkəː** . . ., **gəːgəːgəː** . . . keeping the tip of the tongue against the lower teeth.

350. Some foreign learners use a vowel which is too open and **ʌ**-like or **ɑ**-like. Such a fault can generally be remedied by taking care not to open the mouth too wide; in fact it is often advisable to practise the sound **əː** with the teeth kept actually in contact.

---

[76] More usually pronounced **'ʃoufə**.

[77] **œ** is a lip-rounded **ɛ**; **ø** is a lip-rounded **e**. **œ** is the sound of *eu* in the French *neuf* **nœf** and of *ö* in the German *zwölf* **tsvœlf**. **ø** is the sound of *eu* in the French *peu* **pø** and of *ö* in the German *schön* **ʃøːn**.

351. Other foreign people, Spaniards and Greeks, for example, use a vowel which is more front than central, which has too much resemblance to e or æ. For them it is useful to practise the sound arrived at by unrounding an uː, or in other words, to do their best to say uː through spread lips. (Unrounded u is represented in phonetic transcription by ɯ.) The English əː is between this ɯː and e, and may therefore be learnt by the process described in §§ 110–114.

352. Germans should note that the English sound əː is very similar in quality to the variety of ə heard in the second syllable of the German word *bitte* ˈbitə (stage pronunciation). This fact may be utilised in learning to pronounce the English əː.

353. It is helpful for all foreign learners, and particularly for Germans and Scandinavians, to practise energetically the exercise uːəːuːəːuːəː . . . with the teeth in contact, taking care that the corners of the mouth move *horizontally* and that there is no vertical opening of the mouth. Another effective exercise is to practise iːəːiːəːiːəː . . . keeping the lips stationary in the position shown in Fig. 36.

354. Words for practising the vowel əː; *pearl* pəːl, *bird* bəːd, *turn* təːn, *dearth* dəːθ, *curb* kəːb, *kernel*, *colonel* ˈkəːnl,[78] *girl* gəːl (see § 346), *church* tʃəːtʃ, *germ* dʒəːm, *myrrh* məː, *nurse* nəːs, *learn* ləːn, *fur*, *fir* fəː, *verse* vəːs, *thirst* θəːst, *sir* səː,[79] *deserve* diˈzəːv, *shirt* ʃəːt, *hurt* həːt, *yearn* jəːn, *work* wəːk.

English Vowel No. 12: ə

355. The letter ə without length-mark is employed to denote those members of the English ə-phoneme which are used when the vowel is relatively short. It is sufficient for practical purposes to distinguish three of these members, which we may indicate, when necessary, by the notation $ə_1$ (the principal member), $ə_2$, $ə_3$. An ə of intermediate quality is often called 'the neutral vowel' or 'schwa.'

---

[78] *Colonel* is the only word without an *r* in the spelling in which the sound əː is used.

[79] This word has also a weak form sə.

356. ə₁ is similar to the German sound of *e* in *bitte* ꞌbitə. It

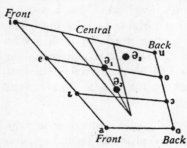

Fig. 52. Relation between the English sounds ə₁, ə₂, ə₃. (The small dots represent Cardinal Vowels.)

is very near to ə: in tamber, but it is always extremely short in English, so that its exact value is difficult to observe or describe; the vowel is subject to slight variations depending on the individual speaker[80] and on the nature of the adjoining sounds.[81] The approximate tongue-position of ə₁ is shown in Fig. 52. Its lip-position is similar to that of ə₃ shown in Fig. 53.

357. ə₁ is the sound of *a* in *along* əꞌlɔŋ, *attempt* əꞌtempt, *admit* ədꞌmit, *gentleman* ꞌdʒentlmən, *Thomas* ꞌtɔməs, *salad* ꞌsæləd, *breakfast* ꞌbrekfəst, *malady* ꞌmælədi; of *ar* in *particularly* pəꞌtikjuləli, *forward* ꞌfɔːwəd, *standard* ꞌstændəd; of *e* in *pavement* ꞌpeivmənt; of *er* in *modern* ꞌmɔdən,[82] *concert* ꞌkɔnsət, *manners* ꞌmænəz, *Underground* (railway) ꞌʌndəgraund; of *i* in *horrible* ꞌhɔrəbl; of *o* in *method* ꞌmeθəd, *protect* prəꞌtekt, *melody* ꞌmelədi, *lemon* ꞌlemən; of *or* in *effort* ꞌefət; of *oar* in *cupboard* ꞌkʌbəd; of *u* in *chorus* ꞌkɔːrəs, *minimum* ꞌminiməm; of *ou* in *famous* ꞌfeiməs. ə₁ is also the usual vowel of the articles *the* (before consonants) and *a*; examples: *the table* ðə ꞌteibl, *a window* ə ꞌwindou.

358. ə₂ is a vowel which has a higher and more retracted tongue-position than ə₁, a vowel which is therefore a kind of ɯ (see Fig. 52 and § 351). It is a member of the English ə-phoneme frequently heard when the adjoining consonant is k or g, as in *condemn* kənꞌdem, *to go* tə ꞌgou, *back again* ꞌbæk əgein, *the ground* ðə ꞌgraund, *hypocrite* ꞌhipəkrit,[83] *suffocate* ꞌsʌfəkeit; the ə in these words is almost equivalent to a very short ɯ (kɯnꞌdem, tɯ ꞌgou, ꞌbæk ɯgein, ðɯ ꞌgraund, etc.).

---

[80] These variants being therefore members of the same *diaphone*.

[81] These variants being therefore members of the same *phoneme*.

[82] Also pronounced ꞌmɔdn when in close grammatical connexion with the following word (as in *modern languages* ꞌmɔdn ꞌlæŋgwidʒiz).

[83] Also pronounced ꞌhipukrit.

359. Sounds intermediate between ə₁ and ə₂ are also common, but it is difficult to say precisely in what cases they are used. Moreover the pronunciation varies considerably from speaker to speaker. In the words *hammock* ˈhæmək, *Jacob* ˈdʒeikəb, I think I generally use a sound nearer to ə₁ than to ə₂ in spite of the fact that there is an adjacent **k**. On the other hand there are many speakers who use a sound approximating to ə₂ in *breakfast, pavement, method* and many other words in which the majority would use ə₁.

360. Owing to these divergences of pronunciation it is unnecessary for the foreign learner to distinguish between ə₁ and ə₂. His pronunciation will sound quite English if he uses ə₁ in all the above-mentioned cases.

361. ə₃ is an opener and more ʌ-like sound than ə₁; it is also pronounced less short than ə₁. It may be placed on the Vowel Figure as shown in Fig. 52. It is used in final position, whereas ə₁ and ə₂ never occur in final position. The following are examples of words pronounced with ə₃; it is to be understood that they only have this vowel when a pause follows: *china* ˈtʃainə, *villa* ˈvilə, *collar* ˈkɔlə, *over* ˈouvə, *manner* ˈmænə, *bitter* ˈbitə, *father* ˈfɑːðə, *actor* ˈæktə, *honour* ˈɔnə, *borough* ˈbʌrə, *thorough* ˈθʌrə, *picture* ˈpiktʃə, *centre* ˈsentə.

Fig. 53. Lip-position of the English 'neutral' vowel ə (ə₃).

362. Many English speakers actually use ʌ in such words, pronouncing ˈtʃainʌ, ˈvilʌ, ˈkɔlʌ, etc.

363. When such words are immediately followed by another word in the same sense-group, the vowel is replaced by ə₁.[84] Thus ə₁ is used in *china tea* ˈtʃainə ˈtiː, *over there* ˈouvə ˈðɛə, *a picture we like* ə ˈpiktʃə wiː ˈlaik, *my father and I* mai ˈfɑːðər ənd ˈai.

---

[84] Not as a rule by ə₂. It seems as if the words ending in ə (except *a* and *the*) never occur in sufficiently close grammatical connexion with a following word to induce a pronunciation with ə₂, even if the following word begins with **k** or **g**. Thus *alpaca coat* ælˈpækə ˈkout is said with ə₁, while *I'll pack a coat* ail ˈpæk ə ˈkout would generally be said with ə₂. Cases in which this distinction is made are so uncommon that they may be for practical purposes disregarded.

364. Sounds intermediate between əₗ and ə₃ exist, but are for the most part of no importance as they may always be replaced by əₗ or ə₃. One, which we may denote by ə₄, is sometimes heard in place of əₗ when words ending in -rə are immediately followed by another word. Example: *borough council* 'bʌrə 'kaunsl, *an error of judgment* ən 'erə əv 'dʒʌdʒmənt, *Dora is here* 'dɔːrə z hiə.

365. In such a word as *honoured* (which I should pronounce 'ɔnəd with əₗ) some speakers use a vowel almost identical in quality with ə₄ but somewhat lengthened. Being relatively rather long, yet quite distinct in quality from əː, it has to be regarded as belonging to a separate phoneme unconnected with the above described members of the ə-phoneme. It is therefore necessary in transcribing the pronunciation of these speakers to use a special phonetic symbol for this vowel. ɐ is the appropriate international phonetic letter for it.

366. ɐ is then a sound intermediate in tamber between əₗ and ə₃ (see Fig. 52). It is always distinctly longer than əₗ and ə₂, but, unlike ə₃, it is never replaced by ʌ. ɐ is found chiefly in derivatives formed by adding d or z to words ending in ə₃, e.g. *honoured* 'ɔnəd or 'ɔnɐd, *delivered* di'livəd or di'livɐd, *manners* 'mænəz or 'mænɐz, *father's* 'faːðəz or 'faːðɐz. Some words not derived in this way are also pronounced with ɐ by some English people; they all appear to be literary or rather uncommon words. Examples are: *laggard* 'lægəd or 'lægɐd, *rampart* 'ræmpət or 'ræmpɐt, *hazard* 'hæzəd or 'hæzɐd and the adjective *divers* 'daivəz or 'daivɐz.[85]

367. ɐ is only used in words where there is an *r* in the spelling It cannot be used in such words as *breakfast, salad, method*. The use of ɐ is probably a spelling pronunciation. It is mentioned here because it is not uncommon, but it must be understood that the use of this vowel is in no way necessary for an acceptable pronunciation of English. Foreign learners are recommended for

---

[85] Commoner words like *leopard* 'lepəd, *standard* 'stændəd, *mustard* 'mʌstəd, *awkward* 'ɔːkwəd, have əₗ. *Convert* (noun) and *bulwark* are generally pronounced with əː ('kɔnvəːt, 'bulwəːk) and occasionally with ɐ ('kɔnvɐt 'bulwɐk) but not as a rule with əₗ. *Forward* is generally pronounced with əₗ ('fɔːwəd) and occasionally with ɐ ('fɔːwɐd); the word is distinct from *foreword* 'fɔːwəːd or 'fɔːəwəːd.

the sake of simplicity to use ə₁ in all cases where ɐ is a possible variant.

368. The foreign learner therefore need only learn two of the numerous varieties of ə occurring in English, namely ə₁ and ə₃. ə₃ is to be used in final position (see § 361), and ə₁ in all other cases in which the ə-phoneme occurs short.

369. ə₁ and ə₃ are both easy sounds for most foreign people. In the case of ə₁ hardly any difficulty arises, owing to the fact that it is extremely short and that slight deviations from the normal value pass unnoticed by English hearers. ə₁ is moreover almost identical with the North German sound of *e* in *bitte* 'bitə. French people generally make the mistake of using the French variety of ə ('*e* mute') which is said with rounded lips; they must remember that all the English varieties of ə are made with spread lips.

370. ə₃ lies between əː and ʌ, and is therefore easy to learn when once the two latter vowels have been acquired. The method described in §§ 110–114 may be used. Foreign learners who have difficulty in distinguishing between the ə-sounds and ʌ (Spaniards, Greeks and the Japanese, for instance) may always use ʌ in place of ə₃ (see § 362).

371. The chief difficulty for foreign people in regard to short ə lies not in making the sound, but in knowing *when to use it*. Ordinary English spelling gives no indication as to when ə is to be used, and consequently foreigners continually replace it by some other vowel which the spelling suggests to them. Misled by the spelling, they say *doctor, consider, particularly, amusement* with some such pronunciations as 'dɔktɔr, kɔn'sider, par'tikjularli, e'mjuːzment instead of 'dɔktə, kən'sidə, pə'tikjuləli, ə'mjuːzmənt. Moreover they are not generally aware of the differences between such words as *experiment* (noun) iks'perimənt and *experiment* (verb) iks'periment, *workman* 'wəːkmən and *coal-man* 'koulmæn.

372. Some guidance is to be found in the fact that ə only occurs in unstressed syllables. The following comparisons illustrate this:

present (noun, adj.) 'prez(ə)nt		*present* (verb) pri'zent	
company 'kʌmpəni		*companion* kəm'pænjən	
history 'hist(ə)ri		*historical* his'tɔrikl	
August (month) 'ɔːgəst		*august* (adj.) ɔː'gʌst	

photograph ˈfoutəgræf[86]	*photography* fəˈtɔgrəfi[87]

photographic ˌfoutəˈgræfik

chronology krəˈnɔlədʒi	*chronological* ˌkrɔnəˈlɔdʒikl
illustration ˌiləsˈtreiʃn	*illustrious* iˈlʌstriəs
labour ˈleibə	*laborious* ləˈbɔːriəs
magic ˈmædʒik	*magician* məˈdʒiʃn
Japan dʒəˈpæn	*Japanese* ˌdʒæpəˈniːz

373. Too much reliance must not, however, be placed on the fact that a syllable is unstressed. All other vowels occur quite frequently with weak stress (see, however, footnote 3 to § 920). Examples are: *insect* ˈinsekt, *torment* (noun) ˈtɔːment, *ferment* (noun) ˈfəːment, *comment* ˈkɔment, *contract* (noun) ˈkɔntrækt, *asphalt* ˈæsfælt, *knapsack* ˈnæpsæk, *Afghan* ˈæfgæn, *Zodiac* ˈzoudiæk, *cannot* ˈkænɔt, *epoch* ˈiːpɔk, *chaos* ˈkeiɔs, *record* (noun) ˈrekɔːd, *statute* ˈstætjuːt, *hubbub* ˈhʌbʌb, *convert* (noun) ˈkɔnvəːt, *Exmouth* ˈeksmauθ,[88] Greek proper names such as *Logos* ˈlɔgɔs, *Pythagoras* paiˈθægəræs, *Thucydides* θjuːˈsididiːz; *exotic* egˈzɔtik, *anticipate* ænˈtisipeit, *carnation* kɑːˈneiʃn, *Norwegian* nɔːˈwiːdʒən, *mercurial* məːˈkjuəriəl. Foreign learners who have accustomed themselves to the frequent occurrence of ə and i in unstressed syllables often have difficulty in pronouncing words such as the above. In their anxiety to use ə properly they will sometimes produce non-existent pronunciations such as nəˈwiːdʒən,[89] ˈnæpsək,[89] ˈstætʃət (for ˈstætjuːt), ˈhændikəp (for -kæp), ˈeiprikət (for -kɔt), kəmpənˈseiʃn (for kɔmpenˈseiʃn or kɔmpənˈseiʃn), ˈgrænsən (for ˈgrænsʌn). Such mistakes are just as un-English as the failure to use ə in words which ought to have it.

374. The use of some other vowel instead of ə is particularly un-English in terminations like -əbl, -əns. *Miserable, consequence* are pronounced ˈmizərəbl, ˈkɔnsikwəns and not, as many foreign people say, ˈmizərabl, ˈkɔnsekwens. Foreign learners can often improve their pronunciation very much by omitting altogether the ə's in such words, and practising ˈmizrbl, ˈkɔnskwns. Similarly

---

[86] Also pronounced ˈfoutəgrɑːf.

[87] Also pronounced fˈtɔgrfi.

[88] Also pronounced ˈeksməθ. Compare *Bournemouth* which is pronounced ˈbɔːnməθ or ˈbuənməθ or ˈboənməθ.

[89] Noted many years ago by Sweet.

preferable, afterwards, solicitor, successful, sufficient, comfortable may with advantage be practised as 'prefrbl, 'ɑːftwdz, 'slistə, sk'sesfl, 'sfiʃnt, 'kʌmftbl. The word *difficult* 'difikəlt is nearly always pronounced badly by foreign people; it should be practised as 'difiklt or 'difklt.

375. Attention should be given to two special cases in which the sound ə may *not* be omitted, namely

  (i) when followed by a nasal consonant and preceded by another nasal consonant, as in *woman* 'wumən, *German* 'dʒəːmən,

  (ii) when preceded by a nasal consonant + plosive and followed by another nasal consonant, as in *incumbent* in'kʌmbənt, *London* 'lʌndən, *Hampton* 'hæmptən, *Islington* 'izliŋtən.

Germans are apt to drop out the ə in such words and to pronounce 'wumn (or 'βumn), 'dʒəːmn (or 'dʒœʀmn), 'lʌndn (or 'lœndn or 'lœnn), etc.

376. Especially noteworthy is the fact that foreign people continually use 'strong forms' in the case of words which have 'strong' and 'weak' forms. They generally fail altogether to use the weak forms of such words as *them, have, and, of, from, for* (ðəm, həv or əv or v, ənd or ən or n, əv, frəm, fə). The subject of strong and weak forms is discussed at length in Chap. XVI. All that need be said here is that English people use weak forms such as those just mentioned much more often than the strorg forms, though there are a certain number of cases in which the strong forms must be used (see for instance §§ 996, 997).

377. The proper use of ə in words which have only one pronunciation may be learnt from a pronouncing dictionary. The proper use of ə in words which are said sometimes with this vowel and sometimes with another is acquired by extensive reading of phonetically transcribed texts.

Chapter XV

THE ENGLISH DIPHTHONGS

General Remarks

378. A common form of Received Southern English contains twelve essential diphthong phonemes. Nine of these are included in the vowel table on p. 61, where they are represented by the symbols **ei, ou, ai, au, ɔi, iə, ɛə, ɔə, uə**, and are numbered 13 to 21. To these must be added three 'rising' diphthongs, **ĭə, ŭə** and **ŭi**, which may be identified by the numbers 22, 23 and 24. These latter are dealt with in §§ 466a–466v. If it is desired to show in writing that the diphthongs 13 to 21 are of a 'falling' type, this can be done by placing the I.P.A. mark ˘ over the second letter of each digraph thus **eĭ, oŭ, aĭ**, etc.

378a. Of the above diphthongs two, **ɔə** and **ŭi**, may be ignored by the foreign learner, the first because many Southern English people (including myself) never use it but replace it by **ɔ:** (§ 458), and the second because it can always be replaced by disyllabic **u-i** (§ 466v).

378b. There exist nine further unessential diphthongs in Southern English, namely **oi, ui, eə, aə, ɐə, oə, ŏi, ĕə** and **ŏə**. They are reductions of **oui** (stressed), **u:i, eiə** (stressed), **aiə, auə, ouə** (stressed), **oui** (unstressed), **eiə** (unstressed) and **ouə** (unstressed) respectively; they are unessential because they may always be replaced by these fuller forms. Reference is made to them in §§ 403, 327a, 392a, 414, 430, 403, 466x. It is necessary to mention the existence of these diphthongs, since they may often be heard from English people, but it is not needful for foreign learners to use them.

379. The diphthongs **iə, ɛə, ɔə, uə** have been aptly termed 'centring' diphthongs.[1]

380. In some of the English diphthong-phonemes we may distinguish more than one member; for instance my **ei** in *gate* **geit** is not quite the same as that in *pay* **pei**.

---

[1] This term was invented by H. E. Palmer. See his *First Course of English Phonetics* (1920), p. 23.

381. The mode of forming the principal members of the English diphthong-phonemes is shown in Figs. 54, 61. The dots show the starting-points, and the arrows show the direction in which the diphthongs proceed.

382. The positions of the ends of the arrows in Fig. 54 show the limits of movement of the diphthongs **ei, ou, ai, au, ɔi.** The sound is not heard to be essentially different if the movement falls somewhat short of the limit; in fact, in the pronunciation of most English speakers, the limit is not nearly reached.

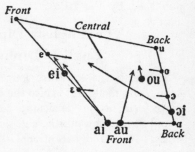

Fig. 54. Diagram showing the nature of the English Diphthongs **ei, ou, ai, au, ɔi.**

383. The limit of movement of the centring diphthongs (**iə, ɛə, ɔə, uə**) is **ə₃** (§ 361). This limit is usually reached when the diphthongs are final, as for instance when the words *near* **niə,** *fair* **fɛə,** *door* **dɔə,** *tour* **tuə** are said by themselves. In non-final position **ə₃** is generally not quite reached; thus many speakers make a slight difference between the diphthongs in *near* **niə** (said alone) and *nearly* **ˈniəli** or *near together* **ˈniə təˈgeðə.** The difference is, however, negligible from the point of view of the foreign learner of English.

384. Some speakers continue the diphthongs **iə** and **ɛə** as far as **ʌ,** especially in final position. Thus it is not uncommon to hear *near, fair* pronounced as **niʌ, fɛʌ;** the pronunciation **ˈniʌli** for **ˈniəli** is less common and would be considered by many English people to be an 'affected' way of speaking.

385. For the purpose of practical language teaching it is convenient to regard a diphthong as a succession of two vowels, in spite of the fact that, strictly speaking, it is a gliding sound. When diphthongs are described in this rough way, the less prominent part of a diphthong is commonly said to be 'consonantal.' Thus in practical teaching it is convenient to regard the diphthong **ei** as a succession of two vowels, **e** and **i,** of which the **i** is consonantal; and the diphthong may be easily taught by telling the pupil to say a certain variety of **e** followed by **i**.

385a. Sometimes it is difficult to distinguish a true diphthong from a sequence of two separately pronounced vowels. For a discussion of this question see my article *Falling and Rising Diphthongs in Southern English* in *Miscellanea Phonetica* II, 1954, published by the I.P.A.

The English Diphthongs in Detail
English Diphthong No. 13: **ei**

386. **ei** is the so-called 'long' sound of the letter *a*, as in *came* keim, *make* **meik**. It is also the usual sound of *ai* and *ay*; examples: *plain* **plein**, *daisy* **'deizi**, *day* **dei**, *play* **plei**. *Ei* and *ea* have the sound **ei** in a few words, e.g. *weigh* **wei**, *veil* **veil**, *great* **greit**, *break* **breik**. Note the exceptional words *bass* (in music) **beis**,[2] *gauge* **geidʒ**.

387. The diphthong **ei** starts at about the English **e** (Vowel No. 3) and moves in the direction of **i** (see Fig. 54).

388. Speakers of Received Southern English do not, however, all use the same variety of diphthong. In other words the notation **ei** stands for a diaphone with several members. Many English people use a diphthong which begins with a lower variety of **e** than this; their varieties of pronunciation may be represented (in 'comparative' notation) by **ɛi**. But if the initial sound of **ɛi** is lower than cardinal **ɛ**, the pronunciation must be considered dialectal (London and Eastern Counties). There are others who use a variety of **ei** beginning with a somewhat closer variety of **e** than that shown in Fig. 54. Others again use a very slightly diphthongal sound which may be symbolized by **ɛe**; this is a comparatively recent development, and is becoming very common among RP speakers.

389. In consequence of the existence of all these variants, the teaching of **ei** to foreigners presents no particular difficulty. If the learner is told to pronounce the English **e** (Vowel No. 3) with **i** (No. 2) immediately after it, the result will be a sufficiently near approximation to **ei**.

---

[2] *Bass* (fish) is **bæs**.

390. But the foreign learner must not forget that the Southern English sound is a diphthong. Foreign people commonly replace **ei** by a long 'pure' **e:**, like the vowel in the German *See* **ze:**. The diphthongal nature of the English **ei** may be well seen by asking any Southern English person to repeat the sound a number of times in rapid succession, thus **ei-ei-ei**. . . . It will be observed that the lower jaw keeps moving up and down.

391. It should be noticed that the German sound of *ee* and the French *é* are closer than the beginning of the English **ei**. Their tongue-positions are in fact higher even than that of cardinal **e**.

392. Words for practice: *pay* **pei**, *bathe* **beið**, *table* **'teibl**, *day* **dei**, *scale* **skeil**, *game* **geim**, *change* **tʃeindʒ**, *James* **dʒeimz**, *maid*, *made* **meid**, *neighbour* **'neibə**, *late* **leit**, *railway* **'reilwei**, *face* **feis**, *veil*, *vale* **veil**, *they* **ðei**, *same* **seim**, *haste* **heist**, *Yale* **jeil**, *wake* **weik**, *player* **'pleiə**, *they're* (= *they are*) **'ðeiə**.

392a. The sequence **eiə** is often replaced by a diphthong **eə**, thus **pleə**, **ðeə**. This diphthong has to be distinguished from **ɛə** (§ 446).

English Diphthong No. 14: ou

393. **ou** is the so-called 'long' sound of the letter *o*; examples: *so* **sou**, *home* **houm**, *noble* **'noubl**, *roll* **roul**,[3] *bolt* **boult**, *post* **poust**, *both* **bouθ**, *only* **'ounli**, *don't* **dount**. **ou** is the regular sound of *oa* when not followed by *r*; examples: *road* **roud**, *toast* **toust**.[4] *Ow* is pronounced **ou** in many words; examples: *know* **nou**, *sow* (verb) **sou**,[5] *growth* **grouθ**. *Ou* is pronounced **ou** in the following words: *dough* **dou**, *mould* **mould**, *moult* **moult**, *poultice* **'poultis**, *poultry* **'poultri**, *shoulder* **'ʃouldə**, *smoulder* **'smouldə**, *soul* **soul**, *though* **ðou**. Note the exceptional words *oh* **ou**, *brooch* **broutʃ**, *sew* **sou**, and words recently i ntroduced from French such as *bureau* **bjuə'rou** or **'bjuərou**.

394. The English diphthong **ou**, as I pronounce it, starts with a tongue-position in advance of and somewhat lower than that of

---

[3] **ou** is used in all words ending in -*oll* except *doll* **dɔl**, *loll* **lɔl** and *Poll* (parrot) **pɔl**.

[4] *Broad* **brɔ:d** is an exception.

[5] *Sow* (pig) is **sau**.

cardinal **o** (Fig. 54), and **a** lip-position of medium rounding (Fig. 55); the speech-organs then move in the direction of **u** (Figs. 54, 56).

Fig. 55. Lip-position of the beginning of the English diphthong **ou**.

Fig. 56. Lip-position of the end of the English diphthong **ou**.

395. The formation of the beginning of the diphthong **ou** may be described formally as follows:

(i) *height of tongue*: a little nearer to 'half-close' than to 'half-open' (see Fig. 54);

(ii) *part of tongue raised*: the fore part of the back;

(iii) *position of lips*: slightly rounded (Fig. 55);

(iv) *opening between the jaws*: medium.

The tip of the tongue is touching or nearly touching the lower front teeth, and, as in the case of all ordinary vowels, the soft palate is in its raised position and the vocal cords are in vibration. In normal speech the opening between the jaws is not so wide as for ɔ, ɔ:, and ʌ.

396. People often do not realize that the vowel in *so, home,* etc., is diphthongal. The fact may be demonstrated by asking any Southern English person to say *Oh! Oh! Oh!* . . . rapidly. It will be observed that the lips do not remain in one position, but keep closing and opening.

397. Foreign people generally replace the English diphthong **ou** by a pure vowel **o:**, such as that heard in the French *côte* **ko:t**, German *wohl* **vo:l**. This is another sound of the half-close type, but it has the tongue further back and higher than the English **o**, and the lips are very much more rounded than for the English sound. The differences between it and the English **o** are summed up by some writers by describing this foreign sound as 'tense.'

398. It is important that foreign learners, and particularly Germans, should remember that in the English **o** the tongue is not in the standard back position, but is advanced towards the central position ('narrowly' ö). This gives to the English o a trace of œ-quality (§ 338). Many foreigners who recognize the diphthongal character of the English ou, fail to advance the tongue sufficiently and so to make the first element enough like œ; the result is that the diphthong which they produce sounds too much like ɔu.[6]

399. In such cases it is well to start by practising the diphthong œu. When this diphthong œu is mastered, learners usually do not have much difficulty in modifying its quality until the true sound of the English ou is arrived at. French people may obtain a near approximation to the English diphthong ou by pronouncing their so-called 'e mute' (the usual vowel in le lə) followed by the English u, thus əu. Those of other nationalities can often learn to make the diphthong by noticing that it is not far removed from ə:u, a sequence of the English vowels Nos. 11 and 8. Most foreign learners find it helpful to keep the tip of the tongue firmly pressed against the lower teeth when practising this diphthong.

400. The diphthong ou is particularly difficult for foreign people when followed by the 'dark' l (§ 668) as in *old* **ould**, *whole* **houl**, *rolls* **roulz**. In practising such words a break should at first be made, thus **ou-ld, hou-l, rou-lz**, and then the sounds should be gradually joined together.

401. Foreign learners should avoid overdoing the diphthongal character of ou or replacing it by forms like ɑu, au, ʌu, all of which may be heard in London and other dialects. It is better to use the continental o: than these exaggerated forms. o: is actually used in Scottish pronunciation.

402. Many foreign people (especially the French, Spaniards, Italians and Japanese) have extreme difficulty in distinguishing ou from ɔ:. Those who have this difficulty should study carefully the differences between the two sounds (§§ 305, 394).

403. The English vowel o occasionally appears without a following u, but only in unstressed syllables or before another vowel. Such cases are comparatively rare, and there are always alternative forms with ou or ə. Thus *November, obey, molest* are often pronounced **no'vembə, o'bei, mo'lest**, but the forms

---

[6] A diphthong of the type ɔu is used for ou in various dialectal varieties of English, but it is hardly to be recommended for foreign learners.

nou'vembə, nə'vembə, ou'bei, ə'bei, mou'lest, mə'lest are also common. Again *going* 'gouiŋ, *slower* 'slouə may be pronounced goiŋ, sloə with diphthongs oi, oə (see § 466x).

404. Some Southern English people use a subsidiary member of the ou-phoneme when dark 1 follows. This subsidiary member starts with a more retracted tongue-position than the ordinary ou; it is consequently a kind of ɔu. Some English speakers, then, use a different diphthong in *bowl* boul, *bolt* boult from that which they use in *bowling* 'bouliŋ, *roll it* 'roul it. It is well for foreign learners to know of the existence of this distinction, but it is not advisable for them to try to make it, since an exaggeration of the retracted pronunciation would become a mispronunciation.

405. Words for practising the diphthong ou: *post* poust, *both* bouθ, *tone* toun, *don't* dount, *cold* kould, *go* gou, *choke* tʃouk, *Joseph* 'dʒouzif, *motion* 'mouʃn, *no, know* nou, *loaf* louf, *roll* roul, *foe* fou, *vote* vout, *though* ðou, *sole, soul* soul, *zone* zoun, *show* ʃou, *hope* houp, *yoke, yolk* jouk, *won't* wount.

English Diphthong No. 15: ai

406. The English diphthong denoted here by ai is the so-called 'long' sound of the letters *i* and *y*; examples: *time* taim, *idle* 'aidl, *night* nait, *child* tʃaild, *find* faind, *fly* flai. *Ie* has the value ai when final, as in *pie* pai, and in inflected forms such as *tried* traid, *cries* kraiz. *Ei* is pronounced ai in the words *height* hait, *sleight* slait, *either* 'aiðə,[7] *neither* 'naiðə,[7] *eider* 'aidə. Exceptionally spelt words are *buy* bai, *eye* ai, *choir* 'kwaiə, *aisle* ail.

407. We have here the case of a diaphone with several members. That is to say different speakers of Received English do not all pronounce ai in the same way. In the pronunciation of many the diphthong begins at Cardinal Vowel No. 4 (a) and immediately proceeds in the direction of i (Fig. 54). With some speakers the diphthong begins at a point between Cardinal a and Cardinal ɑ, while with others the beginning is at a point between a and æ. Others again, especially in the North of England, use a sound nearer to ʌi or əi.

408. With each individual speaker ai represents a phoneme comprising one of the above-mentioned forms as the principal

---

[7] Also pronounced 'iːðə, 'niːðə.

member and at least one notable subsidiary member, namely the
variety used when ə follows (see §§ 414, 415).

409. In the practical teaching of English pronunciation to
foreign learners it is generally convenient to take as the normal
value of **ai** the variety which begins at Cardinal **a**. The formation
of the beginning of this diphthong may be described formally as
follows:

  (i) *height of tongue*: low;

  (ii) *part of tongue raised*: the front;

  (iii) *position of lips*: spread to neutral (Fig. 57);

  (iv) *opening between the jaws*: rather wide.

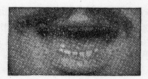

Fig. 57. Lip-position of the
beginning of the English
diphthong **ai**.

Fig. 58. Lip-position of the
end of the English diph-
thong **ai**

The tongue-tip is touching or nearly touching the lower front teeth,
and, as in the case of all ordinary vowels, the soft palate is in its
raised position and the vocal cords are in vibration. The nature
of the diphthong is seen in Fig. 54, and by comparing Figs. 57
and 58.

410. To pronounce the English diphthong **ai** correctly it is not
necessary that i should actually be reached. A certain portion of
the movement towards i is sufficient to give the proper effect.
In other words, a diphthong of the type **ae** will suffice. Even **as**
would not strike an Englishman as wrong, as long as the ɛ-element
is not too open.

411. The English diphthong **ai** does not present difficulty to
most foreign learners, owing to the fact that the pronunciation
of English people varies (§ 407). Some foreigners, however, start
the diphthong too near to **ɑ** (Vowel No. 5). The pronunciation
then becomes dialectal. To correct this mistake, the learner should
make the diphthong sound more like **æi**; he must learn to make

a sound intermediate between ai and æi, by the process described in §§ 110–114.

412. It should be noted that the sound a occurs in Southern English only as the first element of the diphthongs ai and au. In some languages the sound occurs as a pure vowel, e.g. French *la patte* la pat. In many types of Northern English a is used where Southern English has æ.

413. Words for practice: *pile* pail, *bite* bait, *tie* tai, *dine* dain, *kind* kaind, *quite* kwait, *guide* gaid, *child* tʃaild, *mine* main, *nice* nais, *like* laik, *right*, *rite*, *wright*, *write* rait, *five* faiv, *vine* vain, *thy* ðai, *side* said, *resign* ri'zain, *height* hait, *while* wail.

414. ai sometimes forms a so-called triphthong[8] with a following ə, as in *fire* which is generally transcribed 'faiə. In pronouncing this triphthong, the tongue never really goes near to the i-position; aɛə more nearly represents the actual pronunciation. The 'levelling' of the triphthong is often carried so far that it is replaced by a diphthong aə or even simply a lengthened aː; thus *fire* is often heard as faə or faː (which is distinct from *far* faː), and *empire* is often pronounced 'empaə or 'empaː.[9] This levelling of the triphthong is particularly common when a consonant follows, as in *fiery* 'faːri, *society* sə'saːti, *entirely* in'taːli, *violin* va:'lin, *giant* dʒaːnt, *hire it* 'haːr it,[10] etc. (instead of 'faiəri, etc.). The English word *wires*, usually transcribed 'waiəz, is often pronounced in a manner indistinguishable from the French word *Oise* waːz.

415. English people do not as a rule use these reduced forms when the ə is a suffix with a definite meaning. They employ in this case a clearly disyllabic pronunciation which may be symbolized phonetically by ai-ə. These speakers distinguish *higher* 'hai-ə from *hire* 'haiə, *dyer* 'dai-ə from *dire* 'daiə, etc. It is not essential for the foreign learner to make these distinctions.

416. There is another special case in which the reduction of aiə to aə or aː does not take place, namely when 'dark' l follows, as *trial* 'traiəl. The tendency here is rather to drop the ə and pronounce trail. It must be noted, however, that if the word *trial* is

---

[8] It is not a real triphthong, but a sequence of two syllables (see Chap. XII, and especially §§ 232, 233).

[9] Not 'empaː.

[10] Not 'faːri, sə'saːti, in'taːli, 'haːr it, etc.

immediately followed by a word beginning with a vowel, the ə
must be inserted and the aiə may then be reduced to aə or aː,
'dark' l not being used in that case. Thus in *the trial ended* ðə
ˈtraiəl ˈendid, *trial* could not be reduced to **trail**, but might be
reduced to **traəl** or **traːl**.

417. Foreign learners often pronounce **aiə** without making
allowance for the diminution of movement referred to in § 414.
The result is that in their pronunciation *fire, society* sound like
ˈfajə, soˈsajeti. Those who have this tendency should aim at
reducing **aiə** almost to a single long vowel **aː** (in words other than
those referred to in §§ 415, 416).

418. Words for practising **aiə**: *piety* ˈpaiəti, ˈpaəti or ˈpaːti
(distinct from *party* ˈpaːti), *Byron* ˈbaiərən, ˈbaərən or ˈbaːrən,
tyrant ˈtaiərənt, ˈtaərənt or ˈtaːrənt, *diaphragm* ˈdaiəfræm, ˈdaəfræm
or ˈdaːfræm, *liable* ˈlaiəbl, ˈlaəbl or ˈlaːbl, *fiery* ˈfaiəri, ˈfaəri or
ˈfaːri, *violent* ˈvaiələnt, ˈvaələnt or ˈvaːlənt, *scientific* saiənˈtifik,
saənˈtifik or saːnˈtifik, *desirable* diˈzaiərəbl, diˈzaərəbl or diˈzaːrəbl,
iron ˈaiən, aən or aːn.

English Diphthong No. 16: au

419. The English diphthong written phonetically **au** is the usual
sound of *ou*; examples: *loud* **laud**, *house* **haus**, *out* **aut**, *bough* **bau**.
It is also a frequent sound of *ow*; examples: *cow* **kau**, *town* **taun**,
flower ˈflauə. *Eo* has the value **au** in the name *MacLeod* məˈklaud.

420. **au** represents a diaphone with several members. In the
pronunciation of some speakers of Received English the diphthong
begins at Cardinal Vowel No. 4 (**a**) and immediately proceeds in
the direction of **u**. With many others the diphthong begins at a
more retracted point as shown in Fig. 54,[11] or even further back
than this. Some, on the other hand, begin the diphthong at a
point slightly higher than **a**, i.e. at a more **æ**-like sound. When
the starting-point is near to **æ**, the pronunciation is dialectal;
æu is one of the London dialectal variants of **au**.

421. With each individual speaker **au** represents a phoneme
comprising one of the above-mentioned forms as the principal
member and at least one notable subsidiary member, namely the
variety used when ə follows (§ 430).

---

[11] This is my pronunciation.

422. Taking the variety of diphthong shown in Fig. 54 as the normal, we may describe as follows the formation of the vowel with which the diphthong begins:

 (i) *height of tongue*: low;

 (ii) *part of tongue raised*: the hinder part of the 'front';

 (iii) *position of lips*: neutral (Fig. 59);

 (iv) *opening between the jaws*: rather wide.

The tongue-tip is touching or nearly touching the lower front teeth, and, as in the case of all ordinary vowels, the soft palate is in its raised position and the vocal cords are in vibration. The nature of the diphthong is seen in Fig. 54, and by comparing Figs. 59 and 60.

Fig. 59. Lip-position of the beginning of my English diphthong **au**.

Fig. 60. Lip-position of the end of my English diphthong **au**.

423. To pronounce the English diphthong **au** correctly it is not necessary that **u** should actually be reached. The proper effect will be given as long as a considerable portion of the movement towards **u** is performed. In other words a diphthong of the type **ao** will suffice.

424. In the practical teaching of English pronunciation to foreign people the most suitable variety of **au** to learn depends to some extent on the nationality of the learner. Thus, if the learner is French, it is well to teach an **au** with a somewhat retracted **a**, for the reason given in § 425. If the learner is German, the variety beginning with Cardinal **a** should be taught (see § 427).

425. French people generally make the beginning of **au** too near to **æ**.[12] They may improve the sound by starting from the French **a** (the sound of *â* as in *pâte*). This may or may not give

 [12] This is a good example of a case where in practice the results are not what one would expect from theoretical considerations, since ordinary French contains **a** but no **æ**.

the correct pronunciation; it depends on the variety of ɑ used by the French speaker. If his ɑ is too retracted to produce a diphthong near enough to the English au, he must aim at a diphthong intermediate between ɑu and æu, using the method described in §§ 110–114.

426. French learners sometimes extend the movement of the diphthong as far as a very close u. To correct this they should aim at pronouncing ao.

427. Many foreign people, and especially Germans, mispronounce the English au by using a diphthong which begins at or near Cardinal Vowel No. 5 (ɑ). In other words, the initial element of their diphthong is too retracted. To correct this they should aim at making a sound intermediate between ɑu and æu, after the manner indicated in §§ 110–114.

428. Many Germans also extend the movement of the diphthong as far as a close u. Other Germans, on the other hand, do not make sufficient movement in the diphthong and pronounce aɔ. The diphthong, as I pronounce it, lies between these two extremes. Germans may learn an adequate variety of the English diphthong best by pronouncing in sequence an advanced a and English short u.[13]

429. Words for practice: *pound* paund, *bough, bow* (bend the body) bau,[14] *town* taun, *doubt* daut, *cow* kau, *gown* gaun, *mouth* mauθ, *now* nau, *loud* laud, *row* (noise) rau,[15] *wound* (past tense of the verb *wind* waind) waund,[16] *fowl, foul* faul, *vow* vau, *thousand* 'θauznd, *thou* ðau, *sow* (pig) sau,[17] *resound* ri'zaund, *shout* ʃaut, *how* hau.

430. In the so-called triphthong[18] auə the tongue never reaches the u position. aoə or aɔə more nearly represents the pronunciation usually heard. The levelling is often carried so far that a diphthong of the type aə results. This diphthong is distinguished,

---

[13] Not a and o, on account of the full back position of German o.

[14] But a *bow* for shooting, etc., is bou.

[15] But a *row* of houses, etc., is rou, as also is the verb meaning to propel a boat with oars, and the corresponding noun.

[16] But the verb *to wound* and the noun *wound* are wuːnd.

[17] But the verb *to sow* is sou.

[18] It is not a real triphthong, but a sequence of two syllables (see Chap. XII, and especially §§ 232, 233).

in the pronunciation of many English people, from the other variety of **aə** which replaces **aiə** (§ 414). To show this distinction in writing we may write the reduced **auə** as **a̱ə**, putting under the **a** the mark ̱ denoting retraction. Thus *power* which would usually be transcribed **ˈpauə** is often pronounced **ˈpa̱oə** or **ˈpa̱ɔə** or **pa̱ə**. The levelling is sometimes carried so far that the triphthong becomes reduced to a single long **a̱ː**. Thus *power* may often be heard as **pa̱ː**. This levelling of the triphthong is especially frequent when a consonant follows, as in *powerful* (transcribed **ˈpauəfl**, but usually pronounced **ˈpaoəfl** or **ˈpa̱əfl** or **ˈpa̱ːfl**), *our own* (transcribed **auər ˈoun**, but usually pronounced **aoər ˈoun** or **a̱ər ˈoun** or **a̱ːr ˈoun**).

431. The differences between **a** and **a̱** and the English **ɑ** are so slight that many English people are unable either to distinguish by ear or to make the intermediate **a̱**; either they replace it by **ɑ** or they make the reduced forms of **aiə** and **auə** identical (saying them with a variety of **a**). But with those who do distinguish, and make the three vowels, the sounds belong to separate phonemes; in my pronunciation **ˈtaːriŋ** with the fully front **a** is the reduced form of *tiring* **ˈtaiəriŋ**, **ˈta̱ːriŋ** with a retracted **a̱** is the reduced form of *towering* **ˈtauəriŋ**, and both these words are distinct from *tarring* **ˈtɑːriŋ**.

432. Further examples of the retracted **a** are: *dowry* **ˈdauəri**, **ˈda̱əri** or **ˈda̱ːri** (distinct from **ˈdaːri**, the reduced form of *diary* **ˈdaiəri**), *Gower Street* **ˈgauə striːt**, **ˈga̱ə striːt**, or **ˈga̱ː striːt**, *now-a-days* **ˈnauədeiz**, **ˈna̱ədeiz**, or **ˈna̱ːdeiz**, *flowerpot* **ˈflauəpɔt**, **ˈfla̱əpɔt** or **ˈfla̱ːpɔt**, *devouring* **diˈvauəriŋ**, **diˈva̱əriŋ** or **diˈva̱ːriŋ**.

433. It is not necessary for foreign students to learn to make the distinction between **aə** and **a̱ə**.

434. Some words which may be said with **auə** have alternative pronunciations with a very definite disyllabic **au-ə**. This way of pronouncing is usual when the **ə** is a suffix or belongs to a suffix, as in *plougher* **ˈplau-ə**, *allowable* **əˈlau-əbl**, *allowance* **əˈlau-əns**. The same pronunciation may also be heard in a few other words usually transcribed with **auə**, e.g. *coward* **ˈkau-əd** and the surname *Cowan* **ˈkau-ən**. These words may be said with ordinary **auə**, but they do not as a rule have **a̱ə** and **a̱ː** as alternatives.

435. There is another special case in which the reduction of **auə** to **a̱ə** or **a̱ː** does not take place, namely when the triphthong is followed

by the 'dark' l, as in *towel* 'tauəl, *vowels* 'vauəlz. The tendency
here is to drop the ə and pronounce taul, vaulz. A word such
as *towel* is never pronounced tạːl, since the l in words where u
precedes is rather 'dark' even when the next word in the sentence
begins with a vowel. For instance, English people may often be
heard to pronounce such an expression as *the towel isn't in its place*
as ðə 'taul 'iznt in its 'pleis. (Compare the case of words ending
-aiəl, where the form -aːl may be heard when the following word
begins with a vowel, § 416.)

English Diphthong No. 17: ɔi

436. The English diphthong written phonetically ɔi is the
regular sound of *oi* and *oy*. Examples: *oil* ɔil, *noise* nɔiz, *boy* bɔi,
employs im'plɔiz, *employer* im'plɔiə, *royal* 'rɔiəl or rɔil.

437. The chief member of the ɔi-phoneme is a diphthong
beginning about half-way between the English Vowels Nos. 6
and 7 (ɔ and ɔː) and terminating near to i (see Fig. 54). The
phoneme has subsidiary members, but they do not differ greatly
from the chief member. Thus there certainly is a slight difference
between the diphthong in *choice* tʃɔis and that in *oil* ɔil; in *choice*
the movement of the diphthong is continued nearly as far as the
position of the English short i, while in ɔil the movement does
not reach such a high position. In *employer*, too, i is not reached;
the actual pronunciation might be written im'plɔeə.[19] The so-
called 'triphthong' ɔiə is, however, never reduced to the same
extent as aiə and auə.

438. Foreign learners may ignore the differences mentioned in
the last paragraph, and may learn the diphthong with sufficient
exactitude by starting with the quality of the English long ɔː
(No. 7) and proceeding immediately to i (No. 2). The diphthong does
not as a rule present any difficulty to them. Some Dutch people
and Germans are apt to finish the diphthong with rounded lips[20];

---

[19] It is not written so in ordinary transcriptions, since it is, as a rule, more
convenient in practice to adhere to the principle of admitting only one way
of representing each phoneme. Note that the ɔiə of *employer* is distinct
from the sequence ɔːjə heard in one pronunciation of *lawyer* 'lɔːjə. (Some
English people pronounce the word as 'lɔiə.)

[20] The terminal sound is then the vowel in the German *Hütte* 'hytə,
hübsch hypʃ.

it is easy to correct this as soon as the learner realizes that the
English diphthong ends with the lips *spread*; if necessary, he must
practise the exercise ɔiɔiɔi . . . with energetic motion of the lips.

439. Words for practice: *point* pɔint, *boy* bɔi, *toy* tɔi, *Doyle*
dɔil, *coin* kɔin, *choice* tʃɔis, *joint* dʒɔint, *noise* nɔiz, *loyal* 'lɔiəl,
royal 'rɔiəl, *foil* fɔil, *voice* vɔis, *soil* sɔil, *hoist* hɔist.

English Diphthong No. 18: iə

440. iə is a 'falling' diphthong (§ 223) which starts at about the
position of the English short i and terminates at about ə₃ (§ 361).
Its formation is shown in Fig. 61.   This diphthong-phoneme may

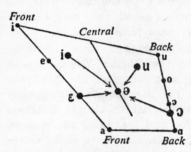

be regarded as consisting of a
single member; there are no
phonemic variants differing to
any marked extent from the
above value.   The slight modification mentioned in § 383 is
negligible from the point of view
of the foreign learner of English.

Fig. 61. Diagram showing the
nature of the English 'centring'
diphthongs, iə, ɛə, ɔə, uə.

440a. The 'falling' character
of iə is effected by the use of
'diminuendo stress.' This means
that the beginning part of the
diphthong is uttered with stronger
stress than the end part. This stress is felt subjectively by the
speaker; it is not always apparent objectively to the hearer on
account of the greater inherent sonority (carrying power) of ə as
compared with i (§§ 100, 101).

441. There exist diaphonic variants of iə; that is to say, there
are English speakers who use a somewhat different diphthong.
The most notable of these variants is one (already noted in § 384) in
which the movement of the diphthong proceeds to a point distinctly
lower than ə₃; this form of diphthong may be represented by iʌ. A
less common variant begins nearer to long iː than to short i; it is
heard from those whose pronunciation has been influenced by some
dialect (generally Northern, but also London and Australian).

442. iə is the usual sound of *eer*; examples: *deer* diə, *peering*
'piəriŋ, *steerage* 'stiəridʒ. *Ear, ere, eir, ier, ea, ia* also have the

sound iə in some words; examples: *ear* iə, *beard* biəd, *here* hiə, *weird* wiəd, *pierce* piəs, *fierce* fiəs, *idea* ai'diə, *Ian* iən.

442a. Some of these words have alternative pronunciations with jəː. For instance, some English people pronounce *here* and *fierce* as hjəː, fjəːs. This does not apply as a rule to words spelt without *r*, such as *idea*, *Ian*, nor to words in which the iə is preceded by r or w, such as *career* kə'riə, *queer* kwiə. But there are some exceptions, e.g. *theatre* 'θiətə or 'θjəːtə. See *Falling and Rising Diphthongs in Southern English* in *Miscellanea Phonetica* II.

443. Foreign learners are recommended to ignore the variants mentioned in §§ 441, 442a and to use always the diphthong described in § 440. It is easily learnt by treating it in the first instance as a succession of the two sounds i and əₐ.

444. Their most usual fault is to begin the diphthong with long tense iː instead of with lax i, besides which they often finish the diphthong with some variety of r-sound. It is very common to hear foreign people pronouncing *here* as hiːər or hiːʀ instead of hiə. Even if they are able to make lax i, they are generally not aware that this is the sound to use at the beginning of this diphthong, if they wish to acquire normal Southern English pronunciation. It is quite easy for the foreign learner to correct the above mispronunciations as soon as he has learnt to make lax i and əₐ correctly.

445. Further words for practice: *pier* piə, *beer* biə, *tier*, *tear* (of the eyes) tiə,[21] *dear* diə, *Keir* kiə, *gear* giə, *cheer* tʃiə, *jeer* dʒiə, *mere* miə, *near* niə, *leer* liə, *real* riəl, *fear* fiə, *veer* viə, *theatre* 'θiətə, *seer* siə, *sheer*, *shear* ʃiə, *here*, *hear* hiə, *year* jiə,[22] *weir*, *we're*[23] wiə, *weary* 'wiəri.

English Diphthong No. 19: ɛə

446. ɛə, as I pronounce it, is a diphthong which starts about half-way between the English Vowels Nos. 3 and 4 (e and æ) and terminates at about əₐ (§ 361). The formation is shown in Fig. 61.

---

[21] *Tear* (verb) is tɛə, as also is the corresponding noun meaning a rent.
[22] Also very commonly pronounced jəː. This is my pronunciation.
[23] The usual conversational form of *we are*.

447. It will be noticed that the starting-point of the diphthong εə is about Cardinal ε. The mode of forming this initial part may therefore be summarized as follows:

Fig. 62. Lip-position of the beginning of my English diphthong εə.

(i) *height of tongue*: half-open;

(ii) *part of tongue raised*: the front;

(iii) *position of lips*: spread to neutral (Fig. 62);

(iv) *opening between the jaws*: rather wide.

The tip of the tongue is touching or nearly touching the lower front teeth, and, as in the case of all normal vowels, the soft palate is in its raised position and the vocal cords are in vibration.

448. The phoneme εə may be regarded as consisting of a single member; there are no phonemic variants differing to any marked extent from the above value.

449. There exist diaphonic variants among speakers of Received English. The most noteworthy is æə, which is by no means uncommon. On the other hand there are some English people who begin the diphthong with a sound nearer to English e (English Vowel No. 3) than to æ. Variations in the termination of the diphthong may also be observed. Thus many speakers finish the diphthong at a point lower than ə₃; this pronunciation may be represented by the notation εʌ.

450. εə is the regular sound of the group of letters *air*; examples: *pair* pεə, *fair* fεə, *cairn* kεən. It is also the sound of *ear* and *are* in many words; examples: *bear* bεə, *spare* spεə. Note the exceptional words *there* and *their* which are both pronounced ðεə,[24] *scarce* skεəs and *aeroplane* 'εərəplein.

451. The manner of teaching εə to foreign students depends considerably on their nationality. Most foreigners make the mistake of sounding some kind of r at the end of it. This must not be done if they aim at pronouncing like normal Southern English people. When this fault has been corrected, others generally remain. French learners usually begin the diphthong

---

[24] *There* has also a weak form ðə (ðər before vowels). *Their* before vowels has occasionally a weak form ðər.

correctly but mispronounce the termination by rounding their lips; and if they have been taught to keep the lips spread at the end of the diphthong, the final sound is often still incorrect owing to the tongue being in too high a position.

452. Mispronunciations of a similar kind are often to be observed with people of other foreign countries—sometimes in cases where theory would lead us not to expect them, e.g. with some Germans. In such cases the pronunciation can generally be greatly improved if the learner will *increase the distance between the jaws as the diphthong proceeds*; in other words, if he will take care that the jaws shall be wider apart at the end of the diphthong than they are at the beginning. To pronounce like this often requires considerable practice on the part of the learner.[25]

453. Another mispronunciation frequently heard from Germans is to begin the diphthong with a very close e; this e is often lengthened by them, giving a pronunciation eːə. The best way of correcting this is to teach the variant pronunciation æə; to do this he should practise saying æ (English Vowel No. 4) with ə₃ or ʌ immediately after it.

454. Words for practice: *air* ɛə, *pair, pear* pɛə, *bear* bɛə, *tear* (verb) tɛə, *dare* dɛə, *care* kɛə, *chair* tʃɛə, *fair* fɛə, *vary* ˈvɛəri, *there* ðɛə, *Sarah* ˈsɛərə, *share* ʃɛə, *hare, hair* hɛə, *wear* wɛə.

English Diphthong No. 20: ɔə

455. The diphthong ɔə starts very near to English Vowel No. 7 (ɔː) and proceeds in the direction of ə₃ as shown in Fig. 61. The lip-rounding of the initial part is less close than for ɔː (No. 7). With many speakers the movement of the diphthong does not reach as far as ə₃; this is especially the case when a voiceless consonant follows, as in *coarse, course* kɔəs.

456. The initial part of the diphthong may be described shortly as follows:

   (i) *height of tongue*: somewhat below half-open;

   (ii) *part of tongue raised*: the back;

---

[25] Here is another case in which practical experience gives a method which on theoretical grounds one would not expect to be effective. English speakers do not as a rule separate the jaws in this manner in pronouncing ɛə or even in pronouncing the variant ɛʌ.

(iii) *position of lips*: open lip-rounding;

(iv) *distance between jaws*: medium to wide.

The tip of the tongue is generally, though not necessarily, somewhat retracted from the lower teeth. As in the case of all normal vowels, the soft palate is in its raised position and the vocal cords are in vibration.

457. The diphthong ɔə may be heard in the pronunciation of many speakers in words written with *oar*, *ore*, and in some words written with *our*. Examples: *coarse* kɔəs, *score* skɔə, *four* fɔə, *course* kɔəs. It may also be heard in the words *door* dɔə and *floor* flɔə.

458. It must be noticed on the other hand that many speakers of Received English, myself among them, do not use the diphthong ɔə at all, but replace it always by ɔː (English Vowel No. 7); we pronounce the above words kɔːs, skɔː, fɔː, kɔːs, dɔː, flɔː. Those who wish to learn to make the sound ɔə may make a sufficiently near approximation to it by pronouncing Vowel No. 7 (ɔː) followed by ə₃.

459. Further examples of ɔə: *pour*, *pore* pɔə or pɔː,[26] *boar*, *bore* bɔə or bɔː, *tore* tɔə or tɔː,[27] *core* kɔə or kɔː,[28] *more* mɔə or mɔː, *Nore* nɔə or nɔː,[29] *lore* lɔə or lɔː,[30] *roar* rɔə or rɔː,[31] *fore* fɔə or fɔː,[32] *soar*, *sore* sɔə or sɔː,[33] *Azores* ə'zɔəz or ə'zɔːz, *shore* ʃɔə or ʃɔː,[34] *your* jɔə or jɔː,[35] *wore* wɔə or wɔː.[36]

English Diphthong No. 21: uə

460. uə is a diphthong which starts at u (English Vowel No. 8) and terminates at a sound of the ə-type. The formation of its usual value is shown in Fig. 61. It is a 'falling' diphthong, its

---

[26] pɔː is also the pronunciation of *paw*.

[27] tɔː is also the pronunciation of *tor*.

[28] kɔː is also the pronunciation of *caw*.

[29] nɔː is also the pronunciation of *nor* and *gnaw*.

[30] lɔː is also the pronunciation of *law*.

[31] rɔː is also the pronunciation of *raw*.

[32] fɔː is also the strong form of *for*.

[33] sɔː is also the pronunciation of *saw*.

[34] ʃɔː is also the pronunciation of *Shaw*; ʃɔə and ʃɔː are also pronunciations of *sure* (§ 463).

[35] Also pronounced juə and joə.

[36] wɔː is also the pronunciation of *war*.

falling character being effected by means of 'diminuendo stress.'
This means that the beginning part of the diphthong is uttered
with stronger stress than the end part. This stress is felt subjectively by the speaker; it is not always apparent objectively to
the hearer on account of the greater sonority (carrying power) of
ə as compared with u (§§ 100, 101).

461. A diphthong of the type uə is used in two categories of
words, which we may call (a) and (b). Category (a) comprises most
words written with *ure*[37] and *oor* and their derivatives; examples:
sure ʃuə, *cure* kjuə, *endure* in'djuə, *poor* puə, *moor* muə, *surely* 'ʃuəli,
cured kjuəd, *poorer* 'puərə. It also comprises many words spelt
with *ur* followed by a vowel; examples: *curious* 'kjuərĭəs, *duration*
djuə'reiʃn, *security* si'kjuəriti. It comprises further some words
spelt with *our*, such as *tour* tuə, *gourd* guəd and *bourse* buəs and
French names like *Lourdes* luəd, when pronounced in English
fashion.

461a. Category (b) comprises words spelt with *ua*, *ue* or *ewe*
followed by a consonant letter, the syllable being stressed. Such
are *truant* truənt, *fluency* 'fluənsi, *jewel* dʒuəl. They all have
variant pronunciations with uːə, e.g. 'truːənt, 'fluːənsi. The
diphthong uə occurs too as a variant of uːə when the termination
-er is added to words ending in *-uː*, as in *doer* duə or 'duːə, *fewer*
fjuə or 'fjuːə, which are formed from *do* duː, *few* fjuː.

462. The words of category (a) do not have variant pronunciations with uːə, but they nearly all have variants with a diphthong
oə. Thus *sure*, *curious*, *tour* are pronounced by some as ʃoə,
'kjoərĭəs, toə.

463. Many of the words of category (a), and especially the
commoner ones, also have alternative pronunciations with ɔə or
ɔː. For instance, a great many Southern English people pro-
nounce *poor*, *sure*, *cure*, *pure*, *endure*, *curious*, *secure* as pɔə, ʃɔə,
kjɔə, pjɔə, etc., or pɔː (like *paw*), ʃɔː (like *Shaw*), kjɔː, pjɔː, etc.
Less common words, such as *tour*, *tourist*, *moor*, are generally
said with uə or oə (tuə or toə, 'tuərist or 'toərist, muə or moə);
the forms tɔə, 'tɔərist, mɔə and tɔː, 'tɔːrist, mɔː also exist, but
are not so frequent as the ɔə and ɔː variants of the commoner

---

[37] Except when unstressed, as in *furniture* 'fəːnitʃə.

words *poor*, *sure*, etc. The same applies to *steward*, which may be heard as **stjɔəd** and **stjɔːd** as well as **stjuəd** and **stjɔəd**. Rarer words such as *gourd* and *bourse* are pronounced with **uə** or **oə**; I do not recall ever hearing these words said with **ɔə** or **ɔː**. The proper names *Stewart* and *Stuart* are generally pronounced **stjuət** or **stjoət**.[38]

464. The forms with **uə** are generally taught as being the most 'correct' for words of category (*a*), and on the whole they seem to be the best for foreign pupils to learn. It is, however, necessary that foreign learners should know of the existence of the forms with **oə, ɔə** and **ɔː**, since they are used by large numbers of people whose speech must be regarded as Received English.[39]

465. The most common mispronunciation of **uə** by foreign people is to begin it with an **uː** (similar to English Vowel No. 9) instead of with lax **u**. They often also add a **r**-sound at the end of the diphthong when there is an *r* in the spelling. Thus it is very common to hear foreign people pronounce *poor* as **puːər** or **puːʀ** instead of **puə**. This should not be done, if they wish to speak with normal Southern pronunciation. It is quite easy for the foreign learner to correct such errors as soon as he has learnt to make **u** (English Vowel No. 8). All he has to do is to pronounce this **u** with **ə₃** immediately after it.

466. The following are some words for practice; those marked * have variants with **oə, ɔə** and **ɔː**, those marked ‡ appear to have variants with **oə** only, those marked † have variants with **uːə**; *poor* **puə,** * *boor* **buə,** * *tour* **tuə,** * *doer* **duə,** † *gourd* **guəd,** ‡ *jewel* **dʒuəl,** † *adjure* **ə'dʒuə,** ‡ *moor* **muə,** * *bluer* **bluə,** † *truer* **truə,** † *sure* **ʃuə,** * *your* **juə** * (less common than **jɔə** and **jɔː**), *pure* **pjuə,** * *endure* **in'djuə,** * *cure* **kjuə,** * *skewer* **skjuə,** ‡ *Muir* **mjuə,** * *newer* **njuə,** † *lure* **ljuə** * or **luə,** ‡ *fewer* **fjuə,** † *sewer* (drain) **sjuə.** ‡

English Diphthong No. 22: ĭə

466a. Resembling the diphthong **iə** (No. 18) but yet differing from it in some respects is another sound which may be represented by the notation **ĭə**. It is heard in such words as *hideous* **'hidĭəs,**

---

[38] Rarely **stjɔət**, and apparently never **stjɔːt**.

[39] **ɔː** was used, for instance, by the late Prof. H. C. Wyld, and this pronunciation is recorded in his *Universal English Dictionary*.

glorious ˈglɔːrɪəs, *happier* ˈhæpɪə, *easier* ˈiːzɪə, *area* ˈɛərɪə, *aquarium* əˈkwɛərɪəm, *radius* ˈreidɪəs, *theoretical* θɪəˈretikl, *axiomatic* æksɪə- ˈmætik, *realistic* rɪəˈlistik (see § 466*i*), *archaeological* ɑːkɪəˈlɔdʒikl, *Neapolitan* nɪəˈpɔlitn, *Leonora* lɪəˈnɔːrə, *Cleopatra* klɪəˈpɑːtrə.

466*b*. ɪə (No. 22) is always unstressed. iə (No. 18) on the other hand is probably to be considered as always either fully or partially stressed; it is in its nature that it should be so (see § 440*a*).

466*c*. The exact nature of ɪə is difficult to establish. Many English people 'feel' it as a sequence of i and ə forming two syllables. They may even at times, especially in precise speaking, use a disyllabic sequence of i and ə in the words here written with ɪə. This way of pronouncing is shown in some dictionaries; it may be denoted phonetically by i-ə, thus ˈhidi-əs, ˈiːzi-ə, ˈɛəri-ə, θi-əˈretikl, etc.[40] To me, however, the sound generally heard in the words such as those in § 466*a* appears to be a 'rising' diphthong, i.e. a diphthong in which the end part has greater prominence than the beginning part (§ 223). I do not feel this prominence at the end to be attributable to *stress*. I find the whole diphthong to be pronounced evenly with weak stress, and that the latter part owes its prominence to the greater sonority (carrying power) of ə as compared with i.

466*d*. In spite of the absence of stress, ɪə taken as a whole has a noteworthy degree of *prominence* on account of its length. This prominence is liable to give the impression of 'secondary stress' (i.e. moderately strong force of utterance) to those who have difficulty in distinguishing prominence by stress from prominence due to other factors. This 'secondary stress' is probably less in degree than that attributable to iə (No. 18) in comparable situations. See next paragraph; also § 440*a* and Chap. XII.

---

[40] In verse the combination of i and ə in such words is sometimes disyllabic (i-ə), though much more often monosyllabic (ɪə or jə). In Shakespeare's verse, for instance, the terminations of such words as *audience, envious,* are always treated as monosyllabic except when they occur at the end of a line. Compare *Arise, fair sun, and kill the envious moon (Romeo and Juliet,* ii, 2, 4) and *Be not her maid, since she is envious (Romeo and Juliet,* ii, 2, 7). Occasionally the monosyllabic pronunciation is needed at the end of a line, as for instance the word *bounteous* in: *and you yourself Have of your audience been most free and bounteous (Hamlet,* i, 3, 93).

466e. The fact that iə (No. 18) probably always has a primary or a secondary stress in English, while ĭə (No. 22) is always unstressed, suggests that the distinction between the two may not be phonemic. There are, however, objections which render it difficult to establish this definitely. It may be said, in particular, that although iə (No. 18) by its nature must have a certain degree of stress (§ 440a), yet in such words as *reindeer* ˈreindiə, *nadir* ˈneidiə, *emir* ˈemiə, *sclerosis* skliəˈrousis, it has *the weakest degree of stress that it is capable of having*; some people might therefore feel that it should be considered as unstressed. Again, if it can be shown that the analysis of ĭə as a diphthong is of doubtful accuracy, its phonemic status must necessarily be obscure. On the other hand, allowance must be made for the fact that in some environments the difference between ĭə and a weakly stressed iə is difficult to perceive; this suggests that the two sounds are not likely to be phonemically different, since as a general rule distinctions between phonemically different sounds are very easy to hear in the same phonetic context. The whole question of the nature of the sounds iə, ĭə and i-ə and their phonemic status in English deserves further investigation.[41]

466f. ĭə has a certain resemblance to the sequence jə, but it is distinct from this. ĭə is a gradual glide, whereas jə begins with a sudden rapid glide. It is noteworthy that many, though not all, of the English words containing ĭə have alternative pronunciations with jə. For instance, some English people pronounce *hideous* as ˈhidjəs and *easier* as ˈiːzjə. Some even use jə after **w**, as in *colloquial* kəˈloukwjəl (more usually kəˈloukwĭəl). Words like *area*, in which ĭə is preceded by **r**, do not have a variant pronunciation with jə. Nor do some of the words in which ĭə immediately precedes a stress, e.g. *Neapolitan*.[42]

466g. Examples of weakly stressed iə (No. 18) are not common. They are found mainly in compound words, such as *reindeer* ˈreindiə, the verb *dog-ear* ˈdɔgiə, *lop-eared* ˈlɔpiəd, *Shakespeare*

---

[41] The subject is discussed at greater length in my article *Falling and Rising Diphthongs in Southern English* in *Miscellanea Phonetica* II, 1954, published by the I.P.A.

[42] *Pianissimo*, however, is often said with jə: pĭəˈnisimou or pjəˈnisimou (also pjææˈnisimou and piəˈnisimou).

'ʃeikspiə, *Ellesmere* 'elzmiə, *Bluebeard* 'bluːbiəd. There are, however, a few simple words (mostly of foreign origin) in which a weak
iə occurs. Such are *nadir, emir* and *sclerosis*, quoted in § 466e;
also *vizier* which is pronounced 'viziə or vi'ziə, and some proper
names such as *Angier* 'ændʒiə, *Gambier* 'gæmbiə.

466h. Sometimes the difference between iə and ĭə is accompanied
by a difference of 'juncture' of syllables or a difference in place
of syllable division. For instance, the distinction between *corn-ear*
(ear of corn) 'kɔːniə and *cornea* (of the eye) 'kɔːnĭə involves not
only the difference iə/ĭə but also a difference in the point of syllable
division: this point is after the n in *corn-ear* but in the middle of
the n in *cornea*. This in turn involves a slight difference in the
length of the ɔː-sounds in the two words, the ɔː in *corn-ear* being
somewhat longer than that in *cornea*. This does not mean that
the differences in juncture can always be held to account for the
difference between iə and ĭə, since cases occur where iə and ĭə are
differentiated in similar environments showing no differences of
juncture.

466i. Most words containing iə and ĭə have alternative pronunciations. Many of those containing strongly stressed iə have
variants with jəː, as already mentioned in § 442a. For instance,
clear is kliə or kljəː, *serious* is 'siəriəs or 'sjəːrĭəs.[43] There exists
a pronunciation (now old-fashioned) of *ear* as jəː (like *year*). Some
words with the weakly stressed iə have other types of variant:
thus *nadir* has a variant 'neidə, *emir* and *vizier* have variants
e'miə, vi'ziə. And, as already mentioned in § 466f, many words
containing ĭə have variants with jə. A few such words have
variants with iə; such are *frontier* 'frʌntĭə which is also pronounced
'frʌntiə and 'frʌntjə (also 'frɔntĭə, 'frɔntiə, 'frɔntjə) and *realistic*
which may be heard as rĭə'listik and riə'listik.

466j. It is probable that many English people do not distinguish
iə from ĭə at all, at any rate in quick speech. For this reason and
for the reason that with some the distinction between iə and ĭə is
probably not phonemic (§ 466e), the distinction between the two is

---

[43] *Fiat* (make of motor-car), the legal term *lien* and the proper name *Ian*
are exceptions. They are normally said with iə (fiət, liən, iən) and
occasionally with iːə ('fiːət, 'liːən, 'iːən), but never with jəː.

often ignored in phonetic transcriptions. I now think it on the whole preferable that the foreign learner should observe the distinction if he can.[43a]

466k. The following are some further words illustrating the use of ɪə: *heavier* 'hevɪə, *morphia* 'mɔːfɪə, *Victoria* vɪk'tɔːrɪə, *nuclear* 'njuːklɪə, *audience* 'ɔːdɪəns, *historian* hɪs'tɔːrɪən, *material* mə'tɪərɪəl, *variable* 'vɛərɪəbl, *Hilliard* 'hɪlɪəd, *requiem* 'rekwɪəm, *alienation* eɪlɪə'neɪʃn, *amiability* eɪmɪə'bɪlɪti, *theological* θɪə'lɔdʒɪkl, *ideological* aɪdɪə'lɔdʒɪkl, *rearrange* rɪə'reɪndʒ. Many of these words have alternative pronunciations with jə. *Rearrange* has an alternative pronunciation riːə'reɪndʒ.

466l. The following are some examples contrasting ɪə with weakly stressed iə: *reindeer* 'reɪndɪə, *windier* (more windy) 'wɪndɪə; *nadir* 'neɪdɪə, *shadier* 'ʃeɪdɪə, *Canadian* kə'neɪdɪən; *wheatear* (name of a bird) 'wiːtɪə, *meatier* (more meaty) and *meteor* 'miːtɪə; *vizier* 'vɪzɪə, *busier* 'bɪzɪə; *Gambier* (surname) 'gæmbɪə, *Gambia* 'gæmbɪə. The words *windier, meteor, Gambia, Canadian* have alternative pronunciations with jə; so do *shadier, meatier* and *busier*, though perhaps less commonly. The words ending in ɪə (No. 18) do not have alternatives with jə.

English Diphthong No. 23: ŭə

466m. Resembling the diphthong uə (No. 21) but yet differing from it in some respects is a sound which may be represented by the notation ŭə. It is heard in such words as *influence* 'ɪnflŭəns, *incongruous* ɪn'kɔŋgrŭəs, *arduous* 'ɑːdjŭəs, *vacuum* 'vækjŭəm, *valuer* 'væljŭə, *valuable* 'væljŭəbl, *arguer* 'ɑːgjŭə, *Papua* 'pæpjŭə, *usual* 'juːʒŭəl, *puerility* pjŭə'rɪlɪti, *Juanita* dʒŭə'niːtə,[44] *fluorescent* flŭə'resnt.

466n. ŭə (No. 23) is always unstressed. uə (No. 21) on the other hand is probably to be considered as always either fully or partially stressed; it is in its nature that it should be so (see § 460).

466o. As with ɪə, the nature of ŭə is difficult to establish with precision. Some English people 'feel' it as a sequence of u and ə forming two syllables, and may even pronounce a disyllabic u-ə

[43a] A short investigation of the status of iə and ɪə has been published by B. S. ANDRÉSEN in *Le Maître Phonetique*, July, 1957, pp. 35-37.

[44] Also pronounced wə'niːtə. (I have heard of three Englishwomen with this name who pronounce it thus.)

in precise speaking: thus 'ınflu-əns, 'ɑːdju-əs, pju-ə'rıliti. This
kind of pronunciation is indicated in some dictionaries. Personally,
I regard the ŭə of my pronunciation as a 'rising' diphthong (§ 223).
The ə-element is more prominent (§ 223) than the u-element on
account of the greater sonority (carrying power) of ə as compared
with u, and not on account of any increase in stress.[45]

466p. In spite of the absence of stress of ŭə as used in English,
the sound taken as a whole has a considerable degree of *prominence*
by reason of its length. This prominence may give the impression
of 'secondary stress' to those who have difficulty in distinguishing
stress-prominence from prominence caused by other factors. See
Chap. XII.

466q. The fact that uə (No. 21) probably always has a primary
or a secondary stress, while ŭə (No. 23) is always unstressed,
suggests that the distinction between them may not be phonemic,
though objections similar to those adduced in the case of iə and ĭə
(§ 466e) render it difficult to prove this as a fact. In particular,
although uə (No. 21) cannot be unstressed in the ordinary sense
of the term (§ 460), it may nevertheless sometimes have the minimum
stress that it is capable of having; and it is a question whether
this degree of stress should not count as complete lack of stress.
Likewise if there is any doubt concerning the correctness of analysing
ŭə as a diphthong, its phonemic status must necessarily be obscure.
On the other hand, in some phonetic contexts uə and ŭə are difficult
to distinguish, and this fact supplies evidence in favour of treating
them as members of a single phoneme, since as a rule phonemic
differences are easily heard in one particular context. The available
evidence leads me to think that the distinction between uə and
ŭə is phonemic with some English people, though not with others.
(The analysis is rendered difficult by the fact that words containing
weakly stressed uə are few in number and for the most part uncommon and subject to variant pronunciations. The case is,

---

[45] In verse the combination of u and ə in such words as those quoted in
§ 466m sometimes counts as two syllables, but more often as one. In Shake-
speare it counts as a single syllable except at the end of a line. Compare:
Valiant and virtuous, full of haughty courage (1 *King Henry VI*, iv, 1, 35).
The flinty ribs of this contemptuous city (*King John*, ii, 1, 384).
O, he was gentle, mild and virtuous (*King Richard III*, i, 2, 104).
Call'd Katharina fair and virtuous (*Taming of the Shrew*, ii, 1, 43).

however, illustrated by such words as *tenure* 'tenjuə, *contour* 'kɔntuə, *penury* 'penjuəri, *manicure* 'mænikjuə, *bureaucracy* bjuə'rɔkrəsi, *neurologist* njuə'rɔlədʒist, and the names *Amoore* 'eimuə and *Tweedsmuir* 'twi:dzmjuə, when pronounced as shown here.)

466*r*. ŭə has a certain resemblance to the sequence wə, though it is distinct from it. ŭə is a gradual glide, whereas wə begins with a sudden rapid glide. It is to be observed that some words normally said with ŭə have alternative pronunciations with wə. For instance, the name *Joshua* is pronounced 'dʒɔʃwə at least as frequently as 'dʒɔʃŭə, and some English people pronounce *influence* as 'inflwəns and *usual* as 'ju:ʒwəl. A preceding r does not preclude the use of the variant wə; for instance, *incongruous* may be pronounced in'kɔŋgrwəs. The variant wə may even be heard occasionally after j, e.g. 'ɑ:djwəs for the more usual 'ɑ:djŭəs.

466*s*. Most words containing uə and ŭə have alternative pronunciations of one sort or another. The words of category (*a*) containing uə (§ 461) generally have variants with oə or ɔə or ɔ:; this applies not only to stressed syllables as shown in §§ 462–464, but also to such words as *manicure, bureaucracy*. Most words containing ŭə followed by a consonant have other types of variant. Thus *valuable* and *vacuum* are often pronounced 'væljubl, 'vækjum, and *usual* has variants 'ju:ʒul and 'ju:ʒl as well as the form 'ju:ʒwəl mentioned in the last paragraph. A few (very few) of the words normally said with ŭə have variant pronunciations with u:ə, like the words of category (*b*) (§ 461*a*); for instance, *fluorescent* is pronounced flu:ə'resnt as well as flŭə'resnt.

466*t*. It is probable that many English people do not distinguish uə from ŭə at all, at any rate in quick utterance. For this reason, and for the reason that with some the distinction between uə and ŭə is probably not phonemic with many speakers (§§ 466*e*, 466*q*), the distinction between the two is often ignored in phonetic transcripts. My present view is that the foreign learner had better observe the distinction if he can.

466*u*. Examples showing clearly the contrast between uə and ŭə are not numerous. The distinction is, however, exemplified by *tenure* 'tenjuə and *valuer* 'væljŭə, *contour* 'kɔntuə and *Mantua* 'mæntjŭə or 'mæntŭə, *rest-cure* 'reskjuə (when pronounced without t) and *rescuer* 'reskjŭə.

English Diphthong No. 24: ŭi

466v. A rising diphthong **ŭi** is not uncommon. It is always unstressed, and it occurs in one pronunciation of such words as *valuing* **'væljŭiŋ**, *issuing* **'isjŭiŋ** or **'iʃŭiŋ**, *casuist* **'kæzjŭist**, *ruination* **rŭi'neiʃn**. It is always replaceable by the disyllabic sequence **u-i**, which is difficult to distinguish from it. It is distinguishable (subjectively at any rate) from the stressed diphthong **ui** referred to in § 327a, but to the hearer the distinction is hardly perceptible. For these reasons the diphthong **ŭi** may be ignored by the foreign learner; it is sufficient that he should use the disyllabic pronunciation, namely **u** followed by **i**.

466w. **ŭi** is often replaced by **uːi** when immediately preceding a stress. Thus **ruː'neiʃn** is an alternative to **rŭi'neiʃn** (*ruination*).

Other Diphthongs

466x. The following diphthongs occur in English in addition to those described above: **oi, ŏi, eə, ĕə, oə, ŏə**. **oi, eə** and **oə** are referred to in §§ 403, 392a, 403; examples of them are *going* **goiŋ**, *player* **pleə**, *slower* **sloə**. **ŏi, ŏə** are heard in such words as *yellowish* **'jelŏiʃ**, *follower* **'fɔlŏə**. **ĕə** is very uncommon; it may be heard in the rare word *forayer* (person who forays) **'fɔrĕə**. As already noted in § 378b, these diphthongs are all colloquial reductions of fuller forms, and are not necessary to an acceptable pronunciation of English. **oi** and **ŏi** are stressed and unstressed reductions of **oui**; **eə** and **ĕə** are stressed and unstressed reductions of **eiə**; and **oə** and **ŏə** are stressed and unstressed reductions of **ouə**. These full forms are quite commonly employed by English people, and are well suited for use by the foreign learner. Readers interested in the theory of all these diphthongs are referred for further particulars and examples to *Falling and Rising Diphthongs in Southern English* in *Miscellanea Phonetica* II (I.P.A.).

Chapter XVI

STRONG AND WEAK FORMS

467. One of the most striking features of English pronunciation is the phenomenon known as *gradation*. By gradation is meant the existence in many common English words of two or more pronunciations, a *strong form* and one or more *weak forms*. Weak forms occur only in unstressed positions; strong forms are used chiefly when the word is stressed, but they also occur in unstressed positions.

468. A weak form of a word is generally distinguished from a strong form either by a difference of vowel-sound, or by the absence of a sound (vowel or consonant), or by the difference in the length of a vowel.

469. When the forms differ in vowel quality, it is generally found that the weak form has ə where the strong form has some other vowel. Examples:

	strong form	weak form (or one of the weak forms)	illustration of weak form
the	ði:	ðə[1]	*the man* ðə ˈmæn
them	ðem	ðəm	*take them* ˈteik ðəm
at	æt	ət	*at once* ət ˈwʌns
are	ɑː	ə	*the boys are ready* ðə ˈbɔiz ə ˈredi
of	ɔv	əv	*out of date* ˈaut əv ˈdeit
for	fɔː	fə	*it's for me* it s fə ˈmiː
should	ʃud	ʃəd	*I should think so* ai ʃəd ˈθiŋk sou
do	duː	də	*nor do you* ˈnɔː də ˈjuː
but	bʌt	bət	*all but one* ˈɔːl bət ˈwʌn
Sir	səː	sə	*Sir James* sə ˈdʒeimz
a	ei	ə	*a house* ə ˈhaus
by	bai	bə	*sold by the pound* ˈsould bə ðə ˈpaund
there	ðɛə	ðə	*there's no time* ðə z ˈnou ˈtaim
and	ænd	ənd	*you and I* ˈjuː ənd ˈai

[1] The weak form used before consonants.

126

470. In a few cases the vowel of a weak form is **i**. Examples:

	strong form	weak form	illustration of weak form
the	ði:	ði[2]	*the order* ði 'ɔːdə
be	biː	bi	*I shan't be long* ai 'ʃɑːnt bi 'lɔŋ
been	biːn[3]	bin	*I've been out* ai v bin 'aut
me	miː	mi	*show me the way* 'ʃou mi ðə 'wei
she	ʃiː	ʃi	*she said so* ʃi 'sed sou
my	mai	mi[4]	*I must do my work* ai məs 'duː mi 'wəːk

471. Usage in regard to these weak forms with i varies considerably both with individuals and according to the situation of the word in the sentence. Many speakers pronounce ði: (with i: somewhat shortened[5]) instead of ði before vowels, pronouncing *the order, the end* as ði: 'ɔːdə, ði: 'end rather than ði 'ɔːdə, ði 'end; this is particularly common when the following vowel is i, as in *the ink* ði: 'iŋk. Some English people use bin as a strong form of *been*; others (apparently an increasing number) use the strong form bi:n in unstressed positions. Thus some would pronounce *I've been there* as ai v 'bin ðɛə instead of the more frequent ai v 'biːn ðɛə; others would pronounce *I've been out* as ai v biːn 'aut instead of ai v bin 'aut. *Be* is generally pronounced bi when unstressed, except in final position; examples: *you'll be late* juː l bi 'leit, *it ought to be finished* it 'ɔːt tə bi 'finiʃt, *Be sure to come* bi 'ʃuə tə 'kʌm, but *it ought to be* it 'ɔːt tə biː. It is also usual to pronounce biː instead of bi when the following word begins with i as in *I shall be in* ai ʃl biː 'in; ai ʃl bi 'in is also possible, but would, I think, be less frequent. *Be* often occurs in a position where it may be either unstressed or pronounced with secondary stress; in such cases the pronunciation with i: is possible even when the stress is too slight to mark in a phonetic transcript. Thus *he wants to be a teacher* may be pronounced either hiː 'wɔnts tə bi ə 'tiːtʃə or hiː 'wɔnts tə biː ə 'tiːtʃə. The most convenient rule for foreign learners is to use bi whenever the word is unstressed and not final.

---

[2] Only used before vowels.
[3] Pronounced bin by some.
[4] See § 473.
[5] See § 870.

472. The treatment of *me, he, she, we* is different from that of *be.* Weak forms with short lax **i** are fairly common in the case of *me* and *she*, but they are not regularly used like **bi**; the use of the strong forms **miː**, **ʃiː** (with vowel shortened owing to lack of stress) is also quite frequent in unstressed positions. Thus *show me the way* may be pronounced either **'ʃou mi ðə 'wei** or **'ʃou miː ðə 'wei**; *she said so*, though usually said with **ʃi**, may also be said with **ʃiː**, even when the word is quite unstressed. In the case of *he* and *we*, the strong forms **hiː**, **wiː** are commonly used in unstressed positions; weak forms **hi**, **wi** exist but are not often used. Thus the usual pronunciation of *he said so, we thought so* is **hiː 'sed sou, wiː 'θɔːt sou**. The most convenient rule for foreign learners is to pronounce unstressed *me, he, she, we* always with **iː**.

473. The use of a weak form (**mi**) for *my* is not by any means universal; many English people, always use **mai** in unstressed as well as in stressed positions.[6] On the stage in serious drama it is customary to use **mi** in all unstressed positions.[7]

474. The short lax **u** occurs in certain weak forms of *to, do, who* and *you*.

475. The principal weak forms of *to* are **tu** and **tə** (with **ə₁** or **ə₂**, see §§ 356, 358), and the general usage (which incidentally gives the most practical rule for foreign learners) is to pronounce **tu** before vowels and before **w** and finally, but **tə** (with **ə₁** or **ə₂**) before consonants other than **w**. Examples: *to eat* **tu 'iːt**, *close to us* **'klous tu əs** and **'klous tu 'ʌs**, *to win* **tu 'win**, *Where are you going to?* **'wɛər ə ju: 'gouiŋ tu**, *to give* **tə 'giv**, *going to London* **'gouiŋ tə 'lʌndən**.

476. It must be noted, however, that English people do not always observe this rule consistently. In the first place the unstressed *to* before a consonant is sometimes said with a vowel that

---

[6] Except in the special expressions *my lord*, which is generally pronounced **mi 'lɔːd**, and (at Eton College) *my tutor* **mi 'tjuːtə** and *my dame* **mi 'deim**. I do not use **mi** except in these and one or two other common expressions such as *never in my life* **'nevər in mi 'laif**.

[7] It is likewise customary on the stage in serious drama to give a weak form **min** to the unstressed *mine* which in older literature replaces *my* before words beginning with a vowel, thus *mine eyes* **min 'aiz**, *mine own* **min 'oun**.

is neither ə₁ nor u, but is a sound between them; with some speakers the sound is ə₂, but it is ə₂ used as separate phoneme and not an ə₂ dependent upon the adjacent sounds as described in § 358. This usage may be illustrated by the words *amend, the men, to mend.* Most English people would probably pronounce ə'mend, ðə 'men, tə 'mend, using ə₁ in all three cases; but some would distinguish tə 'mend from the other cases by using ə₂ in it. (With such speakers ə₂ is a separate phoneme and should be written with a special sign, say ə̣, in phonetic transcription.[8])

477. Again, in slow speaking tu may often be heard instead of tə as a weak form of *to* before consonants, but there is no consistent rule in regard to its use.

478. In ordinary talking, when *to* is unstressed and followed by a consonant, the vowel is extremely short and sometimes almost disappears altogether. It may sometimes be a help to the foreign learner if this special shortness is marked in transcriptions, thus 'gouiŋ tə̆ 'lʌndən, 'wel-tə̆-'du: (*well-to-do*). It seems possible that this extreme shortness may be distinctive, though I have not met with two sentences distinguished by it. Compare, however, *a later day* ə 'leitə 'dei with *from day to day* frəm 'dei tə̆ 'dei; the ə in the first example is distinctly longer than the ə̆ in the second.[9]

479. *Do* has a strong form du: (and occasionally du before another vowel) and weak forms du, də and d (d being a variant of də). The weak form du is used before vowels and before w; də is used before consonants, the variant d being commonly used before the word *you.* Examples: *nor do I* 'nɔ: du 'ai, *so do we* 'sou du 'wi:, *What do others think?* 'wɔt du 'ʌðəz θiŋk; *How do they do it?* 'hau də ðei 'du: it (or . . . 'du it), *Why do people go there?* 'wai də pi:pl 'gou ðɛə, *What do you want?* 'wɔt də ju: 'wɔnt (more commonly 'wɔt d ju: 'wɔnt).

480. As with *to*, the use of ə in the weak form of *do* before consonants is not invariable. The weak form də may be said with either ə₁ or ə₂, and sometimes a sound between ə and u may be heard. These shades of sound appear to be used by some

---

[8] The use of a dot under a vowel letter to indicate a closer variety of vowel was recommended by the International Phonetic Association in 1927 (see *Le Maître Phonétique*, April, 1927, p. 14).

[9] There is a further difference between these examples, namely that the ei preceding the t is shorter in ə 'leitə 'dei than in frəm 'dei tə̆ 'dei (see §§ 892, 893).

speakers without any apparent consistency. Foreign learners are recommended to use the following consistent rule: Pronounce unstressed *do* as **du** before vowels, **du** before **w**, **d** before the word *you*, and **də** before consonants in all other cases.

481. The strong form **du:** is used in final unstressed position. Example: *I do* (with emphasis on *I*) **'ai du:**.

482. *Who* has weak forms **u:, hu, u**, which may be used in place of **hu:** in unstressed position. The four forms are interchangeable, except that **u:, u** do not occur initially. See example on p. 135. Foreign learners are recommended to use always the strong form **hu:**, which can never be incorrect.

483. *You* has a weak form **ju** which may be used in place of **ju:** in unstressed position. Thus *I'll see you to-morrow* may be pronounced either **ai l 'si: ju: tə'mɔrou** or **ai l 'si: ju tə'mɔrou**.

484. The following are the chief words in which one of the weak forms differs from the strong form by the absence of a vowel: *am, an, and, can, do, for, from, had, has, have, is, ma'am, many, not, of, Saint, shall, should, some, than, the, them, till, us, will, would*. The forms will be found in the list in § 487, and illustrations of their use are given in § 488 (p. 133).

485. The following are the chief words in which weak forms lack a consonant which is present in the strong forms: *and, had, has, have, he, her, him, his, must, of, Saint, shall, them, who, will, would*. See §§ 487, 488.

486. The following are words of which the strong forms are frequently used in unstressed position (with some shortening of the vowel owing to the lack of stress): *be, been, do, he, her, me, or, she, we, who, you*. All these words also have weak forms with a different vowel, see §§ 471–483, 487, 488.

487. We now give a list of all the English words which have weak forms differing notably from the strong forms. Some people do not use weak forms of the words marked *.

	Strong Forms	Weak Forms
a	ei	ə
am	æm	əm, m
an	æn	ən, occasionally ṇ
and	ænd	ənd, nd, ən, ṇ

	Strong Forms	Weak Forms
are	ɑː (before vowels ɑːr)	ə (before vowels ər or sometimes r)
as	æz	əz
at	æt	ət
be	biː	bi (see § 471)
been	biːn, bin	bin (see § 471)
but	bʌt	bət
*by	bai	bə, bi
can (be able)	kæn	kən, rarely kn, kŋ
could	kud	kəd
do (auxiliary)	duː	du, də, d (see §§ 479, 480)
does (auxiliary)	dʌz	dəz
for	fɔː (before vowels fɔːr or fɔr)	fə (before vowels fər)
from	frɔm	frəm, frm
had (auxiliary)	hæd	həd, əd, d
has (auxiliary)	hæz	həz, əz, z, s
have (auxiliary)	hæv	həv, əv, v
he	hiː	iː, hi, i (see § 472)
her	həː (before vowels həːr)	əː, hə, ə₃ (before vowels əːr, hər, ər)[10]
him	him	im
his	hiz	iz
is	iz	z, s
ma'am	mæm	məm, m[11]
*many	'meni	məni, mni
me	miː	mi (see § 472)
must	mʌst	məst, məs
*my	mai	mi (see § 473)
*nor	nɔː (before vowels nɔːr)	nə (before vowels nər)
not	nɔt	nt, n
of	ɔv	əv, v, occasionally ə

---

[10] The forms without **h** are not used initially. Thus *her hair is brown* is pronounced **həː 'hɛə z 'braun**. For **ə₃** see example in § 488.

[11] Only used by servants addressing mistresses. When addressing members of the royal family, the full form **mæm** is used when unstressed.

	Strong Forms	Weak Forms
or	ɔː (before vowels ɔːr)	ə (before vowels ər)
per	pəː (before vowels pəːr)	pə (before vowels pər)
Saint	seint	sənt, sən, sint, sin, snt, sn
shall	ʃæl	ʃəl, ʃl, occasionally ʃ
she	ʃiː	ʃi (see § 472)
should	ʃud	ʃəd, ʃd
Sir	səː (before vowels səːr)	sə (before vowels sər)
*so	sou	so, sə
some[12]	sʌm[12]	səm, sm[12]
*such	sʌtʃ	sətʃ
than	ðæn	ðən, ðn
that (conj., relative pron.)[13]	ðæt	ðət
the	ðiː	ði, ðə, ð (see §§ 469–471, 492)
them	ðem	ðəm, ðm, very colloquially sometimes əm, m
there	ðɛə (before vowels ðɛər)	ðə (before vowels ðər, ðr)
till	til	tl (occasionally)
*time(s)	taim(z)	təm(z)
to	tuː	tu, tə (see §§ 475–478)
upon	əˈpɔn	əpɔn
us	ʌs	əs, s
was	wɔz	wəz
we	wiː	wi (see § 472)
were	wəː[14] (before vowels wəːr)[14]	wə (before vowels wər)
who	huː	uː, hu, u
will	wil	l, occasionally əl
would	wud	wəd, əd, d

---

[12] In reality sʌm and səm (sm) are different words. See p. 135, footnote 21.
[13] *That* (demonstrative pronoun) has no weak form.
[14] Less commonly wɛə (before vowels wɛər).

	Strong Forms	Weak Forms
you	juː	ju, very colloquially sometimes jə
your	jɔː (before vowels jɔːr)[15]	jə (before vowels jər)

488. The following are examples illustrating the use of important weak forms, to supplement those already given in preceding paragraphs.

am	*I'm coming* ai m 'kʌmiŋ
an	*an egg* ən 'eg, *I have got an egg* ai v gɔt ən 'eg or ai v gɔt n̩ 'eg
and	*three and eight* 'θriː ənd 'eit, *two and six* 'tuː ən 'siks, *for good and all* fə 'gud nd 'ɔːl, *bread and butter* 'bred n 'bʌtə, *cut and dried* 'kʌt n 'draid
are	*the boys are here* ðə 'bɔiz ə 'hiə, *the boys are over there* ðə 'bɔiz ər ouvə 'ðɛə, *the shops are all shut* ðə 'ʃɔps r 'ɔːl 'ʃʌt
as	*it is as well* it s əz 'wel
at	*at home* ət 'houm, *look at that* 'luk ət 'ðæt
but	*tired but successful* 'taiəd bət sək'sesfl
can	*George can stay* 'dʒɔːdʒ kən 'stei, *we can do it* wiː kn 'duː it, *we can get it* wiː kŋ 'get it
could	*he could have told me* hiː kəd əv 'tould miː
does	*What does it matter?* 'wɔt dəz it 'mætə
for	*I did it for fun* ai 'did it fə 'fʌn, *out for a walk* 'aut fər ə 'wɔːk or 'aut fr ə 'wɔːk
from	*a long way from London* ə 'lɔŋ 'wei fr(ə)m 'lʌndən
had	*the train had gone* ðə 'trein əd 'gɔn, *before we had finished* bi'fɔː wiː d 'finiʃt, *I had got to* ai d 'gɔt tu
has	*George has come* 'dʒɔːdʒ əz kʌm, *he has come to-day* hiː z 'kʌm tə'dei, *the fire has gone out* ðə 'faiə z gɔn 'aut, *it has been very good* it s bin 'veri 'gud, *the book has disappeared* ðə 'buk əz disə'piəd or ðə 'buk s disə'piəd

---

[15] Also jɔə (before vowels jɔər). Also less commonly juə or joə (before vowels juər or joər).

have	*What have you done?* 'wɔt əv ju: 'dʌn, *I have bought a book* ai v 'bɔ:t ə 'buk
her	*she had her hat in her hand* ʃi: 'hæd ə: 'hæt in ə: 'hænd,[16] *he paid her what he owed her* hi: 'peid ə: wɔt i: 'oud ə,[17] *take her out* 'teik ər 'aut or 'teik ə:r 'aut, *give her her hat* 'giv ər ə: 'hæt[18]
him, his	*Give him his coat* 'giv im iz 'kout
is	*he's never there* hi: z 'nevə 'ðɛə, *Alfred is not well* 'ælfrid z 'nɔt 'wel, *it's all right* it s 'ɔ:l 'rait
*many	*How many more?* 'hau məni 'mɔ: or 'hau mni 'mɔ:
must	*I must go now* ai məs 'gou 'nau
*nor	*neither he nor I know anything about it* naiðə 'hi: nər 'ai nou 'eniθiŋ ə'baut it
not	*are not* ɑ: nt, *does not* 'dʌz nt, *it does not matter* it 'dʌz n 'mætə, *he used not to* hi: 'ju:s nt tu[19]
of	*cup of tea* ə 'kʌp əv 'ti: (very colloquially ə 'kʌp ə 'ti:), *first of all* 'fə:st əv 'ɔ:l or 'fə:st v 'ɔ:l
or	*two or three more* 'tu ə θri: 'mɔ:, *one or two others* 'wʌn ə tu: 'ʌðəz, *or else* ər 'els
per	*five per cent per annum* 'faiv pə 'sent pər 'ænəm
Saint	*St. Alban* snt 'ɔ:lbən or sənt 'ɔ:lbən or sint 'ɔ:lbən, *St. Paul's* sn 'pɔ:lz or sənt 'pɔ:lz or sint 'pɔ:lz, *St. John's Wood* sn 'dʒɔnz 'wud
shall	*Shall I come with you?* ʃəl 'ai kʌm 'wið ju:,[20] *Where shall we go?* 'wɛə ʃl wi 'gou or 'wɛə ʃ wi 'gou
should	*I should have thought so* ai ʃəd əv 'θɔ:t sou or ai ʃd əv 'θɔ:t sou
sir	*Yes, sir* 'jes sə (with ə₃), *Sir John* sə 'dʒɔn (with ə₁), *Sir Edward* sər 'edwəd (with ə₁)

---

[16] *Her* can hardly be reduced to ə in this case. If ə were used, the sentence would sound like *she had a hat in a hand.*

[17] In final position *owed her* is pronounced like *odour* (with ə₃). The *her* in *paid her* would also be pronounced with ə₃ if it were in final position.

[18] Not 'giv ər ə 'hæt which would mean *Give her a hat.*

[19] Also pronounced hi: 'ju:st nɔt tu.

[20] Also pronounced 'ʃæl ai kʌm 'wið ju: (or . . . 'wið ju).

some	*some paper* səm ˈpeipə or sm ˈpeipə[21]
*such	*I never heard of such a thing* ai nevə ˈhəːd əv sətʃ ə θiŋ
than	*more than that* ˈmɔː ðən ˈðæt or ˈmɔː ðn ˈðæt
that (conj., rel. pron.)	*I found that I was wrong* ai ˈfaund ðət ai wəz ˈrɔŋ, *the book that was on the table* ðə ˈbuk ðət wəz ɔn ðə ˈteibl
them	*Take them away* ˈteik ð(ə)m əˈwei or (very collo- quially) ˈteik əm əˈwei
there	*there wasn't one* ðə ˈwɔz nt wʌn, *there is no one there* ðə z ˈnou wʌn ˈðɛə, *if there isn't there ought to be* if ðər ˈiz nt ðər ˈɔːt tə biː
till	*I'm staying there till Tuesday* ai m ˈsteiiŋ ðɛə tl ˈtjuːzdi
*time(s)	*the first time I went there* ðə ˈfəːs(t) təm ai ˈwent ðɛə, *three times four are twelve* ˈθriː təmz ˈfɔːr ə ˈtwelv
upon	*piled up one upon another* ˈpaild ˈʌp ˈwʌn əpən əˈnʌðə
us	*Give us one* ˈgiv əs wʌn, *let us go* ˈlet s ˈgou[22]
was	*he was right* hiː wəz ˈrait
were	*they were very kind* ðei wə ˈveri ˈkaind, *the books were on the table* ðə ˈbuks wər ɔn ðə ˈteibl
who	*the man who did it* ðə ˈmæn uː ˈdid it or ðə ˈmæn hu ˈdid it or ðə ˈmæn u ˈdid it
will	*that will do* ˈðæt l ˈduː, *the church will be full* ðə ˈtʃəːtʃ əl bi ˈful
would	*it would be a pity* it əd bi ə ˈpiti, *you would like to* juː d ˈlaik tu
your	*Make up your mind* ˈmeik ʌp jə ˈmaind

---

[21] Meaning a certain quantity of paper. If the word *paper* were used in
the sense of a journal, *some* would have the strong form sʌm; example: *I saw
it in some paper* ai ˈsɔː it in sʌm ˈpeipə, meaning 'I saw it in a journal, but
I don't remember *which* journal.' Note that sʌm is unstressed in this case.
sʌm and səm (sm) should really be considered as different words.

[22] Meaning 'we had better go' (addressed to a member of the party denoted
by *us*). ˈlet əs ˈgou would mean 'allow us to go' (addressed to someone other
than a member of the party denoted by *us*). This difference was first pointed
out by Y. R. Chao (*Le Maître Phonétique*, January, 1931, p. 4).

489. It is to be noticed that the words *on*, *when*, and *then* have no weak forms; they are pronounced ɔn, wen (or hwen) and ðen even in the weakest positions. *Not* has a common weak form nt after certain verbs (as in *can't* kɑːnt, *did not* 'didnt). Some English people use a weak form nət in the single word *cannot* 'kænət (more usually 'kænɔt). These words are mentioned here because foreign learners sometimes make mistakes in regard to them.

490. There are other words which have weak forms when they occur as the second element of certain compound words.   Such are:

	Strong form	Weak form	Example
berry	'beri	-bəri or -bri	*gooseberry* 'guzbəri or 'guzbri
board	bɔːd or bɔəd	-bəd	*cupboard* 'kʌbəd
ford	fɔːd	-fəd	*Oxford* 'ɔksfəd
land	lænd	-lənd	*Scotland* 'skɔtlənd
man	mæn	-mən	*gentleman* 'dʒentlmən
men	men	-mən	*gentlemen* 'dʒentlmən[23]
most	moust	-məst	*topmost* 'tɔpməst[24]
mouth	mauθ	-məθ	*Plymouth* 'pliməθ
pan	pæn	-pən	*saucepan* 'sɔːspən
pence	pens	-pəns or -pns	*twopence* 'tʌpəns or 'tʌpns *fivepence* 'faifpəns
penny	'peni	-pəni or -pni	*halfpenny* 'heipəni or 'heipni
sense	sens	-səns or -sns	*nonsense* 'nɔnsəns or 'nɔnsns
shire	'ʃaiə	-ʃiə or -ʃə	*Devonshire* 'devnʃiə or 'devnʃə
where	wɛə or hwɛə (before vowels (h)wɛər)	-wə (before vowels -wər)	*anywhere near* ˌeniwə 'niə,[25] *anywhere else* ˌeniwər 'els[25]
yard	jɑːd	-jəd	*vineyard* 'vinjəd

491. The proper use of weak forms is essential for a correct pronunciation of English, and is one of the most difficult features

---

[23] Some public speakers say 'dʒentlmen.
[24] Also pronounced 'tɔpmoust.
[25] Also pronounced ˌeniwɛə 'niə, ˌeniwɛər 'els.

of English pronunciation for foreigners to acquire. Foreign people generally have an almost irresistible tendency to use strong forms in their place. Such a pronunciation gives to the English ear the impression that unimportant words and syllables are receiving undue prominence, and in consequence the important words and syllables lose some of the prominence they ought to have.

492. When a weak form contains an ə which may be omitted, foreign learners will generally do well to use the form without ə. Thus though *away from the city, I should have thought so* are commonly pronounced ə'wei frəm ðə 'siti, ai ʃəd əv 'θɔːt sou, yet foreigners generally pronounce better by practising ə'wei frm ð 'siti, ai ʃd v 'θɔːt sou. This latter pronunciation will strike an English person as much more natural than the common foreign pronunciation with strong forms instead of weak ones; the long successions of consonants arising in such exercises are not so difficult as they look.

493. The correct use of weak forms is best acquired by continual reading of phonetic transcriptions. In a few cases there are rules which help the learner, e.g. the rule as to the use of strong forms of prepositions given in §§ 996, 997.

Chapter XVII

THE ENGLISH PLOSIVE CONSONANTS

Detailed Descriptions

494. Plosive consonants are formed by completely closing the air passage, then compressing the air and suddenly opening the passage, so that the air escapes making an explosive sound.

495. There are six plosive consonant phonemes in English. They are represented in phonetic transcription by the letters **p, b, t, d, k, g**. The 'glottal stop' (ʔ) also occurs, but it is not a significant sound of the language.

p

496. In pronouncing the principal member of the English **p**-phoneme the air passage is completely blocked by closing the lips and raising the soft palate; the air is compressed by pressure from the lungs, and when the lips are opened the air suddenly escapes from the mouth, and in doing so makes an explosive sound; the vocal cords are not made to vibrate. The formation of the sound may be expressed shortly by defining it as a *voiceless bilabial plosive* consonant.

497. In Southern English when **p** is followed by a stressed vowel as in *pardon* **'pɑːdn**, *payment* **'peimənt**, it is pronounced with considerable force, and a noticeable puff of breath or 'aspiration' (i.e. a slight **h**) is heard after the explosion of the **p** and before the beginning of the vowel. The pronunciation might be shown thus: **pʰɑːdn, pʰeimənt**. This aspiration is less strong when the **p** is preceded by **s** (e.g. in *spider* **'spaidə**). Also the aspiration is less strong when a very short vowel follows, as in *picked* **pikt**. When **p** is followed by an unstressed vowel, as in *upper* **'ʌpə**, the aspiration is weak—with some speakers almost imperceptible. It is not usually necessary to indicate the aspiration of **p** in practical phonetic transcription, since the less aspirated varieties are determined by their situations; they are 'members of the same phoneme.'

(For further discussion of aspirated plosives see Theory of Plosive Consonants, §§ 561–568.)

498. Many Northern English people pronounce **p** (also t and k) with little or no aspiration.

499. A subsidiary member of the **p**-phoneme with nasal plosion is heard when **m** or **n** follows as in *topmost* **'tɔpmoust**, *hypnotize* **'hipnətaiz**. Another subsidiary member with hardly any plosion is heard when **t** or **k** follows, as in *wrapped* **ræpt**, *napkin* **'næpkin**, and yet another with no plosion at all before **p** and **b** (§§ 579, 582).

500. **p** is the usual sound of the letter *p*; example: *pipe* **paip**. *P* is silent in the initial groups *pt*, *pn*, generally also in initial *ps*; examples: *ptarmigan* **'tɑ:migən**, *pneumatic* **nju'mætik**, *psalm* **sɑ:m**,[1] also in the single words *raspberry* **'rɑ:zbri** and *cupboard* **'kʌbəd**. Note the exceptionally spelt word *hiccough* **'hikʌp**.[2]

501. Scandinavians and some Germans are apt to aspirate initial **p** too strongly, pronouncing **'pɑ:dn** as **'phɑ:dn** or **'phɑ:dn**. Other Germans, on the contrary, especially South Germans, replace **p** by a feebly articulated sound not followed by any **h**, a consonant which sounds to an English ear rather like **b** (phonetic symbol **b̥**[3]). Scandinavians also have a tendency to replace **p** by **b̥** when it occurs at the beginning of an unstressed syllable as in *upper* **'ʌpə**, *apple* **'æpl** and after **s** as in *spend* **spend**. They should practise aspirating the **p** in these cases, and should not take notice of the diminution of aspiration referred to in § 497.

502. French people, on the other hand, pronounce the consonant **p** strongly as in English, but they usually do not insert the aspiration as Southern English people do (§ 497). They should rather aim at saying **'phɑ:dn**, etc.: they are never likely to exaggerate **h** like the Scandinavians and Germans.

503. Words for practising **p** with ordinary plosion: *peel* **pi:l**, *pill* **pil**, *pencil* **'pensl**, *patch* **pætʃ**, *pass* **pɑ:s**, *pocket* **'pɔkit**, *paw* **pɔ:**, *pull* **pul**, *pool* **pu:l**, *public* **'pʌblik**, *purse* **pə:s**, *pail* **peil**, *post* **poust**,

---

[1] Some people, and particularly psychologists, pronounce **ps** in words beginning with *psych-*; thus *psychology* is **sai'kɔlədʒi** or (less commonly) **psai'kɔlədʒi**.

[2] Now often spelt *hiccup*.

[3] ₒ is the sign devoicing, so that **b̥** denotes 'voiceless *b*'. It is its weak force of articulation that distinguishes it from **p**.

pie **pai**, *power* **'pauə**, *point* **pɔint**, *pier* **piə**, *pair* **pɛə**, *pour* **pɔə**,[4] *poor* **puə**[5]; *capable* **'keipəbl**, *happy* **'hæpi**, *pepper* **'pepə**, *people* **'piːpl**; *lip* **lip**, *map* **mæp**, *top* **tɔp**, *help* **help**; *spin* **spin**, *spend* **spend**, *spot* **spɔt**, *sport* **spɔːt**, *spoon* **spuːn**.

$$\boxed{\text{b}}$$

504. The principal English **b** is formed like the principal English **p** (§ 496) except that the force of exhalation is weaker and the vocal cords are made to vibrate (§ 82) so that 'voice' is produced during the articulation of the sound.   The formation of the principal English **b** may therefore be expressed shortly by defining it as a *voiced bilabial plosive* consonant.

505. A subsidiary member of the English **b**-phoneme with nasal plosion is used when **m** or **n** follows, as in *submit* **səb'mit**, *abnormal* **æb'nɔːməl**.   Other subsidiary members with no plosion occur before **p** and **b** (§ 578), and with hardly any plosion before other plosives, as for instance in *obtain* **əb'tein**.   Yet other subsidiary **b**'s with partial voice are used in initial and final positions, and when a voiceless consonant precedes, as in *Whitby* **'witbi**.   Many English people use a completely devoiced **b** (**ḇ**) in these positions (see §§ 573, 576).

506. As the chief members of the **b**-phoneme are wholly or partially voiced, they cannot have 'aspiration' in the ordinary sense of the term.

507. **b** is the usual sound of the letter *b*; example: *baby* **'beibi**. *B* is silent when final and preceded by *m* as in *lamb* **læm**, *comb* **koum**, *Coombe, Combe* **kuːm**[6]; also before *t* in a few words such as *debt* **det**, *doubt* **daut**, *subtle* **'sʌtl**.

508. Many foreign people, and especially Germans, do not voice **b** properly, but replace it by **ḇ** (§ 501).   This sounds wrong to English people when voiced sounds precede and follow, as in *above* **ə'bʌv**, *table* **'teibl**, *the boat* **ðə 'bout**.   But the use of **ḇ** does not matter when a word like *bring* **briŋ** is said by itself or is initial in a sentence, nor when a word like *rub* **rʌb** is said by itself or is

---

[4] Also pronounced **pɔː**.

[5] Also pronounced **poə** or **pɔə** or **pɔː**.

[6] *Iamb* **'aiæmb** is an exception.

final in a sentence (see § 505).   For exercises for acquiring a fully voiced **b** see § 177.

509. Spaniards and Portuguese people do not always make the full contact which is necessary for the proper pronunciation of the sound **b**. This is especially the case when the **b** comes between two vowels in an unstressed position, as in *labour* **'leibə**. The result is that the **b** is replaced by the bilabial fricative **β** (§ 692). Some Germans, especially Bavarians, have a similar tendency.

510. Words for practice: *bee* **biː**, *bid* **bid**, *bed* **bed**, *bad* **bæd** or **bæːd**, *bark* **baːk**, *box* **bɒks**, *bought* **bɔːt**, *bull* **bul**, *boot* **buːt**, *bud* **bʌd**, *burn* **bəːn**, *bay* **bei**, *boat* **bout**, *buy* **bai**, *bough* **bau**, *boy* **bɔi**, *beer* **biə**, *bare* **bɛə**, *boar* **bɔə** or **bɔː**, *boor* **buə**; *October* **ɔkˈtoubə**, *robin* **ˈrɔbin**, *bubble* **ˈbʌbl**; *web* **web**, *bulb* **bʌlb**, *hubbub* **ˈhʌbʌb**, *tribe* **traib**.

$$\boxed{t}$$

511. In pronouncing the principal member of the English **t**-phoneme, the air passage is completely blocked by raising the soft palate and raising the tip of the tongue to touch the teeth-ridge, as shown in Fig. 27; the air is compressed by pressure from the lungs, and when the tongue is removed from the teeth-ridge, the air suddenly escapes through the mouth, and in doing so makes an explosive sound; the vocal cords are not made to vibrate. The formation of the sound may be expressed shortly by defining it as a *voiceless alveolar plosive* consonant.

512. In English when **t** is followed by a vowel in a stressed syllable, as in *taken* **ˈteikn**, it is 'aspirated' in the same way as **p**, that is to say, a slight **h** is inserted between the explosion and the beginning of the following vowel. This articulation may be regarded as an essential element of the principal member of the English **t**-phoneme. A subsidiary member with less aspiration is used in unstressed positions, as in *letter* **ˈletə**, *quantity* **ˈkwɔntiti**; also after **s**, as in *step* **step**, *stood* **stud**.

513. Other subsidiary members are (1) a dental **t** which is used before **θ** and **ð**, as in *eighth* **eitθ**, *look at this* **ˈluk ət ˈðis**, (2) a post-alveolar **t** which is used before **r**, as in *rest-room* **ˈrest-rum**, *at Rome* **ət ˈroum**, (3) a nasally exploded **t** which is used before nasal consonants, as in *mutton* **ˈmʌtn**, *that man* **ˈðæt ˈmæn**, (4) a laterally exploded **t** which is used before **l**, as in *bottle* **ˈbɔtl**, *at last* **ət ˈlaːst**,

(5) a **t** without plosion which is used when **t, d, tʃ** or **dʒ** follows, as in *that time* **'ðæt 'taim**, *not done* **'nɔt dʌn**, *that church* **'ðæt 'tʃəːtʃ**, *that gentleman* **'ðæt 'dʒentlmən**, and with many speakers before other plosive consonants, as in *at present* **ət 'preznt**, *at Brighton* **ət 'braitn**, *Atkinson* **'ætkinsn**, *it goes* **it 'gouz**.

514. **t** is the usual sound of the letter *t*; example: *tent* **tent**. It is, however, represented by *-ed* in the past tenses and past participles of verbs ending in voiceless consonants (other than **t**); examples: *packed* **pækt**, *missed* **mist**, *rushed* **rʌʃt** (but compare *waited* **'weitid**).[7] Note also the exceptionally spelt words *eighth* **eitθ**, *thyme* **taim**, *Thames* **temz**, *Thomas* **'tɔməs**, *Mathilda* **mə'tildə**, *Esther* **'estə**. *T* is silent in words ending in *-stle*, *-sten*: *castle* **'kɑːsl**, *thistle* **'θisl**, *fasten* **'fɑːsn**, *hasten* **'heisn**, *listen* **'lisn**[8]; also in *Christmas* **'krisməs**, *chestnut* **'tʃesnʌt** and many similar words.

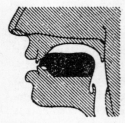

Fig. 63. Tongue-position of dental **t** (variety with tip of tongue against lower teeth).

515. Many foreign people, e.g. the French, Italians, Hungarians, and some Germans, use a **t** articulated by the tip of the tongue against the upper teeth, somewhat as shown in Fig. 26 (less commonly against the lower teeth, as shown in Fig. 63). They pronounce a dental consonant instead of an alveolar consonant. This articulation produces a very unnatural effect when used in English, especially when **t** is final, as in *what* **wɔt**.

516. The difference between the articulation of **t** in French and English may be shown by palatograms. Figs. 64, 66 show palatograms of the English *two* **tuː** and the French *tout* **tu**. Figs. 65, 67 show palatograms of the English *tea* **tiː** and the French *type* **tip**.[9]

---

[7] This only applies to verbs, not to the termination *-ed* generally. Thus *wicked* is **'wikid** (see footnote 10 to § 525).

[8] The only exception of importance is *pestle*, which is pronounced **'pestl** by many.

[9] Incidentally, these palatograms corroborate a curious point previously ascertained by direct observation, that while the English **t** is articulated further back when followed by sounds of the **u** type than when followed by sounds of the **i** type, yet in French the opposite is the case.

517. Indians generally use a 'retroflex' t (phonetic symbol ʈ) in place of the English t. In pronouncing the retroflex sound the tongue-tip touches the roof of the mouth further back than for the English t (Fig. 114, p. 214). Norwegians and Swedes also use ʈ in some cases (see § 829).

Fig. 64. Palatogram of the English word *two*.

Fig. 65. Palatogram of the English word *tea*.

Fig. 66. Palatogram of the French word *tout*.

Fig. 67. Palatogram of the French word *type*.

518. Scandinavians and some Germans are apt to exaggerate the aspiration of t and to pronounce *taken* as ˈtheikn (or ˈtheːkn). There are, however, other Germans who pronounce t very feebly, and do not insert any h after it; the consonant then sounds to an English ear like a weak d (phonetic symbol ḍ). These latter must be careful to pronounce the English t with considerable force of the breath. Scandinavians have a tendency to replace t by ḍ when it occurs at the beginning of an unstressed syllable, as in *matter* ˈmætə, *bottle* ˈbɒtl; also after s, as in *storm* stɔːm. They should practise aspirating the t in all such cases, and should not take notice of the diminution of aspiration referred to in § 512.

519. French people on the other hand pronounce the consonant strongly as in English, but they usually do not insert the aspiration properly. The sound they produce is known as 'unaspirated' **t**. They should therefore rather aim at pronouncing **'theikn, thi:** (*tea*), **thu:l** (*tool*), etc.

520. The difficulties experienced by foreign learners in connexion with the nasally and laterally exploded **t**'s and with the unexploded **t** are dealt with in §§ 578–590.

521. Words for practising **t** with ordinary plosion: *tea* **ti:**, *tin* **tin**, *tell* **tel**, *attack* **ə'tæk**, *task* **tɑ:sk**, *top* **tɔp**, *talk* **tɔ:k**, *took* **tuk**, *two* **tu:**, *tumble* **'tʌmbl**, *turn* **tə:n**, *take* **teik**, *toast* **toust**, *time* **taim**, *town* **taun**, *toy* **tɔi**, *tear* (of the eye) **tiə**, *tear* (to rend, a rent) **tɛə**, *tore* **tɔə** or **tɔ:**, *tour* **tuə**; *writing* **'raitiŋ**, *water* **'wɔ:tə**, *native* **'neitiv**, *theatre* **'θiətə**, *constitute* **'kɔnstitju:t**, *potato* **pə'teitou**; *print* **print**, *profit* **'prɔfit** (= *prophet*), *doubt* **daut**.

d

522. The principal member of the English **d**-phoneme is formed like the principal English **t** (§ 511) except that the force of exhalation is weaker and the vocal cords are made to vibrate so that 'voice' is heard. The formation of the principal English **d** may therefore be expressed shortly by defining it as a *voiced alveolar plosive* consonant.

523. The chief subsidiary members of the English **d**-phoneme are (1) a dental **d** which is used when **θ** or **ð** follows, as in *width* **widθ**, *add them* **'æd ðəm**, (2) a post-alveolar **d** which is used before **r**, as in *he would write* **hi: d 'rait**, (3) a **d** with nasal plosion which is used when **m** or **n** follows, as in *admire* **əd'maiə**, *road-mender* **'roud,mendə**, *sudden* **'sʌdn** (see § 586), (4) a laterally exploded **d**, as in *middle* **'midl** (see § 590), (5) a **d** without plosion which is used when **t**, **d**, **tʃ** or **dʒ** follows, as in *bed-time* **'bedtaim**, *good jam* **'gud 'dʒæm**, (6) partially voiced varieties of **d**, which are often used in initial and final positions and when a voiceless consonant precedes, as in *birthday* **'bə:θdei**. Many English people use a completely devoiced **d** in these positions (see §§ 573, 576).

524. As the chief members of the **d**-phoneme are wholly or partially voiced, they cannot have 'aspiration' in the ordinary sense of the term.

525. d is the regular sound of the letter *d*; example: *deed* **diːd**. Note that final *-ed* is pronounced **-d** in the past tenses and past participles of all verbs ending in vowels or in voiced consonants (other than **d**); examples: *played* **pleid**, *seized* **siːzd**, *begged* **begd**.[10]

526. Like **t**, the English sound **d** is articulated by the tip of the tongue against the teeth-ridge (Fig. 27); but many foreign people, and especially those speaking romance languages, replace it by a sound made with the tip or blade of the tongue against the teeth (Figs. 26, 63). This articulation produces an unnatural effect in English, especially when the **d** is final as in *good* **gud**.

527. The palatograms for **d** are practically identical with those for **t** (Figs. 64, 65, 66, 67).

528. Many foreign people, and especially Germans, do not voice the sound **d** properly, but replace it by **d̥** (§ 518). This sounds wrong to English people when voiced sounds precede and follow, as in *addition* **ə'diʃn**, *hide it* **'haid it**. But the use of **d̥** does not matter when such a word as *do* **duː** is said by itself or is initial in a sentence, or when such a word as *card* **kɑːd** is said by itself or is final in a sentence. For exercises for acquiring a fully voiced **d**, see § 177.

529. Spaniards and Portuguese people are apt to reduce **d** to a weak form of the corresponding fricative **ð** (§ 702), especially when intervocalic and unstressed, as in *ladder* **'lædə**.

530. Words for practice: *deal* **diːl**, *did* **did**, *debt* **det**, *dash* **dæʃ**, *dark* **dɑːk**, *dog* **dɔg**, *door* **dɔː**, *doom* **duːm**, *dust* **dʌst**, *dirt* **dəːt**, *date* **deit**, *dome* **doum**, *dine* **dain**, *down* **daun**, *dear* **diə**, *dare* **dɛə**; *hiding* **'haidiŋ**, *louder* **'laudə**, *garden* **'gɑːdn**, *middle* **'midl**[11]; *lead* (to conduct) **liːd**, *lead* (metal) **led**, *hard* **hɑːd**, *load* **loud**, *wood* **wud**.

---

[10] When the verb ends in **d** (or in **t**) the termination is pronounced **-id**; examples: *added* **'ædid**, *fitted* **'fitid**. When the verb ends with a voiceless consonant (other than **t**), the termination is pronounced **-t** (§ 514).

Note that the termination *-ed* in adjectives is almost always pronounced **-id**. Hence a difference in pronunciation is made between *aged* (participle) **eidʒd** and *aged* (attributive adjective) **'eidʒid**, *blessed* (participle) **blest** and *blessed* (adjective) **'blesid**, etc. Similarly, the adverbs formed from participles take the pronunciation **-idli**, whatever the form of the simple participle may be; compare *unfeigned* **ʌn'feind**, *unfeignedly* **ʌn'feinidli**, *marked* **mɑːkt**, *markedly* **'mɑːkidli**, *composed* **kəm'pouzd**, *composedly* **kəm'pouzidli**.

[11] See § 590.

531. As regards the variety of **d** known as retroflex **d** (phonetic symbol **ɖ**), see Chap. XXV.

$$\boxed{k}$$

532. In pronouncing the common varieties of **k** the air passage is completely blocked by raising the back of the tongue to touch the fore part of the soft palate, the soft palate being at the same time raised so as to shut off the nose passage (see Fig. 31); the air is compressed by pressure from the lungs and when the contact of the tongue with the palate is released by lowering the tongue, the air suddenly escapes through the mouth and in doing so makes an explosive sound; the vocal cords are not made to vibrate. The formation of the principal English **k** may be expressed shortly by defining it as a *voiceless velar plosive* consonant.

533. The English k-phoneme contains several easily distinguishable members. Firstly, there are variations in the place of tongue-articulation dependent upon the nature of a following vowel. Taking the **k** in *come* **kʌm** as the principal member of the phoneme, we find that a more forward **k** is used before **iː** (as in *keep* **kiːp**) and a more backward **k** before **ɔ** (as in *cottage* **'kɔtidʒ**); other intermediate sounds are used before other vowels according to their nature. Secondly, there exist varieties of **k** with different degrees of lip-rounding, the most notable being a strongly lip-rounded **k** used before **w** (as in *queen* **kwiːn**). The precise sound used also depends to some extent on preceding vowels. The k-sound used finally when a consonant precedes (as in *ask* **ɑːsk**) is about the same as that in **kʌm**, that is to say the principal member.

534. Thirdly, the amount of 'aspiration' of **k** before a vowel varies like that of **p** and **t** (see §§ 497, 512). Thus the principal **k** (as in **kʌm**) has considerable aspiration, while an unstressed **k** with the same tongue-position (as in *baker* **'beikə**) and a **k** following **s** (as in *sky* **skai**) have less aspiration. The same applies to the fronter and backer members of the phoneme; compare *kingdom* **'kiŋdəm** in which the **k** has fairly strong aspiration with *talking* **'tɔːkiŋ** and *skin* **skin** in which the **k** has less aspiration.

535. Fourthly, **k** has nasal plosion before nasal consonants (as in *acme* **'ækmi**, *Faulkner* **'fɔːknə**, *bacon* **'beikn** or **'beikŋ**). And fifthly, a **k** with little or no plosion is used before other plosives (see §§ 578, 579, 581, 582).

536. The principal English **k** pronounced by itself gives no palatogram on my artificial palate, but forward members of the phoneme give palatograms. A palatogram of the word *key* **ki:** pronounced by me is shown in Fig. 68.

537. Members of the **k**-phoneme are regularly used where the ordinary spelling has *k*, and where it has *c* followed by one of the letters *a*, *o* or *u* or a consonant letter or finally; examples: *king* **kiŋ**, *cat* **kæt**, *coat* **kout**, *cut* **kʌt**, *fact* **fækt**, *electric* **i'lektrik**. *Ch* is pronounced **k** in some words, e.g. *character* **'kæriktə**, *chemist* **'kemist**, *Christmas* **'krisməs**,

Fig. 68. Palatogram of the English word *key*.

ache **eik**. *Qu* is generally pronounced **kw** (e.g. *queen* **kwi:n**, *quarter* **'kwɔ:tə**), but there are a few words in which it is pronounced **k** (e.g. *conquer* **'kɔŋkə**, *liquor* **'likə**, *antique* **æn'ti:k**). *X* is generally pronounced **ks** (e.g. *box* **bɔks**); for the exceptional cases in which it is pronounced **gz**, see § 547.

538. In French the subsidiary **k**'s preceding front vowels are more forward than in English; in fact with many French people the contact is so far forward that the sound is the true palatal consonant **c** (Fig. 29). The use of such a sound gives to the ordinary English ear the effect of **kj**; thus when a Frenchman pronounces *kept* as **cɛpt**, it sounds to English people like **kjept**. French people are also liable to use a fronted **k** before **ʌ**, **ai**, and **au**, as in *cut* **kʌt**, *kind* **kaind**, *count* **kaunt**. The nature of this mistake will be realized by comparing Figs. 29, 30, and 31.

539. Some Scandinavians and Germans exaggerate the aspiration of **k**, and say **'khiŋdəm**, **'khɔtidʒ**, etc. Other Germans on the contrary, and especially those from Central Germany, are apt to pronounce the sound very feebly, and not to insert any aspiration after it; the consonant then sounds to an Englishman like a weak **g** (phonetic symbol **g̊**). Those who have a tendency to pronounce in this way must therefore be careful to pronounce the initial **k** with considerable force of breath. Scandinavians are also liable to

replace **k** by **g̊** when the sound occurs at the beginning of an
unstressed syllable, as in *thicker* **'θikə**, *pocket* **'pɔkit**; also when
preceded by **s** as in *school* **sku:l**. They should practise aspirating
the **k** in such cases, and should not take notice of the diminution
of aspiration referred to in § 534.

540. French people on the other hand pronounce the consonant
k strongly as in French, but they usually do not insert the aspiration.
They should therefore rather aim at pronouncing **'khiŋdəm,
khaind, 'khɔtidʒ**, etc., with exaggerated aspiration.

541. Words for practice: *key* **ki:**, *kill* **kil**, *kettle* **'ketl**, *cat* **kæt**,
cart **kɑ:t**, *collar* **'kɔlə**, *cushion* **'kuʃin**,[12] *cool* **ku:l**, *cut* **kʌt**, *curl* **kə:l**,
cave **keiv**, *cold* **kould**, *kind* **kaind**, *cow* **kau**, *coil* **kɔil**, *Keir* **kiə**, *care*
kɛə, *course* **kɔəs** or **kɔ:s**; *acre* **'eikə**, *cooking* **'kukiŋ**, *rocky* **'rɔki**; *leak*
li:k, *cake* **keik**, *pack* **pæk**, *duke* **dju:k**.

$$\boxed{\text{g}}$$

542. The principal English **g** is formed exactly like the principal
English **k** (§ 532) except that the force of exhalation is weaker
and the vocal cords are made to vibrate so that 'voice' is heard.
The formation of the principal English **g** may therefore be expressed
shortly by defining the sound as a *voiced velar plosive* consonant.

543. The English **g**-phoneme, like the **k**-phoneme, has subsidiary
members with places of articulation different from that of the
principal member. Thus if we take the **g** in *govern* **'gʌvən** as
the principal member of the English **g**-phoneme, we find that the
sound in *geese* **gi:s** has a fronter articulation and the sound in
got **gɔt** has a backer articulation. There are other varieties of **g**
with intermediate places of articulation, and their use depends
upon the nature of adjacent vowels. There exist also varieties of
g with different degrees of lip-rounding, the most notable being
a strongly lip-rounded **g** used before **w**, as in *language* **'læŋgwidʒ**.

544. Other subsidiary members of the **g**-phoneme with partial
voice or occasionally without voice are used by many speakers

---

[12] Also pronounced **'kuʃən** and **'kuʃn**.

in initial and final positions and when a voiceless consonant precedes (see §§ 573, 576).

545. As the chief members of the g-phoneme are wholly or partially voiced, there cannot be any 'aspiration' in the ordinary sense of the term.

546. A further subsidiary member of the g-phoneme with nasal plosion is used when m or n follows, as in *dogmatic* dɔg'mætik, *Agnes* 'ægnis. Other g's with little or no plosion occur before other plosive consonants (see §§ 578, 581, 583).

547. Members of the g-phoneme are the regular sounds of the letter *g* when followed by one of the letters *a, o* or *u* or a consonant or when final (as in *game* geim, *go* gou, *good* gud, *gum* gʌm, *green* griːn, *big* big). The g-phoneme is also used in some words spelt with *ge* and *gi*, for instance *get* get, *give* giv, *girl* gəːl,[13] *finger* 'fiŋgə.[14] The *x* in the prefix *ex-* is generally pronounced gz when immediately followed by a stressed or semi-stressed vowel, except in words beginning with *exc-*; examples: *exact* ig'zækt, *examine* ig'zæmin, *examination* igˌzæmi'neiʃn, *exhaust* ig'zɔːst, *exhibit* ig'zibit (but *except* ik'sept, *excite* ik'sait); compare *exhibition* eksi'biʃn, *exercise* 'eksəsaiz, in which the vowel following the prefix is quite unstressed.

548. As in the case of k some French people articulate g too far forward for English, and sometimes even replace it by the

---

[13] Pronounced gɛəl by some.

[14] The principal words in which g before *e* or *i* is pronounced g are *gear* giə, *geese* giːs, *get* get, *gibberish* 'gibəriʃ (also 'dʒibəriʃ), *gibbous* 'gibəs, *giddy* 'gidi, *gift* gift, *gig* gig, *giggle* 'gigl, *gild* gild, *gill* (of a fish) gil (*gill*, liquid measure, is dʒil), *gimlet* 'gimlit, *gimp* gimp, *begin* bi'gin, *gird* gəːd, *girder* 'gəːdə, *girdle* 'gəːdl, *girl* gəːl, *girth* gəːθ, *give* giv, *gizzard* 'gizəd; *anger* 'æŋgə, *conger* 'kɔŋgə, *eager* 'iːgə, *finger* 'fiŋgə, *hunger* 'hʌŋgə, *linger* 'liŋgə, *longer* 'lɔŋgə, *longest* 'lɔŋgist, (*fish-)monger* -mʌŋgə, *stronger* 'strɔŋgə, *strongest* 'strɔŋgist, *tiger* 'taigə, *younger* 'jʌŋgə, *youngest* 'jʌŋgist; all words ending with *-gger, -gging*, e.g. *dagger* 'dægə, *digging* 'digiŋ; also the names *Gertrude* 'gəːtruːd, *Gibbon(s)* 'gibən(z), *Gibbs* gibz, *Gibson* 'gibsn, *Gilbey* 'gilbi, *Gilchrist* 'gilkrist, *Gillespie* gi'lespi, *Gillow* 'gilou, *Gilpin* 'gilpin, *Girton* 'gəːtn, *Gissing* 'gisiŋ and a number of less common names. *Gill* in 'Jack and Gill' (now more usually written *Jill*) is dʒil, otherwise the proper name *Gill* is gil; *Gifford* is 'gifəd and 'dʒifəd, *Gilson* is 'dʒilsn and 'gilsn, *Gimson* is 'gimsn and 'dʒimsn.

voiced *palatal* plosive ɟ, when a front vowel follows, as in *gay* gei,
guest gest, *gallop* 'gæləp.   Some French people do this also before
ʌ, ai and au, as in *gun* gʌn, *guide* gaid, *gown* gaun.   (ɟ has the
same tongue-position as c, see Fig. 29.)

549. Many foreign people, and especially Germans, do not voice
the sound g properly, but replace it by g̊ (§ 539). This sounds
wrong in English when voiced sounds precede and follow, as in
regard ri'gɑːd, *eager* 'iːgə. But the use of g̊ does not matter when
such a word as *go* gou is said by itself or is initial in a sentence,
or when such a word as *jug* dʒʌg is said by itself or is final in a
sentence.   For exercises for acquiring a fully voiced g, see § 177.

550. Spaniards and Portuguese people often reduce g to the
corresponding *fricative* sound (phonetic symbol ɣ), especially when
intervocalic and unstressed, as in *sugar* 'ʃugə. Danes and some
Germans have a similar tendency.

551. Words for practice: *geese* giːs, *give* giv, *guess* ges, *gas* gæs,
guard gɑːd, *got* gɔt, *gauze* gɔːz, *good* gud, *goose* guːs, *gum* gʌm, *girl*
gəːl, *gate* geit, *goat* gout, *guide* gaid, *gown* gaun, *gear* giə; *eager*
'iːgə, *tiger* 'taigə, *organ* 'ɔːgən, *sugar* 'ʃugə; *big* big, *egg* eg, *log* lɔg,
mug mʌg.

ʔ

552. The sound commonly known as the 'glottal stop' or 'glottal
catch,' but more accurately termed the *glottal plosive* consonant,
is not an essential sound of the English language, but it is necessary
to say a few words about it here.

553. In forming the sound ʔ the glottis is closed completely
by bringing the vocal cords into contact, the air is compressed
by pressure from the lungs, and then the glottis is opened (by
separating the vocal cords) so that the air escapes suddenly.   It
is neither breathed nor voiced.

554. An exaggerated form of this consonant constitutes the
explosive sound heard in coughing. Some coughs can be
represented in phonetic transcription. A common kind of cough is
ʔʌhəʔʌh.

555. The consonant ʔ occurs as an essential sound of many languages; but in Received English it is not an essential sound, though it may often be heard incidentally. It sometimes occurs in Received English when a word which normally begins with a stressed vowel is specially emphasized. Thus *it is absolutely false* spoken with emphasis on *absolutely* would often be pronounced it s 'ʔæbsəluːtli 'fɔːls. The sound ʔ is also often prefixed to initial vowels when people speak with hesitation.

556. Most foreign people, and more particularly Germans, have a tendency to insert the sound ʔ at the beginning of all words which ought to begin with vowels. Thus they will pronounce *it was all our own fault* as it wəz 'ʔɔːl ʔauə 'ʔoun 'fɔːlt. Sometimes they insert the sound in the middle of a word before a stressed vowel, saying for instance, wɛəʔʼʔæz, kriʼʔeit, fiziʼʔolədʒi instead of wɛəʼræz, kriʼeit, fiziʼolədʒi (*whereas, create, physiology*).

557. It is important that the foreign learner should remedy this error. The mistake is one which will effectually spoil what is otherwise a good pronunciation, and it is one which often necessitates a great deal of practice on the part of the learner. It must be remembered that in normal English there is no break between consecutive words which are closely connected by the sense. The normal English way of pronouncing may often be acquired by dividing up the sounds into syllables, thus: it wə 'zɔː lauə 'roun 'fɔːlt.

558. In phonetic transcriptions the absence of the glottal stop may be marked, if desired, by ‿: thus, it wəz‿ɔːl‿auər‿oun 'fɔːlt.

559. Further examples for practice: *far away* 'fɑːr‿ə'wei, *anywhere else* 'eniwɛər‿els, *the ends of the earth* ði‿endz‿əv ði‿əːθ, *to eat an apple* tu‿iːt‿ən‿æpl, *all over again* 'ɔːl‿ouvər‿ə'gein, *not at all* 'nɔt‿ə'tɔːl, *to live on an island* tə 'liv‿ɔn‿ən‿ailənd, *he put on an overcoat* hiː 'put‿ɔn‿ən‿ouvəkout.

560. Very frequently in dialectal English ʔ is used as a substitute for t in unstressed positions. Some speakers of received English pronounce like this, especially when m, n, r, j, or w follows, as in *fortnight* 'fɔːʔnait, *Tottenham* 'tɔʔnəm, *quite right* 'kwaiʔ 'rait, *not yet* 'nɔʔ 'jet, *that one* 'ðæʔ wʌn. It is not necessary for foreign learners to adopt this pronunciation, but they should know of its existence.

Theory of Plosive Consonants

561. To pronounce a complete plosive consonant (§ 183) two things are necessary: (i) contact must be made by the articulating organs, (ii) the articulating organs must subsequently be separated. Thus, in pronouncing an ordinary **p** the lips must be first closed and then opened.

562. While the organs articulating a plosive consonant are actually in contact they form what is termed the *stop*. In the case of voiceless consonants, e.g. **p**, no sound is heard during the stop; in the case of voiced consonants, e.g. **b**, some voice (a greater or less amount according to circumstances, §§ 572 ff.) is heard during the stop.

563. The explosion of a plosive consonant is formed by the air as it suddenly escapes at the instant when the stop is released. The rush of air, however, necessarily continues for an appreciable time after the contact is released. A plosive consonant therefore cannot be fully pronounced without being followed by another independent sound, namely the sound produced by this rush of air. This independent sound may be either breathed or voiced.

564. When we pronounce a *voiceless* plosive, e.g. **p**, "by itself," it is generally followed by a short breathed sound which may be represented by ^h, thus **p**^h. When we pronounce a voiced plosive, e.g. **b**, by itself, it is generally followed by a short vowel, which may be represented by ˚, thus **b**˚.

565. When a *voiced* plosive consonant is followed by a vowel, as in the group **bɑː**, the vowel itself constitutes the necessary independent sound.

Voiceless Plosives

566. It is possible to pronounce a *voiceless* plosive consonant followed by a vowel, e.g. the group **pɑː**, in such a way that the vowel constitutes the additional sound necessary for the full pronunciation of the consonant; the effect of this manner of pronouncing the sequence is that the vowel-sound begins at the instant of the explosion of the consonant. It is also possible to pronounce a voiceless plosive consonant followed by a voiced consonant, e.g. the group **pl**, in such a way that the voice begins at the instant of the plosion. Voiceless plosive consonants pronounced in such a way that voice begins at the instant of the plosion are said to be *unaspirated*.

567. Unaspirated voiceless plosives fall into two classes, viz. those uttered with considerable force of exhalation, and those in which the force of exhalation is weak.[16] The former strike the English ear as belonging to the **p, t, k** class; the latter, though voiceless, strike the English ear as belonging to the **b, d, g** class. Examples of the first kind are the French initial **p, t, k**, as in *père* pɛːr, *tard* taːr, *cas* kɑ (see §§ 502, 519, 540); examples of the second are the sounds ḅ, ḍ, g̊, referred to in §§ 501, 518, 539, which are heard in many parts of Germany instead of the distinctly voiced **b, d, g** of normal North German.

568. In English, initial voiceless plosives are not generally pronounced in this way, but as already remarked in §§ 497, 512, 534, breath is heard immediately after the plosion. The sounds are then said to be *aspirated*. Thus *part, pair* could be written 'narrowly' as pʰɑːt, pʰɛə; *praise* might be written 'narrowly' as transcription pᵇreiz. In Denmark and some parts of Germany aspiration of this kind is so strong that there is practically a full independent **h** inserted between **p, t, k**, and following vowels (§§ 501, 518, 539).

Ejective Sounds

569. It is possible to pronounce consonants of plosive nature in which the necessary air pressure is produced by some other means than by the lungs. Sounds in which the air is forced outwards by these means are called *ejective* consonants.

570. The most important ejective sounds are those formed by a closure in the mouth (as for **p, t**, or **k**, for instance), keeping the soft palate raised and *closing the glottis*. The air in the

---

[16] With *voiced* plosive consonants the amount of force does not appreciably influence the effect of the sound on the European ear.

completely enclosed cavity thus formed is slightly compressed, chiefly through muscular action in the throat causing the larynx to rise somewhat; when the closure in the mouth is released, the air therefore escapes with a plosive noise, although the glottis remains closed.   When exaggerated these ejective sounds have a peculiar hollow quality resembling the sound made in drawing a cork out of a bottle.

571. These sounds are mentioned here because French people occasionally use them instead of ordinary voiceless plosives when final.   Such a pronunciation may be corrected by pronouncing a distinct **h** after the explosion, e.g. practising the words *up* ʌp, *get* **get**, *look* **luk**, as ʌph, **geth, lukh**.

Voiced Plosives

572. In voiced plosive consonants the amount of voice heard during the stop may vary.   In English and French when a voiced plosive, e.g. **b**, occurs between two vowels (as in *about* əˈbaut), voice sounds throughout the whole of the stop.   Many French people also pronounce *initial* voiced plosives in this way, e.g. the **b** in *bas* **ba**, the **d** in *doute* **dut**.

573. In English when **b, d**, and **g** occur initially, as when *bee* **biː**, *day* **dei**, *go* **gou** are said by themselves, they are partially devoiced in the pronunciation of most people, that is to say, voice is not heard during the whole of the stop but only during part of it, generally the latter part.   With some speakers the voice disappears altogether, so that the sounds are replaced by **b̥, d̥, g̊**.

574. In the cases mentioned in the two preceding sections, the voice of the following vowel begins at the instant of the plosion.

575. Another variety of plosive consonant may be made, in which the stop is voiced but breath is heard when the contact is released.   Final voiced plosives are often pronounced in this way in English.   This is especially the case when another consonant precedes, as in *bulb* **bʌlb** (narrowly **bʌlbʰ**).

576. With many speakers the stop itself is partially or even completely devoiced in these circumstances.   In the latter case the consonants are very weak voiceless plosive consonants, or sometimes weak 'ejective' sounds (§ 570).   These weakened forms of final voiced consonants may be represented by b̦, d̦, g̦, without inconvenience, being very similar in acoustic effect to the sounds b̦, d̦, g̦, previously described.   Thus when *bulb* is said by itself, it is generally pronounced bʌlb̦.

577. In French, final voiced plosives are generally completed by the addition of a weak central vowel ᵊ, *herbe* for instance being pronounced ɛrbᵊ.   French people should be careful not to make this final ᵊ at all strong in saying such English words as *globe* gloub, *knob* nɔb.

Incomplete Plosive Consonants

578. Sometimes plosive consonants are not fully pronounced. This happens in normal English when a plosive consonant is immediately followed by another plosive consonant or by an affricate.   Thus in the usual pronunciation of such words as *act* ækt, *picture* 'piktʃə, the tongue does not leave the roof of the mouth in passing from the **k** to the **t** or **tʃ**.   There is therefore no explosion of the **k**; only the stop of it is pronounced.   In *Act 2* 'ækt'tuː there is in normal pronunciation no explosion to the **k** or to the first **t**; the first **t** is in fact only indicated by a silence. Similarly in *empty* 'empti there is no explosion to the **p**; its presence is indicated by a silence.[17]   It is a case of a sound and a silence belonging to the same phoneme.   Similarly in *cub-pack* 'kʌbpæk, *begged* begd there are no explosions to the **b** and **g**; only the stops of the sounds are pronounced.

579. In *that time* 'ðæt 'taim, *red deer* 'red 'diə, the first **t** and **d** are not exploded; in fact, the only difference between the **tt**, **dd** here and the **t**, **d** in *satire* 'sætaiə, *red ear* 'red 'iə, *readier* 'rediə, is that in the former cases the stop is very much longer than in the latter.   Further instances of the same kind are *lamp-post* 'læmppoust, *book-case* 'bukkeis, *cockcrow* 'kɔkkrou.

580. In *apt* æpt, *ebbed* ebd the **t**, **d** are formed while the lips are still closed for the **p**, **b**.   The result is that the **p** and **b** do not have normal plosion, that is to say no ʰ or ᵊ is heard when the lips are separated.   Similarly in *suit-case* 'sjuːtkeis the **k** is formed during the stop of the **t**, with the result that little or no plosion is heard when the **t** is released.

---

[17] The word is often reduced to 'emti; there is also a variant 'emm̦ti.

581. In *ink-pot* ˈiŋkpɔt, *big boy* ˈbig ˈbɔi, the lips are closed for the p and b during the stop of the k and g. The result is that no explosion of the k or g is heard.

582. The sequence td in *that day* ˈðæt ˈdei differs from the d in *muddy* ˈmʌdi in having a longer stop, the first part of which is voiceless.[18] In ˈðæt ˈdei, *midday* ˈmiddei (or ˈmidˈdei) the stops are of the same length, but in the former the first part of the stop is voiceless and the second part voiced,[18] while in the latter the stop is voiced throughout. Further instances of the same kind are *scrap-book* ˈskræpbuk, *black gown* ˈblækˈgaun, *soap-bubble* ˈsoupˌbʌbl.

583. The sequence dt in *bedtime* ˈbedtaim only differs from the t in *better* ˈbetə, in having a longer stop, the first part of which is voiced. In ˈbedtaim, ˈðætˈtaim, the stops are of the same length, but in the former the first part of the stop is voiced and the second part voiceless, while in the latter the stop is voiceless throughout. A further instance of the same kind is *egg-cup* ˈegkʌp.

584. Many foreign people pronounce all the above sequences of consonants in an unusual manner, by inserting ʰ or ᵊ between the consonants. The mistake is particularly noticeable in the sequences kt, gd. Foreign people usually pronounce *act* as ækʰt, *picture* as ˈpikʰtʃə, *begged* as begᵊd. The foregoing explanations (§§ 578–583) should enable them without much difficulty to pronounce such words as most English people do.

585. Additional examples for practice: *picked* pikt, *wrecked* rekt, *locked* lɔkt, *cooked* kukt, *worked* wəːkt, *fogged* fɔgd, *tugged* tʌgd, *exactly* igˈzæktli,[19] *expectation* ˌekspekˈteiʃn, *big dog* ˈbig ˈdɔg.

Nasal Plosion

586. In sequences consisting of a plosive immediately followed by a nasal, e.g. the sequence tn in *mutton* ˈmʌtn, the plosive is not pronounced in the normal way. The explosion heard in pronouncing such sequences is not formed by the air escaping through the mouth, but the mouth closure is retained and the explosion is produced by the air suddenly escaping through the nose at the instant when

---

[18] With many speakers the *whole* of the stop is voiceless in these cases.
[19] Also often pronounced igˈzækli or ˈgzækli.

the soft palate is lowered for forming the nasal consonant. This kind of plosion is known as *nasal plosion*.

587. Many foreign people pronounce such English sequences as tn incorrectly. Thus they often pronounce *mutton, topmost*, etc., as 'mʌtən, 'tɔpʰmoust, etc., instead of 'mʌtn, 'tɔpmoust, etc.

588. Those who have difficulty may acquire the correct pronunciation by practising (i) pmpm . . . and bmbm . . . without opening the lips, (ii) tntn . . . and dndn . . . without moving the tip of the tongue, (iii) kŋkŋ . . and gŋgŋ . . . without moving the back of the tongue.

589. Additional examples for practice: *shopman* 'ʃɔpmən, *written* 'ritn, *certain* 'sə:tn, *sudden* 'sʌdn, *hidden* 'hidn, *bacon* 'beikŋ (alternative form of 'beikən), *oatmeal* 'outmi:l, *sharpness* 'ʃɑ:pnis.

Lateral Plosion

590. In the sequences tl, dl, as in *little* 'litl, *middle* 'midl, the explosion of the t is lateral, that is to say the tip of the tongue does not leave the teeth-ridge in pronouncing the sequence. Many foreign people have difficulty in doing this, and consequently replace tl by təl or something similar (thus 'litel, 'midəl). The correct pronunciation of the tl in *little* may be acquired by practising the exercises tltltl . . ., dldldl . . . with the tip of the tongue kept firmly pressed against the upper teeth, where it can be seen. In pronouncing these exercises the tip of the tongue should not move at all.

590a. Many English people reinforce syllable-final p, t, k by means of a simultaneous glottal stop. The onset of this glottal closure may precede that of the oral closure, as in *top* tɔʔp, *eight* eiʔt, *back* bæʔk. A similar glottalization may accompany syllable-final tʃ, e.g. *catch* kæʔtʃ.

Chapter XVIII

THE ENGLISH AFFRICATE CONSONANTS

591. An 'affricate' consonant is a kind of plosive in which the articulating organs are separated more slowly than usual. In pronouncing ordinary plosives the separation is made with great rapidity, and the acoustic effect of the consonant is what might be called 'clean-cut'; the plosion itself may be regarded as an instantaneous noise; if a vowel or an aspiration (**h**) follows, the ear cannot detect any intermediate glide between the plosion and that vowel or aspiration.

592. When, however, the separation of the articulating organs is performed less rapidly, the ear perceives distinctly the glide between the plosion and a following sound. The effect of this glide is essentially the sound of the homorganic fricative consonant, through the position for which the articulating organs necessarily pass.

593. There exist degrees of affrication corresponding to the degrees of rapidity with which the separation of the articulating organs is performed. If affrication is perceptible but only very slight, the sound is classified as a plosive. But if there is strong affrication, such that the effect of the homorganic fricative is distinctly perceived by the hearer, then the sound is classified as an affricate.

594. As there exist fricative consonants corresponding to every plosive, so also there are affricates corresponding to every plosive (with the exception of ʔ which has no corresponding fricative).

595. The nature of an affricate may be well seen by articulating the affricate corresponding to the plosive **b**. Pronounce the syllable **bɑ** firstly in the normal manner and then performing the separation of the lips slowly in such a way that the bi-labial fricative β[1] is heard before the vowel begins; the consonant then becomes an affricated **b**. A similar exercise should be tried with

---

[1] The Middle German sound of *w*, Spanish sound of *b*.

a *dental* **d**. First pronounce the syllable **da** (with a dental **d**), then make a similar movement but withdrawing the tongue slowly from the teeth in such a way that the dental fricative **ð**[2] is heard as a transitory sound before the vowel begins; the consonant then becomes an affricated dental **d**.

596. It is convenient as a rule to represent affricates in phonetic transcription by digraphs consisting of the symbol for the normal plosive followed by the symbol for the homorganic fricative. Thus the affricate corresponding to **b** may be written **bβ**, and the affricate corresponding to dental **d** may be written **dð**. Affricates corresponding to other sounds of the **d**-type may be written **dz**, **dʒ**, **dɹ**, etc. The breathed affricates may be represented in a similar way thus **pɸ**,[3] **tθ**, **ts**, **tʃ**, **tɹ**,[4] **kx**,[5] corresponding to **p**, dental **t**, other varieties of **t**, **k**, etc.

597. The fricative glide which finishes an affricate is an essential part of its pronunciation; this glide gives to each affricate its distinctive character, and it is never suppressed.[6] In this respect affricates differ from plosives (see §§ 578–583). Thus the affricate is pronounced with plosion and off-glide in the past tenses of verbs ending in **tʃ** or **dʒ**, as in *attached* **əˈtætʃt**, *pledged* **pledʒd**. But in the past tenses of verbs ending with the plosives **p**, **b**, **k** or **g**, e.g. in *stopped* **stɔpt**, *rubbed* **rʌbd**, *cracked* **krækt**, *dragged* **drægd**, these consonants have no plosion. The same thing is well seen in compound words and in juxtapositions of words. The affricates **tʃ** and **dʒ** are pronounced with plosion and off-glide in *latch-key* **ˈlætʃkiː**, *which place* **ˈwitʃ ˈpleis**, *lodge-keeper* **ˈlɔdʒ₁kiːpə**, *large town* **ˈlɑːdʒ ˈtaun**, *Bridgetown* **ˈbridʒtaun**, *orange juice* **ˈɔrindʒ dʒuːs**. (The plosive consonants have no plosion in similar combinations, e.g. in *hat-box* **ˈhætbɔks**, *hat-pin* **ˈhætpin**, *that place* **ˈðæt ˈpleis**, *neck-tie* **ˈnek-tai**, *back door* **ˈbæk ˈdɔː**, *cardboard* **ˈkɑːdbɔːd**, *egg-plant* **ˈegplɑːnt**, *pug dog* **ˈpʌg dɔg**, *Egton* **ˈegtən**, *Bridport* **ˈbridpɔːt**.)

---

[2] For **ð** see § 702.

[3] **ɸ** is the symbol for 'bi-labial *f*.'

[4] Generally simplified to **tɹ** or **tr**.

[5] **x** represents the German *ach*-sound.

[6] If we except the case of 'doubling' in languages such as Italian and Hindi.

598. For the above reason the representation of affricates by digraphs is particularly appropriate.

599. At the same time it must be realized that it is sometimes more convenient to represent affricates by single letters. Such representation is feasible in writing the many languages which contain relatively few affricates; it could hardly be applied to a language containing a number of affricates, owing to the difficulty of devising a sufficient number of good symbols. When a language contains only two affricates of the tʃ and dʒ type, the letters c and ɟ are appropriate for representing them, provided that these letters are not required for representing palatal plosives in the same language.[7]

600. In Received English there are six affricates which may be represented phonetically by the digraphs tʃ, dʒ, ts, dz, tr, dr. (tr, dr are written in place of tɹ̥, dɹ, in order to avoid the introduction of the additional symbols ɹ, ɹ̥).

$$\boxed{\text{tʃ}}$$

601. In pronouncing the principal member of the English tʃ-phoneme, the air-passage is completely blocked by raising the soft palate and raising the tip and blade of the tongue into the

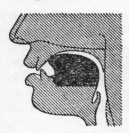

Fig. 69. Tongue-position of the 'stop' of the affricate tʃ.

position shown in Fig. 69, that is to say a closed position in which the main part of the tongue is shaped nearly as for ʃ (Fig. 99); while the 'stop' is being held, air is compressed by pressure from the lungs; when the tongue is removed from the teeth-ridge, the air escapes through the mouth: the removal of the tongue is performed in such a way that the effect of the homorganic fricative ʃ is audible before any following sound is reached (see § 592); the vocal cords are not made to vibrate.

---

[7] Some phoneticians recommend using c and ɟ in transcribing English. I am doubtful if there is anything to be gained by adding these two symbols, and it might be urged that there would be an inconsistency in not also introducing special signs for tr and dr.

The formation of tʃ may be expressed shortly by defining it as a *voiceless palato-alveolar affricate* consonant.[8]

602. Those whose languages contain aspirated and unaspirated plosives regard the English tʃ as aspirated in stressed position, as in *chair* tʃɛə, *enchant* inˈtʃɑːnt. This aspiration is, however, combined with the ʃ-element and is not heard clearly following it. Nevertheless, the notation tʃʰɛə, inˈtʃʰɑːnt may be used when it is desired to show the aspiration. In unstressed position there is little or none of this aspiration in English (e.g. in *kitchen* ˈkitʃin *lecture* ˈlektʃə).

603. tʃ really stands for a diaphone; that is to say the sound varies to some extent with different speakers. In particular there is variation in lip-articulation. With some (probably the majority) the tongue-articulation is accompanied by protrusion of the lips as for ʃ (Fig. 101), while with others the lips are spread. Slight variations may also be observed in the position of the tip of the tongue.

Fig. 70. Palatogram of the English tʃ in the syllable tʃɑː.

604. Fig. 70 shows a palatogram of the English tʃ. It should be compared with the palatograms of English t (Figs. 64, 65), ts (Fig. 72) and tr (Fig. 73).

605. tʃ is the usual English sound of *ch* and *tch*, as in *chain* tʃein, *choose* tʃuːz, *orchard* ˈɔːtʃəd, *watch* wɔtʃ, *wretched* ˈretʃid. It is also the usual sound of t in unstressed *-ture*, as in *furniture* ˈfəːnitʃə, *nature* ˈneitʃə.[9] *Ti* has the value of tʃ when the termination *-tion* is preceded by *s*, as in *question* ˈkwestʃən, *combustion* kəmˈbʌstʃən. *Te* is pronounced tʃ in *righteous* ˈraitʃəs, but not in other words ending in *-teous*.

606. Most foreign learners do not experience difficulty in pronouncing an adequate tʃ. Danes, however, are apt to substitute tj for it, and make *choose* sound too much like tjuːz; to remedy this error it is first necessary to learn to make a good ʃ by the method given in § 735; then a good tʃ may be acquired by prefixing to ʃ the appropriate variety of t. The sound must, if necessary,

---

[8] For glottalization of tʃ, see § 590a, p. 159.

[9] Exceptions are *aperture* ˈæpətjuə, *overture* ˈouvətjuə (rarely with -tʃə).

be somewhat exaggerated by articulating with the tip of the tongue
a little too far back, and care must be taken to round and protrude
the lips well as shown in Fig. 101.

607. Words for practice: *cheap* tʃiːp, *chin* tʃin, *check* tʃek, *chap*
tʃæp, *charm* tʃɑːm, *chop* tʃɔp, *chalk* tʃɔːk, *choose* tʃuːz, *chum* tʃʌm,
church tʃəːtʃ, *picture* 'piktʃə, *chain* tʃein, *choke* tʃouk, *child* tʃaild,
choice tʃɔis, *cheer* tʃiə, *chair* tʃɛə; *each* iːtʃ, *ditch* ditʃ, *sketch* sketʃ,
porch pɔːtʃ, *much* mʌtʃ, *birch* bəːtʃ, *H* eitʃ, *broach, brooch* broutʃ,
couch kautʃ.

608. The affricate tʃ must be distinguished from the sequence
t + ʃ which also occurs in English.   When it is desired in phonetic
transcription to show that this sequence is used, a hyphen must
be placed between the t and the ʃ.   Examples of the group t + ʃ
are *courtship* 'kɔːt-ʃip, *nutshell* 'nʌt-ʃel, *light-ship* 'lait-ʃip, *Dorsetshire*
'dɔːsit-ʃə.

$$\boxed{\text{dʒ}}$$

609. The principal member of the English dʒ-phoneme is formed
like tʃ except that the vocal cords are made to vibrate so that
'voice' is produced during the articulation of the sound. The
formation of the sound may therefore be expressed shortly by
defining it as a *voiced palato-alveolar affricate* consonant.

610. Being a voiced sound it cannot have 'aspiration' in the
ordinary sense of the term.

611. The dʒ-phoneme has subsidiary members with partial voice
which are used in initial and final positions (as when *generally*
'dʒenrəli is initial or when *bridge* bridʒ is final), and when a breathed
consonant precedes (as in *gas-jet* 'gæsdʒet). Many English people
use a completely voiceless d̥ʒ̊ in these situations.

612. dʒ is subject to diaphonic variations similar to those
mentioned in § 603.

613. dʒ is the usual English sound of *j*, and the usual sound
of *g* before *e*, *i*, and *y*[10]; examples: *jump* dʒʌmp, *jaw* dʒɔː, *jet* dʒet,
gem dʒem, *giant* 'dʒaiənt, *page* peidʒ, *pigeon* 'pidʒin, *religion* ri'lidʒən,

---

[10] For the words in which *g* before *e* or *i* has the sound g see footnote 14
on p. 149.

gymnastic dʒim'næstik; *dg* has this sound in *edge* edʒ, *judgment*
'dʒʌdʒmənt, etc.   Note also the miscellaneous words *grandeur*
'grændʒə, *soldier* 'souldʒə, *Greenwich* 'grinidʒ, *Norwich* 'nɔridʒ,
sandwich 'sænwidʒ.[11]

614. Most foreign people, except Danes and South Germans,
pronounce dʒ sufficiently well without difficulty.   Danes are apt
to replace it by dj and make *June* dʒuːn sound too much like *dune*
djuːn; to correct this error, learn ʒ first (§ 742) and then prefix
the appropriate variety of d, taking care to articulate with the
tip of the tongue against the teeth-ridge (not too far forward)
and to protrude the lips as shown in Fig. 101.

615. South Germans are liable to use d̥ʒ̊, a voiceless sound
resembling tʃ, in place of dʒ.   This sounds wrong to English people
when voiced sounds precede and follow, as in *engaging* in'geidʒiŋ),
adjoin ə'dʒɔin.   But the use of d̥ʒ̊ does not matter when such a
word as *join* dʒɔin is said by itself or is initial in a sentence, or
when such a word as *edge* edʒ is said by itself or is final in a sentence.
Foreign learners who have difficulty in giving sufficient voice to
dʒ should practise exercises of the types recommended in §§ 177,
792.

616. Words for practice: *Jean* dʒiːn, *jig* dʒig, *gem* dʒem, *Jack*
dʒæk, *jar* dʒɑː, *job* dʒɔb, *jaw* dʒɔː, *June* dʒuːn, *just* dʒʌst, *journey*
'dʒəːni, *injure* 'indʒə, *James* dʒeimz, *joke* dʒouk, *gibe* dʒaib, *joy*
dʒɔi, *jeer* dʒiə; *bridge* bridʒ, *large* lɑːdʒ, *George* dʒɔːdʒ, *age* eidʒ.

$$\boxed{\text{ts}}$$

617. The sequence of letters ts is used in more than one sense in
transcribing English.   There exists an affricate ts, but it is a rare
sound and only occurs in words and names borrowed from foreign
languages such as *tsetse* 'tsetsi (first ts),[12] *Tsana* 'tsɑːnə, *Tsushima*
'tsuːʃimə.   There exist also sequences consisting of t followed by s;

---

[11] But *Ipswich* 'ipswitʃ, *Droitwich* 'drɔitwitʃ.   Some say 'sænwitʃ in the
singular, but 'sænwidʒiz seems to be universal for the plural.   The place-
name *Sandwich* is more usually 'sænwitʃ, but some say 'sænwidʒ and there
exists an old-fashioned pronunciation 'sænidʒ.   *Ostrich* is usually pronounced
'ɔstritʃ, but the form 'ɔstridʒ may also be heard.
[12] Also pronounced 'tetsi.

in some cases, e.g. in *outside* **ˈautˈsaid**, *outset* **ˈautset**, the two sounds
are clearly separated, while in other cases, e.g. in *cats* **kæts**, *curtsey*
ˈkəːtsi, they are pronounced together in more or less intimate
combination. Thus though the **ts** of *curtsey* is not a true affricate,
it is more like an affricate than the **ts** of *outside* is. In **ˈtsetsi** the
first **ts** is a true affricate, but the second is like the **ts** in *curtsey*.

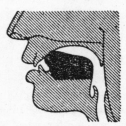

Fig. 71. Tongue-posi-
tion of the 'stop' of the
affricate **ts**.

Fig. 72. Palatogram
of the affricate **ts** in
the syllable **tsɑː**.

618. The affricate **ts** is formed by placing the main part of the
tongue as for **s** (§ 709) and bringing the blade to touch the teeth-
ridge as shown in Fig. 71; air is compressed by pressure from the
lungs, and then the tongue is removed not too rapidly from the
teeth-ridge; at the beginning of the separation there is a plosion,
and as the separation proceeds, the effect of a short **s** is audible;
the vocal cords are held apart during the production of the sound, so
that no 'voice' is present. The formation of the sound may be
expressed shortly by defining it as a *voiceless blade-alveolar affricate*
consonant.

619. Fig. 72 shows a palatogram of the affricate **ts**. It should
be compared with the palatograms of English **t** (Figs. 64, 65), **tʃ**
(Fig. 70) and **tr** (Fig. 73).

620. As the true affricate **ts** is so uncommon in English, and as
it appears to occur exclusively in initial position, it is not necessary
for practical purposes to have a special symbol to distinguish it
from the group **t + s**. When it is desired to show specially that **t**
and **s** are separately pronounced, a hyphen may be introduced,
thus *outset* **ˈaut-set**.

dz

621. The affricate **dz** is formed like the affricate **ts** except that its articulation is accompanied by vibration of the vocal cords so that 'voice' is heard. The formation of the sound may therefore be expressed shortly by describing it as a *voiced blade-alveolar affricate* consonant.

622. The sound is very uncommon in English. It only occurs in foreign proper names beginning with **dz**, e.g. *Dzungaria* **dzʌŋ'gɛərïə**.

623. There also occurs in English the sequence **d + z**, in which the two sounds are in fairly intimate combination, though not sufficiently intimate as to constitute a true affricate. This sequence **dz** is common in final position, as in *reads* **riːdz**, *fields* **fiːldz**, *woods* **wudz**; in this position it is often partially or completely devoiced (see §§ 722, 788, 789). In medial position **dz** is rare, and occurs mainly in compound words, such as *bird's-eye* **'bəːdzai**, and in borrowed foreign words, such as *piazza* **pi'ædzə**.

tr

624. As already mentioned in § 617, it is often difficult to draw a line of demarcation between an affricate and an intimate combination of two sounds. It is, however, probably correct to class the Southern English **tr** (as in *tree* **triː**) as an affricate. The sound **tr** is formed by placing the main part of the tongue as for **r** (§ 747) and bringing the tip of the tongue to touch the back part of the teeth-ridge very much as shown in Fig. 28; air is compressed by pressure from the lungs, and then the tongue is removed not too rapidly from the teeth-ridge; at the beginning of the separation there is a plosion, and as the separation proceeds the effect of **ɹ̥** (breathed fricative **r**) is audible; the vocal cords are held apart during the production of the sound, so that no 'voice' is present. The formation of the sound may be expressed shortly by defining it as a *voiceless post-alveolar affricate* consonant.

625. If the separation of the tongue were performed very rapidly, the corresponding plosive would be produced. This plosive is one variety of Indian retroflex (cerebral) **ṭ** (*ṭ*).

626. Fig. 73 shows a palatogram of the affricate **tr**. It should be compared with the palatograms of English **t** (Figs. 64, 65), **tʃ** (Fig. 70), and **ts** (Fig. 72).

Fig. 73. Palatogram of the affricate **tr** in the syllable **trɑː**.

627. The affricate **tr** is the usual sound of *tr* in English; examples: *tree* **triː**, *straight* **streit**, *entrance* **'entrəns**.

628. Foreign learners who have difficulty in pronouncing the English **r** have also difficulty with **tr**. There are two methods of acquiring **tr**. One is to learn **r** first, by the methods suggested in § 766, and then prefix to it the appropriate variety of **t**. The other is to start from **tʃ** and try to pronounce it with the jaws widely separated. Place two fingers one above the other between the teeth, and try to say **tʃ**; the resulting sound approximates very nearly to the English **tr**. This exercise may be done still better with a cork about an inch in diameter; the endeavour to pronounce *chain* **tʃein** with the cork held between the teeth produces a syllable almost identical with *train* **trein**.

629. Words for practice: *tree* **triː**, *trick* **trik**, *treasure* **'treʒə**, *travel* **'trævl**, *trance* **trɑːns**, *trot* **trɔt**, *trawler* **'trɔːlə**, *true* **truː**, *trust* **trʌst**, *tradition* **trə'diʃn**, *train* **trein**, *trophy* **'troufi**, *try* **trai**, *trout* **traut**, *Troy* **trɔi**, *matron* **'meitrən**, *poultry* **'poultri**, *symmetry* **'simitri**, *actress* **'æktris**.

630. The affricate **tr** must be distinguished from the sequence **t + r** which also occurs in English. When it is desired in phonetic transcription to show that this sequence is used, a hyphen must be placed between the **t** and the **r**, unless there is a stress-mark separating the letters. Examples of the sequence **t + r** are *rest-room* **'rest-rum**, *outrageous* **aut'reidʒəs**.

631. The affricate **dr** is formed like **tr** except that the vocal cords are made to vibrate so that 'voice' is produced during the articulation of the sound. The formation of the sound may therefore be expressed shortly by defining it as a *voiced post-alveolar affricate* consonant.

632. If the separation of the tongue-tip from the roof of the mouth is performed very rapidly, the sound produced is no longer an affricate but is the corresponding plosive. This plosive is one variety of Indian retroflex (cerebral) **ḍ** (*ḍ*).

633. The affricate **dr** is the usual sound of *dr* in English; examples: *dream* **driːm**, *draw* **drɔː**, *hundred* **'hʌndrəd**. It occasionally occurs finally in words borrowed from French, such as *cadre* **kɑːdr**; in these cases the **dr** is often partially or completely devoiced.

634. Foreign learners who have difficulty in pronouncing the English **r** have also difficulty with **dr**. **dr** may be acquired by methods similar to those recommended for **tr** (§ 628). *Jaw* **dʒɔː**, *jug* **dʒʌg** pronounced with a large cork held between the teeth become practically *draw* **drɔː**, *drug* **drʌg**.

635. Words for practice: *dream* **driːm**, *drip* **drip**, *dread* **dred**, *drag* **dræg**, *draft*, *draught* **drɑːft**, *drop* **drɔp**, *draw* **drɔː**, *drew* **druː**, *drum* **drʌm**, *dramatic* **drə'mætik**, *draper* **'dreipə**, *drove* **drouv**, *dry* **drai**, *drought* **draut**, *Droitwich* **'drɔit-witʃ**, *dreary* **'driəri**, *drawer*[13] **drɔə** or (more commonly) **drɔː**, *Drury* **'druəri**; *laundry* **'lɔːndri**, *Andrew* **'ændruː**, *bedroom* **'bedrum**,[14] *kindred* **'kindrid**.

636. The affricate **dr** must be distinguished from the sequence **d + r** which also occurs in English. When it is desired in phonetic transcription to show that this sequence is used, a hyphen must be placed between the **d** and the **r**, unless there is a stress-mark separating the letters. Examples of the sequence **d + r** are *head-rest* **'hed-rest**, *head-room* (room for one's head) **'hed-rum**,[14] *blood-red* **'blʌd'red** or **'blʌd-red**, *hand-writing* **'hænd-raitiŋ**.[14]

---

[13] Meaning a sliding box in a table, etc. *Drawer* meaning a person who draws is **'drɔːə**.

[14] It is noteworthy that *bedroom* is usually said with the affricate **dr**. In other compounds the **d** and **r** are pronounced separately, as shown in § 636.

Chapter XIX

THE ENGLISH NASAL CONSONANTS

637. Nasal consonants are formed by closing the mouth-passage completely at some point, the soft palate being held in its lowered position so that the air is free to pass out through the nose.

638. There are three nasal consonant phonemes in English. They are represented phonetically by the letters **m**, **n**, **ŋ**.

639. The principal member of the English **m**-phoneme is formed as follows. The mouth-passage is completely blocked by closing the lips; the soft palate is lowered so that, when air is emitted by pressure from the lungs, it passes out through the nose; the tongue is held in a neutral position; the vocal cords are made to vibrate so that 'voice' is produced. The formation of the sound may be expressed shortly by defining it as a *voiced bi-labial nasal* consonant.

640. When a vowel follows, the position of the tongue during the production of **m** approximates to the position required for that vowel. To this extent, therefore, it may be said that there are subsidiary members of the phoneme. With most speakers, however, these differences of tongue-position are slight and their effects on the acoustic quality of the sound are negligible.

641. A labio-dental nasal (ɱ) is used by some speakers as a subsidiary member of the **m**-phoneme when **f** or **v** follows, as in *triumph* **ˈtraiəmf**, *comfort* **ˈkʌmfət**, *Dumville* **ˈdʌmvil**, *information* **imfəˈmeiʃn** (a variant of **infəˈmeiʃn**). This subsidiary sound is used chiefly by those whose upper teeth project considerably beyond the lower teeth.

642. A partially devoiced **m** (phonetically **m̥**) sometimes occurs as a subsidiary member of the **m**-phoneme when **s** precedes in the same syllable, as in *small* **smɔːl** (see § 845 (i) *a*).

643. m is the regular sound of the letter *m*; examples: *make* meik, *come* kʌm. *M* is, however, silent in initial *mn-*, as in *mnemonic* niːˈmɔnik.

n

644. The principal member of the English n-phoneme is formed as follows. The mouth-passage is completely blocked by raising the tip of the tongue to touch the teeth-ridge as shown in Fig. 74; the soft palate is lowered so that, when air is emitted by pressure from the lungs, it passes out through the nose; the vocal cords are made to vibrate so that 'voice' is produced. This formation may be expressed shortly by defining the sound as a *voiced alveolar nasal* consonant.

645. Subsidiary members of the English n-phoneme exist, and notably an advanced (dental) variety which is used when θ or ð follows (as in *enthusiasm* inˈθjuːziæzm, *in there* ˈin ˈðɛə) and a retracted variety used before r (as in *enrol* inˈroul). Practically these varieties are of no importance, since they are acoustically almost indistinguishable from the principal n. A partially devoiced n also occurs as a subsidiary member of the phoneme. It is used when s precedes in the same syllable (as in *sneeze* sniːz, see § 845 (i) *a*).

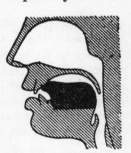

646. Some foreign people, chiefly speakers of Romance languages, regularly use a dental n, i.e. a n articulated by the tip of the tongue against the upper teeth. The difference of sound is unimportant except in final position, where the use of dental n gives an unnatural effect to English ears. These foreign people have no difficulty in pronouncing such words as *own*

Fig. 74. Position of Tongue and Soft Palate for English n.

oun, *done* dʌn with an alveolar n, when once the formation has been explained to them.

647. Some Germans use a slightly palatalized n differing from the usual English n in the same way as the German l does from the English final l (see Chap. XX). The correct English n has a

duller quality than this German variety of **n**. The "clear" quality
of this palatalized variety is often strengthened by lip-spreading.
The effect of the sound is strange to English ears when final or
followed by a consonant, and especially when preceded by a back
vowel, e.g. in *pond* **pɔnd**, *soon* **suːn**. The correct English **n** presents
no great difficulty after the English final 1 has been acquired
(§§ 670–672). Note that lip-spreading should be avoided in
pronouncing the English **n**, and that if a back vowel precedes,
as in **pɔnd**, **suːn**, it is well to maintain the lip position of the back
vowel until the completion of the **n**.

648. The palatograms of the various kinds of **n** are similar to
those of **t** (Figs. 64, 65, 66, 67).

649. French learners have to be told that *-gn-* is pronounced
with **g** followed by **n** in English. Those who do not know this
follow French usage, and use a palatal nasal consonant (**ɲ**) in
such words as *ignorance* **ˈignərəns**.

649a. **n** is the usual sound of the letter *n*; examples: *nine* **nain**,
linen **ˈlinin**.

ŋ

650. The principal member of the English **ŋ**-phoneme is formed
as follows. The mouth-passage is completely blocked by raising
the back of the tongue to touch the fore part of the soft palate as
shown in Fig. 75; the soft palate is in its lowered position, so that
when air is emitted by pressure from the lungs it issues through
the nose; the vocal cords are made to vibrate, so that 'voice' is
produced. The formation of this **ŋ** may be expressed shortly by
defining it as a *voiced velar nasal* consonant.

651. Varieties of **ŋ** with fronter and backer tongue-articulation
occur as subsidiary members of the phoneme. Their use is determined by the nature of the adjacent vowels. Thus the principal **ŋ**
is used after **ʌ**, as in *young* **jʌŋ**, *trunk* **trʌŋk**, and when **ɔ** precedes
and **i** follows, as in *belonging* **biˈlɔŋiŋ** (first **ŋ**); a backer variety
of **ŋ** is used after **ɔ** finally, as in *long* **lɔŋ**; and varieties of different
degrees of advancement are used after the front vowels, the frontest
occurring after **i**, as in *sing* **siŋ**, *bringing* **ˈbriŋiŋ**. These differences
of articulation can easily be felt, but they are of no practical
importance, because the acoustic differences are hardly appreciable.

652. The ŋ-phoneme is represented in spelling by final *ng*, as in *king* **kiŋ**, and very often by *n* before letters representing **k** and **g** sounds, as in *ink* **iŋk**, *anchor* **'æŋkə**, *finger* **'fiŋgə**, *'strongest* **'strɔŋgist**.

653. In regard to the pronunciation of the sequence of letters *ng* when medial, it is to be noted that (i) ŋ alone is used in words formed from verbs by the addition of the suffixes *-er* and *-ing*, e.g. *singer* **'siŋə**, *hanging* **'hæŋiŋ**; (ii) the prefix *con-* when followed by the sounds **k** or **g**, is pronounced by most people with ŋ when the following syllable is quite unstressed, but with **n** when the following syllable has stress (primary or secondary); thus, *congress* **'kɔŋgres**, *congregation* **ˌkɔŋgri'geiʃn** have ŋ, while *concur* **kən'kəː**, *congratulation* **kənˌgrætju'leiʃn** have **n**; (iii) the prefixes *en-*, *in-*, *un-* are pronounced with **n** by most speakers of Received English: thus *engage* **in'geidʒ**, *ingredient* **in'griːdïənt**, *ungrateful* **'ʌn'greitfl** have **n**.   These latter prefixes are also generally pronounced with **n** when **k** follows, as in *encourage* **in'kʌridʒ**, *increase* (noun) **'inkriːs**, *increase* (verb) **in'kriːs**, *uncomfortable* **ʌn'kʌmfətəbl**.   There is, however, a tendency at the present day to use ŋ in place of **n** in cases (ii) and (iii).

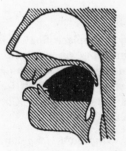

Fig. 75. Tongue-position of Cardinal ŋ.

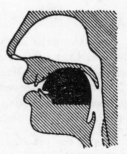

Fig. 76. Tongue-position of Cardinal ɲ.

654. The principal English ŋ gives no palatogram on an ordinary artificial palate, since no part of the contact is against the hard palate.   The subsidiary ŋ used after **i** gives the palatogram shown in Fig. 77.

655. The sound ŋ is often pronounced incorrectly by French people.   They have a tendency to replace it by the palatal nasal ɲ, especially when a front vowel precedes. The difference between ŋ and ɲ will be seen from Figs. 75, 76.

656. ɲ is the ordinary French '*n* mouillé,' as in *montagne* mõtaɲ. French people have to remember that for the English ŋ the contact of the tongue with the palate is much further back than for the French ɲ. It is often useful for them to practise the sound ŋ with the mouth very wide open.[1]

Fig. 77. Palatogram of the 'advanced' ŋ in the English sequence -iŋ (my pronunciation).

Fig. 78. Palatogram of French ɲ in the sequence aɲa.

657. Some Germans have a tendency to replace final ŋ by the sequence ŋk, thus confusing for instance *sing* siŋ and *sink* siŋk. This defect may be remedied by pronouncing final ŋ very long, thus siŋː. It should be observed that the substitution of ŋk for ŋ in *nothing, something, anything* is found in London dialect (Cockney) but is not considered a desirable pronunciation.

658. Words for practice: *bring* briŋ, *sang* sæŋ, *long* loŋ, *rung* rʌŋ; *longing* ˈloŋiŋ, *singer* ˈsiŋə; *longest* ˈloŋgist, *anger* ˈæŋgə, *anchor* ˈæŋkə, *younger* ˈjʌŋgə, *handkerchief* ˈhæŋkətʃif.

---

[1] The mouth may be kept open if necessary by means of a large cork, 1¼ inches wide, placed between the front teeth.

Chapter XX

THE ENGLISH LATERAL CONSONANTS

659. The lateral consonants occurring in English are represented phonetically by the letter l. Several varieties occur in Received Southern English, but for practical purposes it is sufficient to distinguish two. These are known as 'clear' l and 'dark' l. They are members of the same phoneme, the principle governing their use being that clear l occurs only before vowels and before j, while dark l is only used before all other consonants and finally. Thus 'clear' l is used in *leave* liːv, *lake* leik, *along* əˈlɔŋ, *million* ˈmiljən, while 'dark' l is used in *feel* fiːl, *field* fiːld, *people* ˈpiːpl.[1]

660. Both these consonants are primarily articulated by the tip of the tongue touching the teeth-ridge in such a way that though there is complete closure in the middle of the mouth, yet a passage for the air is left on one or both sides of the tongue; the soft palate is in its raised position; the vocal cords are made to vibrate so that 'voice' is produced. This formation may be expressed shortly by defining the sounds as *voiced alveolar lateral* consonants. In order to give a *complete* definition of any particular variety of l-sound it is, however, necessary to specify in addition the position of the main body of the tongue (see §§ 665–669).

661. In narrow (allophonic) transcription the clear l and dark l are distinguished as l and ɫ respectively. Thus the word *little*, which is usually transcribed simply ˈlitl, might be written in narrow transcription ˈlitɫ.

662. The English l-phoneme is always represented in current spelling by the letter *l*. Examples: *let* let, *look* luk, *collar* ˈkɔlə, *bell* bel (narrow transcription beɫ), *belt* belt (beɫt), *people* ˈpiːpl (ˈpiːpɫ). *L* is silent in *calf* kɑːf, *half* hɑːf, *behalf* biˈhɑːf, *chalk* tʃɔːk, *walk* wɔːk, *Fa(u)lkner* ˈfɔːknə; *balm* bɑːm, *calm* kɑːm, *palm* pɑːm, *psalm* sɑːm, *qualm* kwɔːm,[2] *Malmesbury* ˈmɑːmzbəri, *salmon* ˈsæmən; *could* kud and kəd, *should* ʃud and ʃəd, *would* wud and

---

[1] Many English people use a very dark l when it is syllabic (as in ˈpiːpl) and a less dark variety in other cases (as in fiːl, fiːld).

[2] Also kwɑːm.

173

wəd and əd, *Holborn* 'houbən³; *folk* fouk, *yolk* jouk, *Folkestone*
'foukstən; *holm* houm; *Lincoln* 'liŋkən; *calve* kɑːv, *halve* hɑːv, *salve*
(soothe) sɑːv⁴; *colonel* 'kəːnl.

663. Many foreign people articulate their l-sound with the tip or
blade of the tongue against the *teeth*. It should be noticed,
however, that such variations in the position of the tip of the
tongue do not appreciably affect the quality of l-sounds. Variations in the quality of l-sounds are due chiefly to the position of
the *main part of the tongue* (see § 665, also footnote 6 on p. 176).

664. l-sounds are pronounced *unilaterally* by many. In this
pronunciation the tongue obstructs the air passage in the middle
of the mouth and on one side, the air being free to pass out on
the other side. The sounds thus produced are not appreciably
different from the normal lateral sounds, in which both sides are
open.

665. Many varieties of l-sounds may be formed with the tip
of the tongue in the lateral position against the teeth-ridge or
teeth. These varieties depend on the position of the *main part
of the tongue* and not on the position of the tip; this is a point
of considerable importance. While the tip is touching the teeth-
ridge or teeth, the main part is free to take up any position, and
in particular it may take up any vowel-position. The l-sound
produced with a given vowel-position of the main part of the
tongue always has a noticeable acoustic resemblance to that vowel;
it may be said to have the 'resonance' of that vowel. It is not
difficult to pronounce a whole series of l-sounds having the resonance
of all the principal vowels, i, e, ɑ, ɔ, u, ə, etc. These varieties
of l may be represented, when necessary, by the notation lⁱ, lᵉ,
lᵃ, lᵒ, lᵘ, lᵉ, etc.⁵

666. Figs. 79, 80 and 81 show the approximate positions of
the tongue in pronouncing lⁱ, lᵘ, and lᵉ with the tip of the tongue
against the teeth-ridge. Similar diagrams may be drawn to show
the formation of lⁱ, lᵘ, lᵉ pronounced with the tip of the tongue
against the teeth.

---

³ 'houlbən is now sometimes heard from speakers of Received English,
and this pronunciation seems to be gaining ground.

⁴ But *salve* in the sense of 'to save a ship' is sælv. *Valve* is vælv.

⁵ It is often convenient in oral work to refer to these sounds as 'l with
i-resonance,' 'l with u-resonance,' etc.

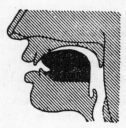 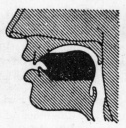 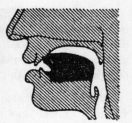

Fig. 79. Tongue-posi-
tion of 'clear' l (l^l).

Fig. 80. Tongue-posi-
tion of 'dark' l (l^u).

Fig. 81. Tongue-posi-
tion of intermediate
l (l^e).

Fig. 82. Palatogram
of l^l with tip of
tongue placed as in
English.

Fig. 83. Palatogram
of l^e with tip of
tongue placed as in
English.

Fig. 84. Palatogram
of l^a with tip of
tongue placed as in
English. The palato-
gram of l$^{ɔ:}$ (l with
resonance of English
long ɔ:) is very
similar to this.

Fig. 85. Palatogram
of l^ɔ (l with resonance
of English short ɔ)
with tip of tongue
placed as in English.

Fig. 86. Palatogram
of l^u with tip of
tongue placed as in
English.

Fig. 87. Palatogram
of l^ə with tip of
tongue placed as in
English.

667. Figs. 82 to 87 are palatograms showing the differences between some of the chief varieties of l pronounced with the tip of the tongue placed as in English. A similar set of diagrams may be obtained showing the differences between the same varieties of l pronounced with the tip of the tongue placed further forward.

668. The difference between 'clear' varieties of l and 'dark' varieties of l is thus simply a difference of vowel resonance. In clear varieties of l there is a raising of the front of the tongue in the direction of the hard palate (in addition to the tongue-tip articulation), while in dark varieties of l there is a raising of the back of the tongue in the direction of the soft palate. In other words, clear l-sounds have the resonance of front vowels, whereas dark l-sounds have the resonance of back vowels.[6]

669. The English 'dark' l, which is used finally and before consonants,[7] generally has the resonance of a back vowel approaching u. The Southern English 'clear' l, which is used before vowels, generally has the resonance of a front vowel approaching i.[8]

---

[6] It must not be thought that the peculiar quality of the dark l as compared with the clear l is due to the retraction of the tip of the tongue. A dark l with u resonance pronounced with the tip of the tongue against the back part of the teeth-ridge is indistinguishable as regards acoustic effect from a dark l with u resonance pronounced with the tip of the tongue right against the teeth. Similarly a clear l with i resonance pronounced with the tip of the tongue against the back part of the teeth-ridge is indistinguishable acoustically from a clear l with i resonance pronounced with the tip of the tongue against the teeth. The same applies to all the other varieties. Note that the English dark l is articulated with the tip of the tongue against the teeth in such a word as *health* helθ; note also that if a foreign learner is unable to pronounce the English dark l with the tip of the tongue right against the teeth, he may be quite certain that he is forming the sound incorrectly (see § 670).

[7] Other than j.

[8] Both are subject to slight variations depending on the nature of the adjoining vowel. The only cases of note are when the adjoining vowel is ɑ or ɔ. When the dark l is preceded by ɑ or ɔ, its resonance tends towards these vowels; and when the clear l is followed by ɑ or ɔ, it tends towards a 'neutral' l with the resonance of ə. These varieties are other subsidiary members of the Southern English l-phoneme.

It should be remarked here that the treatment of l-sounds is different in other types of English. In particular, in Scottish English and in American English dark l is commonly used in all positions. In Irish English l is clear in all positions. There are, moreover, English people, especially in the North, who use intermediate l-sounds in all situations.

670. Most foreign people use a clear l in English in all situations, instead of using a dark l when final or followed by a consonant. It is often a matter of considerable difficulty to them to acquire the pronunciation of dark l. The best way of obtaining it is to place the tip of the tongue *between the teeth*[9] in the lateral position, and, while the tip of the tongue is pressed firmly against the upper teeth, to try to pronounce the vowel u without rounding the lips.

671. Many foreign learners find it easier to acquire l° first, by pressing the tip of the tongue firmly against the upper teeth in the lateral position and trying to pronounce simultaneously the vowel ɔ. When l° is obtained, the quality of the sound has then to be gradually modified until the correct lᵘ is arrived at. It should be remarked, however, that the sound l° should only be used as an exercise and should not be used instead of lᵘ in speaking. (The Portuguese have a tendency to do this.)

672. Other foreign learners find it more helpful to press the tip of the tongue firmly against the upper teeth in the lateral position and try to pronounce a series of vowels, beginning with i, e.g. i, e, a, ɔ, u. With a little practice they are generally able to produce readily the various varieties of l, namely lⁱ, lᵉ, lᵃ, l°, lᵘ, and can therefore in particular pronounce the lᵘ of Received English.

673. The easiest words for practising the dark l are those in which the sound is syllabic (§ 211) and not preceded by t or d (§ 590), e.g. *people* ˈpiːpl, *table* ˈteibl, *knuckle* ˈnʌkl, *struggle* ˈstrʌgl; the most difficult words for most foreign people are those in which the preceding vowel is ɔː or ou, e.g. *all* ɔːl, *old* ould.

674. The Japanese are generally unable to make any kind of l with certainty. They confuse it with r, and use varieties of l and r indiscriminately for both l and r when speaking English. It is not difficult to teach a Japanese to make a l by explaining

---

[9] The reason for saying 'between the teeth' is that many foreign learners try to obtain the peculiar resonance of the English lᵘ by curling back or 'inverting' (§ 827) the tip of the tongue. The sound so formed is quite different from a dark l. The tendency to invert the tongue is avoided if the tip of the tongue is placed between the teeth, and when once l can be correctly pronounced with the tip of the tongue between the teeth, there is no difficulty in retracting it to the more usual position just behind the upper teeth. See footnote 6 on previous page.

the manner in which the sound is produced. In the first instance
the best results are obtained if the Japanese learner practises l
with the tip of the tongue pressed firmly against the upper teeth.
When he has mastered the sound pronounced in this way, he
may proceed to form a l in the normal English position against
the teeth-ridge.

675. The chief difficulty for the Japanese is not to learn to
make l, but to remember to *use* it in the proper places in connected
speech. It is a help to practise reading from phonetic texts in
which every l is underlined and every **r** is marked in some distinctive
way (e.g. by drawing a circle round it).

676. Russians have difficulty in making the English clear l.
Before sounds of the i and e type they substitute a 'palatalized' l
which is followed by a distinct j-glide; their pronunciation of
live, *let* sounds like ljiv, ljet. Before other vowels they use a
dark l; thus they pronounce *like*, *lock* as ɫaik, ɫɔk. To improve
their pronunciation they should learn to use a l of intermediate
resonance, such as l° or l°, by the method indicated in § 672.

677. Words for practising clear l[10]: *leave* liːv, *lick* lik, *let* let,
lamb læm, *large* lɑːdʒ, *long* lɔŋ, *law* lɔː, *look* luk, *lose* luːz, *love*
lʌv, *learn* ləːn; *lake* leik, *loaf* louf, *line* lain, *loud* laud, *employ*
im'plɔi; *clear* kliə, *flare* flɛə, *floor* flɔə or flɔː; *cellar* 'selə' *calling*
'kɔːliŋ, *jelly* 'dʒeli.

678. Words for practising dark l: *double* 'dʌbl, *noble* 'noubl,
possible 'pɔsəbl, *struggle* 'strʌgl, *eagle* 'iːgl, *angle* 'æŋgl, *vessel* 'vesl,
partial 'pɑːʃl, *little* 'litl, *settle* 'setl, *middle* 'midl, *candle* 'kændl;
feel fiːl, *fill* fil, *fell* fel, *shall* ʃæl, *snarl* snɑːl, *doll* dɔl, *fall* fɔːl,
full ful, *fool* fuːl, *dull* dʌl, *curl* kəːl, *fail* feil, *foal* foul, *file* fail, *fowl*
faul, *foil* fɔil; *field* fiːld, *milk* milk, *health* helθ, *Alps* ælps, *scald*
skɔːld, *bulk* bʌlk, *pulpit* 'pulpit, *ruled* ruːld; *nails* neilz, *cold* kould,
child tʃaild, *owls* aulz, *coils* kɔilz.

---

[10] Most foreign learners, other than the Russians and the Japanese, do not
need to practise the words with clear l. The l which they are accustomed
to use in their own language generally suffices.

Chapter XXI

THE ENGLISH FRICATIVE CONSONANTS

Detailed Descriptions

679. Fricative consonants are formed by a narrowing of the air-passage at some point so that, when air is expelled by pressure from the lungs, it escapes with a kind of hissing sound.

680. All fricative consonants may be pronounced with a varying amount of audible friction. In the case of voiced fricative consonants, when the friction is so reduced as to become practically imperceptible, the sounds become 'frictionless continuants' (Chap. XXII).

681. There exist in English ten fricative consonant phonemes. They are represented in phonetic transcription by the letters **f, v, θ, ð, s, z, ʃ, ʒ, r, h.**

$$\boxed{\mathbf{f}}$$

682. The sound **f** is formed by pressing the lower lip against the upper teeth and allowing the air to force its way between them and through the interstices of the teeth; the soft palate is in its raised position and the glottis is left open. This formation may be expressed shortly by defining the sound as a *breathed labio-dental fricative* consonant. The lip-position is shown in Fig. 88.

Fig. 88. Formation of **f**.

683. The positions of the tongue and lips during the articulation of **f** approximate to those required for adjacent vowels. To this extent therefore it may be said that there exist subsidiary members of the phoneme (considering the **f** with neutral tongue-position to be the principal member). These differences of tongue and lip positions are, however, slight, and their effects on the acoustic

179

quality of the sound are negligible for the ordinary linguist.[1]
For practical linguistic purposes it may therefore be said that the
English f-phoneme consists of a single sound and has no subsidiary
members differing appreciably from the principal member.

684. f is the regular sound of *f* and *ph*; examples: *far* fɑː,
faithful 'feiθful, *philosophy* fi'lɔsəfi. *Gh* is pronounced f in the
following common words: *enough* i'nʌf, *rough* rʌf, *tough* tʌf, *cough*
kɔf,[2] *trough* trɔf,[2] *laugh* lɑːf, *draught* drɑːft; also in the less common
words *chough* tʃʌf, *slough* (skin of a snake) slʌf.[3] Note the pronunciation of *lieutenant* lef'tenənt.[4]

685. The Japanese generally replace f by a breathed *bilabial*
fricative ɸ (Fig. 89). (One form of ɸ is the sound made in

blowing out a candle; ɸ is the breathed
consonant corresponding to the voiced
sound β described in §§ 692, 806.) The
error may be remedied by holding the
upper lip out of the way, and practising
the sound with the lower lip firmly
pressed against the upper teeth.

Fig. 89. Formation of ɸ
('bilabial f').

686. The same error is occasionally
met with from Germans and Norwegians, especially when the sound
is preceded by a consonant, e.g. in *useful* 'juːsfl.

687. Words for practice: *feed* fiːd, *fit* fit, *fence* fens, *fat* fæt,
farm fɑːm, *fond* fɔnd, *force* fɔːs, *foot* fut, *food* fuːd, *fun* fʌn, *fir*
fəː; *fail* feil, *fold* fould, *fine* fain, *found* faund, *foil* fɔil; *fear* fiə,
fair fɛə, *four* fɔə or fɔː, *Balfour* 'bælfuə[4a]; *safe* seif, *loaf* louf, *half* hɑːf.

688. The principal English v is formed like the principal English
f (§ 682 and Fig. 88) except that the vocal cords are made to

---

[1] I have been informed by Miss Iza Thompson, a particularly able teacher
of the deaf, that it is useful to point out the existence of these subsidiary
members in teaching speech to the deaf.

[2] Also pronounced kɔːf, trɔːf.

[3] But *slough* meaning a 'morass' is slau.

[4] In the army. In the navy there existed until recently the pronunciations
luːtenənt and 'luːtnənt. Now the form lef'tenənt is usual in the navy as
well as in the army. There exists also a pronunciation lə'tenənt.

[4a] Also 'bælfəə, 'bælfɔə, 'bælfɔː.

vibrate so that 'voice' is produced during the articulation of the sound. The formation of **v** may therefore be expressed shortly by defining it as a *voiced labio-dental fricative* consonant.

689. There exist unimportant subsidiary members of the English **v**-phoneme formed by approximating the positions of the tongue, and to some extent the lips, to the positions required for adjacent vowels in connected speech.

690. Partially voiceless varieties of **v** (**v̥**) occur in the speech of some as subsidiary members of their **v**-phoneme in initial and final positions (see §§ 788–794).

691. **v** is the usual sound of *v*; example: *voice* **vɔis**, *wave* **weiv**. *Ph* is generally pronounced **v** in *nephew* **'nevjuː**, though some English people pronounce **'nefjuː**.

692. Many Germans have a tendency to replace **v** by the *bilabial* fricative **β**. **β** has the same lip-position as **ɸ** (Fig. 89). The English sound **v** has the same lip-position as **f** (Fig. 88), and is acquired by simply pressing the lower lip firmly against the upper teeth (taking care to keep the upper lip out of the way) and producing voice, forcing the air through the narrow passage thus formed. In practising the sound the upper lip may, if necessary, be held out of the way with the finger. The German tendency to use **β** is particularly strong when the sound occurs in the neighbourhood of the sound **w**, as in *equivalent* **i'kwivələnt**.

693. Indians generally replace **v** by a *frictionless continuant* **ʋ** in which the lower lip touches the centre front teeth lightly and is so held as to allow the air to escape chiefly at the sides (see Fig. 90). I am informed that Austrians

Fig. 90. Formation of the Frictionless Continuant **ʋ**.

of the Tirol also use this sound. To pronounce **v** correctly, they must observe carefully the difference between Figs. 88 and 90.

694. Words for practice: *veal* **viːl**, *vicar* **'vikə**, *vest* **vest**, *van* **væn**, *vase* **vɑːz**, *volume* **'vɔljum**, *vault* **vɔːlt**, *vulgar* **'vʌlgə**, *verse* **vəːs**; *vain* **vein**, *vote* **vout**, *vine* **vain**, *vow* **vau**, *voice* **vɔis**; *veer* **viə**, *various* **'vɛəriəs**; *give* **giv**, *glove* **glʌv**, *prove* **pruːv**, *wives* **waivz**, *very well* **'veri 'wel**; *a very vivacious and vain villain visited various* *villages of the valley* ə ˈveri viˈveiʃəs ənd ˈvein ˈvilən ˈvizitid ˈvɛərïəs ˈvilidʒiz əv ðə ˈvæli.

| θ |

695. The English phoneme represented by θ may be regarded as comprising only one sound. There are no members of the phoneme differing to any marked extent from this sound.

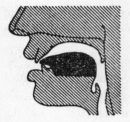

Fig. 91. Tongue-position of θ.

696. The sound θ is articulated by the tip of the tongue against the upper teeth, the main part of the tongue being fairly flat (see Figs. 91, 92); the air passage between the tip of the tongue and the upper teeth is narrow; the soft palate is in its raised position and the vocal cords are not made to vibrate. The formation of θ may be expressed shortly by defining it as a *breathed dental fricative* consonant.

697. Fig. 93 is a palatogram of the English θ.

698. θ is one of the sounds of *th*. *Th* is pronounced in this way (i) initially except in the words mentioned in § 704, e.g. *thin* θin, *thank* θæŋk, (ii) medially in non-Germanic words, e.g. *method* ˈmeθəd, *author* ˈɔːθə, *sympathy* ˈsimpəθi, (iii) finally in all words except those mentioned in § 704, e.g. *mouth* mauθ, *month* mʌnθ.

Fig. 92. Front view of mouth in pronouncing θ.

Fig. 93. Palatogram of θ.

699. Plurals of words ending in *th* take the pronunciation θs in the following cases. (i) If one of the short vowels precedes, e.g. *smiths* smiθs, *breaths* breθs, *moths* mɔθs, *mammoths* ˈmæməθs; (ii) if a consonant precedes, e.g. *lengths* leŋθs, *healths* helθs, *months* mʌnθs; (iii) if the letter *r* precedes in the spelling, e.g. *births* bəːθs, *hearths* hɑːθs (compare *baths* bɑːðz), an exception being *berths* which is bə:θs or bə:ðz; (iv) in the exceptional words *heaths* hi:θs, *faiths* feiθs, *growths* grouθs, *sloths* slouθs.   In other cases ðz is used, e.g. *baths* bɑ:ðz, *mouths* mauðz, *youths* ju:ðz (compare the singular bɑ:θ, mauθ, ju:θ).   In *wreaths, sheaths,* the pronunciation varies; some say ri:ðz, ʃi:ðz and others say ri:θs, ʃi:θs.   My pronunciation is with ðz.[5]   In *cloths* and *broths* the pronunciation varies according to the vowel used.   These words are now generally said with short ɔ, and the plurals are klɔθs, brɔθs; those who, like me, use the more old-fashioned pronunciation with long ɔː generally make the plurals klɔ:ðz, brɔ:ðz.   Some of the latter, however, distinguish two plurals of *cloth*, klɔ:ðz meaning 'pieces of cloth' and klɔ:θs meaning 'kinds of cloth.'

700. Many foreign people replace θ by f or by some variety of s. They may learn to acquire θ by starting with an exaggerated form of it, placing the tip of the tongue so that it projects out between the upper and lower teeth.   When the tongue is in this position, they must blow so that a stream of air passes out between the tongue-tip and the edge of the upper teeth.   The lower lip must be kept out of the way when practising this exercise.   The quality of sound produced in this manner is about the same as that of the ordinary English θ.   When the learner has become familiar with the sound formed in this exaggerated way, he can soon learn to modify the articulation and articulate with the tongue in the normal English position shown in Fig. 91.

700a. It should be observed that in making θ the teeth are separated more widely than in the articulation of s.

701. Words for practice: *theme* θi:m, *thin* θin, *theft* θeft, *thank* θæŋk, *thong* θɔŋ, *thought* θɔ:t, *thumb* θʌm, *third* θə:d, *thermometer* θə'mɔmitə; *Thane* θein,[6] *three* θri:, *thwart* θwɔ:t; *heath* hi:θ, *smith* smiθ, *breath* breθ, *bath* bɑ:θ, *north* nɔ:θ, *truth* tru:θ, *birth* bə:θ; *both* bouθ, *mouth* mauθ; *method* 'meθəd, *author* 'ɔ:θə, *sympathy* 'simpəθi, *ether* 'i:θə; *thirty-three things* 'θə:ti 'θri: 'θiŋz.

---

[5] There is a growing tendency to use the θs forms in many other words, e.g. *truths, baths, oaths.*

[6] But the English river *Thames* is temz, as also are the rivers of that name in Canada and New Zealand; the river *Thames* in Connecticut is θeimz. *Thame* in Oxfordshire is teim.

$$\boxed{\eth}$$

702. The principal member of the English phoneme represented by ð is the voiced consonant corresponding to the breathed θ. Its formation may be expressed shortly by defining it as a *voiced dental fricative* consonant. (See Figs. 91, 92.)

703. Some English people use partially voiceless varieties of ð as subsidiary members of their ð-phoneme in initial and final positions (see §§ 788–794).

704. ð is one of the sounds of *th*. *Th* is pronounced in this way (i) initially in pronouns such as *this* ðis, *they* ðei, and in *than*, *that*, *the*, *then*, *thence*, *there*, *thither*, *though*, *thus*, and their derivatives such as *themselves* ðəm'selvz, *thenceforth* 'ðens'fɔːθ, *therefore* 'ðɛəfɔː, (ii) medially in words of Germanic origin, e.g. *father* 'faːðə, *northern* 'nɔːðən, (iii) in plurals of nouns ending in -*th* not preceded by *r* containing a long vowel or a diphthong, e.g. *paths* paːðz, *youths* juːðz, *oaths* ouðz, *mouths* mauðz (exceptions are *faiths*, *heaths*, *growths*, *sloths* and with some speakers *sheaths*, *wreaths*, *cloths*, see § 699), (iv) finally when there is a mute -*e* in the spelling (e.g. *bathe* beið), and in the single words *with* wið,[7] *bequeath* bi'kwiːð, *booth* buːð, *smooth* smuːð and the rare verbs *mouth* mauð and *south* sauð.[8]

705. Foreign people have the same difficulty with ð as with θ, and the correct sound may be acquired as directed in § 700.

706. Some foreign people, especially Scandinavians and Germans, do not always voice the sound ð properly. They will find it useful to practise singing the sound, sustaining it on various notes.

707. Words for practice: *these* ðiːz, *this* ðis, *then* ðen, *that* ðæt, *thus* ðʌs; *they* ðei, *though* ðou, *thy* ðai, *thou* ðau, *there* ðɛə; *breathe* briːð, *with* wið, *soothe* suːð, *bathe* beið, *loathe* louð, *scythe* saið; *gather* 'gæðə, *worthy* 'wəːði, *hither and thither* 'hiðər ən 'ðiðə.

708. θ and ð are particularly difficult for foreign learners when they occur near the sounds s and z. Students are recommended to practise carefully such phrases as *this is the thing* 'ðis iz ðə 'θiŋ, *the sixth street* ðə 'siksθ 'striːt, *the hyacinths and the chrysanthemums* ðə 'haiəsinθs ən ðə kri'sænθəməmz.

---

[7] Pronounced wiθ in the North of England.

[8] The verb *south* is pronounced sauθ by some.

S

709. The English s-phoneme may be considered for practical language teaching as comprising only one sound.[9] This sound is articulated by the blade (or tip and blade) of the tongue against the teeth-ridge, the 'front' of the tongue being at the same time somewhat raised in the direction of the hard palate (Figs. 94, 95).

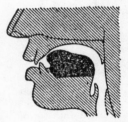

Fig. 94. Tongue-position of s pronounced with tip of tongue raised.

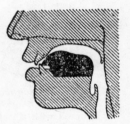

Fig. 95. Tongue-position of s pronounced with tip of tongue lowered.

The teeth are close together; the sound cannot be pronounced with the mouth wide open (see Fig. 96). The space between the blade of the tongue and the teeth-ridge is extremely narrow. The soft palate is in its raised position, and the vocal cords are not made to vibrate. The formation of s may be expressed shortly by defining the sound as a *breathed blade-alveolar fricative* consonant.

710. The tip of the tongue is with some speakers raised towards the teeth-ridge (as shown in Fig. 94), and with others kept against the lower teeth (as shown in Fig. 95). The first formation seems the more usual in English.

Fig. 96. Front view of mouth in pronouncing s.

---

[9] Subsidiary members with varying lip-positions do exist. They are unimportant for ordinary language teaching, but I have been informed that the speech of deaf-mutes can be considerably improved by directing attention to them.

There exists also a weakened form of s which is often used at the ends of words when a breathed consonant precedes, as in *box* bɔks, *books* buks, *shuts* ʃʌts. Some English people use z̦ (§ 722) in such words. See my book *The Phoneme*, §§ 171–175.

711. Fig. 97 is a palatogram of the sound **s**, as pronounced by me (tip of tongue raised). Fig. 98 is a palatogram of the sound **s** as pronounced by a Frenchwoman (tip of tongue lowered). The two sounds though formed slightly differently strike the ear as being very similar.

Fig. 97. Palatogram of English **s** pronounced with tip of tongue raised.

Fig. 98. Palatogram of French **s** pronounced with tip of tongue lowered.

712. There exist many diaphonic variants of **s** differing in the quality of the hiss or the degree of its penetrating power. Some very slight changes in the adjustment of the tongue produce considerable alterations in the acoustic quality of **s**. Moreover, the kinds of **s** which an individual is capable of pronouncing depend to some extent on the formation of his teeth. The occurrence of the various types of **s** in speech is thus partly a matter of language or dialect and partly individual.[10]

713. It may be said that as a general rule the **s** of French people has a more penetrating hiss than that of English people, and the **s** of Germans has a still more penetrating hiss than that of the French. The use of a particularly penetrating **s** is a characteristic of the pronunciation of many Germans, and it sounds incorrect if used in English. An English **s** may be acquired by those who naturally use a sound of more penetrating quality either by diminishing the force of the breath or by articulating with the tip of the tongue raised and held somewhat further back than for the speaker's habitual **s**.

---

[10] Many English people use a variety of **s** involving an articulation by the lower lip against the upper teeth in addition to the tongue articulation. This kind of **s** differs considerably in quality from the normal English **s**.

714. s is the normal sound of the letter *s* in English, as in *so* sou, *sets* sets. *S* is always pronounced s at the beginnings of words, but in other positions it is very frequently pronounced z. Compare *absurd* əb'sə:d, *absolve* əb'zɔlv; *cease* si:s, *please* pli:z, *base* beis, *phrase* freiz; *close* (adj.) klous, *close* (v.) klouz; *use* (noun) ju:s, *use* (v.) ju:z, *used to* (in the senses of 'accustomed to,' 'was in the habit of') ju:st, *used* ('made use of') ju:zd; *this* ðis, *is* iz. Most of the rules regarding the use of s and z are so complicated and subject to such numerous exceptions, that the foreign learner will find the easiest way of acquiring the correct pronunciation is to learn the pronunciation of each word individually as he comes across it.

715. The following points should, however, be noted. (i) The *s* denoting the plural of nouns or third person singular of verbs is pronounced s when the preceding sound is a voiceless consonant, e.g. *cats* kæts, *takes* teiks, *laughs* lɑ:fs. (ii) The *s* in the terminations -*sive*, -*sity* is nearly always pronounced s, e.g. *conclusive* kən'klu:siv, *curiosity* kjuəri'ɔsiti. (iii) Final *s* preceded by one of the letters *a, i, o, u* or *y* is pronounced s (when not mute[11]), e.g. *gas* gæs, *atlas* 'ætləs, *this* ðis, *basis* 'beisis, *chaos* 'keiɔs, *us* ʌs or əs,[12] *genius* 'dʒi:njəs, *precious* 'preʃəs,[13] *Gladys* 'glædis. The only exceptions are the inflected forms of nouns and verbs (e.g. *plays* pleiz, *was* wɔz or wəz), and the single words *his* hiz (weak form iz), *as* æz (weak form əz), *whereas* wɛə'ræz, *avoirdupois* ˌævədə'pɔiz.

716. The following is a list of the chief words ending in -*se* in which the final consonant is s: *abase* ə'beis, *base* beis, *case* keis (and compounds, e.g. *encase* in'keis, *staircase* 'stɛəkeis), *chase* tʃeis, *purchase* 'pə:tʃəs or 'pə:tʃis; *cease* si:s, *crease* kri:s, *decease* di'si:s, *decrease* (noun) 'di:kri:s, *decrease* (v.) di:'kri:s, *grease* (noun) gri:s,[14] *increase* (noun) 'inkri:s, *increase* (v.) in'kri:s, *lease* li:s, *release* (noun and v.) ri'li:s[15]; *Chersonese* 'kə:səni:s, *geese* gi:s, *obese* ou'bi:s; *anise* 'ænis, *concise* kən'sais, *paradise* 'pærədais, *practise* 'præktis, *precise*

---

[11] For examples of mute final *s* see § 718.

[12] Reduced to s in the expression *let us* . . . lets . . . meaning 'we had better' (see footnote 21 on p. 135).

[13] Foreign people often say ʌz, 'preʃəz, etc.

[14] *Grease* (v.) is gri:z.

[15] When the noun is used in the technical legal sense, opposed to *lease*, it is commonly pronounced 'ri:'li:s.

pri'sais, *premise* (noun) **'premis**,[16] *promise* **'promis**; *tortoise* **'tɔːtəs**; *bellicose* **'belikous**, *close* (noun meaning 'enclosed place,' and adj.) **klous**,[17] *dose* **dous**, *jocose* **dʒə'kous**, *morose* **mə'rous**, *purpose* **'pəːpəs**, *verbose* **vəː'bous**; *goose* **guːs**, *loose* **luːs**, *noose* **nuːs** (also pronounced **nuːz**); *obtuse* **əb'tjuːs**, *profuse* **prə'fjuːs**, *recluse* **ri'kluːs**, *refuse* (noun) **'refjuːs**,[18] *use* (noun) **juːs**, *grouse* **graus**, *house* **haus**, *louse* **laus**, *mouse* (noun) **maus**,[19] *souse* **saus**; also all words ending in -*lse*, -*nse*, -*pse*, -*rse* (with the single exceptions of *cleanse* **klenz** and *parse* **pɑːz**), e.g. *else* **els**, *dense* **dens**, *lapse* **læps**, *course* **kɔːs**.

717. The sound *s* is also the usual sound of *c* before *e*, *i*, and *y*, as in *cell* **sel**, *face* **feis**, *cinder* **'sində**, *mercy* **'məːsi**.

718. *S* is silent in *isle* **ail**, *island* **'ailənd**, *aisle* **ail**, *corps* (sing.) **kɔː**,[20] *chamois* **'ʃæmwɑː**,[21] *rendezvous* (sing.) **'rɔndivuː**,[22] *debris* **'debriː**, *demesne* **di'mein**, *viscount* **'vaikaunt**.

719. Some foreign learners tend to voice the sound **s**, especially when it occurs between two vowels, thus replacing it by **z**; others will use a partially voiced **z** or an 'unvoiced **z**,' a sound which has an effect intermediate between **s** and **z** (phonetic symbol **z̥**). Those who have this tendency should practise words like *necessary* **'nesisəri** or **'nesisri**, *ceaseless* **'siːslis**.

720. Further words for practice: *see* **siː**, *sit* **sit**, *set* **set**, *sat* **sæt**, *psalm* **sɑːm**, *song* **sɔŋ**, *saw* **sɔː**, *soot* **sut**, *soon* **suːn**, *son* **sʌn**, *certain* **'səːtn**, *say* **sei**, *so* **sou**, *sigh* **sai**, *sound* **saund**, *soil* **sɔil**; *serious* **'siəriəs**, *Sarah* **'sɛərə**, *soar*, *sore* **sɔə**[23]; *this* **ðis**, *less* **les**, *pass* **pɑːs**, *gross* **grous**, *course* **kɔəs**,[24] *scarce* **skɛəs**, *places* **'pleisiz**, *ceases* **'siːsiz**, *exercises* **'eksəsaiziz**.

> [**Z**]

721. The principal English **z** is the voiced consonant corresponding to the breathed **s**. The formation of the sound may

---

[16] Chiefly used in the plural *premises* **'premisiz**.

[17] *Close* (noun meaning 'end,' and v.) are pronounced **klouz**.

[18] *Refuse* (v.) is **ri'fjuːz**.

[19] The rare verb meaning 'to catch mice' is **mauz** (also **maus**).

[20] The plural is **kɔːz**.

[21] Often pronounced **'ʃæmi** in the expression *chamois leather*.

[22] The plural is **'rɔndivuːz**.

[23] Or **sɔː**.

[24] Or **kɔːs**.

therefore be expressed shortly by defining it as a *voiced blade-alveolar fricative* consonant. It is articulated by the blade (or tip and blade) of the tongue against the teeth-ridge, the front of the tongue being at the same time slightly raised in the direction of the hard palate (see Figs. 94, 95). The teeth are brought close together, and the passage between the blade of the tongue and the teeth-ridge is extremely narrow. The soft palate is in its raised position, and the vocal cords are made to vibrate so that 'voice' is produced. Some English people use some lip articulation in addition (see footnote 10 to § 712).

722. Partially voiceless varieties of z occur as subsidiary members of the English z-phoneme in initial and final positions (see § 788). Completely devoiced z̥ may be heard from some English speakers in these positions.[25]

723. z is the sound of the letter *z*; examples: *zone* zoun, *razor* ˈreizə. It is also very frequently represented by the letter *s*, when not initial; examples: *raise* reiz, *easy* ˈiːzi, *observe* əbˈzəːv, *his* hiz. Final *s* denoting the plural of nouns or third person singular of verbs is pronounced z when preceded by a vowel or by a voiced consonant; examples: *trees* triːz, *plays* pleiz, *rushes* ˈrʌʃiz, *dogs* dɔgz, *ideas* aiˈdiəz, *falls* fɔːlz, *gives* givz; also *does* dʌz, *has* hæz, *is* iz, *was* wɔz. Final *s* is pronounced z in other words whenever it is preceded by a pronounced *e*, e.g. *species* ˈspiːʃiːz, *Hades* ˈheidiːz, *aborigines* æbəˈridʒiniːz.[26] Note the exceptional words with final z mentioned at the end of § 715; also *Mrs.* ˈmisiz. Note that *ss* is pronounced z in the words *dessert* diˈzəːt, *dissolve* diˈzɔlv, *hussar* huˈzɑː, *possess* pəˈzes, *scissors* ˈsizəz, and that *house* haus has the irregular plural ˈhauziz.

724. Some foreign people, and especially Scandinavians and Germans, do not voice the sound z properly, but replace it habitually by a consonant which sounds like a weak s (phonetic symbol z̥). They go beyond the permissible devoicing referred to in § 722. Those who have this tendency will find it useful to practise singing the sound z, sustaining it on various notes.

---

[25] z̥ differs from s in being uttered with weaker air-pressure.

[26] The only exceptions are *yes* jes and a few proper names such as *Agnes* ˈægnis, *Elles* ˈelis. Foreign learners should note that the letter *c* is never pronounced z. Note the pronunciation of Latin plurals in -*es* (-iːz), e.g. *axes* (plural of *axis*) ˈæksiːz. Compare *axes* (plural of *axe*) ˈæksiz.

725. Words for practice: *zeal* ziːl, *zest* zest, *Zoo* zuː, *zones* zounz; *scissors* ˈsizəz, *reserves* riˈzəːvz, *diseases* diˈziːziz.

ʃ

726. The English phoneme represented by the letter ʃ may be considered as comprising only one sound. There are no subsidiary members of the phoneme differing to any marked extent from the principal member.

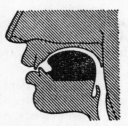

Fig. 99. Tongue-position of English ʃ pronounced with tip of tongue raised.

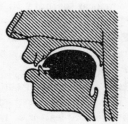

Fig. 100. Tongue-position of English ʃ pronounced with tip of tongue lowered.

727. The normal English ʃ is articulated by the tip and blade of the tongue against the hinder part of the teeth-ridge, the whole of the main body of the tongue being simultaneously held in a raised position after the manner shown in Fig. 99. The teeth are close or fairly close together; the sound cannot be properly pronounced with the mouth wide open. The space between the blade of the tongue and the teeth-ridge is narrow, though wider than for s; on the other hand the air channel in the region of the palate is narrower than in the case of s. There is protrusion of the lips as shown in Fig. 101. The soft palate is in its raised position, and the vocal cords are not made to vibrate. The formation of ʃ may be expressed shortly by defining the sound as a *breathed palato-alveolar fricative* consonant.

Fig. 101. Lip-position of English ʃ.

728. With most speakers the tongue-tip is raised and articulates against the teeth-ridge. Some people, however, make the sound with the blade only, keeping the tip lowered as shown in Fig. 100. This formation does not entail any perceptible difference in acoustic effect.

729. Some English people use a variety of ʃ made with spread lips. It has a 'clearer' acoustic quality than the normal ʃ.

730. Figs. 102 and 103 are palatograms of ʃ, the first being my own and the second being that of a Frenchwoman. Not withstanding the considerable differences of tongue position shown by these palatograms, there is not much acoustic difference between the sounds.

Fig. 102. Palatogram
of English ʃ pro-
nounced with tip of
tongue raised.

Fig. 103. Palatogram
of French ʃ pro-
nounced with tip of
tongue lowered.

731. The chief differences between the articulation of ʃ and s are well seen by comparing the sectional diagrams (Figs. 99 and 94) which are adapted from X-ray photographs, the palatograms (Figs. 102 and 97), and the photographs of lip-positions (Fig. 101 and 96).

732. ʃ is the usual sound of *sh* in English; examples: *shoe* ʃuː, *wish* wiʃ. It is also often used where the spelling has -*si*-, -*ci*-, -*sci*-, -*ti*-, etc., followed by an unstressed vowel or syllabic consonant; examples: *mansion* ˈmænʃn, *Persia* ˈpəːʃə, *special* ˈspeʃl, *provincial* prəˈvinʃl, *musician* mju(ː)ˈziʃn, *precious* ˈpreʃəs, *ancient* ˈeinʃənt, *ocean* ˈouʃn, *permission* pəˈmiʃn, *conscious* ˈkɔnʃəs, *nation* ˈneiʃn, *vexatious* vekˈseiʃəs, *partial* ˈpɑːʃl,[27] *partiality* pɑːʃiˈæliti,

---

[27] And all other words ending in -*tial* except *bestial* ˈbestjəl and *celestial* siˈlestjəl.

associate (verb) ə'souʃieit, (noun) ə'souʃiit[28]; so also in words
like *censure* 'senʃə, *pressure* 'preʃə. *S* is pronounced ʃ in *sure*
ʃuə, *assure* ə'ʃuə, etc., and in *sugar* 'ʃugə. *Ch* is pronounced
ʃ in various recently borrowed French words, such as *champagne*
ʃæm'pein, *chandelier* ʃændə'liə, *machine* mə'ʃiːn, *moustache* məs'taːʃ.
Chivalry used to be pronounced with tʃ, but is now usually pronounced with ʃ ('ʃivlri).

733. ʃ may be considered as an element of the affricate tʃ.
For details see §§ 601 ff.

734. Some Central and South Germans replace ʃ by the corresponding voiced sound ʒ, especially in intervocalic position. They
must master the difference between the voiced and breathed
sounds, if necessary making use of the tests mentioned in § 91.
They must give special attention to the pronunciation of such
words as *nation* 'neiʃn, *marshes* 'maːʃiz, *social* 'souʃl.

735. Danes generally make ʃ too palatal, with the result that
it sounds to an English ear like ʃj; thus they pronounce *shine*,
which should be ʃain, in such a way that it sounds very like ʃjain.
A correct English ʃ may be acquired by trying to keep the tongue
very loose, and by retracting the tip of the tongue and exaggerating
the lip-protrusion.

736. Words for practising ʃ: *sheaf* ʃiːf, *ship* ʃip, *shell* ʃel, *shadow*
'ʃædou, *sharp* ʃaːp, *shock* ʃɔk, *Shaw* ʃɔː, *shoes* ʃuːz, *shut* ʃʌt, *shirt*
ʃəːt; *shake* ʃeik, *show* ʃou, *shy* ʃai, *shout* ʃaut; *shear* ʃiə, *share* ʃɛə,
shore ʃɔə,[29] *sure* ʃuə[30]; *fish* fiʃ, *ash* æʃ, *marsh* maːʃ, *squash* skwɔʃ,
bush buʃ.

$$\boxed{\text{ʒ}}$$

737. The principal English ʒ is formed like ʃ (§ 727) except
that the air-pressure is weaker and the vocal cords are made to
vibrate so that 'voice' is produced during the articulation of the
sound. It may be described as a *voiced palato-alveolar fricative
consonant*.

---

[28] Note *associate* (verb) ə'souʃieit, *appreciate* ə'priːʃieit, *appreciation*
əpriːʃi'eiʃn, *negotiate* ni'gouʃieit, *negotiation* nigouʃi'eiʃn, but *association*
əsousi'eiʃn (less commonly əsouʃi'eiʃn), *pronunciation* prənʌnsi'eiʃn.

[29] Or ʃɔː.

[30] Also pronounced ʃɔə, ʃɛə, and ʃɔː.

738. Partially voiceless varieties of ʒ occur in initial and final positions (see § 788); they are subsidiary members of the English ʒ-phoneme. Completely voiceless ʒ̊ may be heard from some English speakers in these positions.[31]

739. ʒ is the sound of *s* in words like *measure* ˈmeʒə, *pleasure* ˈpleʒə, -*si*- in *occasion* əˈkeiʒn, *hosier* ˈhouʒə and numerous other words in which -*si*- is immediately preceded by a stressed vowel.[32] ʒ is also heard in the miscellaneous words *usual* ˈjuːʒul or ˈjuːʒŭəl, *azure* ˈæʒə, *seizure* ˈsiːʒə, *transition* trænˈsiʒn,[33] and words recently borrowed from French such as *rouge* ruːʒ, *garage* (noun) ˈgærɑːʒ.[34]

740. ʒ may be considered as an element of the affricate dʒ. For details see §§ 601, 609.

741. Some foreign people, and especially Scandinavians and Germans, do not voice ʒ properly, but replace it by a weak ʃ. Those who have this tendency will find it useful to practise singing the sound ʒ, sustaining it on various notes.

742. Danes generally use a variety of ʒ which is too palatal. The sound which they use sounds to an English ear like ʒj when a vowel follows; thus their pronunciation of *measure* sounds too much like ˈmeʒjə. To correct this the tongue should be held loosely and the articulation should be made with the tip of the tongue rather retracted; the lips should be rounded and protruded as shown in Fig. 101.

743. Words for practice: *seizure* ˈsiːʒə, *pleasure* ˈpleʒə, *treasure* ˈtreʒə, *leisure* ˈleʒə, *enclosure* inˈklouʒə, *composure* kəmˈpouʒə; *prestige* presˈtiːʒ, *barrage* ˈbærɑːʒ, *massage* ˈmæsɑːʒ, *camouflage* ˈkæmuflɑːʒ, *espionage* espiəˈnɑːʒ,[35] *rouge* ruːʒ, *gamboge* gæmˈbuːʒ, *cortège* kɔːˈteiʒ, *beige* beiʒ, *Vosges* vouʒ.

r

744. There exist a number of sounds which fall under the general heading of r-sounds. The one with which we are chiefly

---

[31] ʒ̊ differs from ʃ in being uttered with weaker air-pressure.

[32] Not, however, in words like *rosier* ˈrouziə (comparative of *rosy*).

[33] Pronounced by some trænˈziʃn; also trɑːnˈsiʒn and trɑːnˈziʃn.

[34] Also ˈgæridʒ. The verb *to garage* is usually ˈgæridʒ.

[35] Also pronounced ˈespiənidʒ and esˈpaiənidʒ.

concerned here is the most usual English r-sound which is a fricative consonant.

745. The International Phonetic Alphabet provides special letters for representing various kinds of r-sound in narrow ('allophonic' or 'comparative') transcriptions. It is, however, not as a rule necessary to employ these, since it does not often happen that two of these varieties occur as separate phonemes in a language. The particular variety or varieties used in each language can generally be specified once for all.

746. The chief varieties of r-sound are as follows:

	special symbol
rolled lingual r	r
flapped lingual r	ɾ
fricative lingual r	ɹ
rolled uvular r	ʀ
fricative uvular r	ʁ

There exists also a retroflex flap (ɽ), which though easily confused by Europeans with flapped lingual r, should not be regarded as a 'variety' of r; in most languages in which it occurs it is a separate phoneme from one of the above-mentioned r-sounds.[36]

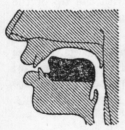

Fig. 104. Tongue-position of English fricative r.

747. The most usual English r is a 'fricative lingual' sound. It is articulated by the tip of the tongue against the back part of the teeth-ridge, the main body of the tongue being kept low and the 'front' being held concave to the palate, as shown in Fig. 104, and the whole tongue being laterally contracted (§73). The distance between the jaws is immaterial; the sound can be pronounced with a wide separation between the upper and lower teeth. The soft palate is in its raised position, and the vocal cords are made to vibrate so that voice is produced during the articulation of the sound. The formation of this r may be expressed shortly by defining the sound as a *voiced post-alveolar fricative* consonant.

---

[36] ɽ is the Swedish dialectal 'thick *l*' and the Indian sound commonly represented romanically by ṛ.

748. A partially voiceless variety of **r** occurs as a subsidiary member of the English **r**-phoneme when a voiceless consonant precedes in the same syllable, as in *prove* **pruːv**, *crowd* **kraud**. See § 845 (i).

749. Many English people pronounce **r** with a certain amount of lip-protrusion, especially in stressed position. Others regularly use a frictionless continuant **r** (§ 796), which is likewise generally accompanied by lip-protrusion in stressed position (§ 797).

750. Many speakers of Received English use a 'flapped' **r** (§ 753) as a subsidiary member of the **r**-phoneme; it occurs chiefly in unstressed intervocalic position, as in *very* **'veri**, *period* **'piəriəd**, and when inserted at the end of a word (§ 756). The use of this subsidiary **r** is not essential; the fricative **r** is also quite commonly used in such cases.

751. In the North of England and in Scotland rolled **r** is generally used in initial position in place of the Southern fricative **r**. The use of rolled **r** is also generally recommended by teachers of singing and elocution in all parts of the country. The sound is also often used in making telephone calls by those who can pronounce it.

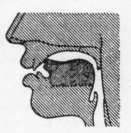

Fig. 105. Action of tongue in pronouncing Rolled Lingual **r**.

752. Rolled lingual **r** is formed by a rapid succession of taps of the tip of the tongue against the teeth-ridge, as shown in Fig. 105. The taps are not made by any conscious muscular movement of the tip of the tongue; the tongue is held loosely in the appropriate position, and the air-stream causes the tip to vibrate. The action is similar to that of a musical reed.

753. Flapped **r** is formed like rolled **r** but consists of only one single tap of the tip of the tongue against the teeth-ridge.

754. Figs. 106 and 107 are palatograms of fricative **r** and flapped **r** (my pronunciation).

755. In non-dialectal Southern English a **r**-sound is the usual pronunciation of the letter *r* when a vowel-sound follows, as in *red* **red**, *round* **raund**, *write* **rait**, *grow* **grou**, *arrange* **ə'reindȝ**, *story*

ˈstɔːri, *for instance* fər ˈinstəns or ˈfrinstəns. In this type of English no r-sound is ever used finally or before a consonant, except occasionally when ə is elided. Thus *far, fir, err, fear, fair, four* are pronounced fɑː, fəː, əː, fiə, fɛə, fɔə or fɔː, and *farm, cord, first, erred, fierce, scarce, fours* are pronounced fɑːm, kɔːd, fəːst, əːd, fiəs, skɛəs, fɔəz or fɔːz; *nearly* ˈniəli rhymes exactly with *really* ˈriəli. Exceptionally r occurs before n and l in one pronunciation of words like *barren* ˈbærn, *quarrel* ˈkwɔrl (more usually ˈbærən, ˈkwɔrəl).

Fig. 106. Palatogram
of English Fricative
r (ɹ).

Fig. 107. Palatogram
of Flapped r (ɾ) in the
sequence ɑːrɑː.

756. But when a word ending with the letter *r* is immediately followed by a word beginning with a vowel, then a r-sound (generally the flapped variety, § 750) is usually inserted in the pronunciation. Thus though *pair* by itself is pronounced pɛə, yet *a pair of shoes* is usually pronounced ə ˈpɛər əv ˈʃuːz. Similarly *your* by itself is pronounced jɔː,[37] *your book* is pronounced ˈjɔː ˈbuk, but *your own* is pronounced jɔːr ˈoun; similarly *our* by itself is auə but *our own* is auər ˈoun[38]; *far* by itself is fɑː, but *far away* is ˈfɑːr əˈwei; *other* by itself is ˈʌðə, but *the other end* is ði ˈʌðər ˈend.[39] r is also generally inserted in compound words, such as *over-eat* ˈouvərˈiːt, *razor-edge* ˈreizərˈedʒ. r inserted in this way is called ‘linking r.’

---

[37] Also jɔə or (less commonly) juə.

[38] Or aər ˈoun or aːr ˈoun (§ 430).

[39] Note the various possible pronunciations of *for him* in *it's very good for him*, when the *him* is unstressed. They are fɔː him, fə him, fɔːr im, for im, fər im, fɔː im; of these for im is perhaps the best for foreign learners to use. *Perhaps* is pəˈhæps or præps; either form may be used in any position; pəˈhæps is fairly common parenthetically (as in *you know, perhaps, . . .* juː ˈnou, pəˈhæps. . . .), and præps is more usual in other cases (e.g. *perhaps we shall* ˈpræps wiː ˈʃæl).

757. There are, however, special circumstances in which a final *r* has no consonantal value even when the following word begins with a vowel. The principal cases are: (i) when the vowel of the syllable in question is preceded by **r**, e.g. *the emperor of Japan* ði 'empərə əv dʒə'pæn, *a roar of laughter* ə 'rɔː əv 'lɑːftə, *a rare animal* ə 'rɛə 'æniml, *nearer and nearer* 'niərə ən 'niərə, *there are at least four of them* ðɛər ə ət 'liːst 'fɔːr ɔv ðəm, (ii) when a pause is permissible between the two words (even though no pause is actually made), e.g. *he opened the door and walked in* hiː 'oupnd ðə 'dɔː ənd 'wɔːkt 'in.

758. Cases may also be found which do not seem to admit of any satisfactory explanation. Thus very many speakers say 'mɔː ən 'mɔː for 'mɔːr ən 'mɔː (*more and more*), bi'fɔː it s tuː 'leit for bi'fɔːr it s tuː 'leit (*before it's too late*). Some people say ə 'pɛə əv 'buːts instead of ə 'pɛər əv 'buːts and ai 'dounou 'wɛə i'tiz for -'wɛər i'tiz (*I don't know where it is*). There appears to be an increasing tendency, especially among younger people, not to use linking **r** at all, particularly when the vowel following the word ending in *r* is unstressed. Sometimes even compound words such as *fire-engine, hair-oil* may now be heard without the **r**: 'faiə,endʒin, 'hɛɔil instead of the more normal 'faiər,endʒin, 'hɛərɔil.

759. Many English people add **r** to words ending in ə when the following word in the sentence begins with a vowel, even if there is no *r* in the spelling. Thus *the idea of it* is very often pronounced ði ai'diər əv it instead of ði ai'diə əv it. Other examples are *china and glass* 'tʃainər ən 'glɑːs, *the sofa over there* ðə 'soufər ouvə ðɛə, *a vanilla ice* ə və'nilər 'ais, *Asia and Africa* 'eiʃər ənd 'æfrikə, *a diploma of honour* ə di'ploumər əv 'ɔnə, *a banana or an apple* ə bə'nɑːnər ɔː ən 'æpl, *Lena Ashwell* 'liːnər 'æʃwəl, *the sonata in F* ðə sə'nɑːtər in 'ef. **r** inserted in such cases is called 'intrusive **r**.' Most teachers discourage its use, but it cannot be denied that a very large number of people, educated as well as uneducated pronounce in this way.

760. An intrusive **r** may also sometimes be heard after ɑː and ɔː. Thus *the Shah of Persia, the law of England* are sometimes pronounced ðə 'ʃɑːr əv 'pəːʃə, ðə 'lɔːr əv 'iŋglənd instead of ðə 'ʃɑː əv 'pəːʃə, ðə 'lɔː əv 'iŋglənd. The use of intrusive **r** after these vowels is less frequent than its use after ə. For further information concerning linking **r** and intrusive **r**, see my *Pronunciation of English* (1950 and subsequent editions), §§ 357–366, and Explanations XV in the 11th (1956) edition of my *English Pronouncing Dictionary*.

761. It is not necessary for foreign people to learn to use intrusive **r**. They should, however, know of its existence; otherwise they may sometimes fail to understand what is said to them by English people who insert it.

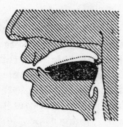

Fig. 108. Position of
tongue and action of
uvula in pronouncing
Uvular Rolled **r** (**ʀ**).

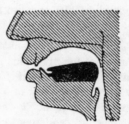

Fig. 109. Tongue-posi-
tion of Uvular Fricative
r (**ʁ**).

762. Many European foreigners, including most French people and most Germans, replace the English **r**-sound by a *uvular* rolled consonant (special phonetic symbol **ʀ**). This sound is formed by a vibration of the uvula against the back of the tongue, somewhat as shown in Fig. 108.[40] This vibration may be seen in a looking-glass, when the sound is pronounced with the mouth wide open.

763. Some European foreigners use the corresponding fricative (narrow phonetic symbol **ʁ**), Fig. 109.

764. The sounds **ʀ** and **ʁ** give no palatograms.

765. The use of **ʀ** or **ʁ** is one of the commonest mistakes made by French, German and Danish people in pronouncing English. It may be added that foreign people often make their pronunciation

---

[40] This action is made possible by holding the tongue in a 'sulcal' position; that is to say, the tongue is held so that the two sides are rather high, but there is a depression or groove down the centre. It is in this groove that the uvula vibrates. The height of the sides of the tongue is indicated by the dotted line in Fig. 108.

still more un-English by pronouncing or giving some indication of
the sound where the letter *r* is final or followed by a consonant—
positions in which **r**-sounds do not exist in non-dialectal Southern
English (§ 755); thus European foreigners often pronounce *part*,
bird as **paαt, bœɐd**, instead of **pɑːt, bəːd**.

766. Experience has shown that the foreign learner who uses a
uvular **r** must first dismiss from his mind his foreign sound of *r*,
and persuade himself that the English sound to be learnt is something entirely different and related only to **z** and **ʒ**. Keeping
this idea in mind, and remembering also the manner of forming
the English **r** described in § 747, many foreign learners are able
to acquire the English sound without much difficulty. For those
for whom these directions are insufficient the following exercise
is generally effective. Keep the mouth very wide open by placing
the bent knuckle of the thumb, or a cork about an inch in diameter,
between the teeth and try as hard as possible to articulate a **ʒ**
with the tip of the tongue against the teeth-ridge. The resulting
sound is very nearly the English fricative **r**. Some foreign people
obtain the sound more easily by trying the same exercise with **z**
or a retracted **ð** instead of **ʒ**. The sound may often be improved
by pushing the tip of the tongue backwards with the end of a
pencil (the end of the pencil being placed underneath the tongue).

767. Thus foreign people may learn to pronounce **r** correctly in
rock, *rat* by inserting the cork between the teeth and trying to
produce the syllables **ʒɔk, ʒæt**, or **zɔk, zæt**, or **ðɔk, ðæt** (with a
retracted **ð**).

768. Foreign learners who are still unable to pronounce a
satisfactory fricative **r** may use a rolled or flapped lingual **r**.

769. Rolled lingual **r** is best acquired by imitation. If simple
imitation is not successful, the following well-known method may
be tried. Pronounce **təˈdɑː** . . . **təˈdɑː** . . . **təˈdɑː** . . . with dental
t's and alveolar **d**'s, at first slowly and then with gradually increasing
speed. By keeping the tongue loose, and pronouncing this exercise
very fast, the **d** tends to become a kind of flapped **r** (§ 753), thus
ˈtrɑː . . . **ˈtrɑː** . . . **ˈtrɑː** . . . . When the flapped **r** has been thus
acquired, after a little practice the action can generally be extended
to the fully rolled sound.

770. If this exercise is not successful, the best thing to do is to practise all kinds of voiced alveolar fricative sounds (ʒ, z, ð and other similar sounds), using considerable force of the breath and trying to keep the tongue loose. It is useful to practise with sudden jerks of the breath. After a little practice students usually manage to hit upon the position in which the tongue will begin to vibrate slightly. To attain a clear sustained r: often requires considerable practice, say five or ten minutes a day for several weeks.

771. Some learners can acquire rolled r more easily when d is prefixed. Others again find it quite easy to make a *breathed* rolled r (either with or without a prefixed t), and can by practice acquire the voiced sound from it.

772. Words for practice: *reason* 'riːzn, *rid* rid, *red* red, *rash* ræʃ, *raft* raːft, *wrong* rɔŋ, *raw* rɔː, *room* rum,[41] *rule* ruːl, *run* rʌn; *race* reis, *rope* roup, *right* rait, *round* raund, *royal* 'rɔiəl or rɔil; *real* riəl, *rarer* 'rɛərə, *roar* rɔə or rɔː, *brewery* 'bruəri; *recruit* ri'kruːt, *retrograde* 'retrougreid, *literary* 'litərəri or 'litrəri.

773. Some foreign people, when they have learnt to realize the fact that in London English the letter *r* is never sounded when final or followed by a consonant, nevertheless still persist in trying to give the effect of a r-sound by curling back, or 'inverting' as it is technically called, the tip of the tongue while pronouncing the vowel (see §§ 831–834).

774. Words for practising the omission of r: *car* kaː, *tar* taː, *war* wɔː, *fur* fəː, *stir* stəː, *over* 'ouvə, *later* 'leitə, *beer* biə, *care* kɛə, *more* mɔə or mɔː, *tour* tuə; *part* paːt, *mark* maːk, *short* ʃɔːt, *corn* kɔːn, *warm* wɔːm, *port* pɔːt,[42] *force* fɔːs,[42] *court* kɔːt or kɔət,[42] *source* sɔːs or sɔəs,[42] *earn* əːn, *fern* fəːn, *girl* gəːl, *world* wəːld, *church* tʃəːtʃ, *hurt* həːt, *concert* 'kɔnsət, *lizard* 'lizəd; *pierce* piəs, *beard* biəd, *weird* wiəd, *scarce* skɛəs, *stairs* stɛəs, *dared* dɛəd, *pears* pɛəz (= *pairs* and *pares*), *gourd* guəd, *assured* ə'ʃuəd.

775. Fricative r may be considered as an element of the affricate dr, and unvoiced fricative ɹ as an element of the affricate tr. For details see §§ 624 ff.

---

[41] Also pronounced ruːm.

[42] Pronounced with ɔə in some parts of the country (see footnote 36 on p. 80).

$\boxed{\text{h}}$

776. The letter **h** denotes the sound of pure breath having a free passage through the mouth. This letter is used in transcribing English and many other languages to represent any one of the sounds produced when the mouth is held in a vowel-position and air is emitted through the wide open glottis. The different varieties of **h** are known as *breathed glottal fricative* consonants, since the friction produced by the air passing through the glottis is the feature common to all of them.

777. There are as many varieties of **h** as there are vowels. In fact, **h**-sounds may be regarded as breathed (devoiced) vowels, and they might in very narrow notation be represented by ị, ạ, ụ, ẹ, etc.

778. The English **h**-phoneme comprises a great many members, the variety used in any particular case being that which corresponds to the vowel immediately following. Thus the **h** in *hit* hit is a breathed i, the **h** in *hard* hɑːd is a breathed ɑ, the **h** in *hook* is a breathed u, and so on.[43] The variety of **h** which has the mouth in the neutral vowel position (as in *hurt* həːt) may be considered as the principal member of the phoneme.

779. There exists also a 'voiced **h**,' which is represented in narrow transcription by the letter ɦ. It has the mouth-position of a vowel but is pronounced with such strong exhaling-force that the air produces considerable friction in the glottis besides causing the vocal cords to vibrate.

780. Voiced **h** occurs in the speech of many English people as a subsidiary member of the **h**-phoneme, when voiced sounds both precede and follow. Thus voiced **h** may often be heard in such words as *behind* biˈhaind, *boyhood* ˈbɔihud, *perhaps* pəˈhæps,[44] *inhabit* inˈhæbit, *the hedge* ðə ˈhedʒ, *two hundred* ˈtuː ˈhʌndrəd. Some speakers would use the ordinary breathed **h** in such cases, especially when speaking slowly. There is therefore no need for the foreign learner to make any special effort to use voiced **h**.

---

[43] These words might be written in very narrow (allophonic) transcription ịit, ɑ̣ːd, ụuk, but such a mode of representation would be both inconvenient and unnecessary.

[44] Also very commonly præps. See footnote 39 on p. 196.

781. The h-phoneme is represented in ordinary English spelling by the letter *h*; examples: *heap* hiːp, *heavy* 'hevi, *hard* haːd, *home* houm, *inhabit* in'hæbit, *dishearten* dis'haːtn. It is represented by *wh* in *who* huː, *whole* houl and their derivatives. The letter *h* is silent in *hour* 'auə, *heir* ɛə, *honour* 'ɔnə, *honest* 'ɔnist and their derivatives; it is also often silent in unstressed syllables, and notably in names ending in -*ham*, such as *Balham* 'bæləm, *Wykeham* 'wikəm (= *Wickham* and *Wycombe*) and in the words *hedgehog* 'hedʒɔg or 'hedʒhɔg, *vehicle* 'viːikl, *annihilate* ə'naiəleit.[45]

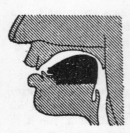

Fig. 110. Tongue-position of the Velar Fricative x.

782. Speakers of French and other Romance languages usually have considerable difficulty in pronouncing h. They generally leave it out altogether. Spaniards usually replace it by the breathed velar fricative (phonetic symbol x), that is, the sound heard for instance in the Scottish *loch* lɔx, Spanish *jabón* xa'βon (Fig. 110). Those who have this difficulty should bear in mind that the h-sounds are simply vowels pronounced with strong breath instead of with voice. A near approach to the h-sounds in *hard* haːd, *he* hiː, *hook* huk, etc., may be obtained by *whispering* the vowels aː, iː, u, etc.

783. There is a peculiarity of French pronunciation which may be made use of for acquiring the English h-sounds. In French, final vowels are often devoiced, e.g. *tant pis* is often pronounced 'tɑ̃ 'pi̥ with devoiced i, *c'est tout* is often sɛ 'tu̥ with devoiced u. In such cases the final sounds are simply varieties of h, i̥ being the same as the h in hiː and u̥ being the same as the h in huː.

784. Most foreign people do not pronounce the h nearly strongly enough in words beginning with hj, e.g. *huge* hjuːdʒ, *human* 'hjuːmən, *hue* hjuː (= *hew*, *Hugh*). Those who have difficulty in acquiring the correct pronunciation should notice that the h in the group hj is very similar to the sound ç (the German *ich-*

---

[45] The letter *h* of ordinary spelling often has no separate consonantal value at all, but is used in conjunction with other letters to form digraphs with special values: thus *ch*, *th* and *sh* generally stand for tʃ, θ or ð, and ʃ respectively.

sound, §§ 820, 821). Many English people, in fact, actually use the sound ç, pronouncing çuːdʒ, etc. It is, therefore, often advisable for foreign learners to adopt the forms with ç rather than those with hj.

785. Words for practice: *heat* hiːt, *hill* hil, *help* help, *hat* hæt, *hard* hɑːd, *hot* hɔt, *hall* hɔːl, *hook* huk, *hoof* huːf, *hut* hʌt, *hurt* həːt; *hay* hei, *hold* hould, *high* hai, *how* hau, *hoist* hɔist; *here* hiə, *hair* hɛə (= *hare*); *behave* biˈheiv, *childhood* ˈtʃaildhud, *buttonhook* ˈbʌtnhuk.

786. In educated English h is often dropped in unimportant words such as *him, her, have,* when unstressed: thus *I should have seen him* is generally pronounced ai ʃəd əv ˈsiːn im. This omission of the h of unstressed words is especially frequent when stressed words beginning with h occur in the same sentence; thus in such a sentence as *she had her hat in her hand* ʃiː hæd əː ˈhæt in əː ˈhænd it would sound pedantic to sound the h in the words *her*. See further, §§ 485, 487, 488.

787. h is occasionally dropped in initial unstressed syllables of longer words, such as *horizon, historical, hotel*. Thus it would be quite usual to pronounce *on the horizon, from the historical point of view* as ɔn ði əˈraizn, frəm ði isˈtɔrikl pɔint ə(v) vjuː. Those who pronounce the h in *hotel* when said by itself would often drop it in *a good hotel* ə ˈgud ouˈtel.

Initial and Final Voiced Fricatives

788. When one of the phonemes z or ʒ occurs initially or finally, partially voiceless sounds are generally used. When initial, as the z in *zeal* ziːl, the sound usually begins without voice and ends with voice; when final, as the z in *please* pliːz, the sound usually begins with voice and ends without voice. Similarly the ʒ in *garage* ˈgærɑːʒ usually begins with voice and ends without voice.

789. When the phoneme is final and preceded by another consonant, a completely voiceless sound is generally used. Thus with most English speakers the z of *heads* hedz or *sounds* saundz (when those words are said by themselves) is completely voiceless and resembles a weak s. This voicelessness may be indicated in narrow transcription by the mark ˳, and the pronunciation of the above words may be shown thus: hedᶎ, saundᶎ (also pronounced saundᶎ and saunᶎ).

790. With some English speakers initial z and all final z and ʒ, whether preceded by consonants or not, are completely voiceless.

791. French people often pronounce initial and final z and ʒ with very full voice; the effect is unnatural to English ears. The ordinary English pronunciation may be acquired by pronouncing the sounds with very weak force.

792. Many other foreign people, and notably Germans and Scandinavians, have difficulty in giving any voice to these sounds. It is necessary for them to learn to make fully voiced z and ʒ in isolation. This may be done as follows. Pronounce a long ə:, and, while this sound is going on, gradually bring the lower lip against the upper teeth in the v-position; the ə:-sound (voice) must be continued while the lip is pressed close enough to the upper teeth to give rise to friction as the air emerges. By this means it is easy to acquire a fully voiced v. Then a similar exercise will give the other fully voiced fricatives ð, z, and ʒ.

793. Very often foreign learners who have taken pains to acquire fully voiced z and ʒ use them without modification in initial and final positions. In fact they do purposely what so many French people do unconsciously (§ 791). They can generally attain a good pronunciation of the z-sounds in *zeal*, *please* by trying to use a sound intermediate between z and s. Similarly they can acquire the partially devoiced varieties of ʒ by aiming at a sound intermediate between ʒ and ʃ. The sounds should be pronounced with weak force, and should have greater resemblance to voiced z and ʒ than to s and ʃ.

794. v and ð are subject to devoicing in similar circumstances, though not to the same degree as z and ʒ. It does not sound wrong to an English ear to hear such words as *veal* vi:l, *wave* weiv, *then* ðen, *smooth* smu:ð pronounced with fully voiced v and ð.

Chapter XXII

FRICTIONLESS CONTINUANTS

795. There exist voiced consonants which have the same or very nearly the same articulatory positions as fricatives, but in which no friction is audible; the absence of audible friction is due either to the fact that less exhaling-force is used than for the corresponding fricative, or to the fact that the aperture at the place of articulation is somewhat wider, or to a combination of both these features.

796. Many English people pronounce **r** as a frictionless continuant instead of as a fricative. The tongue-position required for this variety of **r** is almost identical with that of fricative **r** described in § 747, but the aperture between the tip of the tongue and the teeth-ridge is slightly wider and the sound is produced with less exhaling-force than fricative **r**. The sound is equivalent to a weakly pronounced 'retroflexed' ə (§ 831). It may be denoted, when necessary, by the special symbol ɹ.

797. Many of those whose **r** is a frictionless continuant use a variety which has a certain protrusion of the lips when it occurs at the beginning of a stressed syllable, as in *red* **red**, *arrange* ə'reindʒ. In unstressed position, as in *very* **'veri**, *miracle* **'mirəkl**, a **r** without lip-protrusion is generally used.

798. Examples of other frictionless continuants are a frictionless ʁ (corresponding to the fricative ʁ mentioned in § 763) and the labio-dental frictionless continuant represented phonetically by ʋ (§ 693). Frictionless ʁ is used by many Germans in final position; consequently they often introduce it in such English words as *more*, *better*, pronouncing **mo:ʁ**, **'betʁ** instead of **mo:**, **'betə**. ʋ is used by many Indians in place of both **w** and **v**.

799. Frictionless continuant variants of **w** and **j** are also sometimes heard in English in place of the ordinary semi-vowels (§§ 802, 813). These variants may be indicated phonetically by writing a length-mark after the letters **w** and **j**. Thus the interjections *well* and *yes* are occasionally pronounced **w:el**, **j:es**. These are single syllables, and are distinct from the sequences **u:el**, **i:es** which would be disyllabic. It is weakness of exhaling-force which causes the continuant **w:** and **j:** to be consonantal.

Chapter XXIII

SEMI-VOWELS

800. Semi-vowels are defined as independent vowel-glides in which the speech-organs start by forming a weakly articulated close or fairly close vowel and immediately move to another sound of equal or greater prominence; the initial vowel-position is not held on for any appreciable time. It is the rapid gliding nature of these sounds, combined with the use of rather weak force of exhalation, that renders them consonantal. (See § 102.)

801. In English there exist two semi-vowels; they are represented phonetically by the letters **w** and **j**.[1]

802. In pronouncing **w** the speech-organs start in position for a variety of **u** and immediately leave this for some other vowel position, or occasionally for one of the consonants **l** or **j**. The starting point varies slightly with different speakers and according to the vowel following, but for the purposes of practical teaching it may be considered to be a variety of **u** with the lips pursed up to about the same degree as for the English 'long' **uː** (Fig. 49). The position of this starting point may therefore be described as follows. The lips are closely rounded; there is considerable raising of the back of the tongue in the direction of the soft palate; the soft palate is in its raised position; the vocal cords are made to vibrate so that voice is heard. The formation of **w** may be expressed shortly by defining the sound as a *labio-velar semi-vowel*.

803. The glide away from the above-mentioned starting point may be considered as the principal member of the English **w**-phoneme. The subsidiary members are not important. It may, however, be noted that the lip-rounding is closer when long **uː** follows (as in *woo* **wuː**), and may be less close before vowels remote from **u** (as in *wide* **waid**).

---

[1] In speaking of these sounds they must be called **wə, jə**, on account of their gliding nature.

804. On the other hand, if **w** is pronounced emphatically before any vowel the lip-rounding may be closer than that of **u:** (compare Figs. 111 and 49). For practical purposes therefore the existence of subsidiary members of the **w**-phoneme may be ignored.

Fig. 111. Lip-position of the beginning of **w** in emphatic pronunciation.

805. **w** is the consonantal sound of the letter *w*. It is used when *w* occurs at the beginning of a syllable (except in the group *wr*, in which the *w* is silent) or is preceded by a consonant, e.g. *wait* **weit**, *away* ə**ʹwei**, *twelve* **twelv**. *U* is generally pronounced in this way when preceded by *q*, e.g. *quite* **kwait**,[2] and often when preceded by *g* in unstressed syllables, e.g. *language* **ʹlæŋgwidʒ**. Note the exceptional words *one* **wʌn**, *once* **wʌns**, *choir* **ʹkwaiə**, *suite* **swi:t** (= *sweet*).[3] Examples of **w** followed by **l** and **j** are *equal* (**ʹi:kwl**), *colloquial* (**kəʹloukwjəl**) (alternative forms of **ʹi:kwəl**, **kəʹloukwiəl**).

806. The English sound **w** causes difficulty to many foreign people, and especially to Germans. They generally replace it by a different kind of bi-labial fricative, namely one in which the lips are kept flat instead of being rounded and pushed forward, and in which the tongue is in a neutral position instead of being raised at the back. The phonetic symbol for this consonant is **β**. Its lip-position is the same as that of **φ** (Fig. 89). It is a sound intermediate in acoustic effect between **w** and **v**; it is very frequently heard in German words like *Quelle* **ʹkβɛlə** or **ʹkvɛlə**, *zwei* **tsβai** or **tsvai**. Sometimes foreign learners replace **w** by **v**.

807. The best way of acquiring **w** is to substitute the vowel **u:** for it, and gradually to shorten this **u:**. Germans should begin by practising *win* **win**, *well* **wel**, for instance, as **u:in**, **u:el**, etc. It is also very useful to practise the exercise **u:ə:u:ə:** . . . with energetic motion of the lips. The motion of the lips in this exercise should be entirely *horizontal* (exactly as for **u:i:u:i:** . . .); most foreign learners have an almost irresistible tendency to pass from

---

[2] Not however in *conquer* **ʹkɔŋkə**, *etiquette* **etiʹket**, *exchequer* **iksʹtʃekə**, *liquor* **ʹlikə**, and a few other words.

[3] Note also that the verb *will* (strong form **wil**) has a weak form **l**.

the **uː** to the **əː** by a *vertical* motion of the lower jaw. It will be found helpful to practise this exercise with the teeth kept tightly together.

808. The English sound **w** must be distinguished from the French consonantal sound which is heard at the beginning of *huit*

Fig. 112. Palato-gram of French **ɥ** in the group **ɥə**.

(phonetically **ɥit**) and which French people often substitute for **w** in some English words, such as *persuade* **pəˈsweid**, *Swiss* **swis**. **ɥ** is the semi-vowel corresponding to the French sound of *u* (**y**); in forming its starting-point the lips have a position similar to that of **w**, but there is a simultaneous raising of the 'front' of the tongue towards the hard palate. Fig. 112 is a palatogram of **ɥ**. The English **w** gives no palatogram.

809. Words for practising **w**: *we* **wiː**, *with* **wið**, *wet* **wet**, *wag* **wæg**, *quaff* **kwɑːf**, *want* **wɔnt**, *warm* **wɔːm**, *wool* **wul**, *wound* (injury) **wuːnd**, *won, one* **wʌn**, *word* **wəːd**; *wake* **weik**, *won't* **wount**, *wife* **waif**, *wound* (past of verb *wind*) **waund**; *weird* **wiəd**, *wear* **wɛə**, *wore* **wɔə**,[4] *wooer* **wuə**[5]; *waver* **ˈweivə**, *equivalent* **iˈkwivələnt**. The following sentence affords good practice for foreign learners who have difficulty with **w**: *we would work if we were wise* **wiː ˈwud ˈwəːk if wiː wə ˈwaiz**.

810. The breathed consonant corresponding to **w** (phonetic symbol **ʍ**) is used by many English people in words spelt with *wh*. Thus *what, which* are often pronounced **ʍɔt, ʍitʃ**. This pronunciation, with a variant **hw** which is difficult to distinguish from it, is regularly used in Scotland, Ireland, the North of England and in America. In the South the more usual pronunciation of these words is **wɔt, witʃ**, etc., though the use of **ʍ** or **hw** is some-times taught as being more 'correct'.

811. **ʍ**, being a breathed sound, is a fricative consonant and not a semi-vowel. The friction is always clearly audible. (Semi-vowels have no audible friction, see definition of a vowel, § 97.)

812. **ʍ** may be defined shortly as a *breathed labio-velar fricative* consonant.

---

[4] Or **wɔː**.

[5] Or **ˈwuːə**.

$\boxed{\text{j}}$

813. In pronouncing the most usual English j the speech-organs start at or near the position for the English 'short' i (§§ 254, 255) and immediately leave this for some other sound of equal or greater prominence. The sound following j is generally a vowel, but it may on occasion be one of the consonants l or w. It is the glide away from i that constitutes the consonant j. The starting-point of the principal English j may be described as follows. The front of the tongue is raised rather high in the direction of the hard palate (as for i, Fig. 34); the lips are spread; the soft palate is in its raised position; the vocal cords are made to vibrate, so that voice is heard. The formation of j may be expressed shortly by defining the sound as an *unrounded palatal semi-vowel*.

814. The above is a description of the principal member of the English j-phoneme. The actual sound used in particular words depends to some extent on the nature of the following vowel. The starting-point of j is generally closer than the following vowel. Thus it is very close indeed before i:, as in *yield* ji:ld, but much less close before such sounds as ɑ or ɔ, as in *yard* jɑ:d, *yacht* jɔt. In such a case as *four yards* 'fɔ: 'jɑ:dz the j hardly rises above the position of English Vowel No. 3 (e). It is thus possible to distinguish several subsidiary members of the English j-phoneme. The distinctions, however, are unimportant, and may be ignored in the practical teaching of English.

815. The palatogram of the j in the group jɑ: is practically identical with the palatogram of lax i (Fig. 39).

816. j is the consonantal sound of the letter *y*; examples: *yes* jes, *vineyard* 'vinjəd. *I* and *e* often have the value j when the following sound is ə; examples: *onion* 'ʌnjən, *familiar* fə'miljə, *simultaneous* siməl'teinjəs.[6] Examples of j followed by l and w are *labial* ('leibjl), *arduous* ('ɑ:djwəs) (alternative forms of 'leibjəl or 'leibĭəl, 'ɑ:djŭəs).

817. In words spelt with *u, ue, ui, ew,* and *eu,* representing long u:, j is sometimes inserted before the u: (as in *uniform* 'ju:ni-

---

[6] Note that *i* does not usually have the value of j when followed by vowels other than ə. Thus *peculiarity, pronunciation* are with most speakers pi,kju:li'æriti, prə,nʌnsi'eiʃn (not pikju:'ljæriti, prənʌn'sjeiʃn as sometimes pronounced by foreign people).

fɔːm, *few* fjuː) and sometimes not (as in *rule* ruːl, *chew* tʃuː). The rules with regard to this are as follows. (i) The j is never inserted after tʃ, dʒ, or r, or after l preceded in turn by a consonant; examples: *chew* tʃuː, *June* dʒuːn, *rule* ruːl, *blue* bluː. (ii) The j is regularly inserted after p, b, t, d, k, g, m, n, f, v, h; examples: *pew* pjuː, *beauty* 'bjuːti, *tune* tjuːn, *due* djuː, *queue* kjuː, *argue* 'ɑːgjuː, *music* 'mjuːzik, *new* njuː, *few* fjuː, *fugue* fjuːg, *view* vjuː, *huge* hjuːdʒ. (iii) The j is regularly inserted after l preceded by a vowel, when that preceding vowel is stressed (examples: *deluge* 'deljuːdʒ, *value* 'væljuː[7]) or semi-stressed (example: *aluminium* ˌæljuˈminjəm[8]). (iv) Usage varies in words in which l is initial or preceded by an unstressed vowel; thus *lute*, *absolute* are pronounced ljuːt, 'æbsəljuːt by some, and luːt (like *loot*), 'æbsəluːt by others; the forms with j are recommended by some teachers, but the forms without j appear to be the more usual in ordinary speech, at any rate in the commoner words. (v) After s, z, and θ usage also varies; thus *suit*, *presume*, *enthusiasm* are pronounced sjuːt, priˈzjuːm, inˈθjuːziæzm by some and suːt, priˈzuːm, inˈθuːziæzm by others; I use the forms with j.

818. Some foreign people, and especially North Germans, use a *fricative* j; the effect is somewhat strange to English ears. Fricative j is made by holding the tongue in position for a rather close i and producing voice with considerable exhaling-force. The English semi-vowel j may easily be acquired by observing its gliding nature and by diminishing the force of exhalation.

819. Words for practising j: *yield* jiːld, *Yiddish* 'jidiʃ, *yet* jet, *yak* jæk, *yard* jɑːd, *yacht* jɔt, *yawn* jɔːn, *yew* juː (= *you*), *young* jʌŋ, *yearn* jəːn; *Yale* jeil, *yolk* jouk; *year* jiə or jəː, *your* jɔə,[9] *you're* juə; *beyond* biˈjɔnd,[10] *million* 'miljən, *India* 'indjə.

820. The breathed consonant corresponding to j (phonetic symbol ç) is used by some English people in place of hj in such words as *huge* hjuːdʒ or çuːdʒ, *human* 'hjuːmən or 'çuːmən. A gliding ç (corresponding to the semi-vowel j) must be considered as a fricative consonant, since the friction is clearly audible; in

---

[7] Also pronounced 'væljuː.
[8] More often pronounced with short u (ˌæljuˈminjəm).
[9] Or jɔː, also jɔə and (less commonly) juə.
[10] Also biˈɔnd.

fact it is almost impossible in ordinary connected speech to distinguish by ear between a gliding ç and a continuous fricative ç (corresponding to fricative j).

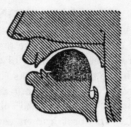

Fig. 113.　Tongue-position of the Palatal Fricative ç

821. The continuant ç may be termed the *breathed palatal fricative*. It is one variety of the German '*ich*-sound.' Its tongue-position is that shown in Fig. 113 or somewhat opener than this.[11]

---

[11] The opening may be as wide as for cardinal i or even slightly wider.

Chapter XXIV

NASALIZATION

822. When sounds (other than plosive and nasal consonants) are pronounced with simultaneous lowering of the soft palate, so that the air passes through the nose as well as through the mouth, they are said to be *nasalized*. Nasalized sounds are generally represented in phonetic transcription by the mark ˜ placed above the symbol of the normal sound. The best known cases of nasalized sounds are the French vowels ɛ̃, ɑ̃, õ (or ɔ̃), œ̃ heard in *vin* vɛ̃, *sans* sɑ̃, *bon* bõ (or bɔ̃), *un* œ̃. Such sounds do not occur in Received English.

823. Some foreign people are apt to nasalize vowels whenever a nasal consonant follows: thus French people often pronounce *jam*, *hand*, *won't* as dʒæ̃m, hæ̃nd, wõnt, instead of dʒæm, hænd, wount; the Portuguese regularly pronounce the English word *tense* (which should be tens) as tẽns or even tẽs. The Dutch and many South Germans have a similar tendency; with these the nasalization is especially noticeable in the diphthongs, e.g. wãĩn or βãĩn instead of wain (*wine*). Some foreign people nasalize all vowels or at any rate all the more open vowels independently of any nasal consonant. Such nasalization is abnormal when introduced into English.

824. Those who habitually nasalize their vowels[1] often have difficulty in getting rid of the fault. It can be cured by constant practice of isolated vowel sounds. It is better to start practising with close vowels, such as iː, uː, there being always less tendency to nasalize these. It is also a good plan to pronounce z before each vowel, because z is a sound which cannot be nasalized without losing most of its characteristic quality. When by means of exercises such as ziːzi: . . . zuːzu: . . . the student is enabled to pronounce a pure iː and uː, which should not require much practice, the opener vowels may be rendered pure by exercises such as

---

[1] We are here speaking of nasalization which is merely the result of habit and not due to any physical defect.

ieie . . ., uouo . . ., iaia . . ., uɔuɔ . . . pronounced without break
between the i and e, u and o, etc. When all the isolated vowels
can be pronounced without nasalization, easy words should be
practised. The greatest difficulty will probably be found in words
in which the vowel is followed by a nasal consonant, e.g. *wine*
wain, *want* **wɔnt**; such words should therefore be reserved till the
last. In practising a word such as **wain** a complete break should
at first be made between the **ai** and the **n**, thus **wai-n**; this interval
may afterwards be gradually reduced until the normal pronunciation
is attained.

825. It can be shown by experimental methods that slight
nasalization of vowels occurs in English when nasal consonants
follow. Such nasalization is, however, not sufficient to give to
the vowels the characteristic nasal tamber. For the purposes of
practical teaching it is therefore necessary to state definitely that
vowels are not nasalized in normal British English.

826. Words for practice: *stream* **striːm**, *limb* **lim** (= *Lympne*),
stem **stem**, *jam* **dʒæm** or **dʒæːm**, *calm* **kɑːm**, *Tom* **tɔm**, *form* **fɔːm**,
room **rum**,[2] *boom* **buːm**, *come* **kʌm**, *germ* **dʒəːm**; *game* **geim**, *home*
houm, *time* **taim**; *seen*, *scene* **siːn**, *tin* **tin**, *then* **ðen**, *ran* **ræn**, *man*
mæn or **mæːn**, *barn* **bɑːn**, *can't* **kɑːnt**, *on* **ɔn**, *corn* **kɔːn**, *spoon* **spuːn**,
one **wʌn**, *learn* **ləːn**, *rain* **rein**, *alone* **ə'loun**, *wine* **wain**, *town* **taun**,
coin **kɔin**; *end* **end**, *hand* **hænd**, *pond* **pɔnd**, *warned* **wɔːnd**, *under*
'ʌndə; *owned* **ound**, *find* **faind**, *found* **faund**, *joined* **dʒɔind**.

---

[2] Also pronounced **ruːm**.

Chapter XXV

RETROFLEX SOUNDS

827. Retroflex sounds (also called 'cerebral,' 'cacuminal' or 'inverted' sounds) are those in the formation of which the tip of the tongue is curled upwards towards the hard palate. Thus 'retroflex t' and 'retroflex d' are plosive consonants made by articulating with the tip of the tongue against the hard palate as shown in Fig. 114.

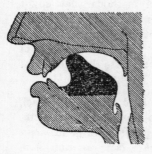

828. The principal retroflex consonants are represented phonetically by the letters t ɖ ɳ ɭ ʂ ʐ. A retroflex rolled consonant is not known to occur in any language, so the letter ɽ is used to represent the 'retroflex flap' formed by placing the tongue in a retroflex position with the tip near the hard palate and then shooting it forwards and downwards in such a way that the under side of the tongue strikes the teeth-ridge producing a flapped sound of very characteristic quality. The retroflex frictionless continuant of this series is near in quality to the alveolar ɹ and does not as a rule require a separate symbol.

Fig. 114. Tongue-position of the retroflex consonant t.

829. Retroflex consonants do not occur in Received English; they may be heard in some foreign pronunciations. Indians generally use t and ɖ in place of the English alveolar t and d; they pronounce *ten* as ten, *did* as ɖiɖ, *to-day* as tuɖeː (instead of təˈdei). Norwegians and Swedes often use retroflex consonants in words which have the spelling *r* + alveolar consonant-letter; thus they pronounce *part, hard, barn, pearl, first* (which are in South-Eastern English paːt, haːd, baːn, pəːl, fəːst) as paʈ or paɻt, haɖ or haɻd, baːɳ or baɻɳ, pəːɭ or pəɻɭ, fəːʂt or fəɻʂt. The correct English alveolar sounds are easily acquired by feeling with the tip of the tongue the appropriate place of articulation on the teeth-ridge.

830. ɽ is sometimes heard from English people in place of the ordinary flapped **r** after short vowels; thus the interjections *hurry up!*, *sorry!* may sometimes be heard as ˈhʌɽi ˈʌp, ˈsoɽi. This pronunciation appears to be merely a peculiarity of individual speakers, and does not belong to any recognized dialect.

831. Vowels may be 'retroflexed,' i.e. pronounced with retroflex modification. In making retroflexed vowels the main body of the tongue is held as for an ordinary vowel, but the tip of the tongue is simultaneously curled up towards the hard palate with lateral contraction (§ 73). The resulting sounds have a peculiar hollow quality.[1] Fig. 115 shows the approximate tongue-position of a retroflexed ɑ.

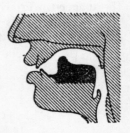

Fig. 115. Tongue-position of a retroflexed ɑ.

832. Retroflexed vowels may be represented in phonetic transcription by superposing ɹ on the vowel letter, thus ɑ̫, ɔ̫, ə̫, etc., or by means of digraphs, ɑɹ, ɔɹ, əɹ, etc., with the convention that each of these sequences of two letters represents only a single sound. Retroflexed ə (əɹ) may be represented more simply by ɹ alone (see § 796). Some writers prefer to represent these sounds by letters with a 'retroflex modifier,' thus ɑ̣, ɔ̣, ə̣.[2]

833. Retroflexed vowels do not occur in the type of English taken as a model for the purposes of this book. They are, however, found in many other types of English in words written with *r* final or *r* + consonant, such as *far*, *garden*, *door*, *sort*, *verse*. The use of retroflexed vowels in such words is not confined to local dialects, but may be heard in the speech of many educated English people, and particularly of those who come from the South-West of England; retroflexed vowels are also a characteristic feature of Irish and American English. Some English people use retroflexed ə(ː), but not any other retroflexed vowels; such speakers pronounce *bird*, *verse*, *murmur*, as bə̫ːd, və̫ːs, ˈmə̫ːmə̫, but *garden*, *door* as ˈgɑːdn, dɔː or dɔə, etc.

---

[1] The same acoustic effect may also be produced by a lateral contraction of the tongue (§ 73) combined with a retraction of the tip without raising it.

[2] An alternative symbol for ə̣ is ɚ (much used by American writers).

834. Some foreign people, and especially Norwegians and Swedes, use retroflexed vowels in speaking English in much the same way as the South-Western Englishman does. If they wish to acquire the ordinary pronunciation of educated Londoners, they must avoid this retroflexion; it may be easily avoided by keeping the tongue-tip firmly pressed against the lower teeth while pronouncing the vowels in such words as *garden, door, verse, murmur, bark, curve*. Words for practice are given in § 774.

Chapter XXVI

SIMILITUDE, ASSIMILATION

Similitude

835. It often happens that a particular sequence of two phonemes involves the use of a certain subsidiary member of one of them which has a greater resemblance to a neighbouring sound than the principal member has. In this case there is said to be *similitude* between that subsidiary member and the neighbouring sound. Thus a partially breathed l ($\underset{\circ}{\text{l}}$) is used in English in such words as *please* pli:z, *play* plei (see § 845 (i) *a*), and we say there is similitude between this $\underset{\circ}{\text{l}}$ and the p.[1]

836. Examples of similitude may be stated by means of a formula of the following type: *the subsidiary sound B belonging to the phoneme whose principal member is the sound A is used when the sound C is adjacent to it or near to it.* Thus the example in § 835 may be stated thus: the subsidiary sound $\underset{\circ}{\text{l}}$ (partially breathed l) belonging to the English phoneme whose principal member is a fully voiced l is used when p precedes in a stressed syllable.

Assimilation

837. *Assimilation* is defined as the process of replacing a sound by another sound under the influence of a third sound which is

---

[1] The term 'similitude' is only used in reference to subsidiary members of phonemes. Sounds which resemble each other but belong to separate phonemes often occur in sequence, but such resemblances between consecutive sounds are not called similitudes. Such are the resemblances between ŋ and k in *conquest* 'kɔŋkwest (where both sounds are velar) or between z and g in *dogs* dɔgz (where both sounds are voiced). Such sequences are often the result of the historical process known as *assimilation*, but the resemblances do not come within the definition of *similitudes*.

Similitudes are to be found both in single words and when two words are put together in forming a sentence. In the latter case the similitudes are brought about by contextual assimilation (§ 838). An example of it is the use of dental n in 'wʌn 'θiŋ, ɔn ðə 'graund quoted in § 845 (ii). Similitudes occurring in single words are not necessarily brought about by assimilation.

near to it in the word or sentence.   The term may also be extended
to include cases where a sequence of two sounds coalesces and
gives place to a single new sound different from either of the
original sounds; this type of change may be termed 'coalescent
assimilation.'

838. Assimilations are of two chief kinds, historical and contextual.   By a 'historical assimilation' we mean an assimilation
which has taken place in the course of development of a language,
and by which a word which was once pronounced in a certain way
came to be pronounced subsequently in another way.   By a 'contextual assimilation' we mean one which is occasioned when words
are juxtaposed in a sentence, or in the formation of compounds, and
by which a word comes to have a pronunciation different from that
which it has when said by itself.

839. An example of historical assimilation is the change of **m**
to **n** which has taken place in the word *ant* ænt.   In the thirteenth
and fourteenth centuries this word was written *amete* and *amte*,
and was no doubt pronounced **'æmətə** and (later) **'æmtə** and æmt;
spellings with *n* in place of *m* first appeared in the fifteenth century,
clearly indicating the change to the modern pronunciation ænt.   An
example of historical coalescent assimilation is the reduction of the
sequence **tj** to the affricate **tʃ** in such a word as *picture* **'piktʃə** which
some hundreds of years ago was doubtless pronounced **'piktjur.**

839a. An example of contextual assimilation is the change of
s to ʃ when *horse* hɔːs and *shoe* are put together and form *horse-shoe*
'hɔːʃʃuː.   An example of contextual coalescent assimilation is when
don't **dount** and *you* **juː** are put together and pronounced **'dountʃu,**
as is frequently done.

840. Changes of the kind mentioned in § 839 which occur when
a word is borrowed from one language into another may be considered as particular cases of historical assimilation.   Such a case
is the change of **s** to **z** when the English *roast beef* is borrowed into
French, where it is pronounced **rozbif.**

841. Historical assimilations are conveniently described by means
of the following formulae: (i) (for ordinary assimilations) *the sound
A has been replaced by the sound B under the influence of the sound C,*
(ii) (for coalescent assimilations) *the sounds A and C have influenced*

each other and coalesced into the single sound B. Thus in the two examples quoted in § 839 the assimilations may be described thus: (1) **m** has been replaced by **n** under the influence of **t**, (2) **t** and **j** have influenced each other and have coalesced into the single sound **tʃ**.

841*a*. Contextual assimilations may be described by the following formulae: (i) (for ordinary assimilations) *the sound A is replaced by the sound B under the influence of the sound C*, (ii) (for coalescent assimilations) *the sounds A and C influence each other and coalesce into the single sound B.* Thus in the two examples quoted in § 839*a* the assimilations may be described thus: (1) **s** is replaced by **ʃ** under the influence of **ʃ**, (2) **t** and **j** influence each other and coalesce into the single sound **tʃ**.

842. The distinction between similitude and assimilation should be carefully observed.[2] The term 'similitude' is used to describe an existing fact; 'assimilation' is a process by which certain pronunciations are evolved. (Thus it would not be accurate to say that the use of a partially breathed **l** in *please* is a case of 'assimilation.' Such a statement would imply that the **l** of *please* had at one time been fully voiced and had subsequently lost part of its voice owing to the presence of the **p**; there is, on the contrary, every reason to believe that the **l** in this word has had its present value ever since the word first appeared in the language.)

843. It is likely that many similitudes have been arrived at by a process of assimilation, but it is generally not possible to tell this with any degree of certainty.

Types of Similitude

844. Similitudes are of various kinds. The most important are (i) resemblances in the matter of voice or breath, (ii) resemblances in tongue-position in the case of a consonant, (iii) resemblances in lip-position in the case of a consonant, (iv) vowel harmony, (v) resemblance of a vowel to an adjacent consonant, (vi) nasality in phonemes of which the principal member is not nasal.

---

[2] Many writers have used the term 'assimilation' loosely to include similitude. It is desirable to avoid this ambiguity by using separate terms.

Examples of Similitude

845. The following are some noteworthy examples of similitudes occurring in English. The types are numbered as in § 844.

(i) *a.* When the phonemes **m n l r w j** are immediately preceded by a voiceless consonant in a stressed syllable, partially breathed varieties of **m n l r w j** are used. Examples: *small* **smɔ:l**, *sneeze* **sni:z**, *place* **pleis**, *cream* **kri:m**, *quite* **kwait**, *pew* **pju:**.[3] The pronunciation may be represented in narrow (allophonic) transcription thus: **sm̥ɔ:l**, **sn̥i:z**, etc.

b. When the **h**-phoneme occurs medially between voiced sounds, a voiced **h** (**ɦ**) is used by most English people (§§ 779, 780). Examples: *behind* **bi'haind**, *adhere* **əd'hiə**, *inhabit* **in'hæbit** (narrow transcription **bi'ɦaind**, **əd'ɦiə**, **in'ɦæbit**).

(ii) Different varieties of **k** and **g** are used before different vowels (§§ 533, 543). Different varieties of **ŋ** are used after different vowels (§ 651). Different varieties of **h** are used before different vowels (§ 778). Special varieties of **t** are used before **θ** and **r**, as in *eighth* **eitθ**, *at rest* **ət 'rest** (§ 513). A labio-dental **m** is used by some speakers before **f** and **v** (§ 641). A dental **n** is used before **θ** and **ð**, as in *one thing* **'wʌn 'θiŋ**, *on the ground* **ɔn ðə 'graund**.

(iii) Lip-rounded varieties of **k**, **g** and other consonants are used before **w**, as in *queen* **kwi:n**, *language* **'læŋgwidʒ** (§§ 533, 543, and footnote 9 on p. 185).

(iv) No example in modern English.[4]

(v) When the long **u:** is preceded by **j**, an advanced variety of vowel (**ü:**) is used (§ 326); examples: *music* **'mju:zik**, *deluge* **'delju:dʒ**. When a front vowel phoneme is followed by dark **l**,

---

[3] The consonant is more breathed after **p t k** than after the fricatives; thus the **l** in *place* has a larger proportion of breath than the **l** in *slate* **sleit**.

The partially breathed members of these phonemes are not used if the preceding consonant belongs to a different syllable, e.g. in *at once* **ət'wʌns**, *at rest* **ət 'rest** (not **ə'twʌns**, **ə'trest**). See § 1094 (1)–(3), also my article on *The Word as a Phonetic Entity* in *Le Maître Phonétique*, Oct.-Dec., 1931.

[4] An example is the use of **e** and **ɛ** in Zulu. In that language **e** is only used when the following syllable contains **i** or **u**, while **ɛ** is used finally and when the following syllable contains some other vowel, e.g. **leli** (this) but **wɛna** (thou).

a somewhat lowered and centralized sound is employed.   Thus the
e in *well* is an opener and more retracted vowel[5] than that in
get, and the æ in *alphabet* 'ælfəbit is more a-like than the æ in
alley 'æli (which has a clear l).   See also the dialectal examples
bowl, rule referred to on p. 224.

(i) Vowels have slight nasality before nasal consonants (§ 825).

Types of Assimilation

846. There exist various types of assimilation parallel to the
various types of similitude.   The most important are (i) assimilations of breath to voice and voice to breath, (ii) assimilations
affecting the position of the tongue in pronouncing consonants,
(iii) assimilations affecting the position of the lips in pronouncing
consonants, (iv) assimilations by which a vowel is affected by
another vowel, (v) assimilations by which a vowel is modified by
an adjacent consonant, (vi) assimilations affecting the position of
the soft palate.

Examples of Historical Assimilation

847. The following are examples of historical assimilation.   The
types are numbered as in § 846.

(i) For the words *width, breadth, amidst,* many people use the
pronunciation witθ, bretθ, ə'mitst instead of the commoner and
presumably older pronunciation widθ, bredθ, ə'midst.   Here d has
been replaced by t under the influence of θ or s.

In *absorption* əb'sɔ:pʃn, *description* dis'kripʃn, *action* 'ækʃn,
election i'lekʃn, *direction* di'rekʃn, *affliction* ə'flikʃn, etc., it may
be presumed that in Latin times an assimilation took place by
which b (or g) was replaced by p (or k) under the influence of a
following t.[6] (The ti has undergone a further change to ʃ in
Modern English—an assimilation of type (ii).)

If, as is likely, the final *s* of plurals such as *dogges, wordes* was
pronounced in Early English as s ('dogəs, 'wordəs), then the
resemblance seen in the modern *dogs* dogz, *words* wə:dz has been

---

[5] The e in *well* is near to cardinal vowel No. 3 (ɛ).

[6] In such a word as *absorptive* no assimilation has taken place.   This
word is a modern invention and has never had a b before the t.   It has
the pronunciation with p by analogy.

arrived at by an assimilation: **s** has been replaced by **z** under the influence of **g**, **d**, etc.[7] (More modern words, such as *globes* **gloubz**, *jugs* **dʒʌgz**, *tunnels* **'tʌnlz**, *schemes* **ski:mz** are formed by analogy, but no assimilation has taken place, since these plurals have never been pronounced otherwise than with **z**.)

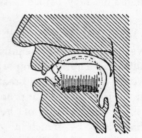

Fig. 116.   Tongue-positions of **t**, **j**, and **tʃ** (characteristic features somewhat exaggerated).
— **t** - - -**j** . . . . .**tʃ**.

(ii) Words like *picture* **'piktʃə**, *question* **'kwestʃən** were no doubt at one time pronounced **'piktjur**, **'kwestjən**, etc. In such cases **tj** has undergone a coalescent assimilation resulting in **tʃ**. The nature of this assimilation is shown in Fig. 116. Similarly in *grandeur* **'grændʒə**, which was doubtless formerly pronounced **'grændjur**, the sounds **d** and **j** have influenced each other and have coalesced into the affricate **dʒ**.

The words *sure* and *sugar*, which are now pronounced **ʃuə**, **'ʃugə**, were probably pronounced in former times **sju:r**, **'sjugər**. There has been a coalescence (§ 837) of **sj** to **ʃ**, the **s** and **j** having influenced each other. The way in which this assimilation has worked may be seen by comparing the tongue-position of **s** (Fig. 94) with those of **j** and **ʃ** (Fig. 99). The same assimilation has taken place in unstressed position in a large number of words, e.g. in most of those ending in *-tion*, *-tial*, *-cial*, *-cian*, and consonant letter + *-sion* or *-sure*, such as *nation* **'neiʃn** (formerly **'nɛ:sjən**),

---

[7] If the supposition as to the value of final **s** in Early English is correct there has been no assimilation in the case of *cats* **kæts**, *books* **buks**, etc. The value of the **s** has simply remained unchanged.

position pə'ziʃn (formerly po'zisjən), *portion* 'pɔːʃn (formerly 'pɔrsjən), *essential* i'senʃl (formerly e'sensjəl), *musician* mjuː'ziʃn (formerly miu'zisjən), *mansion* 'mænʃən (formerly 'mænsjən), *permission* pə'miʃn (formerly pər'misjən), *pressure* 'preʃə (formerly 'presjur).

The corresponding assimilation of the voiced zj to ʒ is also fairly common in unstressed position. Examples are seen in *vision* 'viʒn (formerly 'vizjən), *measure* 'meʒə (formerly 'mezjur), *azure* 'æʒə (formerly 'æzjur or 'ɛːzjur).

The majority of the ʒ's occurring in Modern English have been arrived at by this assimilation.

The word *handkerchief* was doubtless at one time pronounced 'hæn(d)kə:tʃif; it is now 'hæŋkətʃif. This development illustrates a historical assimilation by which n has been replaced by ŋ under the influence of k.

The pronunciation 'beikŋ which is often heard for *bacon* instead of the more usual 'beikən or 'beikn illustrates a similar historical assimilation: here again n has been replaced by ŋ under the influence of k.[8]

The 'fronting' of k in the development of such a word as *chin* is also a historical assimilation of type (ii). This word is believed to be derived from an early form kinn which subsequently became cin[9] and eventually tʃin. A comparison of Figs. 29, 30 with the tongue-position of an i (Fig. 12) shows the nature of the assimilation: k was replaced by c under the influence of i.[10]

(iii) The words *happen, open* are pronounced by some people 'hæpm, 'oupm, instead of in the more usual and presumably older way 'hæpən or 'hæpn, 'oupən or 'oupn. In these cases n has been replaced by m under the influence of p.

---

[8] It does not seem possible to instance the resemblances appearing in such words as *conquer* 'kɔŋkə, *congress* 'kɔŋgres, *congregation* kɔŋgri'geiʃn as the results of assimilation. There does not appear to be any evidence to show that these words were ever pronounced with n.

[9] For c see § 538 and Fig. 29.

[10] The further change c > tʃ is not a case of assimilation. This change was no doubt due to an instinctive desire to make clearer the distinction between words beginning with ci- and those beginning with ki- which appeared in the language at a subsequent time when the tendency to complete fronting was no longer operative.

(iv) The old English mutations are good examples of vowel harmony. It is believed that *men* **men** is derived from an early form **'maniz**, and that **my:s**, the old English form of *mice*,[11] was derived from an earlier **'mu:siz**. In the first case **a** was replaced by **e** under the influence of **i**, and in the second case **u** was replaced by **y** under the influence of **i**.

(v) The common pronunciation of *children* as **'tʃuldrən** furnishes an example of historical assimilation of type (v). Here **i** has been replaced by **u** under the influence of the following dark **l**. The occasional pronunciation of *pretty* (normally **'priti**) as **'pruti** is probably also due to assimilation: **i** has become **u** under the influence of **pr**.

In the pronunciation of those whose speech shows marked traces of London dialect many examples may be found of modifications of other vowels under the influence of a following dark **l**. Thus with many Londoners *bowl* and *rule* have vowel-sounds quite distinct from those in *bowling* and *ruling* (where the **l** is clear); an extreme form of these differences may be shown thus: **bɔul**, **'böüliŋ**, **ro:l**, **'rïüliŋ**. (For **ö** see § 398.) In such pronunciations of *bowl* and *rule*, the normal English **ou** is represented by an **ɔu**-like sound and the normal English **u:** is represented by an **o:**-like sound before dark **l**; the similitudes shown in these words have presumably been arrived at by historical assimilation.

There exists a not uncommon pronunciation of the adverb *just* as **dʒest**. This form is probably the result of an assimilation: **ʌ** has been replaced by **e** under the influence of the adjacent **dʒ** and **s**.

(vi) Historical assimilations affecting the position of the soft palate are not common in English. An example is seen in the pronunciation of some people who substitute **nn** for **nd** before unstressed vowels in some words, who pronounce for instance *individual* as **inni'vidjŭəl**. Here **d** has been replaced by **n** under the influence of **n**.[12]

---

[11] **y** stands for the French sound of *u*; it has the tongue-position of **i** combined with lip-rounding. **my:s** no doubt subsequently underwent changes of the following types, which are isolative and not due to assimilation: **my:s** > **mi:s** > **mïis** > **məis** > **mais**.

[12] This pronunciation was first noticed by H. O. Coleman: see his article entitled 'in:ivid:jul pikju:liæritiz' in *Le Maître Phonétique*, July-August, 1911.

848. It will be seen that historical assimilations account for most of what are known as 'combinative' sound-changes.

Examples of Contextual Assimilation

849. The following are some examples of contextual assimilation. The types are numbered as in § 846.

(i) The full pronunciation of *is* is **iz**. In connected speech the word is generally reduced to **z** when preceded by a voiced sound other than **z** or **ʒ**; e.g. *Who is there?* **ˈhuː z ˈðɛə**, *dinner is ready* **ˈdinə z ˈredi**, *When is he coming?* **ˈwen z (h)iː ˈkʌmiŋ**.[13] And it is reduced to **s** when preceded by a breathed consonant other than **s** or **ʃ**; e.g. *it is ready* **it s ˈredi**, *that is all* **ˈðæt s ˈɔːl**, *What is the time?* **ˈwɔt s ðə ˈtaim**, *the shop is open* **ðə ˈʃɔp s ˈoupn**, *Mr. Smith is coming* **mistə ˈsmiθ s kʌmiŋ**.[14] The latter case illustrates contextual assimilation: the **z** of the full pronunciation is replaced by **s** under the influence of a preceding voiceless consonant.

Has is treated similarly. Its strong form is **hæz**, and its weak forms are **həz, əz, z** and **s**, the latter occurring as the result of contextual assimilation after voiceless consonants (other than **s** and **ʃ**): *Who has been here?* **ˈhuː z bin ˈhiə**, *John has finished* **ˈdʒɔn z ˈfiniʃt**, but *Jack has been here* **ˈdʒæk s bin hiə**, *What has he done?* **ˈwɔt s (h)iː ˈdʌn**.

The expression *used to*, meaning 'accustomed to' or 'was in the habit of,' is now generally pronounced **ˈjuːst tu** or **ˈjuːs tu**.[15] Contextual assimilations from voice to breath thus take place when *to* is added to *used*: **d** is replaced by **t** under the influence of the following **t**, and **z** is replaced by **s** under the influence of **t**.[16]

---

[13] But *Whose is this?* **ˈhuːz iz ˈðis**, *George is here* **ˈdʒɔːdʒ iz hiə**.

[14] But *the price is sixpence* **ðə ˈprais iz ˈsikspəns**, *this fish is very good* **ˈðis ˈfiʃ iz ˈveri ˈgud**.

[15] The older form **ˈjuːzd tu** is still sometimes heard.

[16] By analogy, the pronunciation **juːs(t)** is now employed even where *to* does not immediately follow. Thus we say *Used he to?* **ˈjuːst (h)iː tu**, *Yes he used* **ˈjes hiː ˈjuːst**; and a negative **ˈjuːsnt** has been constructed on the model of *mustn't* **ˈmʌsnt**, etc.: **ˈjuːsnt (h)iː**, **ˈnou hiː ˈjuːsnt**. **ˈjuːsnt** is quite a common word in the spoken language, but I do not remember ever seeing it written; it would presumably have to be spelt *usedn't*. If, as is probable, *used to* was formerly pronounced **ˈjuːzd tu**, the change to **ˈjuːst tu** illustrates historical as well as contextual assimilation.

In *newspaper* ˈnjuːspeipə, *fivepence* ˈfaifpəns we see the effect of contextual assimilation in compound words. *News, five* by themselves are pronounced njuːz, faiv; in the compounds the z and v are replaced by s and f under the influence of the following p.

I should have thought so is sometimes pronounced in rapid colloquial speech ai ʃt f ˈθɔːt sou, instead of the more usual ai ʃəd əv ˈθɔːt sou. Here d and v are replaced by t and f under the influence of the following θ.

(ii) A common instance of contextual assimilation of type (ii) is the replacement of s by ʃ under the influence of a following ʃ. Examples are *horse-shoe* ˈhɔːʃʃuː, and such expressions as *this shop, of course she does, just shut the door,* which are very commonly pronounced ˈðiʃ ˈʃɔp, əv ˈkɔːʃ ʃi dʌz, ˈdʒʌʃ ˈʃʌt ðə ˈdɔː. The replacement of z by ʒ under the influence of a following ʃ is also common: *Does she?, butcher's shop* are generally pronounced ˈdʌʒ ʃiː, ˈbutʃəʒ ʃɔp.

Another contextual assimilation made by many English people is the replacement of a terminal s or z by ʃ or ʒ under the influence of an initial j in the next word: ˈðiʃ ˈjəː for ˈðis ˈjəː (*this year*), ˈtelʒ ju for ˈtelz ju (*tells you*), ˈmisiʒ ˈjʌŋ for ˈmisiz ˈjʌŋ (*Mrs. Young*). (It is not necessary for foreign learners to make this assimilation.)

Many English people make the contextual assimilation of replacing initial unstressed j by ʃ or ʒ when the preceding word in the sentence ends in t or d, or of making tj, dj coalesce into the affricates tʃ, dʒ in such sequences: ˈʃʌt ʃr ˈaiz (or ˈʃʌtʃˈraiz) for ˈʃʌt jər ˈaiz[17] (*shut your eyes*), ˈʃʌt ʃ ˈmauθ (or ˈʃʌtʃˈmauθ) for ˈʃʌt jə ˈmauθ[18] (*shut your mouth*), ˈdidʒuː for ˈdid juː (*Did you?*). (It is likewise not necessary for foreign learners to make this assimilation.)

In careless speech other contextual assimilations of type (ii) are continually made. One further example must suffice. *I am going to buy some* is normally pronounced ai m goiŋ tə ˈbai sʌm, but this is often reduced in careless speech to aiŋənə ˈbai sʌm. Here m is replaced by ŋ under the influence of g, and ŋ is replaced by n under the influence of t, and then the g and t are elided. Assimilations which are confined to careless speech may be termed 'negligent'

---

[17] Or ˈʃʌt jɔːr ˈaiz.
[18] Or ˈʃʌt jɔː ˈmauθ.

assimilations (see my *Pronunciation of English*, 1950 and subsequent editions, §§ 404, 405).

(iii) Contextual assimilations of type (iii) are not unfrequently made, especially by careless speakers. The following are some examples: 'tem 'minits for 'ten 'minits (*ten minutes*), where n is replaced by m under the influence of the following m; sm 'pɔːlz, sm 'pæŋkrəs for sn(t) 'pɔːlz, sn(t) 'pæŋkrəs (*St. Paul's, St. Pancras*), 'stæm-pɔint for 'stæn(d)-pɔint (*standpoint*), 'lʌndəm 'bridʒ for 'lʌndən 'bridʒ (*London Bridge*), ai l 'suːm 'briŋ ðəm for ai l 'suːn 'briŋ ðəm (*I'll soon bring them*), in which cases n is replaced by m under the influence of p or b. *Tadpole*, which is normally 'tædpoul, is sometimes pronounced 'tæbpoul, d being replaced by b under the influence of p. *I don't believe it*, which is normally ai 'dount bi'liːv it, is sometimes reduced to ai 'doump 'bliːv it or ai 'doum 'bliːv it, where t is replaced by p under the influence of b, and n is replaced by m under the influence of p or b. Similarly, *it can't be done* (normally it 'kɑːnt bi 'dʌn) is often reduced to it 'kɑːmp bi 'dʌn.

Foreign learners are not recommended to make any of these assimilations of type (iii), but they should observe to what extent they occur in the speech of English people.

(iv) Contextual assimilations of type (iv) are rare in English. An example is seen in the use of i in the ordinary pronunciation of *we are* (wiə); here iː is replaced by i under the influence of ə.

(v) Contextual assimilations of type (v) are likewise not common. The most noteworthy are the replacement of ə by i or u under the influence of a following j or w. Thus it is not uncommon to hear *What are you doing?*, *Which way are you going?*, *Go away* pronounced 'wɔt i ju 'duiŋ, 'witʃ 'wei i ju 'goiŋ, 'gou u'wei instead of the normal 'wɔt ə ju 'duiŋ, 'witʃ 'wei ə ju 'goiŋ, 'gou ə'wei.

(vi) I have not come across any English example of contextual assimilation affecting the position of the soft palate.[19]

---

[19] An example from French is seen in the frequent pronunciation of *les langues modernes* as le lɑ̃ːŋ mɔdɛrn instead of le lɑ̃ːg mɔdɛrn; g is replaced by ŋ under the influence of the adjoining nasal sounds. The result is a similitude, ŋ being an allophone (subsidiary member) of the g-phoneme in French.

Progressive and Regressive Assimilation

850. Assimilations are termed *progressive* and *regressive* according as the assimilated sound is influenced by a preceding or by a following sound. Thus the assimilations which have taken place in dɔgz (s > z), 'beikŋ (n > ŋ), or which take place contextually in it s 'redi (z > s), 'ʃʌt ʃr 'aiz (j > ʃ) are progressive, while those which have taken place in ænt (m > n), witθ (d > t), 'tʃuldrən (i > u), 'njuːspeipə (z > s), 'hɔːʃʃuː (s > ʃ) are regressive.

Difficulties of Foreign Learners

851. French people speaking English often make assimilations of voice to breath and breath to voice where they are not required. When there are two consecutive consonants, one of which is breathed and the other voiced (neither, however, being a liquid), they have a tendency to assimilate the first to the second as regards presence or absence of voice: thus, they are apt to pronounce

medicine (normal English 'medsin) as met'sin,

anecdote (normal English 'ænikdout) rather like anɛg'dɔt,

absurd (normal English əb'səːd) as ap'sœʀd (compare the French *absurde* ap'syʀd),

absolute (normal English 'æbsəluːt or 'æbsəljuːt) as ap'sɔlyt,

plenty of time (normal English 'plenti əv 'taim) as plen'ti ɔf 'taim,

this book (normal English 'ðis 'buk) as ðiz 'buk,

like that (normal English laik 'ðæt) as laig 'ðat.

The Dutch have a similar tendency. Phonetic transcriptions of the correct and incorrect pronunciation will help foreigners to avoid such errors. French people should also note the English word *observe* əb'zəːv which they generally pronounce ɔp'sɛrv as in French.

852. Foreign learners often have difficulty in remembering which are the words in which assimilation from tj to tʃ or dj to dʒ has been made (§ 847 (ii)) and which are the words where such assimilated forms are to be avoided. There is a general rule that this assimilation has taken place in unstressed syllables, though not often in stressed syllables. Thus assimilation has been made in the words *picture, question, grandeur, pressure* mentioned under (ii) on pp. 222, 223; also in *ocean* ˈouʃn, *pension* ˈpenʃn, *conscience* ˈkɔnʃns, *partial* ˈpɑːʃl, *anxious* ˈæŋkʃəs, *usual* ˈjuːʒul or ˈjuːʒŭəl, *soldier* ˈsouldʒə, *righteous* ˈraitʃəs, *natural* ˈnætʃrəl, *furniture* ˈfəːnitʃə. On the other hand the assimilation has not been made in *mature* məˈtjuə, *endurance* inˈdjuərəns, in which the syllables in question are stressed.

853. There are, however, exceptions. There is a tendency, for instance, for less common words to be pronounced without this assimilation; thus *celestial* is siˈlestjəl, *plenteous*, *beauteous* are ˈplentjəs, ˈbjuːtjəs,[20] and *overture* is generally ˈouvətjuə. *Christian* is generally pronounced ˈkristjən, though ˈkristʃən may also be heard. *Sure* ʃuə and *sugar* ˈʃugə are exceptional words in which the assimilation sj > ʃ has been made in stressed syllables.

---

[20] -tj- is used in all words spelt with *-teous* except *righteous*.

Chapter XXVII

ELISION

854. *Elision* is defined as the disappearance of a sound. There are historical elisions, where a sound which existed in an earlier form of a word was omitted in a later form; and there are contextual elisions, in which a sound which exists in a word said by itself is dropped in a compound or in a connected phrase.

855. A noteworthy example of historical elision is the loss of all r-sounds finally and before consonants in Southern English. It cannot be doubted that up to the fifteenth century the *r*'s of such words as *arm, horse, church, more, other* were always sounded (as indeed they still are in many types of English), and it is believed that the elision of these sounds started in the fifteenth century and became fairly general in court circles in the course of the sixteenth.[1] Similar considerations apply to l in some words, e.g. *walk* (now **wɔːk**), *half* (now **hɑːf**).

855a. The following are a few instances of historical elisions of other sounds. The *p* of *cupboard* (now **ˈkʌbəd**) was doubtless pronounced in Early English, but the sound eventually disappeared (probably about the fifteenth century). It is likely that **ˈtɔːtəʃel**, the usual pronunciation of *tortoise-shell*, is a reduction of a previous form **ˈtɔːtəʃʃel** or **ˈtɔːtəsʃel**; if this is so, this word also illustrates historical elision.[2] The usual pronunciation of *windmill* **ˈwinmil**, *kindness* **ˈkainnis** shows historical elision of d, if, as is probable, d was formerly sounded in these words.

856. Historical elisions of unstressed vowels, especially ə and i, are common in English. Examples are seen in the words *history, university,* which are now generally pronounced **ˈhistri, juːniˈvəːsti,** Formerly, no doubt, the pronunciation was **ˈhistəri, juːniˈvəːsiti.**

---

[1] For the evidence see H. C. Wyld's *History of Modern Colloquial English* (Blackwell, Oxford), pp. 298–300.

[2] The elision is by no means a recent one. The Oxford Dictionary records a spelling *torter shell* in 1652.

and these forms may still be heard in precise speech, though they are not common.

857. Contextual elisions of many kinds are frequent in English, especially in rapid speaking. The following are examples of contextual elisions commonly made in ordinary (not rapid) speech: *blind man* **'blain 'mæn**, *Strand Magazine* **'stræn mægə'ziːn**, *a good deal* **ə 'gu'diːl** (elision of **d**), *take care* **'tei'kɛə** (elision of **k**), *last time* **'lɑːs 'taim**. *Sit down* is pronounced by some people **si'daun** with elision of **t**.

Chapter XXVIII

LENGTH, RHYTHM

858. Sounds which can be held on without alteration during a longer or a shorter period of time are called *continuants*. The chief continuant sounds are the vowels, the nasal, lateral, rolled and fricative consonants, the frictionless continuants (Chap. XXII) and the 'stops' of plosive consonants.

859. The *length* or *quantity* of a sound is the length of time during which it is held on continuously in a given word or phrase. Vowels and continuant consonants have length. Vowel-glides (i.e. diphthongs and semi-vowels) also have length. The non-continuants other than vowel-glides, e.g. flapped consonants and the plosions of plosive consonants, may be regarded for practical linguistic purposes as having no appreciable length.

860. It is easy to distinguish many degrees of length, say five or six, but for practical purposes it is sufficient to distinguish two or sometimes three degrees. When two degrees are distinguished, they are called *long* and *short*. When it is desired to distinguish an intermediate degree, this intermediate degree is termed *medium* or *half-long*.

861. The mark of length is **:** placed immediately after the symbol for the sound which is long; half-length is marked when necessary by **·**; short sounds are generally left unmarked.[1]

Length of English Vowels

862. The principles governing the length of sounds in English are very complex, and considerable differences may be observed in comparing the speech of one person with that of another. The following rules of length of English vowels are, however, sufficiently accurate and sufficiently commonly followed to serve as a guide in the practical teaching of the language.

863. Rule I. The vowels Nos. 1, 5, 7, 9, 11 (iː, ɑː, ɔː, uː, əː) are longer than the other English vowels in similar situations, i.e.

---

[1] In rare cases it is useful to mark extreme shortness. This may be done by placing ˘ over the symbol of the sound.

when surrounded by the same sounds, and pronounced with the same degree of stress. Thus the vowels in *heed* hiːd, *hard* hɑːd, *hoard* hɔːd,[2] *food* fuːd, *heard* həːd are longer than the vowels in *hid* hid, *head* hed, *pad* pæd, *rod* rod, *bud* bʌd, *hood* hud; similarly the vowels in *heat* hiːt, *heart* hɑːt, *short* ʃɔːt, *shoot* ʃuːt, *hurt* həːt are longer than the vowels in *hit* hit, *get* get, *hat* hæt, *hot* hot, *hut* hʌt, *put* put. In consequence of this rule it is customary to designate the vowels iː, ɑː, ɔː, uː, əː as the 'long' vowels and the remaining English vowels as the 'short' vowels. Measurements illustrating this rule are given in my book *The Phoneme*, §§ 398, 403–406. (For exceptions see §§ 874–879.)

864. The diphthongs have about the same length as the 'long' vowels.

865. The absolute lengths of the English 'long' vowels and diphthongs are very variable and depend on their situations in words and sentences (see Rules II–V). This fact may be stated in more technical language by saying that there are two 'chronemes' ('long' and 'short') applicable to the vowels of the type of English with which we are concerned here, and that each chroneme comprises several 'allochrones.' See Chap. XXIII of *The Phoneme*.

866. Rule II. The 'long' vowels (and diphthongs) are shorter when followed by a voiceless consonant than when final or followed by a voiced consonant. When thus shortened, the 'long' vowels may if desired be written with ˙ instead of with ː. Thus, the vowel iː is shorter in *seat* siˑt, than it is in *sea* siː or in *seed* siːd; the vowels and diphthongs in *staff* stɑˑf, *sought*, *sort* sɔˑt, *use* (noun) juˑs, *height* haiˑt, *house* (noun) hauˑs, *scarce* skɛəˑs are shorter than those in *star* stɑː, *saw* sɔː, *yew* juː, *high* hai, *now* nau, *scare* skɛə, *starve* stɑːv, *sawed* sɔːd, *use* (verb) juːz, *hide* haid, *cows* kauz, *scares* skɛəz.[3]

867. Rule III. The 'long' vowels (and diphthongs) are also shorter before a nasal consonant or l followed in turn by a voiceless consonant. Thus the ɔː in *fault* fɔˑlt is shorter than that in *fall* fɔːl or that in *falls* fɔːlz; the əː in *learnt* ləˑnt is shorter than that in *learn* ləːn or that in *learns* ləːnz.

---

[2] Also pronounced hɔəd.

[3] The vowel ɑː appears not to undergo as much shortening as the other vowels. Thus the ɑː in *bark* bɑˑk is shorter than that in *barge* bɑːdʒ, but is longer than the iː in *beak* biːk.

868. Rule IV. 'Long' vowels (and diphthongs) in stressed syllables are also shorter when an unstressed syllable immediately follows in the same word. Thus the iː's in *leader* 'liːdə, *seeing* 'siːiŋ are shorter than those in *lead* liːd, *see* siː or *seen* siːn, the ɔː's in *drawing* 'drɔːiŋ,[4] *causes* 'kɔːziz are shorter than those in *draw* drɔː, *draws* drɔːz, *cause* kɔːz, and the uː in *immunity* i'mjuːniti is shorter than that in *immune* i'mjuːn.[5]

869. When 'long' uː is immediately followed by an unstressed i or ə, there is generally an alternative pronunciation with short lax u forming either disyllabic sequences u-i, u-ə or diphthongs ui, uə. Thus *ruin, truer* are pronounced either 'ruːin, 'truːə (with a shortened uː) or 'ru-in, 'tru-ə or ruin, truə. The diphthongs ei and ou are often reduced to e and o in similar situations, with the result that disyllabic sequences e-ə, o-i, o-ə or diphthongs eə, oi, oə are used. Thus *player* is pronounced either 'pleiə (with a shortened ei) or 'ple-ə or pleə[6]; *poetry, slower* are pronounced either 'pouitri, 'slouə (with a shortened ou) or 'po-itri, 'slo-ə or 'poitri,[7] sloə. Variations of this nature are discussed at greater length in my article *Falling and Rising Diphthongs in Southern English* in *Miscellanea Phonetica* II, 1954 (published by the I.P.A.).

870. Rule V. The 'long' vowels (and diphthongs) are shorter in unstressed syllables than in stressed syllables. This reduced length is particularly noticeable in syllables preceding the stress. Thus the ɔː in *audacious* ɔː'deiʃəs and the ɑː in *carnation* kɑː'neiʃn are shorter than the same vowels in *August* 'ɔːgəst, *scarlet* 'skɑːlit; the ai in *idea* ai'diə, the ou in *ovation* ou'veiʃn,[8] and the uə in djuə'reiʃn are shorter than the same diphthongs in *idle* 'aidl, *over* 'ouvə, *enduring* in'djuəriŋ.

---

[4] *Drawing-room* (salon) is pronounced exceptionally with the diphthong ɔi. *Drawing-room* meaning a room for drawing is pronounced 'drɔːiŋrum according to the rule.

[5] Note. The length varies according to the nature of the sound following the 'long' vowel. When an unstressed vowel immediately follows (as in *seeing, drawing*), the long vowel is distinctly shorter than when a consonant intervenes (as in *leader, causes*).

[6] *Prayer* (supplication) is pronounced prɛə, while *prayer* (one who prays) is 'preiə or preə.

[7] Pronounced 'poitri by some.

[8] Also pronounced o'veiʃn.

871. When the unstressed 'long' vowel or diphthong follows the stress, reduction of length is still observable though less marked. Thus the ɔː in *cardboard* ˈkɑːdbɔːd, and the ou in *fellow* ˈfelou[9] are not so long as the same sounds in *board* bɔːd, *below* biˈlou.

872. The English 'short' vowels (i, e, æ, ɔ, u, ʌ, ə) are also subject to certain variations of length. The variations are similar to those of the 'long' vowels but are less in degree. Thus it will be noticed that the short vowels are generally slightly longer before voiced consonants than before voiceless consonants; for instance the i in *bid* bid and the ʌ in *cub* kʌb are slightly longer than the same vowels in *bit* bit and *cup* kʌp. Measurements illustrating this are given in *The Phoneme*, §§ 405, 406.

873. The variations in the length of short vowels, with the exception of the cases noted in §§ 874–878, are, however, not sufficiently noticeable to be of importance in practical linguistic work. Moreover, usage varies a good deal with different speakers.

874. Some exceptional cases of lengthening of the traditionally 'short' vowels must be noted. The most important is a lengthening of æ in certain words. In the South of England a fully long æː is generally used in the adjectives ending in -*ad* (*bad* bæːd, *sad* sæːd, etc.), and is quite common in some nouns, e.g. *man* mæːn or mæn, *bag* bæːg or bæg, *jam* dʒæːm or dʒæm. Curiously enough the æ appears to be more usually short in *nouns* ending in -*ad* (*lad* læd, *pad* pæd, etc.).

875. Long æː is most frequently found before voiced consonants, but is not confined to these situations. Thus the words *back, that* (meaning 'that thing') at the end of a sentence are often pronounced with long æː by some Southern English people. Foreign learners can sometimes improve the effect of their pronunciation of words containing æ by lengthening the vowel.

876. Some English people, and especially Londoners, make a similar lengthening of e in some words, e.g. *bed, dead* (but apparently not in *fed, tread*). The word *yes* is exceptional; it is sometimes pronounced jes, as usually transcribed, but when said by itself it is more often pronounced with a fully long vowel of opener quality (jɛːs). When French people are speaking English, they

---

[9] Also pronounced ˈfelo.

generally fail to lengthen the vowel of this word; their pronunciation gives an effect of abruptness which is strange to English ears.

877. Similar lengthening may occasionally be observed with other traditionally 'short' vowels. Thus speakers may be found who pronounce *big, good* with longer vowels than *pig, hood. His* and *is* often have lengthened vowels when in final position.

878. The lengthened 'short' vowels referred to in the four preceding paragraphs are used chiefly in syllables which are final in the sentence, and the length is particularly marked when the words are pronounced with the 'fall–rise' intonation (§§ 1054, 1055). Thus, in saying *it isn't bad* in such a way as to imply 'but at the same time it's not very good,' the word *bad* would very commonly be pronounced with a long vowel: **i'tiznt 'bæːd.** Similarly, if *yet* had the 'fall–rise' in *I really can't go to bed yet* (implying 'it's much too early'), many people would pronounce **ai 'riəli 'kɑːnt gou tə 'bed 'jeːt,** *bed* having a short vowel and *yet* a long one.

879. The tendency to lengthen 'short' vowels appears to be on the increase. In the local dialect of London it is much more prevalent than in normal educated speech; it may also be observed in American English. It is, in fact, possible that a new development of the language is beginning to take place, by which the present distinctions of quantity combined with quality will eventually give place to distinctions of quality only. If such a new system of vowel-length were to become the regular usage in educated Southern English, it would become necessary to modify the method of vowel representation in practical phonetic transcription by introducing special letters to distinguish the pairs of sounds which are now sufficiently well distinguished by length-marks.[10]

Length of Consonants

880. The length of consonants also varies, but not to the same extent as that of vowels. The following are the only rules of importance for foreign learners.

881. Rule VI. Final consonants are longer when preceded by one of the 'short' vowels than when preceded by one of the 'long'

---

[10] E.g. by introducing into broad transcriptions some such system as that now used in narrower transcriptions, where 'short' **i, u, ɔ** are written **ı, ꞷ, ɒ** and the vowel in *bird* is written with **ɜ.** See Appendix A, §§ *28, 33, 36.*

vowels or by a diphthong. Thus the n in *sin* sin is longer than the n's in *seen, scene* siːn and *sign* sain.

882. Rule VII. Liquids are longer when followed by voiced consonants than when followed by voiceless consonants. Thus the n in *wind* wind is longer than that in *hint* hint, the l in *bald* bɔːld is longer than that in *fault* fɔːlt, the m in *number* 'nʌmbə is longer than that in *jumper* 'dʒʌmpə.

883. Plosive consonants preceded by a short stressed vowel and followed by another consonant are rather long, e.g. the k in *act* ækt, *actor* 'æktə (compare the k in *jacket* 'dʒækit), the p in *description* disˈkripʃn.

884. Liquid consonants are usually long when preceded by a short vowel and followed by an unstressed syllable beginning with j or w, as the l in *million* 'miljən or the m in *somewhere* 'sʌmwɛə (compare *sillier* 'siliə, *summer* 'sʌmə).

885. Consonants following stressed short vowels are sometimes very much lengthened for the sake of emphasis, e.g. *splendid* 'splenːdid, *a little more* ə 'litːl 'mɔː, *I never heard such a thing* ai 'nevːə 'həːd sʌtʃ ə θiŋ, *numbers and numbers of things* 'nʌmːbəz n 'nʌmːbəz əv θiŋz. Similar lengthening occasionally occurs after 'long' vowels, e.g. *it was awfully good* it wəz 'ɔːfːli gud.

Relation between Rhythm and Length

886. Vowel-length depends to a considerable extent on the rhythm of the sentence. There is a strong tendency in connected speech to make stressed syllables follow each other as nearly as possible at equal distances. Rule IV above (§ 868) is a result of this rhythmical tendency. The usage may be stated more fully as follows: when a syllable containing a long vowel or a diphthong is followed by unstressed syllables, that vowel or diphthong is generally shorter than if the syllable were final or followed by another stressed syllable; moreover, the greater the number of following unstressed syllables the shorter is the stressed vowel.

887. The following are some examples to supplement those in § 868. In pronouncing the series of numbers *eighteen, nineteen, twenty* 'eitiːn, 'naintiːn, 'twenti, the diphthong ai in *nineteen* is not so long as the ai in *nine* in the series *eight, nine, ten* 'eit, 'nain,

ˌten. The **ou** in *there's nobody there* ðɛə z ˈnoubədi ˈðɛə is not nearly so long as that in *there's no time* ðɛə z ˈnou ˈtaim.

888. The differences of length caused in this way may be made evident by representing the rhythm by means of an approximate musical notation. Thus if we take a quaver ♪ to represent the length of time between two consecutive stresses in *eight, nine, ten,* the first two of the above sequences will appear thus:

ˈeitiːn ˈnaintiːn ˈtwenti   ˈeit ˈnain ˈten.

It is clear from this that the diphthongs **ei, ai** are something like twice as long in the second sequence as they are in the first.

889. In like manner the two other sequences appear thus:

ðɛəz ˈnoubədi ˈðɛə   ðɛəz ˈnou ˈtaim.

The **nou** in the second sequence takes up almost as much time as the entire word ˈnoubədi in the first. The **ou** is therefore a good deal longer in the second sequence than it is in the first.

890. Further examples:

wiːl   ˈstaːt iˈmiːdjətli if juə   ˈredi.
We'll   start immediately if you're ready.

Here the two syllables ˈstaːti may be made to occupy almost as long a time as the five syllables ˈmiːdjətliifjuə. The syllable staːt accordingly occupies more time than the syllable miːd, and it can be heard that the iː in miːd is short (for a 'long' vowel) and that the comparative lengthening of the syllable staːt is distributed over the sounds aː and t. If in this sentence the word *start* were replaced by a longer word containing a 'long' vowel, this vowel would be shortened. Thus if we were to substitute *arbitrate* ˈaːbitreit or *harmonize* ˈhaːmənaiz, we should find that the whole of these words might be compressed into a space not very much longer than the monosyllable stɑːt.

ju: kən 'kʌm wið 'miː if juə 'redi.
You can come with **me** *if you're ready.*

Here the length of miː is not much less than the total length of the three syllables 'miːdjətli in the preceding example.

ðə 'siːn wəz 'bjuːtəfl.
The scene was beautiful.

ðə 'siːnəri wəz 'bjuːtəfl.
The scenery was beautiful.

These examples show that the iː in *scene* is considerably longer than the iː in *scenery*.

hiː 'muːvz 'veri 'ræpidli.
He moves very rapidly.

hiz 'muːvmənts ə 'veri 'ræpid.
His movements are very rapid.

The group 'muːvməntsə in the second example is compressed into nearly the same space of time as muːvz in the first example, and the uː of 'muːvmənts is heard to be a good deal shorter than the uː of muːvz.

ðei 'beið in ðə 'siː.
They bathe in the sea.

ðeiə 'beiðiŋ in ðə 'siː.
They're bathing in the sea.

Here 'beiðinðə and 'beiðiŋinðə occupy about the same space of time, so that the ei in beið is longer than that in 'beiðiŋ.

891. The nature of spoken English rhythm, upon which the lengths of sounds are partly dependent, is a very involved subject, and it has not been possible for me to investigate it in any detail. It may be remarked, however, that the rhythm is determined not only by the number and nature of the speech-sounds in the word-group and the positions of the stresses in the words of more than

one syllable, but also by the *grammatical relations* between words. Thus if an unstressed syllable occurs between two stressed syllables, it tends to be shorter if it is grammatically closely connected with the following stressed syllable than if its closer grammatical relationship is with the preceding stressed syllable.

892. To illustrate how rhythm is determined by *grammatical relations* between words we may take the comparatively simple case of such a sequence as **'ei + t + ə +** another stressed syllable, where a stressed long vowel (or diphthong) is followed by a single consonant which is followed in turn by a short unstressed vowel and then another stressed syllable. It will be found that this sequence has different rhythms, and consequently different lengths of the sounds **ei, t, ə,** in the three following expressions:

(*He's a*)*way to-day*	(**hiː z ə**)**'wei tə'dei.**
(*A*) *later day*	(**ə**) **'leitə 'dei.**
(*He uses*) *eight a day*	(**hiː juːziz**) **'eit ə 'dei.**

The rhythm in the first example may be expressed by the approximate musical notation ♪. ♪♪, the rhythm in the second example is approximately ♫ ♩, while the rhythm in the third example is intermediate between the other two.[11] Expressed in terms of length of sounds the differences are as follows: in the first example the first **ei** is distinctly long and the **ə** extremely short; in the second example the first **ei** is much shorter and the **ə** is longer; in the third example the first **ei** is also rather short, but there is a perceptible lengthening of the stop of the **t**, and the **ə** is intermediate in length between the **ə**'s of the first two examples.

893. Further examples of a rhythm approximating to ♪. ♪ in similar circumstances are:

Buy the book	**'bai ðə 'buk.**
(*From*) *day to day*	(**frəm**) **'dei tə 'dei.**
Arm in arm	**'ɑːm in 'ɑːm.**

---

[11] The lengths indicated by the musical notes are not the lengths of the syllables but the lengths separating the 'stress-points' or 'peaks of prominence' of the syllables. The note attached to the last syllable of each example denotes the length of time which would presumably elapse between its stress-point and that of a following stressed syllable if there were one.

894. The rhythm of the type ♩. ♪♩ becomes clearer still when two or more consonants intervene between a stressed long vowel and the unstressed short vowel. Examples are seen in:

(*I*) *quite forgot*	(ai) 'kwait fə'gɔt.
First of all	'fəːst əv 'ɔːl.

895. Further examples of a rhythm approximating to ♫♩ in similar circumstances are:

Either book	'aiðə 'buk.
Take it out	'teik it 'aut.
Is it right?	'iz it 'rait?[12]
Does he like (it)?	'dʌz iː 'laik (it)?

896. The rhythms are similar if the first syllable contains a short vowel and two or more consonants intervene between it and the unstressed vowel.

Examples of ♩. ♪♩ :

Come to-day!	'kʌm tə'dei.
(*It's*) *not for us*	(it s) 'nɔt fər 'ʌs.
What's the time?	'wɔt s ðə 'taim?
Ring the bell!	'riŋ ðə 'bel.
Well-to-do	'wel-tə-'duː.
Twelve o'clock	'twelv ə'klɔk.

Examples of ♫♩ :

What's it for?	'wɔt s it 'fɔː?
Shelter here	'ʃeltə 'hiə.

897. On the other hand, the rhythms that might be expected on syntactic grounds are often replaced by others on account of the nature and grouping of the sounds. Thus we have a rhythm approximating to ♫♩ in many cases where the second syllable is in close grammatical connexion with the third; a notable case is

---

[12] *Is it right?* may be said with the rhythm ♪♪♩ ; this is presumably a consequence of the presence of the two consonants **t, r.**

where the first stressed vowel is short or fairly short and there is no consonant or only one consonant separating it from the following unstressed vowel, as in

How are you?	'hau ə 'juːꞋ
Come along!	'kʌm əˈlɔŋ.
Get away!	'get əˈwei.

(The rhythms in the two latter cases are difficult to distinguish from those of *summer day* 'sʌmə 'dei, (a) *better way* (ə) 'betə 'wei.)

Right away   'rait əˈwei.

(In this case the **ai** is rather short because it is followed by a voiceless consonant in the same word. The rhythm is almost indistinguishable from that of (a) *later day*, § 892.)

One o'clock   'wʌn əˈklɔk.

(Compare *twelve o'clock*, § 896.)

898. Again, in the following examples owing to the number of consonants a rhythm approximating to ♪. ♪♪ is found although the second syllable is in close grammatical relationship with the first:

Take them out!	'teik ðəm 'aut.
(Compare *Take it out*, § 895.)	
(*He*) *locked it up*	(hiː) 'lɔkt it 'ʌp.
Easter Eve	'iːstər 'iːv.
Does she like (*it*)?	'dʌʒ ʃiː 'laik (it)Ꞌ

(Compare *Does he like it?* § 895.)

899. The above examples show that the rules determining the rhythm, and therefore the lengths of the sounds, in the simple case of an unstressed syllable between two stressed syllables are rather complex. The reader may thus form some idea of the extreme difficulty of describing or reducing to rules the innumerable rhythms heard in ordinary connected speech. All we can say here is (1) that there is a general tendency to make the 'stress-points' of stressed syllables follow each other at equal intervals of time, but that this general tendency is constantly interfered with by the variations in the number and nature of the sounds between successive stress-points, and (2) that the rhythms heard within the 'stress-bars' are dependent upon the grammatical relations between the words as well as upon the number and nature of the sounds.[13]

Mistakes in Length made by Foreign Learners

900. The most notable mistakes of length heard from foreign learners are as follows.

901. Many foreign people make the English 'long' vowels and diphthongs fully long when followed by voiceless consonants, instead of shortening them in accordance with the rule in § 866. This is one of the characteristic mistakes made by Germans speaking English. They almost invariably make the vowels and diphthongs far too long in such words as *park* pɑːk, *use* (noun) juːs, *fruit* fruːt, *nation* 'neiʃn, *mouth* mauθ, *right* rait, *roast beef* 'roust 'biːf. French people also occasionally fall into this error.

902. Again, Germans generally fail to lengthen properly final consonants preceded by short vowels. Thus, they are apt to pronounce *thin* θin, *tell* tel, *come* kʌm with very short final consonants, instead of lengthening them in accordance with the rule in § 881.

903. The French are inclined to shorten long vowels when final, pronouncing, for instance, *sea*, *too* with short vowels (like the French *si*, *tout*) instead of with long ones (siː, tuː).

904. On the other hand, when there is a final unstressed -ə written *-er*, they make the vowel too long (besides inserting some kind of r-sound). Thus they often pronounce *paper* pe'pœːʀ instead of 'peipə.

905. The French also have a tendency to shorten the long vowels iː and uː when followed by b, d, g, m, n, and l, as in *tube* tjuːb, *food* fuːd, *league* liːg, *tomb* tuːm, *fifteen* 'fif'tiːn, *feel* fiːl.

906. Words for practice: (for Rule I) *seen* siːn, *sin* sin, *harm* hɑːm, *ham* hæm, *short* ʃɔːt, *shot* ʃɒt, *call* kɔːl, *doll* dɒl, *wall* wɔːl, *quality* 'kwɒliti, *pool* puːl, *pull* pul, *root* ruːt, *foot* fut; (for Rule II) *see* siː, *far* fɑː, *saw* sɔː, *too*, *two* tuː, *fur* fəː, *say* sei, *sow* (verb)

---

[13] For a more detailed discussion of the rhythm of English, readers are referred to A. Classe's *The Rhythm of English Prose* (Blackwell, Oxford).

sou, *sigh* sai, *sow* (pig) sau, *lead* (conduct) li:d, *lard* lɑ:d, *lord*,
laud lɔ:d, *lose* lu:z, *learn* lə:n, *laid* leid, *load* loud, *lied* laid, *loud*
laud, *geese* gi:s, *pass* pɑ:s, *horse* hɔ:s, *loose* lu:s, *verse* və:s, *lace* leis,
toast toust, *nice* nais, *house* haus; (for Rule III) *aunt, aren't* ɑ:nt,
taunt tɔ:nt, *learnt* lə:nt, *paint* peint, *don't* dount, *pint* paint, *ounce*
auns.

907. The rhythm of spoken English is a source of considerable
difficulty to some foreign people. The French, for instance, are
liable to make continual use of the rhythm 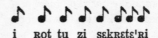 ... where
it is inappropriate in English. Thus they are liable to pronounce
Ring the bell, first of all, What's the time? with the rhythm ♪ ♪ ♪
instead of ♪. ♪♪, and they pronounce *he wrote to the secretary* as

i ʀot tu zi sɛkʀɛtɛˈʀi

instead of the correct English

hi: ˈrout tə ðə ˈsekrətri.

908. The greatest difficulty of all is experienced by the Japanese.
For them and all others to whom English rhythm is difficult is
will be found helpful if the teacher taps the rhythms of sentences
with his finger on the table. The pupil should practise saying
the sentence while tapping in unison with the teacher.

Chapter XXIX

STRESS

The Nature of Stress

909. *Stress* may be described as the degree of force with which a sound or syllable is uttered. It is essentially a subjective action. A strong force of utterance means energetic action of all the articulating organs; it is usually accompanied by a gesture with the hand or head or other parts of the body; it involves a strong 'push' from the chest wall and consequently strong force of exhalation[1]; this generally gives the objective impression of *loudness*. Weak force of utterance involves weak action of the chest wall resulting in weak force of exhalation, and giving the objective acoustic impression of softness.

---

[1] Except in rare cases where strong stress falls on a sound which has no exhalation. It must be observed that cases do occur where a strong stress fails to give much carrying power to a sound, and therefore fails to make it objectively prominent. A strong stress may even occur on a silence, e.g. on the stop of a voiceless plosive. When a strong stress is given to a sound incapable of receiving any noticeable increase of loudness, a person unfamiliar with the language would be unable to tell that a stress was present except by observing the gestures. A hearer familiar with the language would not perceive the stress objectively from the sound apart from the gestures, but he perceives it in a subjective way; the sounds he hears call up to his mind (through the context) the manner of making them, and by means of immediate 'inner speech' he knows where the stress is. The process is analogous to that by which the beats of the bar are felt in syncopated music at points where no notes are played. (This type of process is known to psychologists as "empathy.")

Strong stress without strong force of exhalation and consequent loudness is not often found in English. It may, however, be observed in one pronunciation of *Thank you*, viz. the abbreviated form **ˈk̩kju**. Here a syllabic **k** without plosion is stressed although it has no sound; the stress is generally shown by a gesture. Strong stress without accompanying loudness is a common feature of the Tswana language of South Africa. In that language final low-tone syllables, as for instance the second syllable of the word *thata* ('strong'), are often said without voice and (when plosives precede) with closed glottis. They have a very strong stress, quite as strong as that of the penultimate, but owing to lack of sonority of unvoiced vowels they have **very little loudness.**

910. It was pointed out in §§ 208–210 that one or more sounds in a spoken word or phrase are heard to stand out more prominently than their immediate neighbours; and in the subsequent paragraphs it was shown that a 'syllable' is essentially a small sound-sequence containing a peak of prominence. Now if a word or phrase contains a number of peaks of prominence, it is generally found that the degrees of prominence at the various peaks are unequal; some of the peaks have much greater prominence than others. In other terms, some syllables of a word or phrase are perceived more distinctly than others.

911. The prominence of a given sound may be increased or diminished by means of any one of the three sound-attributes, length, stress, or intonation, or by combinations of these. A common and effective means of increasing prominence is to increase the stress. In English, increase of stress is generally accompanied by a modification of intonation and sometimes by an increase of length.

912. It is important not to confuse *stress* with *prominence* (§§ 100, 101, 208–210). The prominence of a syllable is its degree of general distinctness, this being the combined effect of the tamber, length, stress, and (if voiced) intonation of the syllabic sound. The term 'stress,' as here used, refers only to the degree of force of utterance; it is independent of length and intonation, though it may be, and often is, combined with these.[2] (For a more detailed discussion of the nature of prominence see my book *The Phoneme*, § 434 ff.).

913. Stress without intonation may be heard in English when a clergyman is intoning the prayers in a church service. The relations between stress and intonation found in ordinary spoken English are shown in Chap. XXXI (see especially §§ 1022–1027).

---

[2] Some phoneticians have expressed the view that stress is not independent of pitch, and have shown by experiments with a dead larynx that an increase of stress involves a raising of pitch. This is no doubt the case for a given tension of the vocal cords. But the living speaker does not maintain a fixed tension of his vocal cords; he has complete control of his intonation, whatever the stress may be, and it often happens in a language that strong stresses are found on low-pitched syllables and weak stresses on high-pitched syllables. It appears to me therefore that linguistic stress must be regarded as independent of pitch.

914. Syllables which are pronounced with a greater degree of stress than the neighbouring syllables in a word or sentence are said to be *stressed* or (more accurately) *pronounced with strong stress*. Syllables pronounced with a relatively small degree of stress are said to be *unstressed* or (more accurately) *pronounced with weak stress*. In what follows I am retaining the conventional, though inaccurate, terms 'stressed' and 'unstressed.'

915. It has frequently been suggested that a hearer can distinguish by ear and a speaker can distinguish by sensation quite a number of degrees of stress, say four or five. For instance, I expressed the opinion in previous editions of this book that five degrees of stress may be perceived in the word *opportunity*, and that if we denote the strongest stress by the figure 1, the second strongest by the figure 2, and so on, the stressing of this word
might be indicated thus: ɔpə'tjuːniti. I now think that this view needs modification, on the ground that much of what is commonly thought of as 'stress' is in reality stress (as defined here in § 909) plus 'prominence' effected by means other than stress, and particularly by 'inherent sonority' (§§ 100, 101), by subtle degrees of vowel and consonant length and by intonation.

916. However that may be, I do not find any need in the practical teaching and learning of pronunciation to attempt accuracy of that order. It is generally sufficient to distinguish two degrees only, *stressed* (or *strong*) and *unstressed* (or *weak*). Stressed syllables are marked in this book by placing ' immediately before them, thus *father* 'faːðə, *arrive* ə'raiv, *opportunity* ɔpə'tjuːniti, *Where are you going?* 'wɛər ə juː 'gouiŋ?

917. When for any reason it is found needful to distinguish three degrees of stress, the sign ˌ may be used to denote the intermediate or *secondary* stress. Thus in *examination* the secondary stress is on the second syllable, so that the word may be written, if desired, igˌzæmi'neiʃn. (It is useful to mark the secondary stress in this word, because foreign people usually put the secondary stress on the first syllable.)

918. Marking secondary stress is of particular value in transcribing English words which have three or more syllables preceding the principal stress (see § 941).

Stress in English

A. Word-stress (*simple words*)

919. Most English words of two syllables have one strongly
stressed syllable and one weak one. The strong stress is on the
first syllable in some words and on the second in others. For
instance, in the nouns *increase* and *insult* the first syllable is strong
and the second weak ('**inkri:s**, '**insʌlt**), but in the verbs *increase*
and *insult* the first syllable is weak and the second strong (**in'kri:s**,
in'sʌlt). There exist, however, some disyllabic English words in
which both syllables have strong stress. Such are *fifteen* '**fif'ti:n**,
prepaid '**pri:'peid**. They are said to be 'double-stressed.' Their
stress is subject to rhythmical variations in the sentence (see § 932).

919a. In English words of three or more syllables there is
always one strong syllable and occasionally two. The other
syllables in the words are as a rule weak ('unstressed'), but in
some words there is a syllable with secondary stress. In each
of the following cases, for instance, there is one stressed syllable
and several unstressed ones: *excessively* **ik'sesivli**, *portmanteau*
pɔ:t'mæntou, *philanthropist* **fi'lænθrəpist**, *particularize* **pə'tikjuləraiz**,
symbolically **sim'bɔlikəli**, *uncharitableness* **ʌn'tʃæritəblnis**. There are
secondary stresses in *centralization* **ˌsentrəlai'zeiʃn**, *administration*
əd,minis'treiʃn and the other examples quoted in § 941; probably
also in the numerous single-stressed compounds like *foot-passenger*
'**fut,pæsindʒə**, *kettle-holder* '**ketl,houldə** (§ 946). Occasionally a very
long word may have two secondary stresses. For instance, *intel-
lectuality* may be pronounced **ˌinti,lektju'æliti** (also **ˌintilektju'æliti**
and '**inti,lektju'æliti**).

919b. Examples of double-stressed words of three or more
syllables are given in § 922. Like the disyllables their stresses
are subject to rhythmical variations in the sentence (§ 933).

920. Generally speaking there are no rules determining which
syllable or syllables of polysyllabic English words bear the main
stress. The foreign student is obliged to learn the stress of each
word individually. He has to learn, for instance, that the main
stress is on the first syllable in *photograph* '**foutəgrɑ:f** or '**foutəgræf**,
on the second in *photography* **fə'tɔgrəfi**, on the third in *photographic*
foutə'græfik and on the fourth in *photogravure* **foutəgrə'vjuə**. When

rules of word-stress can be formulated at all, they are generally subject to numerous exceptions.[3]

921. In the case of double-stressed words it is, however, possible to formulate some general principles which are of assistance to the foreign learner. These are given in the following paragraphs.

---

[3] In the above paragraphs (§§ 919–920) I have taken no account of a theory advanced by some that no syllable is really 'unstressed' in English unless it contains one of the vowels ə, i, o (the monophthongal reduction of ou) or u or a syllabic consonant. Those who maintain this theory appear to think that when e, æ, ɔ, ʌ and the long vowels and the falling diphthongs occur in weak positions, they are pronounced in reality with secondary stress. It would seem, for instance, that they consider the second syllables of such words as *insect* 'insekt, *asphalt* 'æsfælt, *teapot* 'tiːpɔt, *hiccup* 'hikʌp, *concrete* 'kɔŋkriːt, *schedule* 'ʃedjuːl, *mundane* 'mʌndein, *fortnight* 'fɔːtnait to have secondary stresses, and the first and third syllables of *portmanteau* pɔːt'mæntou to have secondary stresses.

I am not satisfied that this view is a correct one. It is to be observed in regard to e, æ, ɔ and ʌ that these vowels are undoubtedly more *prominent* (§§ 100, 101, 208) than ə, i, o and u; but this does not necessarily mean that they always derive their prominence from stress as here defined, i.e. from a special push of the chest wall. I submit that they have considerable prominence by reason of their 'inherent sonority' (§§ 100, 101), and that if (say) e and ə₁ (§ 356) are uttered with what the speaker judges to be equal push from the chest wall, and the conditions are in other respects comparable, e 'carries' better than ə does, i.e. it is clearly audible at a greater distance than ə is.

The most that can be said in favour of the theory, in so far as it concerns e, æ, ɔ and ʌ, is that these vowels are generally uttered with greater jaw movement than ə, i, o and u, and perhaps that it is customary to give them slightly greater length than that which ə, i, o, u have in comparable positions. J. W. Jeaffreson, it is true, has maintained that the extent of jaw movement is an indication of stress, but it is not certain that this hypothesis is always valid. His experiments, valuable as they are, did not demonstrate that the English e, æ, ɔ and ʌ are uttered with stronger push from the chest wall than ə, i, o and u. Readers interested in this question are recommended to study Jeaffreson's remarkable results. They are set out in his paper *Stress and Rhythm in Speech* in the *Transactions of the Philological Society*, 1938, and in his unpublished *Mensuration of French Verse* (thesis for the London M.A., 1924) which may be consulted in the Library of the University of London. See also some remarks in my book *The Phoneme*, §§ 204, 205 and footnote 14 on p. 60.

The English vowels iː, ɑː, ɔː, uː and əː have considerable prominence by reason of their length, but I would suggest that there is nothing to prevent them from being 'unstressed,' i.e. uttered with very weak push from the chest wall. The same applies to the diphthongs ei, ou, ai, au and ɔi,

922. Words formed by adding to a word in common use a prefix having a distinct meaning of its own[4] very usually have two strong stresses, namely a stress on the prefix and the stress of the original word. Examples of such prefixes are: *anti-, arch-* (in the sense of 'chief'), *dis-* (when equivalent to *un-* or implying separation), *ex-* (in the sense of 'former'), *half-, joint-, in-* (*il-, im-, ir-*) (in the sense of 'not'), *inter-* (in the reciprocal sense), *mal-, mis-* (implying 'error' or 'falseness'), *non-, out-* (in verbs, with the sense of 'outdoing'), *over-* (in the sense of 'too much'), *pre-* (meaning 'beforehand'), *re-* (denoting 'repetition'), *sub-* (in the sense of 'subordinate'), *ultra-, un-, under-* (in the sense of 'too little' or in the sense of 'subordinate'), *vice-.*[4]

Examples: *anticlimax* ˈæntiˈklaimæks, *archbishop* ˈɑːtʃˈbiʃəp, *disloyal* ˈdisˈlɔiəl, *disconnect* ˈdiskəˈnekt, *discontented* ˈdiskənˈtentid, *disembark* ˈdisimˈbɑːk, *ex-president* ˈeksˈprezidənt, *half-finished* ˈhɑːfˈfiniʃt, *joint-tenant* ˈdʒɔintˈtenənt, *inexperienced* ˈiniksˈpiəriənst,

---

which are 'falling' (§§ 220, 223) by reason of the relatively small inherent sonority of their terminal elements. The same probably applies also to ɛə and ɔə.

It looks as if the only syllabic sounds of Southern English which can properly be said to have inherent stress are iə (No. 18) and uə (No. 21), since, as explained in §§ 225, 440a and 460, these diphthongs owe their 'falling' character to a certain degree of stress on their initial elements. Those who maintain that they cannot be 'unstressed,' and that therefore such words as *reindeer* ˈreindiə, *contour* ˈkɔntuə, are pronounced with secondary stress on the second syllable, have thus a good case. But even here it might be argued that when a sound is said with the minimum stress it is capable of having, it should be considered as unstressed. The question is discussed at some length in the sections relating to iə and uə in my article *Falling and Rising Diphthongs in Southern English* in *Miscellanea Phonetica* II, 1954 (published by the I.P.A.).

In phonetic transcriptions designed for foreign learners I find it adequate to mark with a secondary stress-mark only such syllables as those exemplified at the end of § 919a together with those which have a reduced primary stress in the sentence. To mark weak syllables with secondary stress-marks solely because they contain e, æ, ɔ or ʌ or long vowels or diphthongs seems to me hardly to represent the facts correctly. In any case, I doubt if such marking would serve any useful purpose in texts intended for the practical teaching of English stress, since such syllables are bound to have sufficient prominence if the vowels are correctly pronounced.

[4] The prefixes here referred to may be conveniently termed the 'separable' prefixes.

insincere 'in-sin'siə, *insufficient* 'in-sə'fiʃnt, *illogical* 'i'lɔdʒikl, *imperceptible* 'im-pə'septəbl, *irreligious* 'iri'lidʒəs, *intermingle* 'intə'miŋgl, *malformation* 'mælfɔ:'meiʃn, *misquote* 'mis'kwout, *misrepresentation* 'misreprizen'teiʃn, *non-payment* 'nɔn'peimənt, *outgeneral* 'aut'dʒenərəl, *overestimate* (v.) 'ouvər'estimeit, *overripe* 'ouvə'raip, *prepaid* 'pri:'peid, *rearrange* 'ri:ə'reindʒ,[5] *sub-dean* 'sʌb'di:n, *ultra-fashionable* 'ʌltrə'fæʃnəbl, *unfruitful* 'ʌn'fru:tful, *unknown* 'ʌn'noun, *unpack* 'ʌn'pæk, *unobjectionable* 'ʌnəb'dʒekʃnəbl, *underestimate* (v.) 'ʌndər'estimeit, *under-secretary* 'ʌndə'sekrətri, *vice-chancellor* 'vais'tʃɑ:nslə.

923. It must be observed that if the word to which the prefix is added is not in common use or is only used in a sense different from that attributed to it when the prefix is added, then double stress is not generally used.

Examples: *discourage* dis'kʌridʒ (*courage* not being used as a verb), *inordinate* i'nɔ:dinit (the adjective *ordinate* being rare), *unwieldy* ʌn'wi:ldi (the word *wieldy* being very rare, and in fact unknown to most people), *undoubted* ʌn'dautid (*doubted* not being used as an attributive adjective), *underline* ʌndə'lain (the verb *line* not being used in the sense of 'to draw a line').

924. For a similar reason some adverbs have single stress while the corresponding adjectives have double stress. Thus *unaccountably* is usually ʌnə'kauntəbli, while *unaccountable* is quite commonly 'ʌnə'kauntəbl; so also *invariably* is regularly pronounced in'vɛərïəbli, though the adjective *invariable* is pronounced either 'in'vɛərïəbl or in'vɛərïəbl.

925. Very common words formed from other words by the addition of some of the above-mentioned prefixes, and particularly words in which the stress of the simple word is on the first syllable, are exceptions to the principle stated in § 922, and take no stress on the prefix. Thus it is not usual to stress the prefixes of *impossible* im'pɔsəbl, *unusual* ʌn'ju:ʒuəl, *unfortunate* ʌn'fɔ:tʃnit. Some put *imperceptible* (§ 922) into this category, pronouncing it im-pə'septəbl.

926. In many words which are not uncommon but yet not very common, usage varies. Thus some speakers pronounce

---

[5] Compare *recover* ('get back') ri'kʌvə with *recover* ('cover again,' said of umbrellas, etc.) 'ri:'kʌvə. In *reproduction* the *re-* is not felt as separable, and the normal pronunciation is accordingly ri:-prə'dʌkʃn.

irregularity, overestimate (v.) with single stress (i,regju'læriti, ouvər'estimeit), even when not under the influence of rhythm (§ 932); others would say 'iregju'læriti, 'ouvər'estimeit. In cases of doubt it is probably safer for the foreign learner to use double stress in preference to single stress.

927. Further exceptions are *archbishopric* aːtʃ'biʃəprik, *archdeaconry* aːtʃ'diːkənri, *archdeaconship* aːtʃ'diːkənʃip, *halfpenny* 'heipəni or 'heipni. The word *archangel* is usually 'aːk-eindʒl, but is pronounced 'aːk'eindʒl by some.

928. The following miscellaneous words[6] are commonly pronounced with double stress (subject to rhythmical variations, see § 932): *amen* 'aː'men or 'ei'men,[7] *daresay* 'dɛə'sei, *hullo* 'hʌ'lou, *inborn* 'in'bɔːn, *inbred* 'in'bred, *inlaid* 'in'leid, *conversely* 'kɔn'vəːsli, *postdate* 'poust'deit, and the numerals *thirteen* 'θəː'tiːn, *fourteen* 'fɔː'tiːn, *fifteen* 'fif'tiːn, *sixteen* 'siks'tiːn, *seventeen* 'sevn'tiːn, *eighteen* 'ei'tiːn, *nineteen* 'nain'tiːn.

929. The following words are pronounced either with stress on the last syllable or with double stress; in any case they are subject to the influence of rhythm: *princess* 'prin'ses or prin'ses,[8] *sardine* 'saː'diːn or saː'diːn, *trombone* 'trɔm'boun or trɔm'boun, *bamboo* 'bæm'buː or bæm'buː, *masseuse* 'mæ'səːz or mæ'səːz. Another variable word is *indiarubber*, which is pronounced 'indjə'rʌbə or indjə'rʌbə. Instances of rhythmical variations in these words are given in § 932.

930. A number of proper names are similarly treated, e.g. *Bantu* 'bæn'tuː or bæn'tuː, *Bengal* 'beŋ'gɔːl or beŋ'gɔːl (or 'ben'gɔːl, ben'gɔːl), *Berlin* 'bəː'lin or bəː'lin, *Bexhill* 'beks'hil or beks'hil, *Blackheath* 'blæk'hiːθ or blæk'hiːθ, *Canton* (in China) 'kæn'tɔn or kæn'tɔn,[9] *Carlisle*,[10] *Carlyle* 'kaː'lail or kaː'lail, *Cheapside* 'tʃiːp'said or tʃiːp'said, *Cornhill* 'kɔːn'hil or kɔːn'hil, *Panama* 'pænə'maː or

---

[6] For miscellaneous *compounds* with double stress see §§ 948 ff.

[7] This word is usually pronounced 'aː'men in Church of England churches; elsewhere both forms are heard, 'aː'men being probably the more usual. *Amen Corner* is however 'eimen 'kɔːnə.

[8] The plural *princesses* is prin'sesiz.

[9] But *Canton* in Wales is 'kæntən. The heraldic term *canton* is 'kæntən. *Canton* meaning a state in Switzerland is generally pronounced 'kænton, but some say 'kæntən.

[10] *Carlisle* in Cumberland is locally 'kaːlail.

pæənə'mɑː, *Dundee* 'dʌn'diː or dʌn'diː, *Peiping* 'pei'piŋ or pei'piŋ, *Piccadilly* 'pikə'dili or pikə'dili, *Scawfell* 'skɔː'fel or skɔː'fel, *Spithead* 'spit'hed or spit'hed, *Stonehenge* 'stoun'hendʒ or stoun'hendʒ, *Torquay* 'tɔː'kiː or tɔː'kiː,[11] *Vauxhall* 'vɔks'hɔːl or vɔks'hɔːl, *Whitehall* 'wait'hɔːl or wait'hɔːl, and many names ending in *-ness*, e.g. *Skegness* 'skeg'nes or skeg'nes, *Shoeburyness* 'ʃuːbəri'nes or ʃuːbəri'nes, also disyllabic adjectives ending in *-ese* formed from proper names, e.g. *Chinese* 'tʃai'niːz or tʃai'niːz, *Maltese* 'mɔːl'tiːz or mɔːl'tiːz.[12] All the above are subject to rhythmical variations; for examples see §§ 932, 933.

Rhythmical Variations

931. The stress of words normally pronounced with double stress is very often modified in sentences. The first of the stressed syllables is apt to lose its stress when closely preceded by another stressed syllable; similarly the second of the stressed syllables is apt to lose its stress when closely followed by another stressed syllable. Thus although the word *fourteen* spoken by itself, or said in answer to the question 'How many people were there?' has double stress (§ 928), yet in *fourteen shillings* it is stressed on the first syllable only ('fɔːtiːn 'ʃiliŋz) and in *just fourteen* it is stressed on the second syllable only ('dʒʌst fɔː'tiːn). Compare similarly *inlaid wood* 'inleid 'wud with *all inlaid* 'ɔːl in'leid, *an unknown land* ən 'ʌnnoun 'lænd with *quite unknown* 'kwait ʌn'noun.

932. The words which, when pronounced by themselves, admit of either single or double stress (§§ 929, 930) are likewise subject to similar rhythmical variations. Compare

Princess Victoria 'prinses vik'tɔːriə with *a royal princess* ə 'rɔiəl prin'ses,

an indiarubber ball ən 'indjərʌbə 'bɔːl with *a piece of india-rubber* ə 'piːs əv indjə'rʌbə,

Piccadilly Circus 'pikədili 'səːkəs with *close to Piccadilly* 'klous tə pikə'dili,

Vauxhall Bridge 'vɔkshɔːl 'bridʒ with *near Vauxhall* 'niə vɔks'hɔːl,

Waterloo station 'wɔːtəlu: 'steiʃn with *the train for Waterloo* ðə 'trein fə wɔːtə'luː,

---

[11] But *Newquay* is 'njuːkiː or 'njuːki.
[12] Also pronounced 'mɔl'tiːz, mɔl'tiːz.

Dundee marmalade 'dʌndiː 'mɑːməleid with *going to Dundee*
'gouiŋ tə dʌn'diː,
sardine sandwiches 'sɑːdiːn 'sænwidʒiz with *a tin of sardines*
ə 'tin əv sɑː'diːnz.

933. Similar changes of stress are sometimes found in the case of
single-stressed words. Examples are *Constitution Hill, Cayenne
pepper* which are commonly pronounced 'konstitjuːʃn 'hil, 'keien
'pepə. In *Salvation Army* the stress 'sælveiʃn 'ɑːmi seems quite
as usual as sæl'veiʃn 'ɑːmi. Similarly many would say ən 'ɑːtifiʃl
'læŋgwidʒ, ə 'dipləmætik 'miʃn, rather than ən ɑːti'fiʃl 'læŋgwidʒ,
ə diplə'mætik 'miʃn (*an artificial language, a diplomatic mission*).
Those who pronounce *finance* as fai'næns will often speak of a
'fainæns 'sʌbkəmiti (*finance subcommittee*).

Emphasis

934. When it is desired to emphasize[13] words which have both
a primary and a secondary stress, and in which the secondary
stress precedes the primary (as is usually the case), the secondary
stress is often reinforced and becomes as strong as the primary
stress. Thus the words *fundamental, distribution, responsibility, disappearance, recommend, artificial* (normally ˌfʌndə'mentl, ˌdistri-
'bjuːʃn, risˌponsə'biliti, ˌdisə'piərəns, ˌrekə'mend, ˌɑːti'fiʃl) would
often be pronounced 'fʌndə'mentl, 'distri'bjuːʃn, ris'ponsə'biliti,
'disə'piərəns, 'rekə'mend, 'ɑːti'fiʃl for the sake of emphasis.

935. The frequent use of double stress in the words mentioned
in §§ 929, 930 is no doubt to be attributed to this tendency.
Occasionally other single-stressed words may receive double stress
for the sake of emphasis: thus *unless* is often pronounced 'ʌn'les
instead of the normal ən'les or ʌn'les; and one may occasionally
hear such words as *spectator, psychology, gesticulate, mutation* said
with double stress ('spek'teitə, 'sai'kolədʒi, 'dʒes'tikjuleit, 'mjuː'teiʃn)
instead of the normal single stress (spek'teitə, sai'kolədʒi,
dʒes'tikjuleit, mju(ː)'teiʃn).

936. In longer words, the greater the distance between the
secondary stress and the primary stress, the more readily does
this reinforcement of the secondary stress take place. Thus in
representation, characteristic, vulnerability the double-stressed forms

---

[13] Either for 'intensity' or for contrast. See § 1046.

'reprizen'teiʃn, 'kæriktə'ristik, 'vʌlnərə'biliti seem quite as common as the single-stressed forms ˌreprizen'teiʃn, ˌkæriktə'ristik, ˌvʌlnərə'biliti. And in very long words in which as many as three syllables intervene between the secondary stress and the primary stress, reinforcement of the secondary stress is so common that it is probably to be regarded as the usual form. Thus *perpendicularity*, *characterization* are usually 'pə:pəndikju'læriti, 'kæriktərai'zeiʃn.

937. When it is desired to emphasize (for contrast) a particular *part* of a word which is not normally stressed, that part may receive a strong stress, and the normal primary stress may become a secondary stress. Thus when *reverse* is contrasted with *obverse*, it is commonly pronounced 'ri:və:s. When *commission* is contrasted with *omission*, it is commonly pronounced 'kɔmiʃn or 'kɔ'miʃn. So also with *ascending and descending*, *offensive and defensive*, which are frequently 'æsendiŋ ən 'di:sendiŋ, 'ɔfensiv ən 'di:fensiv[14] (instead of ə'sendiŋ ən di'sendiŋ, ə'fensiv ən di'fensiv). In the case of *external*, there is practically always a contrast, expressed or implied, with *internal*; consequently the natural stress of the word (eks'tə:nl) is seldom heard, the usual pronunciation being 'eks'tə:nl (less commonly 'ekstə:nl). Similarly *demerits* is almost always pronounced 'di:ˌmerits.

Special Difficulties of Foreign Learners

938. Most foreign people have a tendency to stress the last syllable of words ending in *-ute*, *-ude*, *-ise*, *-ize* when the stress should be on some other syllable. They also generally stress the last syllable of *reconcile*, which is in Southern English 'rekənsail.[15] Examples for practice: *prosecute* 'prɔsikju:t, *substitute* 'sʌbstitju:t, *gratitude* 'grætitju:d, *multitude* 'mʌltitju:d, *criticize* 'kritisaiz,[15] *exercise* 'eksəsaiz, *recognize* 'rekəgnaiz.[15] Foreign people are particularly liable to stress the syllables -ju:t, -ju:d, -aiz in the inflected forms such as *prosecuted* 'prɔsikju:tid, *criticizes* 'kritisaiziz.

939. The French are apt to stress the final syllable wrongly in many other words. Examples for practice: *language* 'læŋgwidʒ, *paper* 'peipə, *collar* 'kɔlə, *distance* 'distəns, *circumstance* 'sə:kəmstəns,

---

[14] Or 'æ'sendiŋ ən 'di:⁽¹⁾sendiŋ, 'ɔ'fensiv ən 'di:⁽¹⁾fensiv.
[15] In the North of England and in Scotland the words *reconcile*, *criticize*, *recognize* are usually stressed on the last syllable.

universe **'juːnivəːs**, *ridicule* **'ridikjuːl**, *goodness* **'gudnis**, *vexation* **vek'seiʃn**, *disgraceful* **dis'greisfl**.

940. French people should pay special attention to the stress of English words of more than two syllables. They often have a tendency to stress the first syllable of any long word beginning with a consonant, and the second syllable of any long word beginning with a vowel. They should thus be careful to stress the second syllable in such words as *remarkable* **ri'mɑːkəbl**, *sufficient* **sə'fiʃnt**, *tremendous* **tri'mendəs**, *reluctance* **ri'lʌktəns**, *successful* **sək'sesfl**, and to stress the first syllable in such words as *absolutely* **'æbsəluːtli** or **'æbsə'luːtli**, *execute* **'eksikjuːt**, *excellent* **'ekslənt**.

941. Foreign learners should give special attention to the position of secondary stress in long words where it precedes the primary stress. They often mispronounce such words by putting the secondary stress on the wrong syllable; and particularly on the first when it ought to be on the second. The following are some examples of words of this type[16]:

Secondary stress on first syllable		Secondary stress on second syllable	
centralization	ˌsentrəlai'zeiʃn	*administration*	əd¡minis'treiʃn
modification	ˌmɔdifi'keiʃn	*affiliation*	ə¡fili'eiʃn
ornamentation	ˌɔːnəmen'teiʃn	*anticipation*	æn¡tisi'peiʃn[17]
perigrination	ˌperigri'neiʃn	*assimilation*	ə¡simi'leiʃn
qualification	ˌkwɔlifi'keiʃn	*consideration*	kən¡sidə'reiʃn
representation	ˌreprizen'teiʃn	*examination*	ig¡zæmi'neiʃn
solemnization	ˌsɔləmnai'zeiʃn	*interrogation*	in¡terə'geiʃn
circumlocution	ˌsəːkəmlə'kjuːʃn	*pronunciation*	prə¡nʌnsi'eiʃn
archaeological	ˌɑːkïə'lɔdʒikl	*ecclesiastical*	i¡kliːzi'æstikl
temperamental	ˌtempərə'mentl	*antagonistic*	æn¡tægə'nistik[18]
aristocratic	ˌæristə'krætik	*materialistic*	mə¡tiərïə'listik
mathematician	ˌmæθimə'tiʃn	*academician*	ə¡kædə'miʃn
disciplinarian	ˌdisipli'nɛərïən	*bacteriology*	bæk¡tiəri'ɔlədʒi[19]
caricature	ˌkærikə'tjuə[20]	*Iphigenia*	i¡fidʒi'naiə

---

[16] A number of other useful words with secondary stress on the second syllable will be found in an article on *Secondary Stress* by L. J. Guittart in *English Studies*, Vol. XII, No. 1, Feb. 1930.

[17] Also pronounced ˌæntisi'peiʃn.

[18] Also pronounced ˌæntægə'nistik.

[19] Also pronounced ˌbæktiəri'ɔlədʒi.

[20] Now perhaps more commonly pronounced **'kærikətjuə**.

Secondary stress on first syllable		Secondary stress on second syllable	
penetrability	ˌpenitrə'biliti	*potentiality*	pəˌtenʃi'æliti
instrumentality	ˌinstrumen'tæliti	*accessibility*	ækˌsesə'biliti
individuality	ˌindividju'æliti	*familiarity*	fəˌmili'æriti
artificiality	ˌa:tifiʃi'æliti	*peculiarity*	piˌkju:li'æriti
heterogeneous	ˌhetərə'dʒi:njəs	*superiority*	sjuˌpiəri'ɔriti
paraphernalia	ˌpærəfə'neiljə	*encyclopedia*	enˌsaiklə'pi:djə[21]
peritonitis	ˌperitə'naitis	*tuberculosis*	tjuˌbə:kju'lousis

942. It is noteworthy that a number of words having i in the first syllable and stress on the third syllable have no perceptible stress on the first syllable. Such are *electricity* ilek'trisiti, *electrician* ilek'triʃn, *electrolysis* ilek'trɔlisis, etc., *elasticity* ilæs'tisiti, *detestation* dites'teiʃn. When pronounced as here shown, neither of the first two syllables of these words can be said to have a stronger stress than the other.[22] These words have alternative pronunciations with i: or e; when so pronounced, there is generally secondary stress on the first syllable which can be shown thus, if desired: ˌi:lek'trisiti or ˌelek'trisiti, etc., ˌdi:tes'teiʃn.

B. Word-stress (*Compound Words*)

943. By a compound word is meant here a word made up of two words written in conventional spelling as one, with or without a hyphen.

944. Some compound words have single stress on the first element, others have double stress.[23]

945. Single-stressed compounds are by far the most common. Examples are: *appletree* 'æpltri:, *bookbinding* 'bukbaindiŋ, *bystander* 'bai-stændə, *Buckinghamshire* 'bʌkiŋəmʃiə,[24] *daybreak* 'dei-breik,

---

[21] Also pronounced ˌensaiklə'pi:djə.

[22] If there is any secondary stress, it is on the first syllable i-, and is only subjective. The second syllables are so prominent by the nature of their sounds that it is difficult to make a stress on the first syllable objectively audible.

[23] A few isolated compounds have single stress on the second element. The chief are: compounds with -*ever* (e.g. *whenever* we'nevə), -*self* (e.g. *himself* him'self, *themselves* ðəm'selvz), and the words *hereafter* hiər'a:ftə, *thereafter* ðɛər'a:ftə, *throughout* θru'aut, *wherein* wɛər'in, *already* ɔ:l'redi, *look-out* luk'aut, *uphold* ʌp'hould, *shortcomings* ʃɔ:t'kʌmiŋz.

[24] Or 'bʌkiŋəmʃə.

dining-room 'daininᵣum, *door-handle* 'dɔ:hændl, *figurehead* 'figəhed, *fireplace* 'faiə-pleis, *flowerpot* 'flauəpot, *footpassenger* 'futpæsindʒə, *flute-player* 'flu:tpleiə, *grasshopper* 'grɑ:shopə, *green-fly* 'gri:n-flai, *hairbrush* 'hɛə-brʌʃ, *housekeeper* 'haus-ki:pə, *jellyfish* 'dʒelifiʃ, *kettle-holder* 'ketlhouldə, *key-hole* 'ki:houl, *lightning-conductor* 'laitniŋ-kəndʌktə, *midnight* 'midnait, *orange-blossom* 'ɔrindʒblosəm, *pains-taking* 'peinzteikiŋ, *pickpocket* 'pikpokit, *schoolmaster* 'sku:lmɑ:stə, *shirt-sleeves* 'ʃə:t-sli:vz, *sitting-room* 'sitiŋrum, *smoking-compartment* 'smoukiŋ-kəmpɑ:tmənt, *snowball* 'snoubo:l, *tea-party* 'ti:-pɑ:ti, *thunder-storm* 'θʌndə-stɔ:m, *washingstand* 'wɔʃiŋ-stænd, *waterproof* 'wɔ:tə-pru:f, *weatherbeaten* 'weðəbi:tn, *wind-screen* 'windskri:n.

946. Special attention is called to the following cases of compound nouns in which single stress is used.

(i) Where the compound noun denotes a single new idea rather than the combination of two ideas suggested by the original words. Examples: *blacksmith* 'blæk-smiθ, *bluebottle* 'blu:botl, *Newcastle* 'nju:kɑ:sl,[25] *greenhouse* 'gri:nhaus, *greengrocer* 'gri:ngrousə, *kingfisher* 'kiŋfiʃə, *walking-stick* 'wɔ:kiŋstik. (Exceptions, in my pronunciation, are *great-coat* 'greit'kout, *greengage* 'gri:n'geidʒ.[26])

(ii) Where the meaning of the whole compound noun is the meaning of the second element restricted in some important way by the first element. Examples: *birthday* 'bə:θdei (a special day), *cart-horse* 'kɑ:thɔ:s (a particular kind of horse), *darning-needle* 'dɑ:niŋni:dl (a special type of needle), *dinner-table* 'dinəteibl (a particular kind of table), *gas-engine* 'gæsendʒin (a particular kind of engine), *cattle-show* 'kætlʃou, *sheepdog* 'ʃi:pdog. Exceptions are words in which the second element is felt to be of special importance (see § 949).

(iii) Where the first element is either expressly or by implication contrasted with something. Example: *flute-player* 'flu:tpleiə (where *flute* is naturally felt to be contrasted with other musical instruments).

947. Double stress is used in compound adjectives of which the first element is an adjective. Examples: *redhot* 'red'hot,

---

[25] *Newcastle-on-Tyne* is pronounced locally nju'kæsl.

[26] *Great-coat* and *greengage* are said with single stress ('greitkout, 'gri:ngeidʒ or 'gri:ŋgeidʒ) by some English people.

good-looking **'gud'lukiŋ**, *old-fashioned* **'ould'fæʃnd**, *bad-tempered* **'bæd-
'tempəd**, *absent-minded* **'æbsnt'maindid**, *first-class* **'fəːst'klaːs**, *second-
hand* **'sekənd'hænd**, *bare-headed* **'bɛə'hedid**,[27] *dead-beat* **'ded'biːt**.
Note also *home-made* **'houm'meid**, *well-bred* **'wel'bred**.[28]

948. There is an exceptional case in which single stress is used,
namely when the compound adjective is practically synonymous
with its first element. Examples: *oval-shaped* **'ouvlʃeipt**, *yellowish-
looking* **'jelouiʃlukiŋ** (which are practically equivalent to 'oval,'
'yellowish').[29]

949. When the second element of a compound is felt to be of
special importance, double stress is used. Thus *gas-stove* is commonly
'gæs'stouv, the importance of the second element *stove* being no
doubt due to the implied contrast with 'fire,' the traditional method
of heating in England. (On the other hand, *gas-engine* **'gæsendʒin**
has only a single strong stress, there being no particular contrast
between 'engine' and anything else, but rather a contrast between
an engine worked by gas and engines worked by other means.)
Further examples are: *indiarubber* **'indjə'rʌbə** (the important part
being *rubber*), *eye-witness* **'ai'witnis** ('witness' being contrasted with
persons who had only heard of the occurrence, etc.), *bow-window*
'bou'windou. *Armchair* **'aːm'tʃɛə** would apparently also belong to
this category. *Churchyard* **'tʃəːtʃ'jaːd** is another example in my
pronunciation, the 'yard' being implicitly contrasted with the
church itself; it seems, however, that **'tʃəːtʃ-jaːd** with single stress
is now the commoner form. (*Graveyard* **'greiv-jaːd** is always said
with single stress, there being no such contrast in the case of this
word.)

950. But when a compound noun of the kind referred to in
§ 950 is commonly or very frequently used attributively, it may
have single stress. Examples are *midsummer* **'midsʌmə**, *midnight*
'midnait. These words are frequently used attributively (e.g. *Midsummer Day*, *midnight sun*). When so used they have single
stress on the first element by the principle of rhythm (§ 931),
and this pronunciation has become permanently attached to them.

[27] But *muddle-headed* is pronounced with single stress (**'mʌdlhedid**).
[28] Exception *long-tailed* (tit) **'loŋ-teild**, due no doubt to the fact that this
word is always attributive and therefore takes stress on the first syllable
by the principle of rhythm (§§ 931, 954).
[29] Compare *good-looking* **'gud'lukiŋ** which is not equivalent to 'good.'

Compare *mid-winter* ˈmidˈwintə, which is not used attributively and which has double stress.

951. It may be added that it is often difficult to give satis-factory reasons for assigning a word to the classes mentioned in § 947 (ii) and (iii) or to the class described in § 950. In numerous cases both elements of the word are felt to be important for reasons of contrast or otherwise, and the treatment of the stress may depend simply on a very small balance of importance which it is not easy to estimate.

952. The following are some miscellaneous compounds having double stress (subject to rhythmical variations and to emphasis, §§ 932, 938), although not coming under the principles in §§ 948, 950: *downhill* ˈdaunˈhil, *uphill* ˈʌpˈhil, *downstairs* ˈdaunˈstɛəz, *upstairs* ˈʌpˈstɛəz; *hereby* ˈhiəˈbai, *herein* ˈhiərˈin, *hereinafter* ˈhiərinˈɑːftə,[30] *heretofore* ˈhiətuˈfɔː, *hereupon* ˈhiərəˈpɔn, *whereabouts* (interrogative adverb) ˈwɛərəˈbauts, *thereabouts* ˈðɛərəˈbauts,[31] *thereby* ˈðɛəˈbai, *therein* ˈðɛərˈin, *thereupon* ˈðɛərəˈpɔn, *whereupon* ˈwɛərəˈpɔn; *hence-forth* ˈhensˈfɔːθ, *henceforward* ˈhensˈfɔːwəd, *thenceforth* ˈðensˈfɔːθ, *thenceforward* ˈðensˈfɔːwəd, *elsewhere* ˈelsˈwɛə (also ˈels-wɛə); *inside* ˈinˈsaid, *outside* ˈautˈsaid, *alongside* əˈlɔŋˈsaid, *seaside* ˈsiːˈsaid; *indoors* ˈinˈdɔːz, *outdoors* ˈautˈdɔːz; *upturn* ˈʌpˈtəːn, *meantime* ˈmiːnˈtaim, *meanwhile* ˈmiːnˈwail,[32] *passer-by* ˈpɑːsəˈbai, *point-blank* ˈpɔintˈblæŋk.

953. Nouns compounded of a verb and an adverb, such as *make-up, setback, set-up, get-away*, are generally said with single stress (ˈmeikʌp, ˈsetbæk, etc.), but some pronounce them with double stress.

954. The stress of double-stressed compounds is subject to rhythmical variations like double-stressed simple words (§ 932). The following are examples of rhythmical variations in double-stressed compounds:

a red-hot poker ə ˈredhɔt ˈpoukə   *just red-hot* ˈdʒʌst redˈhɔt
second-hand books ˈsekəndhænd   *all second-hand* ˈɔːl sekəndˈhænd
ˈbuks

---

[30] Note, however, *hereafter* hiərˈɑːftə, *thereafter* ðɛərˈɑːftə.

[31] Note, however, *hereabouts* ˈhiərəbauts and the noun *whereabouts* ˈwɛər-əbauts. Also ðɛərəˈbauts in the expression *there or thereabouts* (ˈðɛər ɔː ðɛərəˈbauts). *Wherein* is always wɛərˈin.

[32] Also ˈmiːntaim, ˈmiːnwail.

inside out 'insaid 'aut	*right inside* 'rait in'said
the upstairs rooms ði 'ʌpstɛəz 'rumz	*on going upstairs* ɔn 'gouiŋ ʌp'stɛəz
greengage jam 'griːngeidʒ 'dʒæːm	*stewed greengages* 'stjuːd griːn'geidʒiz³³
inland revenue 'inlænd 'revinjuː³⁴	*further inland* 'fəːðər in'lænd
the overhead railway ði 'ouvəhed 'reilwei	*right overhead* 'rait ouvə'hed
an uphill task ən 'ʌphil 'taːsk	*a light great-coat* ə 'lait greit-'kout³³
seaside sports 'siː-said 'spɔːts	*cold plum-pudding* 'kould plʌm-'pudiŋ

955. Compound words consisting of three elements generally take single stress on the second element if the first two elements taken alone form a double-stressed compound. Examples: *ginger-beer-bottle* dʒindʒə'biəbotl, *hot-water-bottle* hɔt'wɔːtəbotl, *waste-paper-basket* weis'peipəbɑːskit. (These words may also be said with stress on the first element as well as on the second: 'dʒindʒə'biəbotl, etc.) Otherwise three word compounds have main stress on the first element. Examples: *teapothandle* 'tiːpothændl, *teaspoonful* 'tiːspuːnful, *lodginghousekeeper* 'lodʒiŋhaus,kiːpə, *sodawaterbottle* 'soudəwɔːtə,botl, *watercressbed* 'wɔːtəkres,bed.

Difficulties of Foreign Learners

956. Some foreign people, and especially Germans, are liable to pronounce double-stressed compounds with single stress on the first element; others (especially the French) are liable to pronounce single-stressed compounds with double stress. These errors may be rectified by observing the relations between stress and intonation described in Chap. XXXI (particularly §§ 1019–1027). The correct intonations of *arm-chair*, *plum-pudding*, pronounced with a falling intonation (Tune 1) may be represented thus:

'ɑːm'tʃɛə   'plʌm'pudiŋ

---

³³ My pronunciation. See, however, footnote 26 on p. 258.
³⁴ Also 'inlənd 'revinjuː.

Germans generally say

'ɑːmtʃɛə   'plʌmpudiŋ

while the correct pronunciations of *dinner-table, lightning-conductor*, pronounced with a falling intonation (Tune 1), may be represented thus:

'dinəteibl   'laitniŋkəndʌktə

French people often say

dinə'teibl   'laitniŋkən'dʌktə.

956a. Readers of this book should supplement what is said here on stress by a study of two recently published specialized books on the subject: R. Kingdon's *Groundwork of English Stress* (Longmans, 1958) and G. F. Arnold's *Stress in English Words* (North Holland Publishing Co., Amsterdam, 1957).

C. Sentence-stress

1. *General Principle*

957. As a general rule it may be said that the relative stress of the words in a sequence depends on their relative importance. The more important a word is, the stronger is its stress. The most important words are usually (in the absence of special emphasis) the nouns, adjectives, demonstrative and interrogative pronouns, principal verbs,[35] and adverbs. Such words are therefore generally strongly stressed (subject to exceptions, see §§ 962 ff.). Thus the first sentence of this paragraph is stressed as follows: əz ə 'dʒenrəl 'ruːl it mei bi 'sed ðət ðə 'relətiv 'stres əv ðə 'wəːdz in ə 'siːkwəns diˈpendz ɔn ðɛə 'relətiv imˈpɔːtns. Similarly *What do you think of the weather?* is usually stressed thus: 'wɔt djuː 'θiŋk əv ðə 'weðə; *this train generally arrives late* is normally stressed as follows: 'ðis 'trein 'dʒenrəli əˈraivz 'leit.

---

[35] *Have* used as a principal verb is exceptional. It is often unstressed, though it generally appears in the strong form **hæv**.

958. When all the important words in a sentence are equally important they all have strong stress. In this way it frequently happens that a number of strong syllables occur consecutively. Thus in the sentence *John has just bought two large brown dogs* every word would be stressed except *has*, thus: **'dʒɔn əz 'dʒʌst 'bɔːt 'tuː 'laːdʒ 'braun 'dɔgz.**

959. Foreign learners should note particularly the case of one word qualifying another. Both the words have as a rule strong stress.[36] Examples: *it's very important* it s **'veri im'pɔːtnt,** *a useful book* ə **'juːsful 'buk,** *the first prize* ðə **'fəːst 'praiz,** *roast beef* **'roust 'biːf,** *a deck chair* ə **'dek 'tʃɛə,** *the boy's book* ðə **'bɔiz 'buk,** *Wednesday evening* **'we(d)nzdi 'iːvniŋ,** *George's dog* **'dʒɔːdʒiz 'dɔg,** *North Western* **'nɔːθ 'westən,** *the castle wall* ðə **'kaːsl 'wɔːl,** *an orphan boy* ən **'ɔːfən 'bɔi,** *all right* **'ɔːl 'rait,** *so far so good* **'sou 'faː 'sou 'gud,** *it was too much* it wəz **'tuː 'mʌtʃ,** *Buckingham Palace* **'bʌkiŋəm 'pælis,** *Hyde Park* **'haid 'paːk,** *York Road* **'jɔːk 'roud,** *Chancery Lane* **'tʃaːnsri 'lein,** *Gloucester Terrace* **'glɔstə 'terəs,** *Kentish Town* **'kentiʃ 'taun,** *Camden Town* **'kæmdən 'taun,**[37] *Ladbroke Grove* **'lædbruk 'grouv,** *Shaftesbury Avenue* **'ʃaːftsbri 'ævinjuː,** *Herne Hill* **'həːn 'hil,** *Hampton Court* **'hæmptən 'kɔːt,** *Bell Yard* **'bel 'jaːd,** *Hampstead Heath* **'hæmpstid 'hiːθ,** *Hampstead Way* **'hæmpstid 'wei.** Many foreign people, and especially Germans, omit the stress on the second word in many expressions of this kind; they say for instance

---

[36] The adverb *most* is exceptional. In *a most important thing* ə **moust im'pɔːtnt 'θiŋ,** *their most valued possessions* ðɛə **moust 'væljuːd pə'zeʃnz** the **moust** would not be stressed, except for special emphasis. The substantival and adjectival *most* are, however, stressed; examples: *most of the houses were empty* **'moust əv ðə** [(1)]**hauziz wər 'emti,** *most bears are brown* **'moust 'bɛəz ə 'braun,** and the special expression *for the most part* fə ðə **'moust paːt.** *More* is treated similarly; examples: *that's a more serious matter* **'ðæt s ə mɔː 'siəriəs mætə** (adverbial *more*), *there were more than I expected* ðɛə wə **'mɔː ðən ai iks'pektid** (substantival *more*), *more haste less speed* **'mɔː 'heist 'les 'spiːd** (adjectival *more*).

The adjective *little* is generally not stressed. Compare *they lived in a little house near the wood* ðei **'livd in ə litl 'haus** [(1)]**niə ðə 'wud** with *they lived in a small house near the wood* ðei **'livd in ə 'smɔːl 'haus** [(1)]**niə ðə 'wud,** *a good little boy* ə **'gud litl 'bɔi** with *a big fat boy* ə **'big 'fæt 'bɔi.** There are, however, exceptions, e.g. *little things please little minds* **'litl 'θiŋz 'pliːz 'litl 'maindz;** stress appears to be put on *little* when the word is used to imply a considerable degree of smallness.

[37] But *Canning Town* is sometimes said with single stress (**'kæniŋ taun**).

'roust biːf, 'ɔːl rait. (They also often use an incorrect intonation, as in the examples in § 956.) Where, however, the qualifying word is *no, so* or *too* the tendency on the part of foreign people is rather to omit the stress on the first word and to shorten unnecessarily its vowel (e.g. to say it 'wɔz tu 'mʌtʃ instead of it wəz 'tuː 'mʌtʃ).

960. The case of a verb followed by an adverb, the two words together forming what is practically a new verb, should be also specially noted.[38] Thus in *go away, give up, put down, leave out, turn round, come on,* etc., both words are normally stressed. Examples: *he got up and went away* hiː 'gɔt 'ʌp ən 'went ə'wei, *Put down that parcel!* 'put 'daun ðæt 'pɑːsl, *Take it off!* 'teik it 'ɔf. Phrases like *get ready, make haste* which are equivalent to single verbs are treated in like manner ('get 'redi, 'meik 'heist).

2. *Exceptions to General Rule*

961. Exceptions to the general rule that nouns, adjectives, demonstrative and interrogative pronouns, principal verbs, and adverbs have strong stress (§ 957) are as follows:

962. 1*st exceptional case.* When it is desired to *emphasize* a word for contrast, its stress is increased, while the stress of the surrounding words may be diminished. Thus in the absence of special emphasis the stress of *I never gave you that book* is ai 'nevə 'geiv juː 'ðæt 'buk; but if it were desired to emphasize the word *I* or the word *you* or the word *that*, we should have three different ways of stressing the sentence, namely: 'ai nevə geiv juː ðæt 'buk (stress on *I* and no stress on *never*), ai 'nevə geiv 'juː ðæt 'buk (stress on *you* and no stress on *gave* or *that*), ai 'nevə 'geiv juː 'ðæt buk (stress on *that* and no stress on *book*). In *I don't object,* if *I* is stressed, *don't* is unstressed, thus 'ai dount əb'dʒekt. In *that's your look-out* 'ðæt s 'jɔː lukaut, *look-out* is not stressed, in order to give greater force to *your.* Similarly with *concerned* in *so far as he's concerned* sou 'fɑːr əz 'hiː z kənsəːnd.

963. In the expression *to make sure* tə meik 'ʃuə the *make* is usually not stressed, presumably in order to give greater force to

---

[38] The case of a verb with a preposition is, however, different; in this case the verb only has stress. Examples: *meet with* 'miːt wið, *enter into* (an agreement) 'entər intu.

sure; similarly with *gave* in *he gave a final touch* . . . **hiː geiv ə ˈfainl ˈtʌtʃ**. . . .

964. In *some people think so* **ˈsʌm piːpl ˈθiŋk sou** there is an implied contrast with 'other people,' therefore *people* is not stressed.[39] So also in *the latter case* **ðə ˈlætə keis** there is a contrast (expressed or implied) with some other case. Similarly with *way* in *this way or that* **ˈðis wei ɔː ˈðæt**, and with *instant* in *it was light one instant and dark the next* it **wəz ˈlait ˈwʌn instənt ən ˈdɑːk ðə ˈnekst**. The absence of stress on *rate* in the expression *at any rate* **ət ˈeni reit** appears to be due to a similar cause.

965. For the same reason when a sentence contains a word which has been used just before, that word is generally not stressed. Examples: *How many times have you been there? Three times* **ˈhau meni ˈtaimz əv juː ˈbiːn ðɛə? ˈθriː taimz** (no stress on the second *times*), *those who have read about everything are commonly supposed to understand everything* **ˈðouz hu əv ˈred əbaut ˈevriθiŋ ə ˈkɔmənli səˈpouzd tu ʌndəˈstænd evriθiŋ** (no stress on the second *everything*), *we think of that as a child thinks* **wiː ˈθiŋk əv ˈðæt əz ə ˈtʃaild θiŋks** (no stress on *thinks*), *the boys shouted to the other boys* **ðə ˈbɔiz ˈʃautid tə ði ˈʌðə bɔiz** (no stress on the second *boys*), *the house called 'The Brambles' was chiefly conspicuous for its lack of brambles* **ðə ˈhaus kɔːld ðə ˈbræmblz wəz ˈtʃiːfli kənˈspikjuəs fər its ˈlæk əv bræmblz** (no stress on the second *brambles*).

966. So also when one word in a sequence of two words is naturally or habitually contrasted with some other word, that word alone receives the stress. Thus *acute angle* would generally be pronounced **əˈkjuːt æŋgl** (without stress on *angle*) even when no contrast with 'obtuse' is intended; similarly with *railway journey* **ˈreilwei dʒəːni**, *pleasure trip* **ˈpleʒə trip**, *lighthouse keeper* **ˈlaithaus kiːpə**, *steamship company* **ˈstiːmʃip kʌmpəni**, *life-saving apparatus* **ˈlaifseiviŋ æpəreitəs**, *high-school teacher* **ˈhai-skuːl tiːtʃə**, *safety razor* **ˈseifti reizə**. *Lady's*

---

[39] *Some* is here used in the collective sense, which is distinct from the indefinite (partitive) sense. The indefinite *some* is pronounced **səm** or **sm**, and the following word is stressed, e.g. *there were some books on the table* **ðɛə wə səm ˈbuks ɔn ðə ˈteibl**. *Some* denoting one of a class is pronounced **sʌm** but has no stress, e.g. *we must try and get hold of some teacher* **wiː məs ˈtrai ən get ˈhould əv sʌm ˈtiːtʃə**. (But *some teachers* meaning 'a few teachers' would be **səm ˈtiːtʃəz**, or if contrasted with 'other teachers,' **ˈsʌm tiːtʃəz**).

maid has single stress ('leidiz meid), like *house-maid* 'hausmeid,
parlour-maid 'pɑːləmeid, etc.[40] These cases are sometimes difficult
to distinguish from those mentioned in § 976.

967. Sequences of three words which are equivalent to compound
words are stressed like the compound words mentioned in § 955.
Examples: *public school man* ⁽ⁱ⁾pʌblik 'skuːl mæn, *high water mark*
⁽ⁱ⁾hai 'wɔːtə mɑːk.

968. The stressing of *this, these, that* (demonstrative), *those*
depends upon the amount of 'demonstrativeness' it is desired to
suggest. Sometimes they are equivalent to little more than the
definite article *the*, and in such cases they are unstressed. This is
especially the case when the noun they qualify refers to something previously mentioned. Examples of lack of stress on these
words: *he managed this matter admirably* hiː 'mænidʒd ðis 'mætər
'ædmərəbli, *it was necessary to take these precautions* it wəz 'nesisri
tə 'teik ðiːz pri'kɔːʃnz, *I don't care for that other one* ai 'dount 'kɛə
fə ðæt 'ʌðə wʌn, *he couldn't bear the gaze of those eyes* hiː 'kudnt
'bɛə ðə 'geiz əv ðouz 'aiz. *This* is not stressed in *this morning,
this afternoon, this evening* (ðis 'mɔːniŋ, ðis 'ɑːftə'nuːn, ðis 'iːvniŋ).

969. When *which* is used as a demonstrative pronoun (= 'and
this,' 'and these,' etc.), it is stressed according to the general rule.
Example: *which diamond was eventually lost* 'witʃ 'daiəmənd wəz
i'ventjŭəli 'lɔst (meaning 'and this diamond was . . .').

970. The exclamatory *what* in such expressions as *What a
dreadful thing!, What beautiful weather!, What crowds of people!*
is not stressed, presumably in order to give greater emphasis to
dreadful, beautiful, crowds (wɔt ə 'dredful 'θiŋ, wɔt 'bjuːtəfl 'weðə,
wɔt 'kraudz əv 'piːpl).

971. When *such* is followed by an emphatic word, it is generally
unstressed. Examples: *such a curious shape* sʌtʃ ə 'kjuərïəʃ ʃeip,
such quantities of sand sʌtʃ 'kwɔntitiz əv 'sænd. But when *such*
is followed by a word incapable of receiving emphasis, e.g. *thing*,
it is usually stressed; example: *such a thing ought to be impossible*
'sʌtʃ ə 'θiŋ 'ɔːt tə biː im'posəbl. It may, however, be unstressed

---

[40] *The French lady's maid* may mean two different things according to
the way in which it is stressed. ðə 'frenʃ 'leidiz meid means 'the lady's
maid who is French'; ðə 'frenʃ leidiz 'meid means 'the maid employed
by the French lady.'

if the noun it qualifies is also unstressed; example: *I don't know anything about such matters* ai 'dount nou 'eniθiŋ ə'baut sʌtʃ mætəz, *I never heard of such a thing* ai 'nevə 'hə:d əv sʌtʃ ə θiŋ.

972. When the expressions *sort of, kind of* are used indefinitely, i.e. not with reference to particular varieties of things, the words *sort, kind* are usually not stressed. Examples: *there was a sort of seriousness in his face* ðɛə wəz ə sɔ:t əv 'siərïəsnis in iz 'feis, *they made a kind of agreement* ðei 'meid ə kaind əv ə'gri:mənt. When these expressions are followed by words which cannot be emphasized, both are unstressed; example: *I don't like that kind of thing* ai dount 'laik ⁽¹⁾ðæt kaind əv θiŋ. Also when *sort of* is used in colloquial speech as an adverb meaning 'in some kind of way,' it is not stressed; examples: *he sort of slipped* hi: sɔ:t əv 'slipt, *he slipped sort of* hi: 'slipt sɔ:t ɔv.

973. *2nd exceptional case.* The double stress in groups of words such as those mentioned in §§ 959, 960 is often subject to *rhythmical variations.* The following are examples of variations in stress due to this cause: *hot roast beef* 'hɔt roust 'bi:f, *John went away* 'dʒɔn went ə'wei (cp. *he went away* normally pronounced hi: 'went ə'wei), *a very good thing* ə 'veri gud 'θiŋ (cp. ə 'gud 'θiŋ), *not very good* 'nɔt veri 'gud, *very much better* 'veri mʌtʃ 'betə, *we can't get out* wi: 'ka:nt get 'aut⁴¹ (cp. *Get out!* 'get 'aut), *he put on his hat* hi: 'put ɔn iz 'hæt (cp. hi: 'put it 'ɔn), *Go and get ready!* 'gou ən get 'redi (cp. *Get ready at once!* 'get 'redi ət 'wʌns), *we didn't see anything at all* wi: 'didnt si: 'eniθiŋ ə'tɔ:l (no stress on *see*) (cp. *we did not see the exhibition* wi: 'didnt 'si: ði eksi'biʃn), *the disaster claimed many victims* ðə di'za:stə kleimd 'meni 'viktimz (no stress on *claimed*), *there was nothing going on* ðɛə wəz 'nʌθiŋ gouiŋ 'ɔn (no stress on *going*), *no one went near it* 'nou wʌn went 'niər it (no stress on *went*), *it seems so funny* it 'si:mz sou 'fʌni (no stress on *so*),⁴² *we all got home without difficulty* wi: 'ɔ:l gɔt 'houm wi'ðaut 'difiklti (cp. *we got home* . . . wi: 'gɔt 'houm . . .).

974. In some cases of this kind two ways of stressing are possible. Thus *he's so much kinder than he used to be* may be

---

⁴¹ In rapid conversation often wi: 'ka:ŋk get 'aut.

⁴² The rhythm of it 'si:mz sou 'fʌni is ♪ ♪ ♪ ♫

pronounced hiː z 'sou mʌtʃ 'kaində ðən iː 'juːs(t) tə biː or hiː z sou 'mʌtʃ 'kaində. . . . In *so many years, so much more,* etc., in the sense of 'such a great many years,' 'such a great deal more,' etc., the stress is more usually on *many* or *much* (sou 'meni 'jəːz, sou 'mʌtʃ 'mɔː). The other stressing, 'sou meni 'jəːz, 'sou mʌtʃ 'mɔː, is also possible but seems to be generally avoided, presumably because when *so many, so much* are pronounced with stressed *so*, they usually have the special meanings 'such and such a number,' 'such and such a quantity.'

975. Loss of stress for rhythmical reasons is not always essential for correct pronunciation. Thus it would not be incorrect to say 'hɒt 'roust 'biːf, it 'siːmz 'sou 'fʌni. When the foreign learner is in doubt as to whether a stress should be suppressed on account of rhythm or not, it is safer for him to retain the stress.

976. *3rd exceptional case.* When two nouns in sequence are felt as being very closely connected by the sense, so that they form practically one word, the second is generally unstressed. (These groups may really be considered as compound words, and many of them may be written in ordinary spelling with hyphens.) Examples: *door handle* 'dɔː hændl, *gooseberry bush* 'guzbri buʃ, *camping ground* 'kæmpiŋ graund, *tennis ball* 'tenis bɔːl, *golf club* 'gɔlf klʌb,[43] *cricket bat* 'krikit bæt, *diamond merchant* 'daiəmən məːtʃənt (even when no contrast between dealers in diamonds and dealers in other goods is intended), *violin string* vaiə'lin striŋ, *the Law Courts* ðə 'lɔː kɔːts, *chimney corner* 'tʃimni kɔːnə, *barrel organ* 'bærəl ɔːgən, *bank note* 'bæŋk nout,[44] *examination paper* igzæmi'neiʃn peipə, *lemon squeezer* 'lemən skwiːzə, *hair-dressing saloon* 'hɛədresiŋ səluːn, *television set* teli'viʒn set. (It is often difficult to distinguish this case from that mentioned in § 966).

977. There are some exceptions, namely cases in which the second element expresses or implies a contrast, e.g. *gooseberry tart* 'guzbri 'taːt, *rice pudding* 'rais 'pudiŋ, *plum cake* 'plʌm 'keik, *port wine* 'pɔːt 'wain ('tart' being commonly contrasted with 'pie,' 'pudding,' etc., and 'pudding' with 'meat,' 'wine' with other beverages, etc.). *Saucepan lid* would usually be 'sɔːspən 'lid, no doubt owing to an implied contrast between the lid and the

---

[43] Also, in old-fashioned pronunciation, 'gɔf klʌb.
[44] Less commonly 'bæŋk 'nout.

saucepan itself (cp. *churchyard*, § 950). *Birthday present* and
Christmas present have double stress in my pronunciation ('bə:θdei
'preznt, 'krisməs 'preznt) presumably because *present* is felt to be
the important word.[45]

978. 4th exceptional case. The word *street* in names of streets
is never stressed, e.g. *Oxford Street* 'ɔksfəd stri:t, *Downing Street*
'dauniŋ stri:t (cp. *York Road*, etc., § 959).

979. 5th exceptional case. In phrases of a parenthetical nature
the words are often unstressed. Examples: *Has he gone to town
this morning?* 'hæz i: gɔn tə 'taun ðis mɔ:niŋ?, *How do you do,
Mr. Smith?* hau dju 'du: mistə smiθ, '*Yes*,' he said 'jes hi: sed,
where the phrases *this morning*, *Mr. Smith*, *he said*, are of a
parenthetical nature.

980. The question of stress in such cases is, however, less important than that of intonation (§ 1071). Thus a certain amount
of stress would often be put on the words mɔ:niŋ, smiθ, sed, in
the above examples, provided that the word taun has the lowest
pitch in the first sentence, and that the whole of the phrases
mistə smiθ, hi: sed are pronounced with low pitch. Thus:

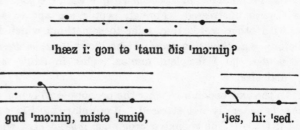

'hæz i: gɔn tə 'taun ðis 'mɔ:niŋ?

gud 'mɔ:niŋ, mistə 'smiθ,   'jes, hi: 'sed.

Further examples are given in § 1071.

981. 6th exceptional case. The various parts of the verb *be*
are generally unstressed even when the word is a principal verb,

---

[45] But *wedding present* has single stress ('wediŋ preznt). Some people,
especially in the North of England, use single stress on *birthday present* and
Christmas present. *Wedding breakfast* has double stress ('wediŋ 'brekfəst)
in my pronunciation. So also have *Christmas dinner* 'krisməs 'dinə,
Christmas pudding 'krisməs 'pudiŋ, *Christmas wishes* 'krisməs 'wiʃiz,
Christmas Day 'krisməs 'dei, *Easter egg* 'i:stər 'eg, *birthday greetings* 'bə:θdei
'gri:tiŋz. *Birthday cake, wedding cake, wedding day* have single stress
('bə:θdei keik, 'wediŋ keik, 'wediŋ dei).

except when it is final. Examples: *the train was late* ðə 'trein
wəz 'leit (cp. *the train arrived late* ðə 'trein ə'raivd 'leit, in which
the verb is stressed), *you are never ready* juə 'nevə 'redi, *What
is the time?* 'wɔt s ðə 'taim? (But it is stressed finally in *I don't
know where it is* ai 'dount nou 'wɛər i'tiz, *here we are* 'hiə wi 'ɑː,
the chances are . . . ðə 'tʃɑːnsiz 'ɑː . . ., *the fact is* ðə 'fækt 'iz, *the
reason being* . . . ðə 'riːzn 'biːiŋ. . . .)

982. The verb *be* is also unstressed when final and immediately
preceded by its subject, if that subject is stressed. Example:
he asked what the time was hiː 'ɑːskt wɔt ðə 'taim wɔz.

983. *7th exceptional case.* When the subject follows the verb,
the verb is generally not stressed. Examples: *'Yes,' said his
father* 'jes, sed iz 'fɑːðə (where *father* may be stressed but *said*
should not be), *after a storm comes a calm* 'ɑːftər ə 'stɔːm kʌmz
ə 'kɑːm (no stress on kʌmz).

3. *Miscellaneous Rules*

984. The following are some miscellaneous facts about stress
which it is necessary for the foreign learner to know.

985. The pronoun *one* in *a good one* ə 'gud wʌn, *everyone* 'evriwʌn,
etc., is always unstressed. Foreign people are apt to stress it.
So also with other words that refer to something which has just
gone before, e.g. *things* in *those things* 'ðouz θiŋz, *matters* in *I'll
explain matters* 'ai l iks'plein mætəz, *affair* in *that's my affair*
'ðæt s 'mai əfɛə.

986. In the expression *each other* the pronoun *each* is not stressed,
and *other* is generally not stressed. Example: *they like each other*
ðei 'laik iːtʃ ʌðə. The reflexive pronouns, *myself*, etc., when used
as object, are generally not stressed. Example: *he hurt himself*
hiː 'həːt imself.

987. Auxiliary verbs are normally not stressed.

988. They are, however, stressed in the following particular
cases:

   (i) In affirmative statements for the sake of emphasis, e.g. *it
   can be done* it 'kæn bi dʌn, *it has been done* it 'hæz bi(ː)n dʌn,[46]

---

[46] The normal (unemphatic) pronunciation of these sentences would be
it kən bi 'dʌn, it s bi(ː)n 'dʌn.

I may have said so ai 'mei əv 'sed sou. The auxiliary *do* is always emphasized in such cases, e.g. *I do want to* ai 'du: 'wɔnt tu; similarly in imperative sentences, e.g. *Do come!* 'du: 'kʌm.

(ii) When immediately followed by *not* pronounced nt, e.g. *I shouldn't have thought so* ai 'ʃudnt əv 'θɔ:t sou, *we haven't been able to* wi: 'hævnt bi(:)n 'eibl tu.[47]

(iii) When introducing a question, e.g. *Have you seen them?* 'hæv ju: 'si:n ðəm?, *Did you like it?* 'did ju: 'laik it? (In this case, however, the stress is not essential.)

(iv) In other questions when there is much curiosity, surprise or anxiety on the part of the speaker and the auxiliary is immediately preceded by the interrogative word, e.g. *What are you doing?* wɔt 'ɑ: ju: 'duiŋ, *What is to be done?* wɔt 'iz tə bi 'dʌn?, *How did they manage it?* hau 'did ðei 'mænidʒ it?[48] (But in *However did they manage it?* hau'evə did ðei 'mænidʒ it? the *did* would not be stressed because it does not immediately follow *how*.)

(v) When the principal verb is suppressed, e.g. *Yes, I have* 'jes ai 'hæv, *he always does* hi: 'ɔ:lweiz 'dʌz.

989. The word *going* in the expression *to be going to* . . . being of an auxiliary nature is often not stressed. Example: *What are you going to do?* 'wɔt ə ju: goiŋ tə 'du:. (It would also be possible to stress *going*.)

990. The adverbs *on, forth*, in the expressions *and so on* ən 'sou ɔn, *and so forth* ən 'sou fɔ:θ are not stressed. The adverb *again* when used to emphasize a contrast is not stressed; examples: *Put it back again* (after having taken it away) 'put it 'bæk əgein, *he's going out again soon* (after having come in) hi: z 'goiŋ 'aut əgein 'su:n, *he was dead and is alive again* hi: wəz 'ded ənd iz ə'laiv əgein.[49]

---

[47] These expressions might also be pronounced ai ʃəd 'nɔt əv 'θɔ:t sou, wi: v 'nɔt bi(:)n 'eibl tu.

[48] The normal (unemphatic) pronunciation of these sentences would be 'wɔt ə ju: 'duiŋ, 'wɔt s tə bi 'dʌn, 'hau did ðei 'mænidʒ it.

[49] But *again* meaning 'a second time' is stressed, e.g. 'put it 'bæk ə'gein (= put it back a second time), hi: z 'gouiŋ 'aut ə'gein 'su:n (= he's soon going out a second time).

991. The adverbs *now* and *then*[50] are normally stressed, e.g. *How are you now?* 'hau ə ju: 'nauꝶ, *I couldn't do it then* ai 'kudnt 'du it 'ðen. The expression *now then* is pronounced 'nau ðen with stress on *now*. The adverb *so* in *do so* 'du: sou, *think so* 'θiŋk sou, etc., is not stressed.

992. Adverbs sometimes do not take stress in final position following a stressed object. Examples: *Put your things on!* 'put jo: 'θiŋz ɔn, *he let the fire out* hi: 'let ðə 'faiər aut.

993. Monosyllabic prepositions and the disyllabic preposition *upon* ə'pɔn (or əpən) are usually unstressed. Examples may be found in any book of phonetic texts. These prepositions may, however, occasionally be stressed when they occur at the beginning of a sentence; examples: *On his way he had an adventure* 'ɔn iz 'wei hi: 'hæd n əd'ventʃə, *In the room they found a dog* 'in ðə 'rum ðei 'faund ə 'dɔg.

994. Monosyllabic prepositions are also occasionally stressed when followed by a pronoun at the end of a sentence (see § 998).

995. Prepositions of two or more syllables (with the exception of *upon*, § 993), such as *after* 'ɑːftə, *into* 'intu,[51] *between* bi'twiːn, *during* 'djuəriŋ, *besides* bi'saidz, *along* ə'lɔŋ, *concerning* kən'səːniŋ, are often stressed in non-final position. Such stress is, however, not essential in many cases; examples: *he went after it* hi: 'went 'ɑːftər it, *I'll do it after tea* ai l 'du it [1]ɑːftə 'tiː, *he ran into them* hi: 'ræn 'intə ðəm, *he put the money into the box* hi: 'put ðə 'mʌni [1]intə ðə 'bɔks, *he searched among his papers* hi: 'səːtʃt ə[1]mʌŋ iz 'peipəz, *he finished it during the holidays* hi: 'finiʃt it [1]djuəriŋ ðə 'hɔlədiz.

996. The final prepositions in sentences like *What are you looking at?* 'wɔt ə ju: 'lukiŋ æt, *Who were you talking to?* 'hu: wə ju: 'tɔːkiŋ tu, *What's all that fuss about?* 'wɔt s ɔːl ðæt 'fʌs əbaut, *we asked where they came from* wi: 'ɑːs(k)t wɛə ðei 'keim frɔm, *he wants looking after* hi: wɔnts 'lukiŋ ɑːftə, are not stressed though they have their strong forms.[52]

---

[50] But not the conjunctions *now*, *then* (see § 1001).

[51] 'intə before consonants.

[52] Except *to*, which is generally said with the weak form tu in such cases. The strong form tuː (unstressed) would also be possible.

997. In sentences ending with a preposition and a pronoun the final pronouns are not stressed unless special emphasis is needed,[53] e.g. *it's very good for you* it s ˈveri ˈgud fɔ: ju (or it s ˈveri ˈgud fə ju:), *What shall we do with it?* ˈwɔt ʃl wi: ˈdu: wið it, *Look at them!* ˈluk æt ðəm (or ˈluk ət ðəm). Foreign learners should note that in these cases the preposition more usually has its strong form and has noticeably stronger stress than the pronoun.

998. Sometimes it is necessary to stress the preposition in sentences of this type in order to bring out a contrast, e.g. *the bills were not large but there were a great many of them* ðə ˈbilz wə ˈnot ˈla:dʒ bət ðɛə wər ə ˈgreit ˈmeni ˈov ðəm.

999. Conjunctions introducing dependent clauses are often stressed when initial. Examples: *When he comes I'll introduce him to you* ˈwen i: ˈkʌmz ai l intrəˈdju:s im tu: ju, *As I was saying . . .* ˈæz ai wəz ˈseiiŋ . . ., *After he had left . . .* ˈɑːftər i: əd ˈleft . . ., *nor do I* ˈnɔ: du ˈai.[54] If the order of the clauses in the first example were reversed, then *when* would not be stressed, because the whole sentence would be pronounced in one breath-group, and the *when* would no longer be initial.

1000. The copulative conjunctions *and* and *but* are not generally stressed. These words may however be stressed, especially when immediately followed by two or three consecutive unstressed syllables. Thus *and at the same time . . .* may be pronounced ˈænd ət ðə ˈseim ˈtaim . . . or ænd ət ðə ˈseim ˈtaim . . . or ənd ət ðə ˈseim ˈtaim. . . . Even in *but it's of the greatest importance* it would be more usual not to stress the *but*, pronouncing bət it s əv ðə ˈgreitist imˈpɔːtns. Foreign learners are recommended to use the weak forms ənd and bət in all such cases, except where special emphasis of the conjunction is required.

1001. Other linking conjunctions, such as *now, then*, introducing the continuation of a narrative or conversation are not stressed, e.g. *Now when he was gone . . .* nau ˈwen i: wəz ˈgɔn . . ., *Then you don't believe it?* ðen ju: ˈdount biˈliːv it, *So he went into the garden* sou i: ˈwent intə ðə ˈgɑːdn.

---

[53] The pronoun *it* would not be stressed in any case. If emphasis were required, it would be replaced by *this* or *that*.

[54] *Nor* introducing a sentence is almost always stressed, unless combined with another word, as in *nor yet* nɔ: ˈjet.

Chapter XXX

BREATH-GROUPS, SENSE-GROUPS

1002. Pauses are continually made in speaking. They are made chiefly (1) for the purpose of taking breath, (2) for the purpose of making the meaning of the words clear.

1003. It is usual to employ the term *breath-group* to denote a complete sentence that can conveniently be said with a single breath, or, in the case of very long sentences, the longest portions that can conveniently be said with single breaths.

1004. Pauses for breath are normally made at points where pauses are necessary or allowable from the point of view of meaning.

1005. Sentences are usually divisible into smaller sequences between which pauses *may* be made, though they are not essential. The shortest possible of such sequences (i.e. sequences which are not capable of being further subdivided by pauses) are called *sense-groups*. Each sense-group consists of a few words in close grammatical connexion, such as would be said together in giving a slow dictation exercise.

1006. The divisions between breath-groups are generally made clear in writing by the punctuation marks. In phonetic transcriptions it is sometimes useful to mark the division of breath-groups by the sign ‖ and the division of sense-groups by the sign |. Another method, which has, however, certain disadvantages, is not to leave any spaces between consecutive words in breath-groups or sense-groups. For this see Chap. XXXII and especially § 1094.

Chapter XXXI

INTONATION

The Nature of Intonation

1007. *Intonation* may be defined as the variations which take place in the pitch of the voice in connected speech, i.e. the variations in the pitch of the musical note produced by the vibration of the vocal cords.

1008. Intonation is thus quite a different thing from stress (§ 909). There are, however, important relations between stress and intonation in English, as indeed in all 'stress languages.' The effect of *prominence* (§§ 101, 208–210) is often produced by certain combinations of the two.

1009. From the above definition it will be seen that there can be no objective intonation when voiceless sounds are pronounced. The number of voiceless sounds occurring in connected speech is, however, small in comparison with the voiced sounds,[1] so that the intonation in any ordinary breath-group may be regarded as practically continuous. It is certainly subjectively continuous.

1010. In ordinary speech the pitch of the voice is continually changing. When the pitch of the voice rises we have a *rising intonation*; when it falls we have a *falling intonation*; when it remains on one note for an appreciable time, we have *level intonation*.

1011. The range of intonation is very extensive. It is a noteworthy fact that most people in speaking reach notes much higher and much lower than they can sing.

1012. The extent of the range in any given case depends on circumstances. It is as a general rule greater in the declamatory style of speech than in conversational style, and in each case it is greater when the speaker is excited than when he is in a serious mood. In reciting a passage of a light or humorous character

---

[1] About 20 per cent. of the sounds used in speaking a connected passage of English are voiceless.

it is by no means unusual for a man with an average voice to have

a range of intonation of over two octaves, rising to F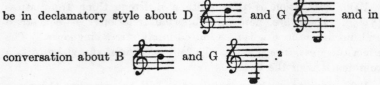

or even higher and going down so low that the voice degenerates
into a kind of growl which can hardly be regarded as a musical
sound at all.   In ordinary conversational English the intonation

(in men's voices) does not often rise above D 🎵 .

1013. In the case of women's voices the range of intonation is
not quite so extensive.   The average limits for English appear to

be in declamatory style about D 🎵 and G 🎵 and in

conversation about B 🎵 and G 🎵 .[2]

1014. A good way of representing intonation for practical
teaching purposes is a system of dots (denoting approximately level
pitches) and curves (denoting rising and falling intonations) placed
above each syllable of a phonetic transcription.   It is convenient
to place these marks on a stave of three lines, the upper and lower
lines representing the upper and lower limits of the voice, and the
middle line representing an intermediate pitch.

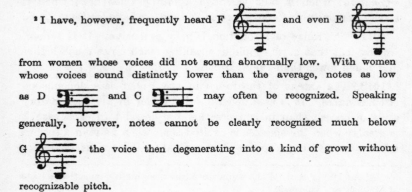

[2] I have, however, frequently heard F 🎵 and even E 🎵

from women whose voices did not sound abnormally low.   With women
whose voices sound distinctly lower than the average, notes as low
as D 🎵 and C 🎵 may often be recognized.   Speaking
generally, however, notes cannot be clearly recognized much below
G 🎵 , the voice then degenerating into a kind of growl without
recognizable pitch.

1015. It is advantageous to show the stress on the intonation-graph. This is conveniently done by indicating the strongly stressed syllables by large dots. If a syllable with a rising or falling intonation is strongly stressed, this may be shown by placing a large dot on the appropriate part of the curve (generally at the beginning); so when a curve has no dot attached to it, it is to be understood that the syllable is unstressed.[3]

1016. Intonations in language have meanings which are super-posed on the dictionary meanings of the words uttered. They may convey subtle shades of meaning which could only be expressed by words in a cumbrous manner, if at all. Compare the following:

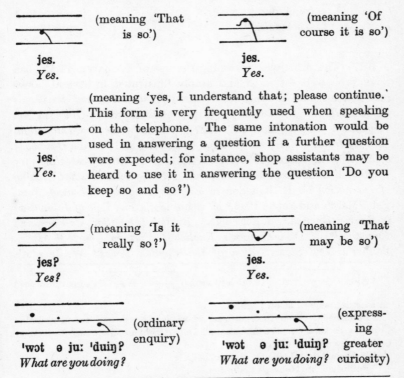

(meaning 'That is so')

jes.
Yes.

(meaning 'Of course it is so')

jes.
Yes.

(meaning 'yes, I understand that; please continue.' This form is very frequently used when speaking on the telephone. The same intonation would be used in answering a question if a further question were expected; for instance, shop assistants may be heard to use it in answering the question 'Do you keep so and so?')

jes.
Yes.

(meaning 'Is it really so?')

jes?
Yes?

(meaning 'That may be so')

jes.
Yes.

(ordinary enquiry)

'wɔt ə juː 'duiŋ?
What are you doing?

(expressing greater curiosity)

'wɔt ə juː 'duiŋ?
What are you doing?

---

[3] This system is a modification of that used by H. Klinghardt in his *Übungen im Englischen Tonfall*, which was first published by Otto Schulze in Cöthen in 1920.

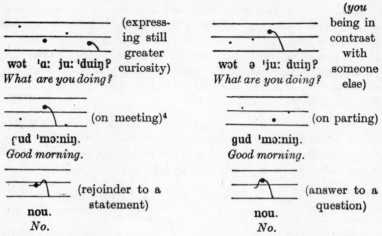

wɔt ˈɑː juː ˈduiŋ? (express-
What are you doing? ing still
                greater
                curiosity)

wɔt ə ˈjuː duiŋ? (*you*
What are you doing? being in
                contrast
                with
                someone
                else)

ɕud ˈmɔːniŋ. (on meeting)[4]
Good morning.

gud ˈmɔːniŋ. (on parting)
Good morning.

nou. (rejoinder to a
No. statement)

nou. (answer to a
No. question)

1017. The principles governing the use of intonation in English have been well set forth and amply illustrated in several books and articles, and notably in Coleman's *Intonation and Emphasis in Miscellanea Phonetica* I (1912),[5] Klinghardt's *Übungen im Englischen Tonfall*, 2nd ed., 1927),[6] Palmer's *English Intonation, with Systematic Exercises* (1922),[7] Armstrong and Ward's *Handbook of English Intonation* (1926),[7] R. Kingdon's *Tonetic Stress Marks for English* in *Le Mâitre Phonetique*, Oct., 1939, articles on *The Teaching of Intonation* by R. Kingdon in *English Language Teaching*, Jan., Feb., March and Sept., 1948,[8] M. Schubiger's *The Role of Intonation in Spoken English*,[9] M. Schubiger's *English Intonation, its Form and Function*,[10] J. D. O'Connor's *English Intonation Course*,[11] H. E. Palmer's *New Classification of the English Tones*,[5] W. Jassem's

---

[4] Also ————— In modern usage ————— is sometimes used

on meeting, as well as on parting.

[5] Published by the International Phonetic Association, and obtainable from the Secretary of the Association, Department of Phonetics, University College, London, W.C.1.

[6] Published by Quelle & Meyer, Leipzig.

[7] Published by Heffer, Cambridge.

[8] Published by the British Council, 65, Davies Street, London, W.1.

[9] Published by Fehr'sche Buchhandlung, St. Gall, 1935.

[10] Max Niemeyer Verlag, Tübingen.

[11] Radiotjänst, Stockholm.

Intonation of Colloquial English,[12] R. Kingdon's *The Groundwork of English Intonation*,[13] Kingdon's *English Intonation Practice*,[13] and K. L. Pike's *The Intonation of American English*.[14]   In this chapter only a bare outline of the subject can be given; those who wish to get a real grasp of English intonation must work through at least the Armstrong–Ward *Handbook*, and Kingdon's *Groundwork*, and preferably several other of the above-mentioned works.

1018. I find the method of classifying the phenomena of English intonation adopted by Armstrong and Ward in their *Handbook* to be effective in practical teaching, and I accordingly follow their system in this chapter.   They have shown, quite correctly in my opinion, that most sense-groups in English are said with one of two fundamental 'tunes' or with other 'tunes' which are formed by modifying the fundamental tunes according to definite principles.

1019. The two fundamental tunes are generally known as 'Tune 1' and 'Tune 2' respectively.[15]   Their particular features are shown by the following graphical illustrations:

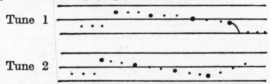

1020. These tunes may be spread over a large number of syllables, or they may be compressed into smaller spaces.   All the essential features of the tunes are shown in the above graphical illustrations.   When the tunes are applied to small groups of syllables or to the extreme case of monosyllables, several of these features disappear.   I find it therefore a good plan in teaching English intonation to start with the intonation of long sentences and proceed subsequently to the intonation of short sentences.

Tune 1 (normal form)

1021. The following are some sentences illustrating the normal form of Tune 1.

[12] No. A45 in the *Prace Wrocławskiego Towarzystwa Naukowego* (publications of the Wrocław Literary and Scientific Society), Wrocław, Poland, 1952.

[13] Published by Longmans, Green & Co., 1958.

[14] University of Michigan Press, 1949.

[15] R. Kingdon has adduced reasons for reversing these numbers.   I suggest that those who favour the Kingdon system should call the present Tunes 1 and 2 'Tune K2' and 'Tune K1.'

(1) Statements:

hi: wəz əbaut ði 'ounli in'telidʒənt 'mæn in ðə 'kʌntri.
He was about the only intelligent man in the country.

it s ðə moust iks'trɔːdnri 'θiŋ ai 'evə 'həːd ov.
It's the most extraordinary thing I ever heard of.

ðei wə 'veri ri'maːkəbl 'səːkəmstənsiz.
They were very remarkable circumstances.

ai v 'dʒʌst 'bɔːt ə 'njuː 'pɛər əv 'glʌvz.
I've just bought a new pair of gloves.

it s 'dʒʌst 'fɔːr ə'klɔk.
It's just four o'clock.

it 'ɔːl 'hæpnd 'jestədi.
It all happened yesterday.

ðɛə z 'nʌθiŋ tə bi 'dʌn əbaut it.
There's nothing to be done about it.

wiː 'did wɔt wiː wə 'tould.
We did what we were told.

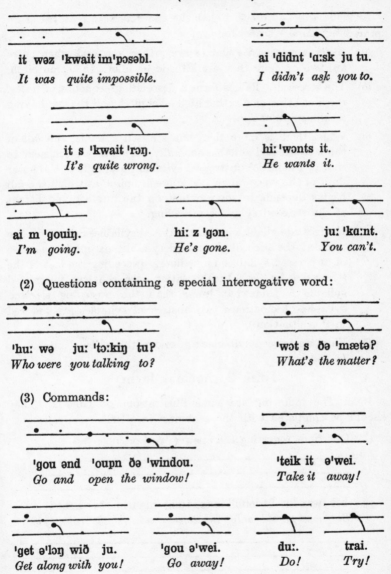

it wəz 'kwait im'posəbl.
It was quite impossible.

ai 'didnt 'ɑːsk ju tu.
I didn't ask you to.

it s 'kwait 'rɔŋ.
It's quite wrong.

hiː 'wɔnts it.
He wants it.

ai m 'gouiŋ.
I'm going.

hiː z 'gɔn.
He's gone.

juː 'kɑːnt.
You can't.

(2) Questions containing a special interrogative word:

'huː wə juː 'tɔːkiŋ tuʔ
Who were you talking to?

'wɔt s ðə 'mætəʔ
What's the matter?

(3) Commands:

'gou ənd 'oupn ðə 'windou.
Go and open the window!

'teik it ə'wei.
Take it away!

'get ə'lɔŋ wið ju.
Get along with you!

'gou ə'wei.
Go away!

duː.
Do!

trai.
Try!

Numerous other examples will be found in Armstrong-Ward, *Handbook*, pp. 11–17.

1022. It will be observed that the characteristic features of an unmodified Tune 1 are as follows:

(a) Initial unstressed syllables are rather low, and when there are two or more they are all said on about the same pitch.

(b) The stressed syllables form a descending sequence of notes, the first being on a rather high level pitch and the last having a falling intonation.

(c) When there is more than one stressed syllable, the fall of the last stressed syllable generally begins at a pitch near to that of the initial unstressed syllables, and falls to the lower limit of the voice-range. The precise pitch at which the fall begins depends to some extent on the number and height of the stressed syllables preceding.

(d) Unstressed syllables between stressed syllables have the same pitch as the preceding stressed syllable, except in the case of unstressed syllables immediately preceding the last of the stressed syllables. In the latter case the last unstressed syllable is somewhat lower than the preceding stressed syllable. (Sometimes two unstressed syllables are lowered in this situation.)

(e) Final unstressed syllables are said with low level pitch.

Tune 2 (normal form)

1023. The following are some illustrations of Tune 2. They should be compared with the sentences in § 1021.

(1) Questions requiring the answer 'yes' or 'no':

bət ˈwɔz hiː ði ˈounli inˈtelidʒənt ˈmæn in ðə ˈkʌntri?
But was he the only intelligent man in the country?

bət ˈiznt it ðə moust iksˈtrɔːdnri ˈθiŋ juː ˈevə ˈhəːd ɔv?
But isn't it the most extraordinary thing you ever heard of?

ˈdid it ˈɔːl ˈhæpn ˈjestədiꞋ
Did it all happen yesterday?

ˈiznt ðɛər ˈeniθiŋ tə bi ˈdʌn əbaut itꞋ
Isn't there anything to be done about it?

ˈdid juː ˈlaik itꞋ   or   did juː ˈlaik itꞋ
Did you like it?

ˈdjuː ˈlaik itꞋ   or   djuː ˈlaik itꞋ
Do you like it?

ˈiz hiː ˈgɔnꞋ   or   iz hiː ˈgɔnꞋ
Is he gone?

ˈduː juːꞋ   ˈhæʒ ʃiːꞋ   ˈkɑːnt wiːꞋ
Do you?   *Has she?*   *Can't we?*

hiː ˈwountꞋ   ouꞋ
He won't?   *Oh?*

(= Do you mean to say that he won't?)   (= Is that really so?)

(2) First parts of sentences:

ai d 'dʒʌst 'bɔːt ə 'njuː 'pɛər əv 'glʌvz, . . .
I'd   just   bought   a   new   pair of   gloves
(and was walking out of the shop).

it s 'dʒʌst 'fɔːr ə'klɔk, . . .
It's   just   four   o'clock
(so I think I'll be going).

əz it wəz 'kwait im'pɔsəbl tə 'finiʃ it, . . .
As   it   was   quite impossible   to finish it
(we didn't hurry ourselves).[14]

wiː 'did wɔt wiː wə 'tould, . . .
We did what we were told
(but it wasn't any use).

ai 'sent him ə'wei, . . .
I   sent   him   away
(but he came back again).

wiː 'gɔt him 'aut əv it. . . .
We got   him   out   of   it
(as soon as we could).

hiː 'went 'in, . . .
He went   in
(but found nobody there).

---

[14] This might also be pronounced

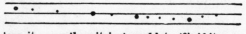

'æz it   wəz 'kwait im'pɔsəbl tə 'finiʃ it, . . .

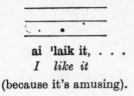

ai 'laik it, . . .
I   like it
(because it's amusing).

(3) Statements with an implication:

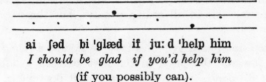

ai ʃəd bi 'glæd if juː d 'help him
I should be glad if you'd help him
(if you possibly can).

it 'iznt 'bæːd.
It isn't bad.

(But at the same time it's none too good.)

Further examples of Tune 2 will be found in Armstrong–Ward, *Handbook*, pp. 22–24.

1024. It will be observed that the characteristic features of Tune 2 are as follows:

(*a*) Initial unstressed syllables are rather low, as in the case of Tune 1.

(*b*) When there is more than one stressed syllable, the first has rather a high pitch and the last has a low pitch. The intervening syllables (both stressed and unstressed) are said on a descending sequence of notes.

(*c*) Unstressed syllables following the last stressed syllable are said on an ascending sequence of notes. When there are no such unstressed syllables, this rising intonation is put on to the last stressed syllable.

(*d*) The pitch of the last stressed syllable (or its initial pitch if it has a rise) is generally lower than that of the initial unstressed syllables. It may, however, be on the same level with them when it is the only stressed syllable in the sense-group.

Variations in the Treatment of Unstressed Syllables

1025. The form of Tune 1 described in §§ 1019–1022 appears to me the most convenient standard form to teach to foreign students, being distinctive and easy to learn. The following variations are, however, permissible in all ordinary cases, but the variations are never essential.

(a) Initial unstressed syllables may be said as a rising sequence, ascending towards the pitch of the first stressed syllable. Thus *It's a most extraordinary thing* it s ə moust iks'trɔːdnri 'θiŋ may be said with the intonation

instead of with the intonation

(b) Unstressed syllables between stressed syllables may be said on a falling sequence between the pitches of the preceding and following stressed syllables,[16] or they may be said on a rising sequence ascending from the pitch of the preceding stressed syllable. Thus it s ðə moust iks'trɔːdnri 'θiŋ ai 'evə 'həːd ɔv may be said with either of the two following intonations instead of with what I have called the 'normal' intonation shown in § 1021:

---

[16] Armstrong and Ward considered this treatment of medial unstressed syllables commoner than the level pitch given here as the normal form (*Handbook*, p. 5, and throughout the examples).

The second of these methods of treating medial unstressed syllables appears to introduce (in the words of Armstrong and Ward) 'an element of surprise, cheerfulness, enthusiasm or more interest.'[17]

1026. In Tune 2, initial unstressed syllables are likewise often said as a rising sequence. Thus *But did you ever see one?* bət did ju: 'evə 'si: wʌn? would often be said with the intonation

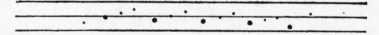

instead of with the intonation

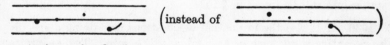

1027. In Tune 2 as in Tune 1 medial unstressed syllables may be said on a rising sequence ascending from the pitch of the preceding stressed syllable. Thus it is possible to pronounce bət 'wɔz hi: ði 'ounli in'telidʒənt 'mæn in ðə 'kʌntri? with the following intonation

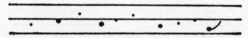

instead of with the normal intonation shown in § 1023. Other examples are:

'put ɔn   jɔ: 'kout.
Put on   your   coat!

wi: 'traid it 'ouvər ənd 'ouvər ə'gein.
We tried it   over and   over   again.

This variation of the tune appears to imply incredulity when applied to questions, encouragement when applied to commands, and cheerfulness or facetiousness or protest when applied to statements.

---

[17] *Handbook,* p. 5.

Long Sentences with Tune 1

1028. When a group requiring Tune 1 is rather long, the tune is often modified by raising the pitch of one of the stressed syllables, as shown in the following example:

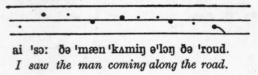

ai 'sɔː ðə 'mæn 'kʌmiŋ ə'lɔŋ ðə 'roud.
I saw the man coming along the road.

This sentence might also be pronounced with an unmodified Tune 1, thus

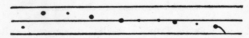

Further examples of this will be found in Armstrong–Ward, *Handbook,* p. 19.

Use of Tune 1 (normal form)

1029. Tune 1 is the intonation of a sense-group which is a plain statement of fact, when there is no unspoken implication and no contrast-emphasis on any particular word. Examples of such statements will be found in § 1021.

1030. It is also the intonation of questions containing a specific interrogative word, such as *how, when, which, why.* Two examples are given in § 1021 (2). The following are some further illustrations. For others see Armstrong–Ward, *Handbook,* pp. 14, 15.

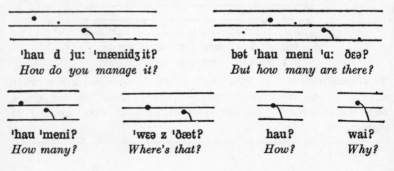

'hau d ju: 'mænidʒ it?
How do you manage it?

bət 'hau meni 'ɑː ðɛə?
But how many are there?

'hau 'meni?
How many?

'wɛə z 'ðæt?
Where's that?

hau?
How?

wai?
Why?

1031. Tune 1 is also the intonation of commands and invitations (as distinguished from requests, see §§ 1040–1041). The following are examples to supplement those in § 1021 (3). Others will be found in Armstrong–Ward, *Handbook*, pp. 16, 17.

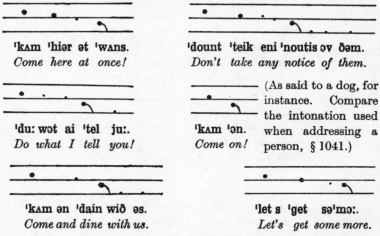

'kʌm 'hiər ət 'wʌns.
Come here at once!

'dount 'teik eni 'noutis ɔv ðəm.
Don't take any notice of them.

'duː wɔt ai 'tel juː.
Do what I tell you!

'kʌm 'ɔn.
Come on!

(As said to a dog, for instance. Compare the intonation used when addressing a person, § 1041.)

'kʌm ən 'dain wið əs.
Come and dine with us.

'let s 'get sə'mɔː.
Let's get some more.

1032. When a plain statement of fact is said in more than one sense-group, Tune 1 is the normal intonation of the last group. Preceding groups are usually said with Tune 2 (§ 1033), but sometimes with Tune 1 (§ 1044). Some examples of the use of Tune 1 in final sense-groups are given in §§ 1034, 1035.

Use of Tune 2 (normal form)

1033. Tune 2 is essentially the intonation of unfinished sentences and of non-final portions of sentences. When a sentence is divisible into two or more sense-groups, Tune 2 is the intonation generally used on the non-final groups.

1034. Examples of Tune 2 in non-final portions of a sentence are seen in the examples in § 1023 (2) and in the first parts of the following:

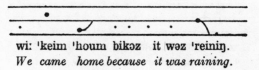

wiː 'keim 'houm bikɔz it wəz 'reiniŋ.
We came home because it was raining.

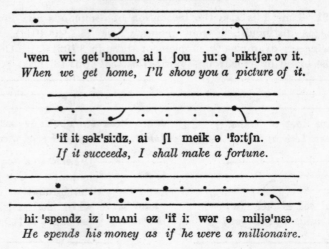

'wen wiː get 'houm, ai l ʃou juː ə 'piktʃər ɔv it.
When we get home, I'll show you a picture of it.

'if it sək'siːdz, ai ʃl meik ə 'fɔːtʃn.
If it succeeds, I shall make a fortune.

hiː 'spendz iz 'mʌni əz 'if iː wər ə miljə'nɛə.
He spends his money as if he were a millionaire.

'wen juː gɔt tə 'lʌndən, 'did juː gou 'streit təðə hou'tel?
When you got to London, did you go straight to the hotel?

1035. In the following examples two or more non-final groups are said with Tune 2:

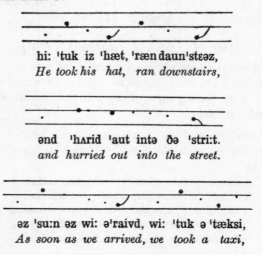

hiː 'tuk iz 'hæt, 'ræn daun'stɛəz,
He took his hat, ran downstairs,

ənd 'hʌrid 'aut intə ðə 'striːt.
and hurried out into the street.

əz 'suːn əz wiː ə'raivd, wiː 'tuk ə 'tæksi,
As soon as we arrived, we took a taxi,

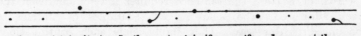

ənd went 'streit tə ðə 'haus tə 'si: if auə 'frend wəz ət 'houm.
and went straight to the house to see if our friend was at home.

Further examples will be found in Armstrong–Ward, *Handbook*, p. 34.

1036. Alternative questions are a particular case of this form of intonation. The last alternative is said with Tune 1, and the preceding alternatives are normally said with Tune 2. The following are examples:

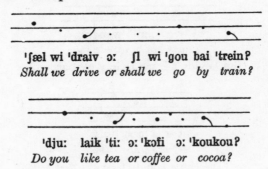

'ʃæl wi 'draiv ɔ: ʃl wi 'gou bai 'trein?
Shall we drive or shall we go by train?

'dju: laik 'ti: ɔ: 'kɔfi ɔ: 'koukou?
Do you like tea or coffee or cocoa?

1037. Another particular case of this normal intonation is seen in enumerations of things. Examples:

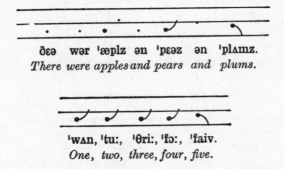

ðɛə wər 'æplz ən 'pɛəz ən 'plʌmz.
There were apples and pears and plums.

'wʌn, 'tu:, 'θri:, 'fɔ:, 'faiv.
One, two, three, four, five.

1038. Very often a sentence which is complete in form is said with Tune 2 because a continuation is implied though not expressed in words, or because the sentence requires a rejoinder from the person addressed. The following are examples of statements pronounced in this way. They imply some such continuations as those shown in brackets.

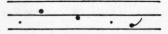

it 'wount 'teik mi: 'lɔŋ.
It won't take me long.
(So you may expect to see me back soon.)

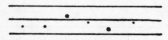

ai wəz 'ounli 'wʌndriŋ.
I was only wondering.
(But couldn't come to any conclusion.)

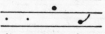

it wəz 'nou 'juːs.
It was no use.
(The thing couldn't be avoided.)

Other examples are enumerations in which the alternatives mentioned do not exhaust the possibilities, e.g.

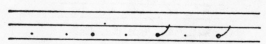

wiː mait gou tə 'lʌndən ɔː 'pæris ɔː bəˈlin.
We might go to London or Paris or Berlin.
(Or some other place.)

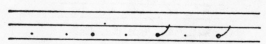

ðɛə wər 'æplz ən 'pɛəz ən 'plʌmz.
There were apples and pears and plums.
(And other kinds of fruit.)

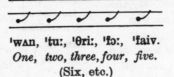

'wʌn, 'tuː, 'θriː, 'foː, 'faiv.
One, two, three, four, five.
(Six, etc.)

The intonations of the last two sentences should be compared with those given in § 1037, where there are no further alternatives.

1039. On the whole, *statements* other than enumerations are not often said with an unmodified Tune 2. They are, however, very often said with a *modified* Tune 2 (§ 1051), since they frequently contain a word requiring contrast-emphasis.

1040. The commonest kinds of sentence pronounced with an unmodified Tune 2 in final position are *ordinary requests* and *questions requiring the answer 'yes' or 'no.'* Requests have Tune 2 presumably because they imply that the person addressed is given the alternative of refusing to accede to them. Questions requiring the answer 'yes' or 'no' have this intonation because they imply the continuation 'or not.'[18]

1041. The following are some examples of requests. They should be compared with the commands in §§ 1021 (3), 1031.

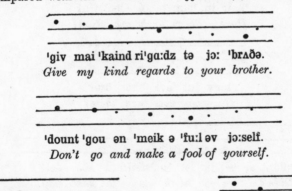

'giv mai 'kaind ri'gɑːdz tə joː 'brʌðə.
Give my kind regards to your brother.

'dount 'gou ən 'meik ə 'fuːl əv joːself.
Don't go and make a fool of yourself.

'dʒʌst 'ʃʌt ðə 'windou.
Just shut the window.

'duː 'kʌm ən 'siː əs.
Do come and see us.

---

[18] This fact was first pointed out by Coleman (*Intonation and Emphasis*, § 60).

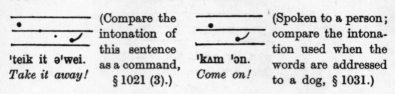

'teik it ə'wei.   (Compare the intonation of this sentence as a command, § 1021 (3).)
Take it away!

'kʌm 'ɔn.   (Spoken to a person; compare the intonation used when the words are addressed to a dog, § 1031.)
Come on!

Further examples of requests will be found in Armstrong–Ward, *Handbook*, p. 24.

1042. The following are some examples of questions requiring the answer 'yes' or 'no,' to supplement those given in § 1023. Further examples will be found in Armstrong–Ward, *Handbook*, pp. 23, 24.

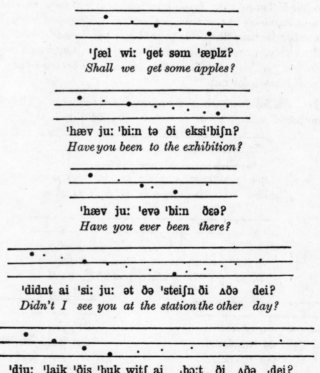

'ʃæl wiː 'get səm 'æplz?
Shall we get some apples?

'hæv juː 'biːn tə ði eksi'biʃn?
Have you been to the exhibition?

'hæv juː 'evə 'biːn ðɛə?
Have you ever been there?

'didnt ai 'siː juː ət ðə 'steiʃn ði ʌðə dei?
Didn't I see you at the station the other day?

'djuː 'laik 'ðis 'buk witʃ ai ˌbɔːt ði ʌðə ˌdei?
Do you like this book which I bought the other day?

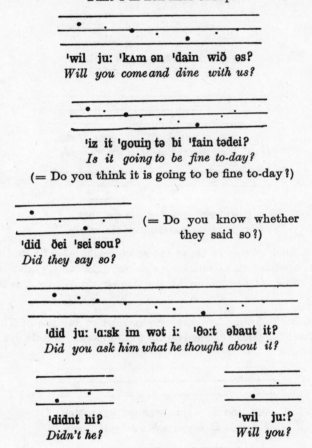

'wil ju: 'kʌm ən 'dain wið əs?
Will you come and dine with us?

'iz it 'gouiŋ tə bi 'fain tədei?
Is it going to be fine to-day?
(= Do you think it is going to be fine to-day?)

'did ðei 'sei sou?
Did they say so?

(= Do you know whether they said so?)

'did ju: 'ɑːsk im wɔt iː 'θɔːt əbaut it?
Did you ask him what he thought about it?

'didnt hi?
Didn't he?

'wil ju:?
Will you?

Tune 1 in non-final Groups

1043. Tune 1 is sometimes used in non-final groups. The commonest case is when the following group expresses a *reservation* as in the following examples:

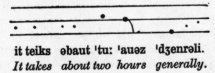

it teiks əbaut 'tuː 'auəz 'dʒenrəli.
It takes about two hours generally.

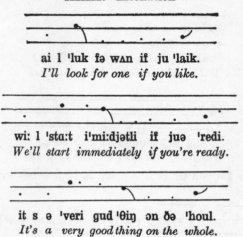

ai l ˈluk fə wʌn if ju ˈlaik.
I'll look for one if you like.

wiː l ˈstɑːt iˈmiːdjətli if juə ˈredi.
We'll start immediately if you're ready.

it s ə ˈveri gud ˈθiŋ ɔn ðə ˈhoul.
It's a very good thing on the whole.

(The non-final groups in these examples might also be said with Tune 1 modified for contrast-emphasis; like the examples in § 1049.) For further examples see Armstrong–Ward, *Handbook*, p. 35.

1044. The following are further examples of the use of Tune 1 in non-final sequences. The reasons for its use are not always easy to establish.

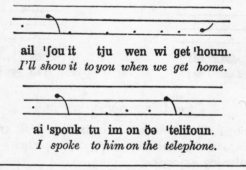

ail ˈʃou it   tju wen wi get ˈhoum.
I'll show it to you when we get home.

ai ˈspouk tu im ɔn ðə ˈtelifoun.
I spoke to him on the telephone.

ˈwen juː ˈgɔt tə ˈlʌndən, ˈdid juː gou ˈstreit tə ðə houˈtel?
When you got to London, did you go straight to the hotel?
(Compare the alternative intonation in § 1034.)

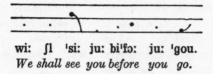

wiː ʃl ˈsiː juː biˈfɔː juː ˈgou.
We shall see you before you go.

Many other examples will be found in the texts in the Armstrong–
Ward, *Handbook*.

Emphasis

1045. When it is desired to give emphasis to a particular word
in a sentence, that word has to be said with greater prominence
than usual. As has already been pointed out in §§ 208–210, 911,
912, special prominence may be given (1) by increasing the length
of one or more sounds, (2) by increasing the stress of one or more
syllables, (3) by using special kinds of intonation, or by combinations of these means. It is also to be noted that when a word
can be pronounced in more than one way, a fuller or strong form
is used in emphasis. Such full or strong forms do not of themselves give prominence[19]; the prominence is effected by means of
the sound-attributes (prosodies) length, stress and intonation.
Of the above-mentioned methods of effecting prominence intonation
is the most important; it is generally, though not necessarily,
combined with extra strong stress on the emphatic word.

1046. There are two kinds of emphasis, which may be termed

---

[19] Except when a sound of a strong form happens to have greater intrinsic
sonority than the corresponding sound of the weak form. In this connexion
it may be repeated here that some sounds are naturally more prominent than
others when said with the same degree of stress or 'push from the chest wall';
in other terms, the inherent sonority of some sounds is greater than that of
others (see §§ 100, 101). Thus if æ and i are pronounced with equal stress,
æ is found to be the more prominent; it will be heard at a greater distance.
It is instructive to try the experiment, suggested by Prof. Lloyd James, of
pronouncing the word *mechanically* (normally miˈkænikəli) on a monotone
or in a whisper, and endeavouring to give artificial prominence to the first
and third syllables by means of stress, while keeping the qualities and normal
lengths of the vowels unchanged. It will be found that though the speaker
may so pronounce the sequence as to experience a subjective impression of
prominence of the first and third syllables, it is very difficult to convey this
as an objective impression to a hearer; the inherent sonority of æ renders
the second syllable the most prominent (objectively) in spite of very strong
stresses that may be put on the adjoining syllables.

emphasis for contrast and *emphasis for intensity*.[20] The first is emphasis intended to show that a word is contrasted with another word (either implied or previously expressed), or that a word introduces a new and unexpected idea. The second is an extra emphasis to express a particularly high degree of the quality which a word expresses; it is equivalent to the insertion of such words as *very, extremely, a great deal of*. Contrast-emphasis may be applied to almost any word, but intensity-emphasis can only be applied to certain words expressing qualities which are measurable, e.g. adjectives such as *huge, enormous, lovely, tremendous, wonderful, marvellous, appalling, awful, tiny, absurd, killing, brilliant, deafening*,[21] adverbs such as *particularly, extremely, hopelessly*, plural nouns such as *quantities, masses, heaps, tons, hundreds*, and a certain number of verbs such as *rush, squeeze, hate*.

1047. Contrast-emphasis is expressed mainly by intonation. The special intonation may be accompanied by extra stress or length, but these are secondary.

1048. It often happens that a word has both kinds of emphasis simultaneously, see § 1061.

Emphasis for Contrast

1049. The following are typical examples of the effect of contrast-emphasis in a sentence which ends with low pitch. The intonation may be regarded as a modification of Tune 1.

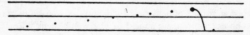

ai θɔːt hiː wəz gouiŋ tə ˈlʌndən.
*I thought he was going to **London**.*

(The other speaker having just said that his friend was going to Edinburgh.)

---

[20] This was first pointed out by Coleman (*Intonation and Emphasis*, §§ 6–15).

[21] Intensity-emphasis cannot be given to *all* adjectives expressing measurable qualities. The majority of adjectives can only have their meaning intensified by prefixing adverbs like *very, extremely, rather*. Such are *good, hot, long, thick, frequent, spacious, troublesome, difficult*. Some are capable of having their meaning intensified by either method; such are *wonderful, absurd*. Students have to learn which adjectives can be said with intensity-emphasis and which have to be intensified by prefixing a qualifying word.

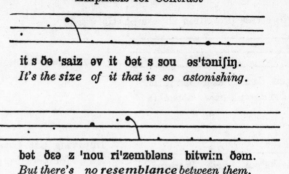

it s ðə 'saiz əv it ðət s sou əs'tɔniʃiŋ.
It's the size of it that is so astonishing.

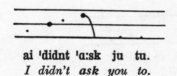

bət ðɛə z 'nou ri'zembləns bitwiːn ðəm.
But there's no resemblance between them.

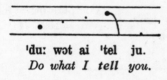

ai 'didnt 'ɑːsk ju tu.
I didn't ask you to.

(Compare other intonations of this sentence shown in §§ 1021 (1), 1051 (1), 1051 (2).)

'duː wɔt ai 'tel ju.
Do what I tell you.

Further examples will be found in Armstrong–Ward, *Handbook*, pp. 52, 53.

1050. It will be seen that in sentences of this kind the only syllable with a really strong stress is the stressed syllable of the emphatic word. Other syllables may have a medium or fairly strong stress, but they have the intonation of unstressed syllables. The intonation is therefore a particular case of that shown in § 1025 (a).

1051. The following are typical examples of the effect of contrast-emphasis in a group with rising intonation. The intonation may be regarded as a modification of Tune 2.

(1) No stress preceding the emphatic word:

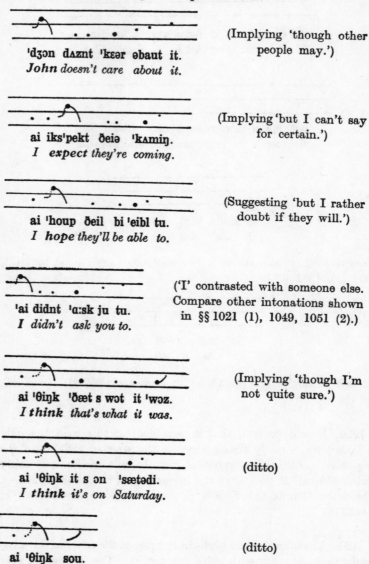

'dʒɔn dʌznt 'kɛər əbaut it.
John doesn't care about it.

(Implying 'though other people may.')

ai iks'pekt ðeiə 'kʌmiŋ.
I expect they're coming.

(Implying 'but I can't say for certain.')

ai 'houp ðeil bi 'eibl tu.
I hope they'll be able to.

(Suggesting 'but I rather doubt if they will.')

'ai didnt 'ɑːsk ju tu.
I didn't ask you to.

('I' contrasted with someone else. Compare other intonations shown in §§ 1021 (1), 1049, 1051 (2).)

ai 'θiŋk 'ðæt s wɔt it 'wɔz.
I think that's what it was.

(Implying 'though I'm not quite sure.')

ai 'θiŋk it s ɔn 'sætədi.
I think it's on Saturday.

(ditto)

ai 'θiŋk sou.
I think so.

(ditto)

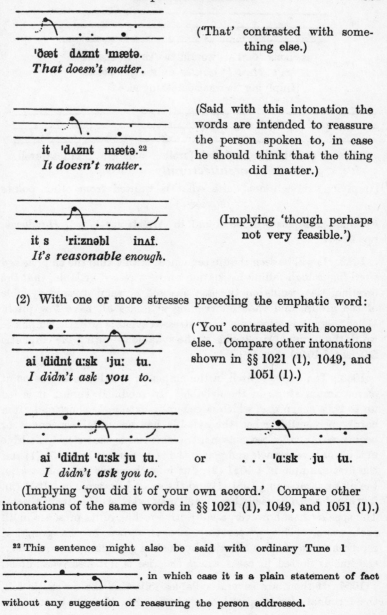

'ðæt dʌznt 'mætə.
That doesn't matter.

('That' contrasted with something else.)

it 'dʌznt mætə.[22]
It doesn't matter.

(Said with this intonation the words are intended to reassure the person spoken to, in case he should think that the thing did matter.)

it s 'riːznəbl inʌf.
It's reasonable enough.

(Implying 'though perhaps not very feasible.')

(2) With one or more stresses preceding the emphatic word:

ai 'didnt aːsk 'juː tu.
I didn't ask you to.

('You' contrasted with someone else. Compare other intonations shown in §§ 1021 (1), 1049, and 1051 (1).)

ai 'didnt 'aːsk ju tu.   or   . . . 'aːsk ju tu.
I didn't ask you to.

(Implying 'you did it of your own accord.' Compare other intonations of the same words in §§ 1021 (1), 1049, and 1051 (1).)

---

[22] This sentence might also be said with ordinary Tune 1

, in which case it is a plain statement of fact without any suggestion of reassuring the person addressed.

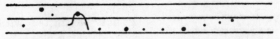

it 'iznt 'ðæt ai 'wɔntid tə 'siː ju əbaut.
It isn't that I wanted to see you about.
(Implying 'it was something else.')

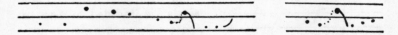

it s ə 'gud 'bildiŋ ɑːki'tektʃərəli.   or ... ɑːki'tektʃərəli.
It's a goodbuilding architecturally.

(Implying 'though not quite what is wanted from other points of view.')

Further examples will be found in Armstrong–Ward, *Handbook*, pp. 58–67.

1052. It will be seen that in sequences of this kind the emphasized word has a high falling intonation on its stressed syllable, that the terminal rise begins on the last stressed or semi-stressed syllable of the group, and that intervening syllables all have low pitch. When there is no stressed or semi-stressed syllable after the emphatic word, the terminal rise begins at the syllable following the emphatic fall (see § 1054).

1053. The highest pitch in the emphatic syllable is at the point of maximum stress in the syllable. In modified Tune 2 it is led up to by a sharp rise, which is generally extremely short and often hardly perceptible when the syllable has no initial consonant or begins with a voiceless consonant. This rise is thus clearly audible in the words *reasonable* and *you* in the last example in § 1051 (1) and the first example in § 1051 (2); but in such words as *think, ask,* in the fifth example in § 1051 (1) and the second example in § 1051 (2), it is too short to be easily heard, and may even be objectively absent. The speaker has, however, a subjective feeling of its presence in all such cases. (This preparatory rise is shown in the graphical representation of the intonation by the line preceding the stress-dot; the line is dotted in cases where the rise is not clearly audible.)

1054. If there are several syllables following the emphatic fall, the terminal rise is spread over them. But if there is only one

unstressed syllable following, the terminal rise is compressed into
it. If there is no following unstressed syllable, the terminal rise
is compressed into the same syllable as the emphatic fall; the
emphatic syllable is therefore said in this case with a fall-rise.
The following are some examples to illustrate these points:

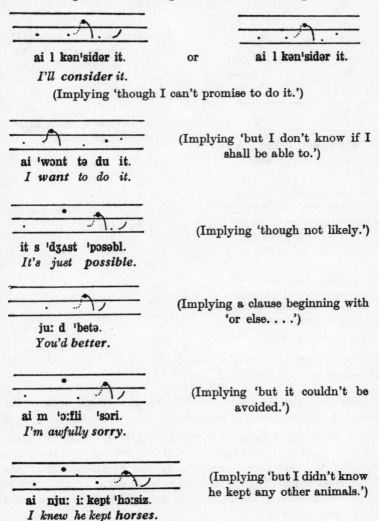

ai l kən'sidər it.   or   ai l kən'sidər it.
I'll consider it.

(Implying 'though I can't promise to do it.')

ai 'wɔnt tə du it.
I want to do it.

(Implying 'but I don't know if I
shall be able to.')

it s 'dʒʌst 'pɔsəbl.
It's just possible.

(Implying 'though not likely.')

juː d 'betə.
You'd better.

(Implying a clause beginning with
'or else. . . .')

ai m 'ɔːfli 'sɔri.
I'm awfully sorry.

(Implying 'but it couldn't be
avoided.')

ai njuː iː kept 'hɔːsiz.
I knew he kept horses.

(Implying 'but I didn't know
he kept any other animals.')

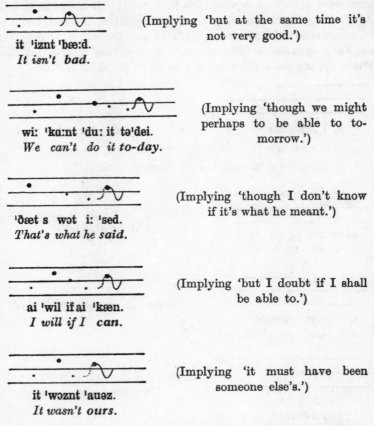

it 'iznt 'bæːd.
It isn't bad.

(Implying 'but at the same time it's not very good.')

wiː 'kɑːnt 'duː it tə'dei.
We can't do it to-day.

(Implying 'though we might perhaps to be able to to-morrow.')

'ðæt s wɔt iː 'sed.
That's what he said.

(Implying 'though I don't know if it's what he meant.')

ai 'wil if ai 'kæn.
I will if I can.

(Implying 'but I doubt if I shall be able to.')

it 'wɔznt 'auəz.
It wasn't ours.

(Implying 'it must have been someone else's.')

Numerous further examples will be found in Armstrong-Ward, *Handbook*, pp. 66–69, 72, 73.

1055. In connexion with the fall–rise on a single syllable the following details should be observed:

(1) When the syllable ends in **m**, **n**, **ŋ** or **l**, the lowest pitch is reached at the beginning of this consonant, and the whole of the rise takes place during the pronunciation of the consonant. Thus in the example *I will if I can* given in the preceding paragraph, the whole of the rise takes place during the **n**.

(2) When the syllable contains a short vowel followed by **b, d** or **g**, the whole of the rise generally takes place during the 'stop' of this consonant. Thus in the example *That's what he said* given in the preceding paragraph, the whole of the rise generally takes place during the 'stop' of the **d**. (In the speech of those who completely devoice final **b, d, g,** the rise takes place on the latter part of the vowel.)

(3) In other cases the rise begins about the middle of the vowel. Examples are seen in the words *bad* and *to-day* in the seventh and eighth examples in § 1054.

(4) When the syllable contains a short vowel followed by a voiceless consonant, the intonation has to be compressed into a particularly short space. The final rising part is then so short as to be difficult to hear. The speaker has, however, a subjective feeling of its presence. This would be the case, for instance, in

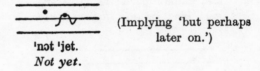

'nɔt 'jet.
Not yet.

(Implying 'but perhaps later on.')

1056. The intonation described in §§ 1051–1055 is sometimes used in situations where there does not appear to be any obvious contrast, and where it is therefore difficult to specify the reason for the use of the intonation. Notable cases are *expressions of regret* and *entreaties* or *urgent requests*.

Examples of expressions of regret:

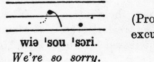

wiə 'sou 'sɔri.
We're so sorry.

(Pronounced in this way even if no excuse is implied; compare *I'm awfully sorry* in § 1054.)

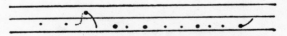

wiː wə 'sou 'sɔri 'nɔt tə bi 'eibl tə 'kʌm.
We were so sorry not to be able to come.

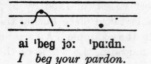

ai 'beg jɔ: 'pɑːdn.
I beg your pardon.

(Meaning 'I'm sorry'; compare the other intonation given in § 1063.)

Examples of entreaties or urgent requests (to be compared with the ordinary requests in § 1041):

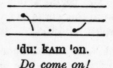

'duː kʌm 'ɔn.
Do come on!

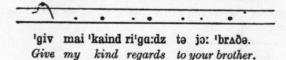

'giv mai 'kaind ri'gɑːdz tə jɔ: 'brʌðə.
Give my kind regards to your brother.

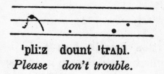

'pliːz dount 'trʌbl.
Please don't trouble.

1057. When a word has to be emphasized for contrast in a question requiring the answer 'yes' or 'no,' the intonation is an ordinary Tune 2 with the emphatic syllable at the point of lowest pitch. All following syllables are generally unstressed, but if any of them have a certain degree of stress, their intonation is as if they were unstressed. The effect of contrast is often made more marked by pronouncing preceding unstressed syllables with high pitch. Examples:

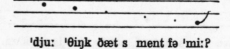

'djuː 'θiŋk ðæt s ment fə 'miː?
Do you think that's meant for me?

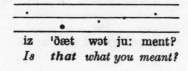

iz 'ðæt wot ju: ment?
Is that what you meant?

hæv 'ju: evə bi:n ðɛə?
Have you ever been there?

(Compare the third example in § 1042.)

did 'ju: laik it?
Did you like it?

(Compare the intonations given in § 1023 (1).)

1058. Tune 1 (with or without an emphatic word) is sometimes applied to questions requiring the answer 'yes' or 'no.' When said in this way the questions embody the idea of some statement or invitation. Examples:

(1) Without contrast-emphasis:

'hæv ju: 'bi:n tə ði eksi'biʃn?
Have you been to the exhibition?

(Suggesting 'I don't expect you have,' or 'You really ought to go.')

'ʃæl wi 'get səm 'æplz?
Shall we get some apples?

(Suggesting 'it would be a good idea to get some apples.' Compare the intonation of the same words in § 1042.)

'wil ju: kʌm ən 'dain wið əs?
Will you come and dine with us?

(= 'I invite you to come and dine with us.' Compare the intonation of the same words in § 1042.)

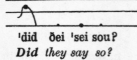

'iz it gouiŋ tə bi 'fain tədei?
Is it going to be fine to-day?

(= 'I wonder if it will be fine to-day.' Compare the intonation
of the same words in § 1042.)

(2) With contrast-emphasis:

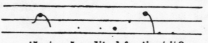

'did ðei 'sei sou?
Did they say so?

(= 'It is open to question whether they
said so.' Compare the other intonation
of the same words in § 1042.)

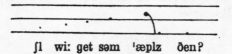

'ðæt s ðə di'rekʃn, 'iznt it?
That's the direction, isn't it?

('Isn't it' being an invitation to assent, and not expressing a desire
for information.[23])

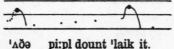

ʃl wi: get səm 'æplz ðen?
Shall we get some apples then?

(= 'In that case I suggest that we get some apples.' Compare
the intonation of the first example in § 1042.)

1059. It happens not unfrequently that two words in the same
sentence have contrast-emphasis. The following are examples:

(1) Single groups:

'ʌðə   pi:pl dount 'laik it.
Other people don't like it.

---

[23] Said as an enquiry, the intonation would be

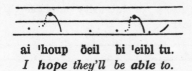

ai 'houp ðeil bi 'eibl tu.
I hope they'll be able to.

ju: 'dount si:mtə 'kɛər əbaut 'ʌðə θinz.
You don't seem to care about other things.

(2) Sentences consisting of two groups:

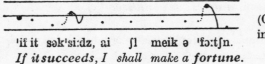

(Compare alternative
intonation in § 1034.)

'if it sək'si:dz, ai ʃl meik ə 'fɔ:tʃn.
If it succeeds, I shall make a fortune.

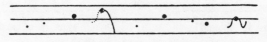

if ðə 'ski:m 'feilz, it 'wount ə'fekt 'ju:
If the scheme fails, it won't affect you.

Further instances will be found in Armstrong–Ward, *Handbook*,
pp. 54–56.

Emphasis for Intensity

1060. Intonation is often employed (in addition to length and
stress) to intensify the meaning of words expressing measurable
qualities as explained in § 1046. The modification of intonation
for this purpose generally takes the form of increasing the pitch
intervals. The pitch of the emphatic syllable is generally led up
to by a rise. For instance, *it's enormous* may be said thus:

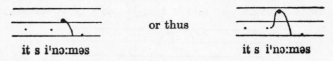

or thus

it s i'nɔːməs   it s i'nɔːməs

the second intonation giving an idea of greater size.

Further illustrations of intensity-emphasis are shown in the following examples:

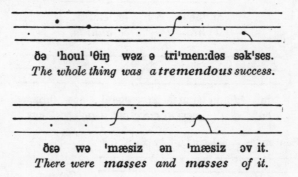

ðə 'houl 'θiŋ wəz ə tri'menːdəs sək'ses.
The whole thing was a tremendous success.

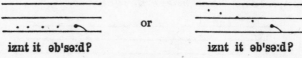

ðɛə wə 'mæsiz ən 'mæsiz ɔv it.
There were masses and masses of it.

In the following example the emphasized word has a low pitch:

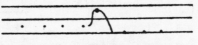   or

iznt it əb'səːd?   iznt it əb'səːd?
Isn't it absurd?

This might also be said with the intonation

In all cases there is very strong stress on the emphatic syllable. There is generally also a lengthening of it. In *enormous* the length is given mainly by an extra long ɔː, in *tremendous* by lengthening the **m** and **n**, in *masses* by lengthening the **m** and **s**, and so on.

1061. Intensified words often have contrast-emphasis as well as intensity-emphasis. In this case the emphatic syllable has to be said with extra length, extra stress and special intonation.

Thus *it was a tremendous success* might be pronounced as follows in reply to someone who said 'I hear it was a great success':

it wəz ə tri'menːdəs sək₁ses.

Similarly in

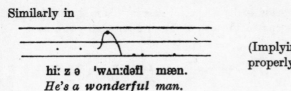

hi: z ə   'wʌn:dəfl mæn.
He's a wonderful man.

(Implying 'though not
properly appreciated.')

Special Intonations

1062. Coleman[24] and others have pointed out that the reasons
for the use of particular intonations are sometimes obscure. The
following are some examples of intonations which are difficult to
explain.

1063. A gradual rise of intonation is used when the speaker
desires the person addressed to repeat what he said before.
Examples:

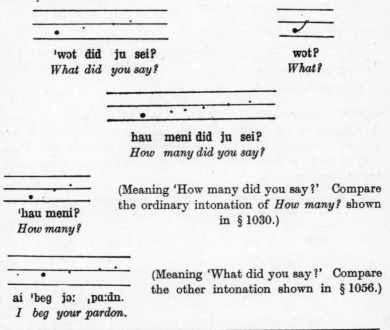

'wɔt did   ju sei?
What did   you say?

wɔt?
What?

hau   meni did ju sei?
How   many did you say?

'hau meni?
How many?

(Meaning 'How many did you say?' Compare
the ordinary intonation of *How many?* shown
in § 1030.)

ai 'beg jɔ: ˌpɑːdn.
I   beg   your pardon.

(Meaning 'What did you say?' Compare
the other intonation shown in § 1056.)

---

[24] *Intonation and Emphasis,* §§ 68–75.

This intonation seems to be a special case of Tune 2, and its use here seems analogous to the use of Tune 2 in such cases as:

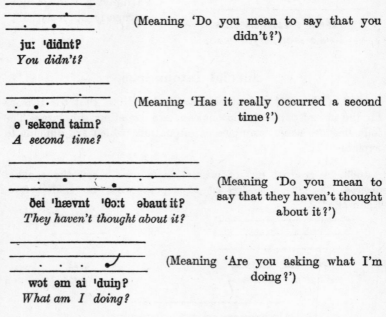

 juː ˈdidnt?
You didn't?

(Meaning 'Do you mean to say that you didn't?')

ə ˈsekənd taim?
A second time?

(Meaning 'Has it really occurred a second time?')

ðei ˈhævnt ˈθɔːt əbaut it?
They haven't thought about it?

(Meaning 'Do you mean to say that they haven't thought about it?')

wɔt əm ai ˈduiŋ?
What am I doing?

(Meaning 'Are you asking what I'm doing?')

1064. The expressions *I do, it's not, he can, they have*, etc., used in replying to a question requiring the answer 'yes' or 'no' are said with Tune 1. But the same expressions are said with Tune 2 when they are used to contradict what the previous speaker has said. Compare:

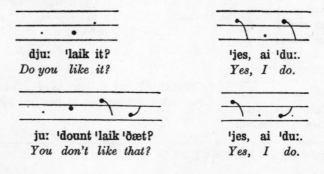

djuː ˈlaik it?
Do you like it?

ˈjes, ai ˈduː.
Yes, I do.

juː ˈdount ˈlaik ˈðæt?
You don't like that?

ˈjes, ai ˈduː.
Yes, I do.

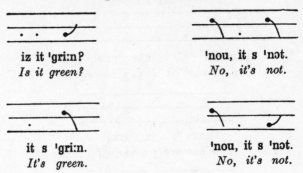

iz it 'gri:nP
Is it green?

'nou, it s 'nɔt.
No, it's not.

it s 'gri:n.
It's green.

'nou, it s 'nɔt.
No, it's not.

1065. In asking a question containing a specific interrogative word, the effect of great curiosity on the part of the speaker is conveyed by saying the interrogative word or the first stressed syllable after it on a very low tone, as shown in the following examples. Preceding unstressed syllables are high-pitched.

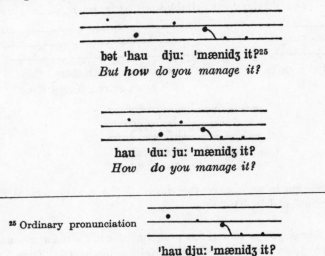

bət 'hau dju: 'mænidʒ itP[25]
*But **how** do you manage it?*

hau 'du: ju: 'mænidʒ itP
How   do you manage it?

[25] Ordinary pronunciation

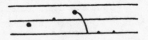

'hau dju: 'mænidʒ itP

The sentence may also be said with contrast-emphasis on *manage,* thus

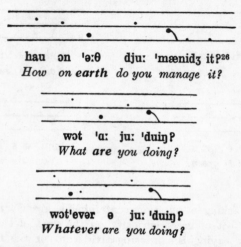

hau ɔn 'əːθ   djuː 'mænidʒ itꟷ[26]
How on earth do you manage it?

wɔt 'ɑː juː 'duiŋꟷ
What are you doing?

wɔt'evər ə juː 'duiŋꟷ
Whatever are you doing?

1066. In exclamations of astonishment a high degree of surprise is expressed by pronouncing the non-final unstressed syllables with high pitch and the stressed syllables with low pitch, as in

hau 'hai it 'luks.
How high it looks!

wɔt n iks'trɔːdnri 'θiŋ.
What an extraordinary thing!

wɔt ə 'veri 'fʌni 'θiŋ.
What a very funny thing!

This intonation is an exaggerated form of the second variant of Tune 1 mentioned in § 1025 (*b*).

1067. *Thank you* is sometimes pronounced with a rising intonation (Tune 2) and sometimes with a falling intonation (Tune 1).

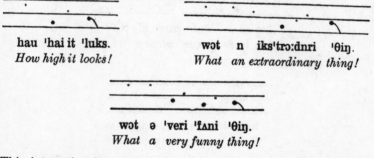

[26] Said with a less degree of curiosity, this sentence would be pronounced with ordinary Tune 1, thus

When a person performs a customary service, the acknowledgement seems to be said more usually with the rising intonation, thus:

'θæŋk ju.

But in acknowledging an unexpected favour the falling intonation seems more usual, thus:

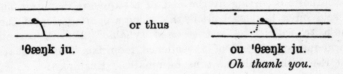

'θæŋk ju.   or thus   ou 'θæŋk ju.
                                           Oh thank you.

1068. *Thank you* with rising intonation is often reduced to ˌŋkju or kju,[27] thus:

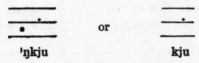

'ŋkju   or   kju

Thank you with a falling intonation is not generally reduced in this way.

1069. *All right* is generally said with Tune 2, thus:

'ɔːl 'rait.

The use of Tune 1 _____ or (with emphasis) _____

may have the effect of a threat.

1070. The usual intonation of *Good morning* as said on parting is

gud 'mɔːniŋ.

---

[27] Also 'k̩kju, see footnote to § 909.

It is not quite clear why this intonation is used, but it appears to imply non-finality or some such continuation as 'I shall hope to see you again soon.'[28] (Cp. § 1072, last example.)

Parentheses

1071. Expressions of a parenthetical nature have no particular intonation of their own. They share the intonation that the main sentence would have if the parenthesis were not there. Thus a parenthesis occurring at the end of a sequence requiring Tune 1 is said on a low level pitch, this being a continuation of the low pitch to which the last stressed syllable falls. A parenthesis occurring at the end of a sequence requiring Tune 2 shares in the rise with which the tune terminates. Examples:

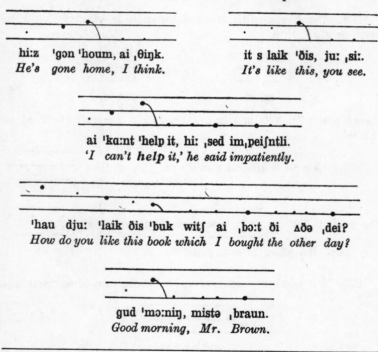

hi:z 'gɔn 'houm, ai ˌθiŋk.
He's   gone home, I think.

it s laik 'ðis, ju: ˌsi:.
It's like this, you see.

ai 'kɑ:nt 'help it, hi: ˌsed imˌpeiʃntli.
'I can't help it,' he said impatiently.

'hau dju: 'laik ðis 'buk witʃ ai ˌbɔ:t ði ʌðə ˌdei?
How do you like this book which I bought the other day?

gud 'mɔ:niŋ, mistə ˌbraun.
Good morning, Mr. Brown.

---

[28] Some English people now use this intonation on meeting. The reason for this is obscure.

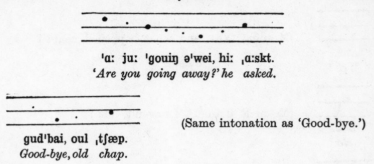

'ɑː juː 'gouiŋ ə'wei, hiː ˌɑːskt.
'*Are you going away?' he asked.*

(Same intonation as 'Good-bye.')

gud'bai, oul ˌtʃæp.
Good-bye, old chap.

For further information about the intonation of parentheses see
Armstrong–Ward, *Handbook*, pp. 27–30.

Interjections

1072. Interjections and exclamatory phrases take as a rule the
intonation of the complete sentences to which they are equivalent.

Examples:

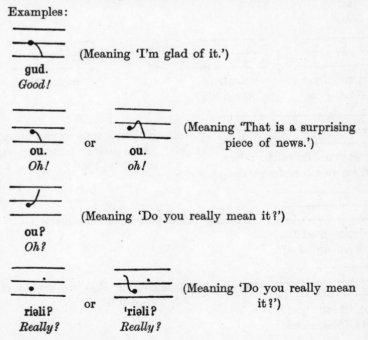

(Meaning 'I'm glad of it.')

gud.
Good!

or (Meaning 'That is a surprising
piece of news.')

ou.   ou.
Oh!   *oh!*

(Meaning 'Do you really mean it?')

ouP
Oh?

or (Meaning 'Do you really mean
it?')

riəliP   'riəliP
Really?   *Really?*

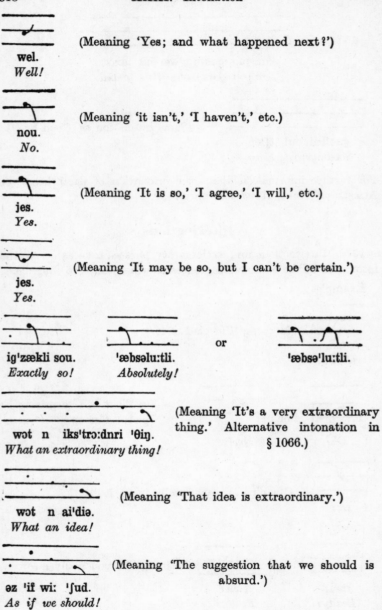

wel.
Well!

(Meaning 'Yes; and what happened next?')

nou.
No.

(Meaning 'it isn't,' 'I haven't,' etc.)

jes.
Yes.

(Meaning 'It is so,' 'I agree,' 'I will,' etc.)

jes.
Yes.

(Meaning 'It may be so, but I can't be certain.')

ig'zækli sou.   'æbsəlu:tli.   or   'æbsə'lu:tli.
Exactly so!   *Absolutely!*

wɔt n iks'trɔːdnri 'θiŋ.
What an extraordinary thing!

(Meaning 'It's a very extraordinary thing.' Alternative intonation in § 1066.)

wɔt n ai'diə.
What an idea!

(Meaning 'That idea is extraordinary.')

əz 'if wiː 'ʃud.
As if we should!

(Meaning 'The suggestion that we should is absurd.')

'wɔt 'nekst.
What next!

(Meaning 'I wonder what impudent thing he'll be doing next.')

gud 'mɔːniŋ.
Good morning.

(Said on meeting.[29] Meaning 'I greet you.' Cp. § 1070.)

Incorrect Forms of Intonation heard from Foreign Learners

1073. The mistakes of intonation made by foreign people when they speak English are very varied. The following are a few examples.

1074. French people often employ an intonation of the type

or

when an intonation of the

type

should be used. The following are examples:

Correct pronunciation

Incorrect intonation often heard from French people

'æbsəluːtli.
Absolutely.

ai v gɔt 'tuː 'tenisbɔːlz.
I've got two tennis balls.

or

Correct pronunciation

Incorrect intonation often heard from Frech people

ai ˈlaik it.
I like it.

ˈwɔt ə juː ˈlukiŋ æt?
What are you looking at?

ai v ˈnevə ˈbiːn ðɛə.
I've never been there.

1075. French people are likewise liable to use an intonation of the type ⟶ in cases where one of the type ⟶ is required. The following are examples:

Correct pronunciation

Incorrect intonation often heard from French people

ˈdount juː ˈθiŋk sou?
Don't you think so?

ˈʃæl wi gou ən ˈluk æt it?
Shall we go and look at it?

Correct pronunciation

Incorrect intonation often heard from French people

'wʌn 'moumənt.
One   moment!

1076. The above incorrect forms of intonation used by French people give the effect of emphasis to the final unstressed syllables.

1077. Germans are liable to make mistakes of an opposite nature, that is to say they have a tendency to use intonations

of the types ———— and ———— where the

intonations ———— and ———— are required. These mistakes are commonly attributed to incorrect stress; it will be found, however, that as long as the intonation is right, the degree of stress is not of much consequence.

Example of the first case:
Correct pronunciation

wiə 'gouiŋ fər ə 'wɔːk in 'ritʃmənd 'paːk.
We're going for a walk in Richmond Park.

Incorrect intonation commonly heard from Germans

Example of the second case:
Correct pronunciation

'ʃæl wi 'gou tə 'ritʃmənd 'paːk?
Shall we go to Richmond Park?

Incorrect intonation commonly heard from Germans

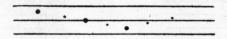

1078. Very often in sequences requiring Tune 2 Germans say the last stressed syllable with high pitch and all following unstressed syllables on the same high pitch. Thus in such an example as:

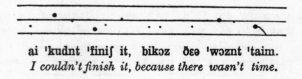

ai 'kʊdnt 'finiʃ it, bikɔz ðɛə 'wɔznt 'taim.
I couldn't finish it, because there wasn't time.

they will pronounce

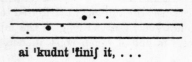

ai 'kʊdnt 'finiʃ it, . . .

1079. Opportunities for these characteristic German mistakes occur very frequently in long descriptive passages. The following taken at random from my *Phonetic Readings in English*[30] will serve to illustrate what happens: *and the sergeant major was heard to say that it kept better time than the station gun.* The intonation should be

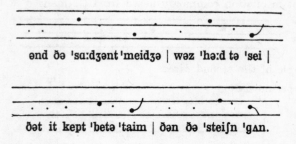

ənd ðə 'saːdʒənt 'meidʒə | wəz 'həːd tə 'sei |

ðət it kept 'betə 'taim | ðən ðə 'steiʃn 'gʌn.

---

[30] Page 7. Published by Carl Winter, Heidelberg (new edition 1956).

Germans are liable to mispronounce the sentence by using the following incorrect intonations:

(1) either

or

ənd ðə ˈsɑːdʒənt meidʒə   ənd ðə ˈsɑːdʒənt meidʒə

(2) either

or

wəz ˈheːd tə ˈsei   wəz ˈheːd tə sei

(3) either

or

ˈbetə taim   ˈbetə taim

(4)

ˈsteiʃn gʌn.

1080. Many Germans also have considerable difficulty in pronouncing stressed syllables on a high level tone as is required in Tune 1. They are apt to say all such syllables with a low rising pitch. Thus in pronouncing *he was about the only intelligent man in the country* they will use an intonation of the following type instead of that shown in § 1021:

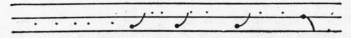

ˈhiː wəz əbaut ði ˈounli inˈtelidʒənt ˈmæn in ðə ˈkʌntri.

1081. Norwegians find Tune 1 difficult. They substitute very high pitch for the low pitch of the final unstressed syllables. Thus they will say

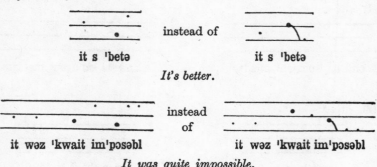

it s 'betə   instead of   it s 'betə

It's better.

it wəz 'kwait im'pɔsəbl   instead of   it wəz 'kwait im'pɔsəbl

It was quite impossible.

1082. Most foreign learners have great difficulty in learning to make a fall-rise on a single syllable, as in the examples in § 1054. The correct pronunciation may be acquired by practising very slowly and then gradually increasing the speed, being careful to observe the rules mentioned in § 1055. Thus the *can* in the example *I will if I can* given in § 1054 should be practised thus:

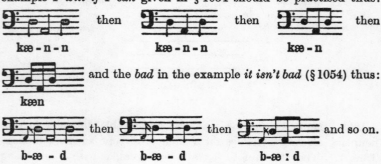

kæ - n - n   then   kæ - n - n   then   kæ - n   then

kæn   and the *bad* in the example *it isn't bad* (§ 1054) thus:

b-æ - d   then   b-æ - d   then   b-æ : d   and so on.

Methods of Recording Intonation

1083. There are various methods of recording intonation.

1084. A notation of dots and lines on a stave, such as that used in this chapter, may be drawn free-hand by anyone with a good musical ear. This method is sufficiently accurate for practical linguistic purposes. The method has the advantage that it records intonations which are subjectively present, even if they are not clearly audible objectively owing to the presence of voiceless sounds or the nature of the pitches of adjacent syllables.

1085. A more accurate method of obtaining intonation-curves is the following. If while a gramophone record is being played the needle is lifted from the revolving disc, the ear retains the impression of the sound heard at the instant when the needle is lifted. If the record is of the speaking voice and the needle is removed in the middle of a voiced sound, the ear retains in particular the pitch of the musical note which the voice is producing at that instant; this may be marked on some kind of musical stave. By taking observations at a large number of points in a sentence and joining the points by lines, a complete intonation-curve of the sentence results. In order to ensure accuracy it is of course necessary to take a number of observations at every chosen point; the chosen points should likewise not be too far apart: thus it is necessary to record the pitch of every vowel and a considerable number of the voiced consonants, and where sounds are long or where the intonation is rising or falling rapidly it may be necessary to record the pitch of two or three portions of one sound. This method was the one followed in preparing my book of *Intonation Curves*.[31]

1086. Certain small inaccuracies are unavoidable with this method, but the method has the advantage that while a considerable degree of scientific accuracy is attained yet the resulting curves are such as can be made use of without difficulty in practical language teaching. The phonetic text is continuous (not irregularly spaced as in the case of the most accurate curves), and the ordinary musical stave being used, the values of the curves are clearly apparent to anyone who has an elementary knowledge of music.

1087. The most accurate methods of obtaining intonation-curves are obtained by measuring the lengths of vibrations on kymographic tracings or enlargements of the lines on gramophone records or records made in other ways. (For details and an example, see

---

[31] Published by Teubner, Leipzig, 1909. Now out of print.

pp. 179–182 of the first and second editions of this book, 1918, 1922.)

1088. Accurate curves obtained by such means have scientific value, but their use in practical language teaching is limited, since they only record what is objectively present. To get good results in practical teaching it is necessary to have regard continually to the intonations *aimed at*, i.e. the intonations which are *subjectively* present to the speaker. These often differ considerably from the objective intonations actually employed. The latter are such approximations to the subjective intonations as are compatible with the length and nature of the sounds in each particular case. (The differences between subjective and objective intonations are especially notable when vowels are very short and voiceless consonants are present.) The graphical representations in the examples in this chapter have been drawn by ear, and they represent the subjective intonations to be aimed at by the learner.

Chapter XXXII

SYLLABLE SEPARATION

1089. It was pointed out in § 212 that it is often impossible to specify points at which a syllable begins and ends. There do exist, however, circumstances where points of syllable separation are well marked in pronunciation, and must be shown in transcriptions in order to render them unambiguous. This happens in some instances of compound words, and in some apparently simple words where two parts, though joined together without pause, are nevertheless pronounced as if they were separate words.

1090. Where such circumstances are present, the points of syllable separation are sometimes made evident in transcriptions by the positions of stress-marks.[1] More often, however, they have to be shown by a special mark. Hyphens are convenient for this purpose.

1091. When two parts of a word are pronounced as if they were separate words, the various rules relating to sound-quality and length in single words apply to each part; the sounds on each side of the place of separation do not affect each other in the ways they would if there were no clear syllable separation. For instance, when the first syllable ends in a long vowel and the second one begins with a breathed consonant, the long vowel does not have a shorter length as described in § 866. And when the first syllable, ends in a breathed consonant and the second begins with **l**, **r**, etc., the fully voiced allophones of these phonemes are used, and not the devoiced sounds which would represent the phonemes if the same breathed consonant were to precede them at the beginning of a word (§ 845 (i) *a*).

1092. These principles are well illustrated by compound words containing sequences of vowel + **s** + **t** + **r** + vowel, such as *toe-strap* **'tou-stræp**, *mouse-trap* **'maus-træp**, *toast-rack* **'toust-ræk**. In **'tou-stræp** the syllable separation is between the **ou** and the **s**. This means that, although there is no cessation of sound at the place of separation, the two syllables are pronounced as if they were separate

---

[1] As long as the system of transcription is one (like that of the I.P.A.) in which stress is shown by marks preceding the stressed syllable.

words, and consequently the **ou** is made fully long as explained in § 866.   In **'maus-træp**, however, the separation being between the **s** and the **t**, the **au** is a rather short diphthong on account of the presence of the **s**.[2]   Moreover, in **'tou-stræp** and **'maus-træp** the **tr**'s are pronounced as if **stræp** and **træp** were said in isolation, which means that they have the sound of the voiceless affricate described in § 624.[3]   In **'toust-ræk** not only is the **ou** rather short in accordance with the principle stated in § 866, but the **r** being pronounced as if it were initial is fully voiced.

1093. It would be ambiguous to transcribe the above words without the hyphens.   If a foreign learner were to say them with syllable separations elsewhere than at the places shown by the hyphens, his pronunciation would be incorrect and possibly unintelligible, since there are no such words as **'tous-træp**, **'toust-ræp**, **'mau-stræp**, **'maust-ræp**, **'tou-stræk** and **'tous-træk**.

1094. The following are some further examples illustrating the effect of syllable separation.

(1) Syllable separation between a vowel and a consonant: *biplane* **'bai-plein**,[4] *eye-sight* **'ai-sait**,[5] *awe-struck* **'ɔ:-strʌk**,[6] *bow-string* **'bou-striŋ**,[7] *door-plate* **'dɔ:-pleit**,[8] *key-stone* **'ki:-stoun**.[9]

(2) Syllable separation after the first of two or three consonants: *horse-truck* **'hɔ:s-trʌk**,[10] *Lakeland* **'leik-lænd**,[11] *heat-wave*

---

[2] I.e. it is said with the shortest 'allochrone' of the long chroneme.   (For 'chronemes' see *The Phoneme*, Chap. XXIII).

[3] Or **t** + voiceless **r**, if it is held that English initial **tr** is a sequence of two sounds.

[4] **'bai-plein** has a fully long **ai** and a voiceless **l**.   The word *pipe-line* **'paip-lain** has a shorter **ai** and a fully voiced **l**.

[5] The first **ai** of **'ai-sait** is fairly long.   If there were a word **'ais-ait** (with the first syllable as in *ice-axe* **'ais-æks**) the first **ai** would be shorter.

[6] **'ɔ:-strʌk** has a fully long **ɔ:**.

[7] **'bou-striŋ** has a fully long **ou**, like **'tou-stræp** (§ 1092).

[8] **'dɔ:-pleit** has a fully long **ɔ:** and a voiceless **l**.   If there were a word **'dɔ:p-leit**, it would have a shorter **ɔ:** and a fully voiced **l**.

[9] **'ki:-stoun** has a fully long **i:**.   If there were a word **'ki:s-toun**, it would have a shorter **i:**.

[10] **'hɔ:s-trʌk** has a rather short **ɔ:**. Compare *awe-struck* (footnote 6).

[11] **'leik-lænd** has a rather short **ei** and a fully voiced **l**.   If there were a word **'lei-klænd**, it would have a fully long **ei** and a voiceless **l** after the **k**.

ˈhiːt-weiv,[12] *leap-year* ˈliːp-jəː,[13] *outrageous* autˈreidʒəs,[14] *boat-race* ˈbout-reis,[15] *Pecksniff* ˈpek-snif,[16] *undomesticated* ˈʌn-dəˈmestikeitid.[17]

(3) Syllable separation after the second of three consonants: *mincemeat* ˈmins-miːt,[18] *bank-rate* ˈbæŋk-reit,[19] *lamp-light* ˈlæmp-lait.[20]

(4) Syllable separation between a consonant and a vowel: *lynx-eyed* ˈliŋks-aid,[21] *cat's-eye* ˈkæts-ai,[21] *stomach-ache* ˈstʌmək-eik,[22] *hair-oil* ˈhɛər-ɔil,[23] *under-masticated* ˈʌndəˈmæstikeitid.[24]

1094. In transcriptions in which words are joined together, hyphens have to be inserted wherever the absence of a hyphen

---

[12] ˈhiːt-weiv has a rather short iː and a fully voiced w. If there were a word ˈhiː-tweiv it would have a fully long ei and a partially voiceless w.

[13] ˈliːp-jəː has a rather short iː and a fully voiced j. If there were a word ˈliː-pjəː, it would have a fully long iː and a partially voiceless j.

[14] *Outrageous* is generally pronounced autˈreidʒəs with a fully voiced r.

[15] ˈbout-reis has a short ou and a fully voiced r. If there were a word ˈbou-treis, it would have a fully long ou and the voiceless affricate tr (or t + voiceless r).

[16] ˈpek-snif has a strong s and a partially voiceless n. If there were a word ˈpeks-nif, it would have a weak s and a fully voiced n.

[17] *Undomesticated* ˈʌn-dəˈmestikeitid has a rather long n, and the ə is very short.

[18] ˈmins-miːt has a short n, and the m of the syllable miːt is fully voiced. If there were a word ˈmin-smiːt, the n would be longer and the second m would be partially voiceless.

[19] ˈbæŋk-reit has a short ŋ and the r is fully voiced. If there were a word ˈbæŋ-kreit, the ŋ would be long and the r voiceless.

[20] ˈlæmp-lait has a short m, and the l of the second syllable is fully voiced. If there were a word ˈlæm-plait, the m would be long and the l following the p would be voiceless.

[21] ˈliŋks-aid and ˈkæts-ai have a weak s (with z̦ as a variant, as explained in footnote 9 to § 709, also *The Phoneme*, §§ 171–175).

[22] The medial k of ˈstʌmək-eik is unaspirated. Compare this word with *summer cake* ˈsʌmə keik which has a longer ə and an aspirated k at the beginning of the final syllable.

[23] ˈhɛər-ɔil is said with a weak variety of r; it is the flapped r (§ 750) in the speech of those who use this sound. If there were a word ˈhɛə-rɔil, it would be said either with a fricative r or with a strong variety of frictionless continuant.

[24] *Under-masticated* ˈʌndəˈmæstikeitid has a medium length n, and the ə is of moderate length. Compare footnote 17.

would render the notation ambiguous in the matter of syllable
separation. The following are a few examples:

ðə'ʃip'sæŋk-wið'ɔːl'hændz (*the ship sank with all hands*),[25]
hiː'sæŋ-kwait'wel (*he sang quite well*),[26]
itsəz'wel-tə'weit (*it's as well to wait*),[27]
hiːzə'weltə-weit (*he's a welter-weight*),[28]
'liː-pleidə'diːp-leid'geim (*Lee played a deep-laid game*).[29]

1095. Similarly, when it is desired to transcribe without spaces
between words, the positions of stress-marks sometimes have to be
chosen so as to show syllable separations. Compare for instance
ə'blækt'ai (*a blacked eye*)[30] with ə'blæk'tai (*a black tie*),[30] and it'slips
(*it slips*)[31] with its'lips (*its lips*).[32]

1096. Further illustrations of phonetic phenomena associated
with syllable separation will be found in §§ 892–898 and in my articles
The 'Word' as a Phonetic Entity in *Le Maître Phonétique*, October,
1931, and *The Hyphen as a Phonetic Sign* in the *Zeitschrift für
Phonetik*, Vol. IX, No. 2 (Berlin, 1956).

1097. The existence of many special shades of sound and degrees
of length near word junctions, as illustrated in this chapter, shows
the necessity for defining the 'phoneme' and the 'chroneme' by
reference to 'words' and not to longer units of connected speech.
See *The Phoneme*, § 34.

---

[25] Here the ŋ is short and the w is fully voiced.
[26] Here the ŋ is long and the w of kwait is partially voiceless.
[27] Here the l is long and the ə of tə very short.
[28] Here the l is short and the ə of 'weltə is of moderate length.
[29] In 'liː-pleid the iː is fully long and the l in the second syllable is voiceless. In 'diːp-leid the iː is rather short and the l is fully voiced.
[30] In ə'blækt'ai the t is unaspirated, but in ə'blæk'tai it is aspirated.
It is worthy of note that ə'blækt'ai is much nearer in sound to ə'blæk'dai
(*a black dye*) than to ə'blæk'tai.
[31] The first s in it'slips is a strong variety, and the l is partially voiceless.
[32] The first s in its'lips is a weak variety, and the l is fully voiced.

APPENDIX A
Types of Phonetic Transcription

1. It has long been known that different types of phonetic transcription are needed for different purposes. Henry Sweet pointed this out in his *Handbook of Phonetics* (1877), in which he published, in their original forms, the systems which he called 'Narrow Romic' and 'Broad Romic.' Narrow Romic was 'scientific,' while the various forms of Broad Romic were 'practical.'

2. In Narrow Romic, Sweet invented means of symbolizing all the speech-sounds and shades of speech-sounds he could think of. In its original form it was composed of Roman lower-case letters supplemented by capitals and italics with special meanings, digraphs, inverted letters and letters with diacritics attached. (In a later revised form he improved it by introducing some new letters to take the place of some of these.) There were also marks denoting degrees of length and stress and certain intonations. From Narrow Romic were derived the 'broad' or 'practical' systems for particular languages. Each 'broad' system was intended to contain only as many symbols[1] as were necessary to represent the particular language without ambiguity, and in selecting the symbols, Sweet took into consideration their familiarity and the convenience of their designs from the point of view of handwriting and the legibility of connected texts.

3. To ensure that his 'broad' texts should be unambiguous, Sweet laid down the principle (now known as the 'phonemic' principle) that only those distinctions of sound should be symbolized which are capable of distinguishing one word from another in the particular language transcribed.[2] To ensure satisfactory letter

---

[1] For the special use of the term 'symbol' as distinguished from 'letter,' see § *19* of this Appendix.

[2] 'In giving passages of any length in phonetic writing, and especially in dealing with a limited number of sounds, as in treating of a single language, it is necessary to have an alphabet which indicates only those broader distinctions of sound which actually correspond to distinctions of meaning' (*Handbook*, p. 103). 'We may lay down as a general rule that only those distinctions of sound require to be symbolized in any one language which are *independently significant*' (*Handbook*, p. 104). The italics are Sweet's; by 'independent' he meant 'not linked with length or stress'.

shapes he restricted his letters as far as possible to those of the
Roman lower case (including æ and œ), making as few additions
as possible.[3]

Broad and Narrow Transcription

4. The terms 'broad' and 'narrow' are convenient, and it is
useful to retain them, giving them the same general meanings that
Sweet did. It is necessary, however, in view of modern develop-
ments in the theory of transcription to introduce some additional
terms to identify types of transcription embodying special features
which at first were but vaguely recognized. Some useful terms
have been proposed by David Abercrombie, Head of the Department
of Phonetics in the University of Edinburgh.[4] I use these and
others in what follows.

5. A 'broad' transcription may be defined precisely as one which
represents only the phonemes of a language, using for this purpose
the minimum number of letter shapes of simplest Romanic form
(consistently with the avoidance of undesirable digraphs for 'single
sounds'[5]) together with such prosodic[6] marks as may be necessary
for the avoidance of lexical ambiguity.[7] This kind of transcription
has been called by Abercrombie 'simple phonemic.' (For 'simple'
see § *13*.)

6. A 'narrow transcription' differs from a 'broad transcription'
in one or both of two ways. (1) A transcription is 'narrow' if it
includes special symbols to denote particular allophones (members
of phonemes, § 197). Abercrombie has proposed the term 'allophonic' for this style of narrow transcription. Such transcriptions
may also be termed 'linguistically narrow.' (2) A transcription is

---

[3] Sweet did not always follow his stated principles with complete consistency, but this was pardonable enough in those early days and did not
invalidate the principles themselves.

[4] See his article *Phonetic Transcriptions* in *Le Maître Phonétique*, July–
December, 1953.

[5] Such as the sh (for ʃ) and ao (for ɔ:) of Sweet's first version of Broad
Romic.

[6] See footnote 2 to § 1 and footnote 23 to § 39.

[7] This concise wording of the definition was suggested to me by J. L. M.
Trim in November, 1954.

also called 'narrow' when use is made of 'exotic' or inconvenient letters when it would be possible to transcribe the language unambiguously with familiar or more convenient ones. Recourse is had to such special letters chiefly when it is desired to show 'external comparisons' by means of separate symbols, i.e. that a sound of one language differs from an analogous sound of another language or from some 'cardinal' sound. Abercrombie has called transcriptions embodying special letters for this purpose 'comparative transcriptions,' and he has pointed out that 'a comparative transcription uses symbols some of which, considered in isolation, are more specific in their reference than those of a simple transcription.' Such transcriptions may also be termed 'typographically narrow.'

7. Recourse may also be had to special letters in order to show 'internal' comparisons between sounds in a single language, e.g. to represent particular allophones or to show that the beginning part of a diphthong is not identical in sound with any 'pure vowel' of the language transcribed.

8. A transcription must also be called 'narrow' if it gives indications of non-significant degrees of length or of any other 'prosodic' distinctions which do not serve to differentiate words.

9. Examples of 'allophonic' transcription would be the use of ł to denote the Southern English 'dark l,' or ţ to denote the dental t in *eighth* eitθ, or ḷ (§ 176) to denote the French 'devoiced l.' Examples of 'comparative' transcription would be the use of ɹ in place of r in transcriptions of English in order to remind readers that the sound is not a rolled one, or of ʀ or ʁ (§§ 746, 762, 763) in transcriptions of French to remind English learners not to use an English r. An example of a transcription which is neither 'allophonic' nor 'comparative' (as defined above), but which calls attention to an 'internal' comparison, is the use of a in writing the English diphthong ai[8] in order to show that the beginning of this diphthong differs both from æ and from ɑ:.

10. The extra symbols needed for narrowing a transcription can always be dispensed with by assuming conventions. When a

---

[8] I.e. the variety of **ai** which begins with cardinal **a** (§ 407). There exist English speakers who start their diphthong with **æ** and others who start theirs with **ɑ** (see *The Pronunciation of English*, 1950 and subsequent editions, §§ 175, 177).

transcription is *allophonic*, the conventions to be stated are the phonetic environments determining the occurrences of each allophone. Thus in transcribing Southern English the narrow symbol ł can be dispensed with and replaced by l, if the conditions under which 'dark l' is used are described once for all, as they are in § 659. When, on the other hand, a transcription is *comparative*, a single symbol can be employed to denote analogous (or occasionally non-analogous) sounds in two or more languages by specifying once for all the value to be attached to it in each. Thus the letter r can be, and generally is, used in transcriptions of English, French and Italian with conventions as to its values in each of these languages.

11. An allophonic transcription may be comparative or non-comparative. For instance, it is allophonic and comparative to denote the fricative and flapped varieties of Southern English r by ɹ (§ 746) and ɾ (§§ 746, 750, 753, 754) respectively, since ɹ is fairly 'specific in its reference' and ɾ is still more so. It is, however, allophonic but not comparative to use o and ou to distinguish the Southern English monophthongal o-sound in *November* from the ordinary diphthongal sound of *below, home*, etc., as is done in EPD transcription of English.[9] This representation is not comparative, since it does not suggest that the o differs from 'cardinal' o or from the o-sounds of French and German or any other language. The value of o in EPD transcription has to be understood once for all.

12. Conversely a comparative transcription may be used in a phonemic manner or in an allophonic manner. For instance, the comparative letter ɹ may be employed either phonemically to denote the Southern English r-phoneme, or allophonically to mean fricative r as distinguished from the flapped sound denoted by ɾ.

Simple and Complex Transcription

13. A form of transcription which comprises only ordinary Roman letters, or Roman letters supplemented by the smallest possible number of new letters is called by Abercrombie 'simple'; it might also be termed 'romanically simple' or 'conservative' or

---

[9] By EPD transcription is meant the type of transcription of English used in my *English Pronouncing Dictionary* (and in this book).

'old-lettered' or 'typographically broad.' The 'simplified transcription' of Southern English described in §§ *44–49* of this Appendix is 'simple' in this sense. It is likewise 'simple' to denote the Spanish **b**-phoneme by the letter **b**, or the Japanese vowel **ɯ** (§§ 145, 351, 358) by **u**, or the Polish vowel **ɨ** (§ 146) by **y**.

14. A 'simple' mode of transcribing on Romanic basis sometimes involves giving to a Roman letter a value differing greatly from that commonly associated with it. For instance, it is 'simple' to use **c** to denote the dental click in Zulu (as is done in the current orthography of that language); this procedure is justifiable on the ground that the letter **c** is not needed for any other purpose in Zulu. Likewise, Sweet wrote 'simply' when in his original Romic systems he took **q** to mean **ŋ** in English and to mean the nasalization of vowels in French. Such uses of Roman letters may be objected to on international grounds, but a transcription employing them in such ways is none the less 'simple,' and may be adequate for the transcriber's purpose.

15. 'Simple transcriptions' are generally phonemic, but they are not necessarily so. It would in rare cases be possible—though I do not say desirable—to arrange an allophonic transcription on a 'simple' basis. Thus it would be 'simple' and allophonic to write the French fronted **k** of *qui, caisse*, etc., with **c**, while retaining **k** in other situations. Likewise it would be 'simple' and allophonic in transcribing Spanish to write **b** for the plosive **b**-sound (used after **m**) and **v** for the non-plosive allophone used in other situations. Similarly, it would be 'simple' to denote the two corresponding members of the Spanish **g**-phoneme by **g** and **q**, or to use **x** to denote the Southern English dark **l**. It is not likely that anyone would seriously contemplate using **q** and **x** in this manner. It would doubtless be generally agreed that their associations render them unsuitable letters for these purposes.

16. When a transcriber wishes to write narrowly (whether allophonically or comparatively), he is however generally obliged to introduce exotic letters.[10] A form of transcription introducing

---

[10] Unless he elects to resort to the unsatisfactory device of using arbitrary digraphs on a large scale, or unless he adopts the unusual course of assigning specialized meanings to superfluous Roman letters after the manner suggested in §§ *14, 15*.

exotic letters when it would be possible by conventions to avoid
doing so may be termed a 'complex' or 'new-lettered' one. A
complex transcription is generally comparative; it may be phonemic
or allophonic. A comparative transcription, however, is not
necessarily complex (see § *15*).

17. It is complex and phonemic to use ɹ to denote the English
r-phoneme, or to write the Japanese close back vowel with ɯ
or the Polish close central vowel with ɨ.[11]

18. On the other hand, it is complex (as well as comparative)
and allophonic to write the English fricative **r** with ɹ (or ɹ) and to
introduce the symbol ɾ to represent the flapped allophone (§ *11*).
It is likewise complex (as well as comparative) and allophonic to
write the Spanish intervocalic **b** with the letter β (§ 692) while
reserving the letter **b** for the plosive **b** occurring after **m**, as has
been done in narrow transcriptions of Spanish.

Uniliteral and Multiliteral Transcriptions

19. It is necessary to draw a distinction between the terms 'letter'
and 'symbol.' Any written sign or sequence of signs or accented
letter used for the representation of a single speech-sound may
be called a 'symbol.'[12] Digraphs such as the tʃ and ai used in
ordinary transcriptions of English,[13] are therefore single symbols,
although they are each composed of two letters. So also are
sequences like hw (often used as a 'simple' substitute for ʍ, § 810)
or ɑŋ, εŋ, etc. (which have been suggested for use in place of ɑ̃, ɛ̃,
etc., to represent nasalized vowels).

20. A system of phonetic transcription which employs for a
given language not only a minimum number of *symbols*, but also

---

[11] As is done in Arend-Choiński's *Polish Phonetic Reader* (University of
London Press).

[12] This special meaning of the word 'symbol' has often been implied but,
as far as I remember, it was not definitely formulated until R. T. Butlin did
so in an article on the phonetics of Malayalam in the *Bulletin of the School of
Oriental Studies*, 1936, p. 437. P. A. D. MacCarthy also drew attention to
it in Appendix C of his *English Pronunciation* (1944).

[13] It is proper in my opinion to consider affricates and diphthongs as 'single
sounds.' Transcribers have at times written them with single letters. This
was done for instance in the Pitman–Ellis phonetic alphabet, which was
used by Alexander Ellis in his *Essentials of Phonetics* (1848) and by Sir Isaac
Pitman in numerous works.

a minimum number of *letters*, may be termed a 'uniliteral' system. Uniliteral systems embody the principle that digraphs, if any are needed, are constructed if possible by putting together letters which are used independently to denote other sounds of the language. When a uniliteral system is based on Roman letters, it need not necessarily be a 'simple' system (§ *13*); it may contain exotic letters introduced to call attention to differences between one language and another. For instance, the 'simplified transcription' of English (§§ *44–49*) would remain uniliteral if all the r's were replaced by ɹ.

21. Systems which employ more than the minimum number of letters needed to represent a given language effectively and unambiguously may be called 'multiliteral.' A system is multiliteral (1) if it comprises any special letters to denote particular allophones, (2) when a letter not otherwise employed is introduced into a digraph. Multiliteral systems, if basically Romanic, are generally 'complex,' since there are seldom enough letters in the Roman alphabet to provide a multiliteral transcription. It is, for instance, multiliteral and complex (but not allophonic) to write the English diphthongs **ai** and **au** with a letter that distinguishes their beginnings from ɑː, as is done in EPD transcription. Uniliteral transcription would require that ɑː should be written as **aː**, or that the diphthongs should be written **ai**, **au**. It would be multiliteral and 'simple' (though not advisable on other grounds) to represent ɑ: by ɋ, while using the customary **ai** and **au** for these diphthongs. It is likewise multiliteral (though convenient) to introduce the letter ʒ into transcriptions of Italian, as is done by those who transcribe the voiced affricate in *giorno* by dʒ.

22. In EPD transcription the following diphthongs are symbolized uniliterally: **ei, ou, ɔi, iə, ɔə, uə**. In other words each of these representations is composed of letters which are used independently for other purposes. On the other hand ɛə, **ai, au** are multiliteral representations,[14] since the letters ɛ and **a** are not employed separately for any other purpose. (A uniliteral representation

---

[14] As long as EPD transcription is used in its full form, i.e. when the sequences **eiə, aiə, auə** are written in full. When the reduced form of **eiə** is written by the reduced symbol **eə**, and when the length-mark is added to **a** to show reduced forms of **aiə** and **auə**, the representations are uniliteral.

of ɛə would be eə. The notation ɛə would be uniliteral only if the letter e were everywhere replaced by ɛ, that is to say if the vowels in *get* and *day* were written with ɛ and ɛi.)

23. Similar considerations apply to the representation of affricate consonants and some other consonant-sounds such as hw and kw. Such sounds may be, and sometimes are, represented by single letters, e.g. c for tʃ, ʍ for hw. It is, however, often convenient to denote them by digraphs. Such digraphs are commonly designed on a uniliteral basis, that is to say by combining two letters which are employed separately for other purposes. But the plan of using special letters in digraphs (i.e. multiliteral representation) has also been tried occasionally.[15]

Exclusive and Inclusive Transcription

24. Since no two speakers of a given language pronounce exactly alike in all respects, anyone seeking to transcribe that language phonetically has to decide what pronunciation to record. When the language is his own, the transcriber may follow the safe course of recording his own way of speaking. Henry Sweet, for instance, did this.[16] Some have sought to record a kind of norm, basing their transcripts on their own speech, but making modifications wherever they have thought their own pronunciation to be unusual. Others again have represented a style of speech specially selected so as to facilitate the task of the language learner; when two ways of pronouncing are possible, they have chosen for representation

---

[15] For instance, Professor C. M. Doke of Johannesburg has used the specially designed letters ƭ and ɗ in his representation of the affricates commonly written tʃ, dʒ. He has written them ƭ·ʃ, ɗʒ, in order to show in his transcripts that the initial parts of these affricates have different articulations from the ordinary t and d in such words as *ten*, *dull*. This is a multiliteral and complex way of symbolizing these sounds. It is presumably to be considered as a 'narrow' representation on account of the 'internal' comparison involved. I am inclined not to consider it an allophonic representation, since the beginnings of tʃ and dʒ have nothing to do with the t and d phonemes. J. L. M. Trim has, however, suggested that it should be considered allophonic, on the ground that the beginning of tʃ may occur by assimilation as an allophone of t when tʃ follows, as in *that cheese* 'ðæt 'tʃiːz.

[16] 'All I can do is to describe that form of London dialect with which I am sufficiently familiar to enable me to deal with it satisfactorily. The only real familiarity we can have is with the language we speak ourselves.' (Sweet, *Primer of Spoken English*, 3rd edition, p. vii.)

the one that is easier or more effective from the point of view of the pupils for whom the transcripts are designed. The 'simplified' transcription of English described in §§ *44–49* of this Appendix makes allowance for considerations of this kind.

25. Whatever the basis of a transcription, it is generally found that some of the symbols can be interpreted by the reader in more than one way. The symbols may be held to cover (within limits) certain deviations from what may be considered as the 'average' values for the particular language transcribed—'diaphonic' variants as they may be called (Chap. XI). It has been pointed out, for instance (in §§ 271, 388, also in my *Pronunciation of English*, 1950 and subsequent editions, §§ 89, 160, 161), that the English sounds of **e** and **ei** both admit of diaphonic variants which would be recognized as coming within the limits of RP; they vary in quality from speaker to speaker. In such cases the foreign learner need not restrict himself rigidly to acquiring one particular shade of sound; it is possible for him to adopt another shade (within limits) without rendering his pronunciation un-English.

26. A transcription which makes allowance for more than one way of pronouncing may be termed an 'inclusive' transcription. One which definitely excludes or provides no means of representing certain possible ways of pronouncing may be termed an 'exclusive' form of transcription. All transcriptions are to a certain extent both inclusive and exclusive. It is advisable therefore to confine the use of these terms to cases where the pronunciations included or excluded are particularly frequent or otherwise noteworthy.

27. A special case of inclusive transcription is one where alternative ways of pronouncing can be shown by means of the symbols employed, and are not merely implicit in the transcription. EPD transcription of English is in some respects adaptable in this way, and this is to a certain extent an advantage. In particular, the following alternative pronunciations in Southern English can be shown by means of it:

(*a*) the lengthening of the traditionally short sounds of *e*, *a* and *u*, as in *red*, *bad*, *run*; this pronunciation may be symbolized by writing **reːd, bæːd, rʌːn** (§§ 874–878), (*b*)   the reduction of **aiə** to a diphthong **aə** or to a monophthong **aː** (distinct from **ɑː**) (§ 414),[17]

(*c*)   the reduction of **eiə** and **ouə** to diphthongs **eə**, **oə** (distinct from **ɛə**, **ɔə**) (§§ 392*a*, 403),

(*d*)   the reduction of **oui** to a diphthong **oi** (distinct from **ɔi**) (§ 403),

(*e*)   the reduction of **ou** to a monophthongal **o**-sound (distinct from **ɔ**) in positions of very weak stress, as in the first syllables of *November, obey, molest* (§ 403).

Characteristics of EPD Transcription

28. EPD transcription of English is exclusive in so far as it does not provide representation for the pronunciation of those Southern English people who lengthen the traditionally short sounds of *i, o* and *u,* as in *this, hot, full* (§ 877, also *The Pronunciation of English,* 1950 and subsequent editions, § 429). To render it inclusive of these variants would involve altering the transcription by the introduction of three extra symbols such as **ɩ, ɒ, ω,** to denote the traditionally short **i, ɔ** and **u,** and to use them throughout. Such a modified system would be narrow ('allochronic') if the length-marks are retained, and would therefore be multiliteral to those who do not lengthen these vowels.

29. EPD transcription of English comprises twenty-two consonant letters (**p b t d k g m n ŋ l r f v θ ð s z ʃ ʒ h j w**), eleven vowel letters (**i e ɛ æ a ɑ ɔ o u ʌ ə**), the length-mark (**ː**) and the marks for primary and secondary stress (**ˈ ˌ**). It is allophonic in one respect only, namely in the use of the letter **o** to denote the monophthongal **o**-sound referred to in (*e*) above. That sound, when consistently used,[18] is a member of the **ou**-phoneme, and can properly be written with **ou** with the convention that it is sounded as the monophthongal allophone in syllables with very weak stress.

30. The multiliteral features of EPD transcription, namely the use of **ɛ, æ** and **ɑ,** are introduced for comparative purposes, and

---

[17] EPD transcription does not allow for the reductions of **auə** as I pronounce them (see § 430). It does cover the speech of those whose reductions of **auə** are identical with those of **aiə** (see § 431).

[18] See my book *The Phoneme,* §§ 252–254.

are thus narrow in one sense; but these letters do not represent allophones (particular members) of any phonemes. ɛ and ɑ are included as being suggestive of the cardinal categories to which the sounds belong—an object which some teachers consider unnecessary.[19] Incidentally, they provide a means by which the transcription is made more inclusive than it would be without them. As to æ, it has been customary to use this letter in order to call the attention of foreign learners[20] to the fact that the sound is an unusual one and likely to give them trouble—again a plan which some consider unnecessary. The use of this sign has the advantage of rendering the transcription inclusive of the speech of the numerous English people who lengthen the vowel.

31. The characteristics of EPD transcription may then be summarized as follows:

(1) it is phonemic except in one point,

(2) it is multiliteral in that three letters are employed which could be dispensed with if the transcription were restricted to the representation of 'common pronunciation,'[21]

(3) it is inclusive in that some of the symbols can by convention be held to represent diaphonic variants, and special arrangements of the letters can be made which indicate the variant pronunciations enumerated in § *27* (*a*)–(*d*).

Narrow Transcription of Southern English

32. In the practical teaching of 'common pronunciation' of Southern English[21] I find the traditional system of regarding i: i,

---

[19] I share this view when it is a question of teaching English to the numerous foreign learners who have no time or inclination to study phonetics. These learners have no need to concern themselves with cardinal categories. What they need is (1) to be taught to make the English sounds, and (2) to be taught to associate each sound with a symbol of a simple phonetic transcription —the simpler the better in my opinion. See §§ 44–49 of this Appendix.

[20] Other than Scandinavians, for whom the letter æ suggests the English e.

[21] I use the term 'common pronunciation' to denote the pronunciation shown by EPD transcription when (1) the vowel letters are given what may be considered to be 'average values' for Southern English, (2) the sequences eiə, ouə, aiə, auə and oui are given their full pronunciation (§§ 392*a*, 403, 414, 430) and (3) the traditionally short vowels, i, e, ɔ, u and ʌ are pronounced short, but æ is pronounced long when appropriate (§§ 874–878).

ɔː ɔ, uː u, əː ə as pairs of corresponding long and short vowels easy and convenient to work with. This manner of transcribing is based on the view that in each pair the length constitutes the fundamental difference, and that the accompanying quality difference is incidental. It is however possible, at any rate in the case of the first three pairs, to take the contrary view—that the quality difference is the fundamental one and that the differences of length are incidental. To those holding this view the qualities of each pair of sounds constitute separate phonemes, requiring therefore separate symbols in transcription, while the vowel lengths, having no significance from the semantic standpoint, do not need to be indicated in broad transcriptions. (See my book *The Phoneme*, §§ 510–516.)

33. Broad transcription of 'common pronunciation' on the latter supposition would involve the adoption of some such system of vowel representation as the following (which should be compared with the chart in § 236). This system is uniliteral (§ *20*) and is phonemic, as long as no indications of length are given;[22] it excludes representation of the monophthongal allophone of **ou** and the reduced forms of **eiə**, **ouə** and **oui**. It presupposes a value of **ə:** differing in quality from all the values of **ə** (see § 342, also § 355, etc.).

34. A similar system of vowel representation also suits well the pronunciation of those who lengthen the traditionally short vowels (§§ 874–879). Here again the system would be phonemic, as long as the lengths are not marked.[22]

35. As far as I know, no author has yet employed a uniliteral system of the above type for transcribing 'common pronunciation.'

---

[22] Except possibly in a few words containing **æ**. It would seem that some Southern English people distinguish **dʒæːm** (fruit preserve) from **dʒæm** (squeeze) and **bæːnd** (*band*) from **bænd** (*banned*).

Transcriptions involving special symbols to denote the qualities of the traditionally short vowels have, however, often been used. But they have been both narrow (in both senses) and multiliteral. They are of value especially in comparative work, e.g. when a teacher or author desires to show in his transcripts differences between different varieties of English pronunciation or between English and foreign languages.

36. Notable among such systems is one in which the vowels of RP are denoted by a system of the following type, with length-marking of **i ɑ ɔ u** and **ɜ**, and with **o** to represent the monophthongal variant of **ou**.[23]

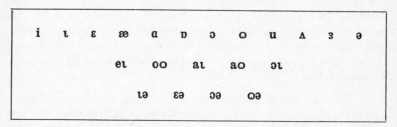

37. This system has generally been called 'Narrow Transcription.' It is, however, not merely narrow (i.e. allophonic and comparative) but also multiliteral and complex. It could be made uniliteral and simple by substituting **e** for **ɛ** and **a** for **ɑ**. It would then remain allophonic (in one respect, namely in its use of **o**) but would cease to be comparative. It could be made uniliteral but complex by substituting **ɛ** for **e** and/or **ɑ** for **a**.

38. At one time (round about 1918) I made considerable use of a narrow transcription of this type. My experience with it originated in the following way. In teaching the pronunciation of foreign languages to English pupils it has generally been my custom to get the pupils to make the foreign sounds and their combinations without teaching them anything about English sounds. I use my own knowledge of phonetics for the purpose, and give the pupils only a minimum of theory. I use a phonemic

---

[23] For the most part using the old symbols ɪ ʊ for the sounds here written ɪ ʊ. The newer symbols date from 1943.

or nearly phonemic transcription of the foreign language, and cause the pupils to associate each sound they learn with the appropriate symbol of that transcription; I do not as a rule give them phonetic representations of any English sounds. I still find this to be the most effective way of teaching the pronunciation of a foreign language for the average learner, i.e. the learner who does not desire to become a specialist in phonetics.[24]

39. However, for several years (from about 1916) I experimented with the plan of showing students phonetic transcriptions illustrating English words in order to demonstrate such differences between the foreign languages and English as can be shown by this means. For this purpose I used a fairly narrow transcription (of the type described in § *36*) of the English words. I did not find it needful to transcribe any connected English texts, but only isolated words and occasionally short sentences. In this way I became accustomed to making a limited use of a narrow transcription for English with some students.

40. To test further the value of this kind of transcription, I subsequently prepared some continuous texts in this type of transcription, and used them both with English students of phonetics and with foreign students desiring to improve their knowledge of English. With English students of phonetics the narrow transcription gave reasonably good results, since with its use various differences between different types of English could be well demonstrated, as also could certain differences between English and foreign languages.

41. With foreign learners of English, on the other hand, I did not find the narrow transcription a success. It did not by any means give the favourable results I had looked for and which might be expected on theoretical grounds. For instance, one would expect the use of a special letter such as ι (or ɪ as it was at that time) to help French pupils to remember that the sound it represents is a difficult one for them and that it differs considerably in quality both from French i and from the English long iː. My

---

[24] My experience thus does not support the theory held by some that a phonetic study of the mother tongue is a useful preliminary to acquiring the pronunciation of a foreign language.

experience was, however, that they persisted in pronouncing it as French i, and they had to be drilled in the use of the opener sound just as much as when the broad transcription (i: i) was used. So after two years' trial of narrow transcription with foreign learners I abandoned it and reverted to broader forms. I continued, however, to use narrow transcription for many years with English-speaking students of phonetics.

42. The first reader to be published employing full narrow transcription of Southern English was P. W. Drew and C. F. Mackenzie's *Phonetic Reader for Junior Classes* (Manchester University Press, 1919). This made a good beginning, but soon proved inadequate for comprehensive courses of instruction. So I asked my colleague, Miss L. E. Armstrong, to prepare a larger *English Phonetic Reader* containing literary texts, so that there should be plenty of material to work with. This she readily consented to do, and the work was published (by the University of London Press) in 1923. I also started contributing English texts in narrow transcription to *Le Maître Phonétique* when its publication was resumed in 1923, and I continued to do so for some years. I did this for two reasons: firstly to make generally known the fact that a narrow method of transcribing English suitable for exact comparative work was available within the framework of the IPA recommendations, and secondly to provide some additional material for experiments in teaching and research with its aid. Some other good books employing narrow transcription were published in the course of the next few years; they included Armstrong and Ward's *Handbook of English Intonation* (Teubner, Leipzig and Heffer, Cambridge, 1926) and the original edition of I. C. Ward's *English Phonetics* (Heffer, 1929).

43. During this period a number of teachers of phonetics expressed themselves as well satisfied with this form of transcription, especially when working with English-speaking students. Some also used it with foreign learners of English, and obtained good results. Some indeed became enthusiastic for it—not sharing my view as to the advisability of symbol economy. There still are to-day (1960) many teachers who advocate the use of this narrow transcription in the teaching of English pronunciation to foreign people.

Simplified Transcription of English

44. About 1930 I began to realize that EPD transcription of
Southern British English, good as it is, is not the *simplest* possible
transcription that can effectively help the foreign learner towards
ability to pronounce English properly. I endeavoured to look at
the question from the point of view of the very numerous foreign
learners whose sole object is to learn to speak English well, and
who have no need either to become specialized phoneticians or to
concern themselves with more than one variety of English pronunciation. It became clearer to me than it had been previously
that a transcription for the use of the foreign learner need not
be so much a precise record of the speech of particular English
people as a guide designed to give him a pronunciation recognizable
as 'good' English; and that consequently when two ways of pronouncing are current in Southern England, the transcriber may
quite properly indicate the form likely to prove easier or otherwise
more effective for the pupil. Viewed from this angle EPD transcription is undoubtedly more 'inclusive' than it need be, and
although it is very nearly 'broad' (for the pronunciations which
it represents), it is for the average foreign learner unduly 'multiliteral' and 'comparative.' I then came to the conclusion that a
still simpler system—one in which the number of special letters is
diminished to an irreducible minimum—is what would meet their
needs best. The value of such a system had indeed been demonstrated long since by Sweet, whose revised Broad Romic as used
in the texts in his *Elementarbuch des Gesprochenen Englisch* (first
published in 1885) fulfilled nearly all the requisite conditions, and
had long enjoyed much success abroad.[25]

---

[25] Sweet's use of ö and ü in this work rendered his system not quite phonemic,
and his use of ɔ rendered it not quite uniliteral nor 'simple.' He might have
rendered it completely uniliteral and simple by substituting oo for ɔ—a plan
which would not have been out of keeping with the rest of his system.

The modified form of transcription adopted in his *Primer of Spoken English*
(first published in 1890) and *Sounds of English* (1908) was narrow in two
respects, namely, that əi and əu were used to denote special varieties of ai
and au occurring in weakly stressed positions. In these books he placed ˇ on
unstressed i, o and u. This was apparently intended as a narrowing, indicating
modified qualities of these vowels when unstressed. Actually it may be
regarded as a stress-mark (denoting lack of stress).

45. It seemed to me necessary therefore to construct and try out a system of vowel representation for Southern English which, while remaining within the framework of the recommendations of the IPA, should completely fulfil all the conditions necessary to simplicity.   These are (1) that the transcription should be 'exclusive' of all varieties of pronunciation needing letters that can be dispensed with by selecting a special form of Southern pronunciation, (2) that the selected form of the language should be transcribed broadly and uniliterally.   Further, it was and is in my opinion desirable that the transcription should be 'simple' (§ *13*), i.e. that the letters used should be, as far as practicable, familiar Roman ones (this in accordance with the provision formulated in *The Principles of the International Phonetic Association*, 1949, §§ 20, 21).

46. The first of these requirements is satisfied by selecting for transcription a form of Received British English from which the following pronunciations are excluded:

(*a*)   lengthening the traditionally short vowels,

(*b*)   reduced pronunciations of eiə, ouə, aiə, auə, oui,

(*c*)   the reduction of ou to a monophthongal o-sound in various unstressed positions.

The second and third requirements are met by replacing the vowel letters of EPD transcription as follows:

using a for the æ of EPD transcription

,,   aː   ,,   ɑː   ,,   ,,

,,   eə   ,,   ɛə   ,,   ,,

,,   o   ,,   ɔ   ,,   ,,

,,   oː   ,,   ɔː   ,,   ,,

,,   oə (or oː) for the ɔə of EPD transcription

,,   oi for the ɔi of EPD transcription

47. A chart of the vowel system on the same lines as those of EPD transcription (§ 236) and 'narrow transcription' (§ *36* of this Appendix) is shown overleaf.[26]

---

[26] A modification favoured by some (including P. A. D. MacCarthy) is to show length by doubling the vowel-letters, thus ii, aa, etc. This plan has much to commend it; its chief advantage lies in the fact that doubled letters are more readily legible than letters with a length-mark.   It involves, however, introducing a hyphen or other special mark to separate short i from an adjacent i or ii, as in *hurrying* 'hʌri-iŋ, *seeing* 'sii-iŋ, and one pronunciation of *rabies* 'reibi-iiz.

iː   i   e   a   aː   o   oː   u   uː   ʌ   əː   ə

        ei   ou   ai   au   oi

        iə   eə   (oə)   uə

48. Feeling convinced that this system ought to be tried, I prepared a text in it in 1930 and published it (not without misgivings) in *Le Maître Phonétique*, January, 1931, p. 12. Further specimens by myself and others followed in January, 1932, p. 8, April, 1932, p. 44, July, 1932, p. 60, January, 1938, p. 10, April, 1938, p. 25, January, 1939, p. 12, April, 1939, p. 32, July, 1939, p. 53, July, 1940, p. 51, October, 1940, p. 69, and texts in this form of transcription have been published in most subsequent numbers.[27] Books using this system began to appear in 1942, starting with N. C. Scott's *English Conversations*.[28] Several others are now available, the chief ones being P. MacCarthy's *English Pronunciation*[28] and *English Pronouncing Vocabulary*[28] and *English Conversation Reader*,[29] A. S. Hornby's *Oxford Progressive English*,[30] Hornby and Parnwell's *English-Reader's Dictionary*,[30] E. L. Tibbitts' *Phonetic Reader for Foreign Students of English*,[28] and my book on *The Phoneme*.[28] The system has also been used in the periodical *English Language Teaching* (from 1946 onwards).[31]

49. The simplified transcription of Southern English above described, being phonemic, uniliteral, simple and very exclusive,

---

[27] Trials were also made with two modified forms of this transcription. One represented the speech of the numerous Southern English people who lengthen æ under certain conditions (§ 874). In this transcription æ was represented by a, lengthened æ by aː, ɑː by ɑː, and ai, au by ɑi, ɑu (see *Le Maître Phonétique*, October, 1932, p. 84, January, 1933, p. 14, April, 1933, pp. 28–33, July, 1933, p. 60, October, 1933, p. 82, April, 1934, p. 56, October, 1934, p. 108, January, 1935, p. 16 and April, 1935, p. 33). In the other æ was represented by æ and ʌ by a, as in Sweet's revised Broad Romic (see *Le Maître Phonétique*, October, 1939, p. 73, January, 1940, p. 18, and April, 1940, p. 36).

[28] Published by Heffer, Cambridge.

[29] Published by Longmans, Green & Co.

[30] Published by the Oxford University Press.

[31] Published by the British Council, 65, Davies Street, London, W.1.

combines in a remarkable degree neatness of appearance with
effectiveness as an aid to teaching pronunciation. In fact, I do
not think it possible to construct anything simpler which will do
its work adequately. Specialists in phonetics will continue to need
transcriptions of more elaborate types, but those who teach English
to average foreign learners—learners who wish to pronounce well,
but who have no time or inclination to make a detailed study of
phonetic science—will in my opinion do well to explain the use and
distribution of the English sounds with the aid of this simplified
system of transcription.

Systematic and Impressionistic Transcription

50. The various types of transcription described in the foregoing
paragraphs have one feature in common. They are all designed
for the representation of languages and forms of speech which have
already been analysed phonetically.

51. It is useful to have a general term to express the fact that
a transcription has been, like all these, constructed to suit the
phonetic structure of a particular language. The term 'systematic'
proposed by Abercrombie suits this purpose well. It is to be
observed that systematic types of transcription always have to be
accompanied by sets of conventions, an understanding of which
is necessary to their correct interpretation.

52. Systematic transcriptions have to be distinguished from
transcriptions made on a general phonetic basis, without reference
to the needs of any particular language. The latter may be
described as 'non-systematic' or 'impressionistic' (to use another
term proposed by Abercrombie). An example of impressionistic
transcription is the kind of phonetic writing a research worker
has to use when he begins taking down a language new to him
and about which he has no advance information. Such transcriptions 'are made by drawing on a theoretically unlimited number of
symbols, which are defined with reference to the total range of
human speech sounds. . . . No conventions accompany them, for
they are made on the same basis for every language.'[31]

---

[31] Quotation from D. Abercrombie's article *Phonetic Transcriptions* in *Le
Maître Phonétique*, July–December, 1953.

53. Ear-training exercises (§§ 21–24, Chap. XIII and Appendix B) have to be written largely impressionistically, except when the teacher states expressly that an exercise contains the sounds of a certain language arranged in sequences that are possible in that language.

APPENDIX B
Further Ear-training Exercises (to supplement those in Chapter XIII)

Note.—It is my custom, when giving dictations of this kind, to repeat easy sequences 5 or 6 times, moderately difficult sequences 10–12 times and very difficult sequences 15–20 times.

I. Easy Sequences containing only English Sounds

beilævəː, gəfɑːsɛə, nɔːpʌtə, wemɔilou, ziʃiəkuː, ʒauθurəː, duəhɛəŋɑː fæbəːle, djɔːmuəðɔ, tɑːwʌzei, kounɔviə, wəːŋɔːræ, houðɔːʒɑː, meveilɛə, ʃaibaudei, wɑːgupviz, vlæpeisez, souŋʃeið, fuəsbɔzd, ŋeilruːð, lɔiʃvluf, θɔəgwæst, bʌʒziːnd, fəːðliŋʒ, pɔŋkriːdʒ, hʌlmʃaunt, θɔːdzləːmb, fiəvwʌnd, puəljiːðd, tʃʌŋgəːzd, sɛəpʃɔlst, meiʒwæv, zweidfʌmz, bræzkʃev, hedʃændʒ, sprædɔθs, æskləːndz, ʃəkpufθ, strɛəzneig, psʌðgləːb, mjɔnʒdou.

II. More difficult Sequences containing only English Sounds

(a) *Monosyllables*

tnəð, skrɔːndʒd, tʃrəːld, gŋɔldz, ŋelpstʃ, zweildð, mlʌh, ʒdriːlg, zmæunʒ, tʃuəʃθ, dðɑːmg, zðɔimj, dʒviəb, ʃkeŋgz, gŋʌθʃt, ftrindz, tsnævk, ʃnjupt, pmdsk.

(b) *Disyllables*

njʌrvəːʒ, zistælh, dzwaimiŋzg, bmənfsɛə, tʃʌŋktjuəf, mwɔːsmiksθ, ləmðaiŋkʃ, jɔimpθiːʒ, moutgɑːntʃt, ŋɔpt-ʃəːŋ, ʒdneir, ŋivæh, tnzelp, skseʒbrɛə, ŋθmæək, bmuktn, kroudʒlʃ, mlgŋ, sklɔidʒketʃ, shɔːfʃə, dʒnuːŋviə.

(c) *Sequences of three or more Syllables*

fɔːʃwiːsleid, rizdfuəʒiə, ŋoumrəːʃveil, zmjuːɔːskeʃ, ʒiʒgrɔvmɛəʒ, gwiːiʃtouŋl, θɛəzmʌktail, səðəŋme, tneizdʃɑːtrʌnst, siəvzæʃtaui, mʌŋdʃuənʃhɔi, fsounlgreh, zleivɔlikdə, daisibəðkeil, suːjitnək,

351

zəzɑːtstənaiʃ, dəlkŋiːuːt, nɔːðiklimeu, stirtseiθnjɑːl, niŋidnerəv, ŋɔlənizdɑːm, nəkeivzdɔːlæg, tnwɑːnɔːdjədəθ, zwauniːrɑːznʌ, ɛəd-pʌkŋilei, gŋɑːŋeiðŋikŋauk, priːŋweŋθɔl, blædniplɔʒi, zɛəseiθlɔidɑː, lubʃkrauŋeʃ, irpluəwoumbɔ, tiːuːnæeginæm, snisŋələvenifə, zliːv-tsiteigəð, niːbvɔzʌkiddug, nɔdzaipdibəteiðətə, sjuːniːdʒəːlɔtʃi, əb-sʌnvigzl, znɛərɔpfrəlɔːðəkous, kəːmənjuːtinek, ŋliwɔːpnevikaimfət, siəzənæŋiskwou, ʃenibmɑːglufəʃtsoumi, tjuərəsiːnidəlæs, hiːaibjʌle-ɬʌŋtou, ntlɑːŋktsɛəbjɔildn, ænəːmidreklæɔːnl, haihuːθubjidʒeŋənplis, lidrefəzəstʌdʒ, wɔθsiəkŋet, oubeinðidzaul, liəkniːsvɛəznəːd, tsifaib-tælzmiːb, mʌtəbdəːŋintailŋɔːt, skrbmdlgz.

III. Words containing non-English Sounds as well as English ones

priːxsfsuə,[1] dlistyːntʃ,[2] fɛəndʒʌŋzeɸ,[3] ŋfeʃndøːtailpf,[4] θouxtəːgyx, tjiəçlɑːtnisʃ,[5] kŋæðøyskrʌpt, həxyŋgufyuː, ɸimʒɔçnauð, ŋœheixɔŋ-kɛəθ,[6] dʒuət-ʃøx, æntyŋgwedʒiðz, ɔtluːθsŋʌβiː.[7]

In the following exercise **i, u** are to be taken to have 'tense' values in all cases, when short as well as when long; **e, o, ɔ** are to be taken to have cardinal values (similar to the vowels in French *thé*, *tôt*, German *Gott*); **r** is to be the rolled lingual sound.

pɯɑːʀeːvɛ,[8] taːɣondʒœl,[9] giçɯait,[10] ʌŋgɑɹloəɸynsθ,[11] ʀɑ̃ːkŋe,[12] pɯtgadnʃøːʀdirp,[10] gziʔɔkluncœsf,[13] ɛ̃xoidlçiu, ɣiːɟøŋk,[14] dũzgeːɹ-hœʃ, nzcyrtɑ̃ːwʌcɔ,[15] mjækklœːʀou, einɣyʔar, θĩceːzniɛu, ʒuyxol̥ɛ,[16]

---

1 For **x** see § 782.
2 **y** is obtained by adding lip-rounding to **i**.
3 For **ɸ** see § 685.
4 For **ø** see § 347.
5 For **ç** see §§820, 821.
6 For **œ** see § 347.
7 For **β** see § 692.
8 For **ʀ** see § 762.
9 For **ɣ** see § 550.
10 **ɯ** has tongue-position of **u** but lips spread as for **i** (§ 145).
11 **ɹ** denotes fricative **r**.
12 **˜** denotes nasalization (see Chap. XXIV).
13 For **ʔ** see §§ 552 ff.
14 For **ɟ** see § 548.
15 For **c** see § 538.
16 For **l̥** see § 176.

tnɔːðɛsɸũçfmɛyzŋgŋiç,   sŋurʀiːgɯ,   øyʒwaɛ̆ghug,   thatame̯frwɛx,[17]
zbljorvɲɛl.̥[18]

Any student who can write the whole of the above exercises
to dictation without mistake may be satisfied that his ear has
been very well trained.

---

[17] For m̥ see § 176.
[18] For ɲ̊ see § 655.

APPENDIX C

Catenation Exercises

The following are some specimens of exercises which should be practised by learners who can make difficult sounds in isolation but have difficulty in pronouncing sequences containing them. The syllables should, if necessary, be practised at first very slowly and then with gradually increasing speed, e.g. θ—w—ɑː, θ-w-ɑː, θ-w-ɑː, θwɑː.

Every difficult consonant should be pronounced in conjunction with every vowel and diphthong.

θiː θi θe θæ θɑː θɔ θɔː θu θuː θʌ θəː θə θei θou θai θau θɔi θiə θɛə θɔə θuə.

ðiː ði ðe ðæ ðɑː ðɔ ðɔː ðu ðuː ðʌ ðəː ðə ðei ðou ðai ðau ðɔi ðiə ðɛə ðɔə ðuə.

viː vi ve væ, etc.

wiː wi we wæ, etc.

riː ri re ræ, etc.

iːθ uθ iθ eθ æθ ɑːθ ɔθ ɔːθ uθ uːθ ʌθ əːθ əθ eiθ ouθ aiθ auθ ɔiθ iəθ ɛəθ ɔəθ uəθ.

iːð ið eð æð, etc.

iːv iv ev æv, etc.

iːl il el æl, etc.

θiːs θiːz ðiːs ðiːz, θis θiz ðis ðiz, θes θez ðes ðez, θæs θæz ðæs ðæz, θɑːs θɑːz ðɑːs ðɑːz, θɔs θɔz ðɔs ðɔz, θɔːs θɔːz ðɔːs ðɔːz, θus θuz ðus ðuz, θuːs θuːz ðuːs ðuːz, θʌs θʌz ðʌs ðʌz, θəːs θəːz ðəːs ðəːz, θəs θəz ðəs ðəz, θeis θeiz ðeis ðeiz, θous θouz ðous ðouz, θais θaiz ðais ðaiz, θaus θauz ðaus ðauz, θɔis θɔiz ðɔis ðɔiz, θiəs θiəz ðiəs ðiəz, θɛəs θɛəz ðɛəs ðɛəz, θɔəs θɔəz ðɔəs ðɔəz, θuəs θuəz ðuəs ðuəz.

sθiː θsi iːsθ iːθs, sθi θsi isθ iθs, and so on with other vowels and diphthongs.

zðiː iːðz zði iðz, zðe eðz, etc.

θwiː θviː θriː θliː swiː sviː sriː sliː ðwiː ðviː ðriː ðliː zwiː zviː zriː zliː, and with other vowels and diphthongs.

354

iːlθ ilθ elθ ælθ ɑːlθ, etc.
iːlð ilð elð ælð ɑːlð, etc.
iːlv ilv elv ælv ɑːlv, etc.
iːŋ iŋ eŋ æŋ ɑːŋ, etc.
ŋiː ŋi ŋe ŋæ ŋɑː, etc.

Various combinations such as: θiːlz zilθ θses væsθ wɑːθs θsɔsθ
θsɔːθs sθuθs zuːðz zðʌðz zðəːzð zðəl ðveilθ vðoulz wailðz
raulv θrɔilð ðriəθ ðlousθ ðwails ðrauθl vrɔizð znəːŋ zŋəːn
ðnəːŋz θŋəːnθ, and so on, substituting other vowels and
diphthongs.

θæθez sezæθ ðæθes zʌðæð θesɑːð zæθʌs . . . wævez vewæθ
væweð wʌvæθ wewɑːs vevʌð . . . θəθɔːz sɔːzəθ ðɔθɔːs zouðoð
θɔːsouð zɔːðous. . . .

After practising systematic exercises of the above description,
the learner should practise pronouncing miscellaneous invented
words such as those given in Appendix B.

APPENDIX D

American Pronunciation

1. English is pronounced in the United States in numerous ways, all differing considerably from the pronunciations used in Great Britain. As American ways of speaking cannot fail to be of interest to foreign learners of English, a short account of the main features of American pronunciation is given in the following paragraphs. These paragraphs do not furnish a detailed description of one particular variety of American English speech. They merely present a record of the chief features which are particularly noticeable to the Southern British hearer, and which are observable in the speech of many Americans.

A. *Vowels*

2. The speech of many (or perhaps most) Americans does not exhibit consistent relationships between vowel length and quality such as are found in some types of British English. With these speakers all vowels may occur long. Consequently all the vowel qualities have to be represented by separate letters in phonetic transcription.

3. A very common American vowel system is the following:

Symbol	Example	Transcription of American English pronunciation
i	*feet*	fit
ι	*fit*	fιt
e	*fade*	fed
ɛ	*fed*	fɛd
a	*bad, half*	bad, haf
ɑ	*hot, father*	hɑt, 'fɑðɹ
ɔ	*bought, long*	bɔt, lɔŋ
o	*low*	lo
ɷ	*good*	gɷd

356

Symbol	Example	Transcription of American English pronunciation
u	*food*	fud
ə	*cup, method*	kəp, 'mɛθəd
ɹ¹	*bird, water*	bɹd, 'wɔtɹ

4. The following are short descriptions of these sounds together with notes on their use.

5. i has the quality of the ordinary British long iː, and is used in the same places as this British sound; many Americans use this sound finally in such words as *heavy, policy* ('hɛvi, 'paləsi rather than 'hɛvɪ, 'paləsɪ), and in inflected forms of such words (e.g. 'paləsiz), also in the prefixes re- and pre- in such words as *retain* (ri'ten), *presume* (pri'zum). ɪ has approximately the same quality as the Southern British short i, and is used for the most part in the same places as this sound, except that i often replaces it at the ends of words and in the prefixes re-, pre-. American e corresponds to Southern British ei; it is often slightly diphthongal. ɛ resembles Southern British No. 3, and is used in the same places as this sound. a is often about Cardinal No. 4, but a higher variety resembling the Southern British raised a (æ) is also common. It is used in the same words as Southern British æ and also in most of the words which in Southern British have ɑː when there is no r in the spelling, e.g. *pass, ask* (American pas, ask, Southern British pɑːs, ɑːsk), *half* (American haf, Southern British hɑːf). The quality of American ɑ is similar to that of the Southern British ɑː in *father*. It is used in some of the words which have ɑː in Southern British when there is no r in the spelling, e.g. 'fɑðɹ (*father*), kɑm (*calm*). It also replaces the British short ɔ in a great many words, e.g. *hot* (hɑt), *top* (tɑp), *bother* ('bɑðɹ), *correspondence* (kɑrə'spanənts). *Bother* rhymes with *father* in American English. American ɔ has a quality intermediate between the qualities of Southern British ɔː and ɔ (generally nearer to the latter). It is used where British English has ɔː, e.g. *cause* (kɔz), *walk* (wɔk), *sort* (sɔɹt); it also replaces the British short ɔ in many words, e.g. *long* (lɔŋ), *dog* (dɔg). American o has a good deal of lip-rounding; it is often slightly diphthongal, except when followed

---

¹ Also written ɝ.

by ɹ. It is used for the most part in the same words as Southern British **ou** (see, however, § 7 of this Appendix). ɷ is rather like the Southern British vowel in *book*, but generally has less lip-rounding. It is used in the words where British English has short **u**. American **u** generally has about the same quality as the Southern English long **u:** described in § 323. Many Americans, however, use a more advanced variety (**ü**) resembling the 'crooner's **u.**' American **u** is used for the most part where Southern British has **u:**; it is also used by many Americans in some words where Southern British has **ju:**, e.g. *knew* (**nu**), *duty* (**ˈdüʈi**). ə is a medium central vowel. It stands commonly for the British English ʌ, also for the ə of British English when there is no *r* in the spelling, e.g. *cup* (**kəp**), *butter* (**ˈbəʈɹ**), *come* (**kəm**) and *method* (**ˈmɛθəd**), *precious* (**ˈprɛʃəs**), *drama* (**ˈdramə**). Some Americans, however, distinguish ʌ and ə in much the same way as Southern British people do. The usual American ɹ appears to me to be an 'r-coloured' high vowel near to ɩ; it is pronounced either with simultaneous curling back of the tongue-tip towards the hard palate, or with a general retraction of the whole body of the tongue with simultaneous lateral contraction (see §§ 73, 831, 833); it differs in quality from the South-Western English ɹ, which is definitely an 'r-coloured' ə. The American ɹ stands for the Southern British ə:, and for ə in words spelt with *r*, e.g. **bɹd** (*bird*), **fɹst** (*first*), **stɹ** (*stir*), **ˈstɹɩŋ** (*stirring*), which is distinct from **strɩŋ** (*string*), **ˈpepɹ** (*paper*), **ˈɛfɹt** *effort*), **pɹˈswed** (*persuade*), **ˈɛrɹ** (*error*).

B. *Diphthongs*

6. In American pronunciation the following diphthongs occur, in addition to the diphthongal variants of **e** and **o**: aɩ, aɷ, ɔɩ, ɩɹ, ɛɹ, aɹ, ɔɹ, oɹ, ɷɹ.

7. aɩ, aɷ, ɔɩ are about as Southern British ai, au, ɔi. The other diphthongs begin with ordinary vowels and end with ɹ. ɩɹ, ɛɹ, ɷɹ correspond to Southern British iə, ɛə, uə. ɔɹ corresponds to Southern British ɔ: in words spelt with *r*, e.g. **sɔɹt** (*sort*), **fɔɹm** (*form*). oɹ occurs in the words listed in footnote 36, p. 80, as having alternative pronunciation with close **o**, e.g. **moɹ** (*more*), **poɹt** (*port*), **koɹs** (*course*). Many Americans, however, do not use oɹ, but employ ɔɹ in its place (**mɔɹ, pɔɹt, kɔɹs**). American aɹ corresponds to Southern British ɑ: in words spelt with *r*, e.g. **pɑɹt** (*part*), **ɑɹm** (*arm*).

C. *Nasalization of Vowels and Diphthongs*

8. In American speech vowels and diphthongs are generally nasalized when preceding a nasal consonant, e.g. **stãnd** (*stand*), **tãĩm** (*time*), **'ɛ̃ni** (*any*), **ĩnstõnt** (*instant*); also very often when following a nasal consonant, e.g. **mẽk** (*make*), **smɔ̃l** (*small*). This nasalization is incidental, and need not therefore be marked in phonetic transcription.

D. *Consonants*

9. The American consonant system is the same as that of Southern British with the following exceptions.

10. **t** preceded by a strongly stressed vowel and followed by a weakly stressed vowel is sounded as a voiced flap (a variety of **ɾ**, §§ 746, 753). As this sound belongs to the American **t**-phoneme, it may be conveniently represented by the symbol **ţ**. Examples **'wɔţɹ** (*water*), **'leţəst** (*latest*).

11. When orthographic *nt* occurs in a similar position, it seems usual not to sound the *t*. Examples: **'wɑnəd** (*wanted*), **'twɛni** (*twenty*), **'sɛnə̃ts** (*sentence*), **'ɪnɹvju** (*interview*), **'kwɑnəţi** (*quantity*). The word *sentence* pronounced by an American is often difficult for a British hearer to recognize.

12. Some Americans, like some British people, use **ʔ** in place of **t** before **m, n, l, r, j, w** in words and expressions like **'sɹʔnli** (*certainly*), **'ðaʔ wən** (*that one*). Cp. § 560.

13. The consonantal **r**, as in **rɛd** (*red*), **brek** (*break*), **'vɛri** (*very, vary*) generally has a more retracted articulation than the corresponding British sound, and it has, as a rule, no perceptible friction. Its articulation is sometimes accompanied by considerable lip action. It may be termed a 'semi-vowel,' since its relation to the American vocalic **ɹ** (§ 5 above) is similar to that existing between **j** and **i** or between **w** and **u**.

14. In the speech of very many Americans **l** is a 'dark' variety (§ 659) in all situations. Dark **l** is used, for instance, in such words as **liv** (*leave*), **laɪk** (*like*), **flot** (*float*), **plan** (*plan*), **'sɪli** (*silly*), **bə'liv** (*believe*), **'mɪljən** (*million*). The American **l** often has a very marked effect on the quality of preceding vowels. In particular, front vowels are often much lowered and retracted in this position. For instance, I have heard *element* (**'ɛləmənt**) pronounced with an **ɛ** that was almost **a**-like.

15. Orthographic *wh* in such words as *which, when* are pronounced in America with **hw** or **ʍ** (voiceless **w**), thus **hwɪtʃ** or **ʍɪtʃ, hwɛn** or **ʍɛn**, etc.

16. Very prominent ə-like glides occur in the speech of some Americans when **ɪ, ɛ** and **a** are followed in the same syllable by certain consonants, especially it would seem **p, t** and **f**. These speakers make **bɪt, gɛt**, etc., sound something like **bɪət, gɛət**, etc. I have heard a distinguished American scientific man whose glide in such words as **gɪft, iˈkwɪpt, fɪfθ** approximated to **ʌ**; the words were quite difficult for British listeners to recognize.[2]

E. *Distribution of Sounds in Words*

17. In American English the distribution of sounds in words often differs from that of British English. The following are examples:

	Usual or frequent American pronunciation	Usual Southern British pronunciation
suggest	səgˈdʒɛst	səˈdʒest
inquiry	ˈɪŋkwəri	inˈkwaiəri
garage	gəˈrɑʒ	ˈgæraːʒ, ˈgærɪdʒ
record (noun)	ˈrɛkɪd	ˈrekɔːd
knew	nu	njuː
fertile,	ˈfɪtl,	ˈfəːtail,
hostile, etc.	ˈhɑstl, etc.	ˈhɔstail, etc.
apparatus	ˌapəˈratəs	ˌæpəˈreitəs
anti-, as in	ˈantaɪ-, as in	ˈænti-, as in
anti-social	ˈantaɪˈsoʃəl	ˈæntiˈsouʃl
quinine	ˈkwaɪnaɪn	kwiˈniːn, ˈkwiniːn
advertisement	ˌadvɪˈtaɪzmənt	ədˈvəːtismənt
amenable	əˈmɛnəbl	əˈmiːnəbl
depot	ˈdipo	ˈdepou
morale	məˈral	məˈrɑːl
vacation	veˈkeʃən	vəˈkeiʃn
exeat	ɛkˈsit	ˈeksiæt
leisure	ˈliʒɪ	ˈleʒə

Other examples (involving secondary stress) are shown in § *19.*

---

[2] Some Southern British people have a somewhat similar tendency, but not to the same degree. See my *Pronunciation of English* (1950 and subsequent editions), §§ 86, 90, 93.

18. In this connexion it is noteworthy that Americans make much more frequent use of the strong form of the indefinite article *a* than English people do. I have heard for instance: hi 'kem 'fɔɹwɹd wɪð e kəm'plitli 'nu 'program (*he came forward with a completely new programme*), 'naʧ 'onli e 'tɹnɪŋ-pɔɪnt (*not only a turning-point*), and many other similar examples. English people would as a rule use the weak form ə in such expressions.

F. *Stress*

19. Words with two or more syllables following the chief stress often have a stronger secondary stress than in British English. The vowel bearing the secondary stress is a 'strong' one, i.e. not ə as often in British English. Examples are

	American pronunciation	Southern British pronunciation
library	'laɪˌbrɛri	'laibrəri
dictionary	'dɪkʃəˌnɛri	'dikʃən(ə)ri or 'dikʃnri
territory	'tɛrəˌtoɹi	'terit(ə)ri
category	'kaʧɪˌgori	'kætig(ə)ri
nominative	'naməˌnɛʧɪv	'nɔm(i)nətiv
ceremony	'sɛrəˌmoni	'seriməni

G. *Intonation*

20. The intonation of American English has a general resemblance to that of Southern British. There are, however, three noteworthy points of difference. One is that in the American tune corresponding to Southern British Tune 2 (p. 282, etc.) the voice appears to start as a rule at a mid or rather low pitch and to remain fairly even until the final rise. The evenness of the tone is often not affected by any stressed syllables that may occur. For instance, an American will pronounce

dɪd ɪt 'ɔl hapən 'jɛstɹde
Did it all happen yesterday?

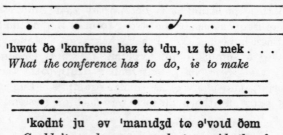

'hwɑt ðə 'kɑnfrəns haz tə 'du, ɪz tə mek . . .
What the conference has to do, is to make

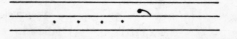

'kʊdnt ju əv 'manɪdʒd tə ə'vɔɪd ðəm
Couldn't you have managed to avoid them?

For the usual Southern British intonation of such sentences, see § 1023.

21. Another, very characteristic, American intonation is one of the type

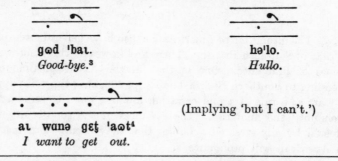

It is used in non-final parts of sentences, where Southern British speakers would employ some variety of Tune 2, i.e. a tune ending with a simple rise. It may occur finally when some continuation is implied; Professor K. L. Pike tells me that it may imply some hesitation, and that it often has a connotation of friendliness. I have heard it in interjectional expressions such as

gʊd 'baɪ.
Good-bye.[3]

hə'lo.
Hullo.

aɪ wɑnə gɛʧ 'aʊt[4]
I want to get out.

(Implying 'but I can't.')

---

[3] I have often heard this from American women; it appears to be much less frequent with men.

[4] I once heard this called out of the window of a train which had just begun to move, by an American woman who had forgotten to get out at her destination. (The guard hearing this remark stopped the train for her.)

This intonation is the same as that recorded for *I want to go* by Pike in his *Intonation of American English*, p. 50.

22. A common variant of this intonation is a tune of the type

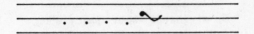

It begins with syllables (stressed or unstressed) at mid or rather low pitch and ends with a high fall-rise. This fall-rise differs from the Southern British one described in § 1054 in two respects: (1) the fall is much less in extent, (2) the entire fall-rise is at a higher pitch-level than that of the preceding syllables. The following are a few out of many examples I have noted:

ɪ? ˈwɑzn ˈmətʃ tə ˈask.[5]
It wasn't much to ask.

wɪɹ ˈglad tə bi ɪn ˈɪŋglənd
We're glad to be in England.

aɪ wəznt ˈrɛdi.
I wasn't ready.

ju kəd əv bɪn ˈfɪm.
You could have been firm.

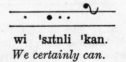

wi ˈsɹtnli ˈkan.
We certainly can.

(Said in reply to the question 'Can you come here?')

---

[5] The speaker from whom I took this example pronounced tə (not tᴡ) before ˈask.

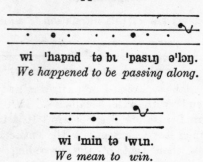

wi 'hapnd tə bɪ 'pasɪŋ ə'lɔŋ.
We happened to be passing along.

wi 'min tə 'wɪn.
We mean to win.

23. Sometimes there is a rise in the course of the syllable preceding the fall-rise. For instance, I have heard

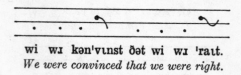

wi wɹ kən'vɪnst ðət wi wɹ 'raɪt.
We were convinced that we were right.

The following is another example noted by one of my colleagues. Doctor addressing patient:

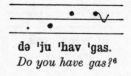

də 'ju 'hav 'gas.
Do you have gas?[6]

24. The precise significance of this intonation is not always clear to me. It seems to differ little from that of the previous intonation (§ *21*), but it implies presumably a higher degree of hesitancy, contrast or friendliness.[7]

---

[6] = Southern British *Do you get flatulence?*

[7] This tune is dealt with (very shortly) by K. L. Pike at the bottom of p. 50 of his *Intonation of American English.* He explains there (1) that the word bearing the fall-rise constitutes the 'centre of attention,' (2) that it is in contrast, and (3) that there is an implication of some sort, e.g. 'that there might be modifying or doubtful circumstances which demand cautious statement.'

25. The above should be compared with the following Southern British intonations:

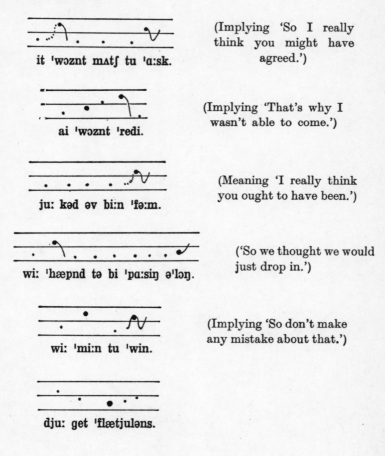

it 'wɔznt mʌtʃ tu 'aːsk.

(Implying 'So I really think you might have agreed.')

ai 'wɔznt 'redi.

(Implying 'That's why I wasn't able to come.')

juː kəd əv biːn 'fəːm.

(Meaning 'I really think you ought to have been.')

wiː 'hæpnd tə bi 'paːsiŋ ə'lɒŋ.

('So we thought we would just drop in.')

wiː 'miːn tu 'win.

(Implying 'So don't make any mistake about that.')

dju: get 'flætjuləns.

INDEX

References are to paragraphs, except when marked p. (page),
App. (Appendix), Fig. (Figure) or Chap. (Chapter)

OTHER WORKS BY THE SAME AUTHOR

The Phoneme, Third Edition (with an Appendix on the history and meaning of the term 'phoneme'), 1967 (Heffer, Cambridge).

The Pronunciation of English, 4th edition, 1956 (Cambridge University Press).

An English Pronouncing Dictionary, 13th edition, re-set, 1967 (Dent, London).

Phonetic Readings in English, new improved edition, 1956 (Winter, Heidelberg).

Intonation Curves (Teubner, Leipzig, 1909).

Shakespeare in the Original Pronunciation. Texts in phonetic transcription with notes, on pp. 36–45 of *English Pronunciation through the Centuries* (Linguaphone Institute, London). Accompanies a double-sided Linguaphone record of passages from Shakespeare in the original pronunciation spoken by D. Jones and E. M. Evans.

New Spelling, by W. Ripman and W. Archer, 6th edition, 1948, revised by D. Jones and H. Orton (Pitman, London).

Dhe Fonetik Aspekt ov Speling Reform (Simplified Spelling Society, c/o 5 Gwyder Road, Beckenham, Kent).

Concrete and Abstract Sounds (*Proceedings of the Third International Congress of Phonetic Sciences*, Ghent, 1938).

The Problem of a National Script for India (Pioneer Press, Lucknow).*

A Colloquial Sinhalese Reader, by D. Jones and H. S. Perera (Manchester University Press, 1919).

* Obtainable from the Department of Phonetics, University College, London, W.C.1.

A Sechuana Reader, by D. Jones and S. T. Plaatje (University of London Press, 1916).

A Cantonese Phonetic Reader, by D. Jones and Kwing Tong Woo (University of London Press, 1912).

The Tones of Sechuana Nouns (International African Institute, 1927).

Cardinal Vowels. Gramophone Records of 8 Primary and 10 Secondary Cardinal Vowels spoken by D. Jones. Linguaphone Records Nos. ENG 252–255. With explanatory Booklet.

The History and Meaning of the Term "Phoneme" (International Phonetic Association, University College, London, 1957).